Digital Classical Philology

Age of Access? Grundfragen der Informationsgesellschaft

Edited by
André Schüller-Zwierlein

Volume 10

Digital Classical Philology

Ancient Greek and Latin in the Digital Revolution

Edited by
Monica Berti

DE GRUYTER
SAUR

ISBN 978-3-11-059678-6
e-ISBN (PDF) 978-3-11-059957-2
e-ISBN (EPUB) 978-3-11-059699-1
ISSN 2195-0210

Library of Congress Control Number: 2019937558

Bibliographic information published by the Deutsche Nationalbibliothek
The Deutsche Nationalbibliothek lists this publication in the Deutsche Nationalbibliografie; detailed bibliographic data are available on the Internet at http://dnb.dnb.de.

Typesetting: Integra Software Services Pvt. Ltd.
Printing and binding: CPI books GmbH, Leck

www.degruyter.com

Editor's Preface

Whenever we talk about information, *access* is one of the terms most frequently used. The concept has many facets and suffers from a lack of definition. Its many dimensions are being analysed in different disciplines, from different viewpoints and in different traditions of research; yet they are rarely perceived as parts of a whole, as relevant aspects of one phenomenon. The book series *Age of Access? Fundamental Questions of the Information Society* takes up the challenge and attempts to bring the relevant discourses, scholarly as well as practical, together in order to come to a more precise idea of the central role that the accessibility of information plays for human societies.

The ubiquitous talk of the "information society" and the "age of access" hints at this central role, but tends to implicitly suggest either that information *is* accessible everywhere and for everyone, or that it *should be*. Both suggestions need to be more closely analysed. The first volume of the series addresses the topic of information justice and thus the question of whether information *should be* accessible everywhere and for everyone. Further volumes analyse in detail the physical, economic, intellectual, linguistic, psychological, political, demographic and technical dimensions of the accessibility and inaccessibility of information – enabling readers to test the hypothesis that information *is* accessible everywhere and for everyone.

The series places special emphasis on the fact that access to information has a diachronic as well as a synchronic dimension – and that thus cultural heritage research and practices are highly relevant to the question of access to information. Its volumes analyse the potential and the consequences of new access technologies and practices, and investigate areas in which accessibility is merely simulated or where the inaccessibility of information has gone unnoticed. The series also tries to identify the limits of the quest for access. The resulting variety of topics and discourses is united in one common proposition: It is only when all dimensions of the accessibility of information have been analysed that we can rightfully speak of an information society.

André Schüller-Zwierlein

https://doi.org/10.1515/9783110599572-201

Preface

More than fifty years have passed since 1968, when Harvard University Press published the Concordance to Livy (*A Concordance to Livy* [Harvard 1968]), the first product of what we might now call Digital Classics. In the basement of the Harvard Science Center, David Packard had supervised the laborious transcription of the whole of Livy's *History of Rome* onto punch cards and written a computer program to generate a concordance with 500,000 entries, each with 20 words of context. Fourteen years later, when in 1982 I began work on the Harvard Classics Computing Project, technology had advanced. The available of Greek texts from the Thesaurus Linguae Graecae on magnetic tape was the impetus for my work – the department wanted to be able to search the authors in this early version of the TLG on a Unix system. There was also a need to computerize typesetting in order to contain the costs of print publication. Digital work at that time was very technical and aimed at enhancing traditional forms of concordance research and print publication.

When I first visited Xerox's Palo Alto Research Center in 1985, I also saw for first time a digital image – indeed, one that was projected onto a larger screen. As I came to understand what functions digital media would support, I began to realize that digital media would do far more than enhance traditional tasks. As a graduate student, I had shuttled back and forth between Widener, the main Harvard library, and the Fogg Art Museum library, a five or ten minute walk away. That much distance imposed a great deal of friction on scholarship that sought to integrate publications about both the material and the textual record. It was clear that we would be able to have publications that combined every medium and that could be delivered digitally. My own work on Perseus began that year with a Xerox grant of Lisp Machines (already passing into obsolescence and surely granted as a tax write-off).

A generation later, the papers in this publication show how far Digital Classics has come. When I began my own work on Perseus in the 1980s, much of Greek and Latin literature had been converted into machine readable texts – but the texts were available only under restrictive licenses. The opening section of the collection, *Open Data of Greek and Latin Sources*, describes the foundational work on creating openly licensed corpora of Greek and Latin that can support scholarship without restriction. Scholars must have data that they can freely analyze, modify and redistribute. Without such freedom, digital scholarship cannot even approach its potential. Muellner and Huskey talk about collaborative efforts to expand the amount of Greek source text available and to begin developing born-digital editions of Latin sources. Cayless then addresses the challenge of applying the methods of Linked Open Data to topics such as Greco-Roman culture.

https://doi.org/10.1515/9783110599572-202

Cataloging and Citing Greek and Latin Authors and Works illustrates not only how Classicists have built upon larger standards and data models such as the Functional Requirements for Bibliographic Records (FRBR, allowing us to represent different versions of a text) and the Text Encoding Initiative (TEI) Guidelines for XML encoding of source texts (representing the logical structure of sources) but also highlights some major contributions from Classics. Alison Babeu, Digital Librarian at Perseus, describes a new form of catalog for Greek and Latin works that exploits the FRBR data model to represent the many versions of our sources – including translations. Christopher Blackwell and Neel Smith built on FRBR to develop the Canonical Text Services (CTS) data model as part of the CITE Architecture. CTS provides an explicit framework within which we can address any substring in any version of a text, allowing us to create annotations that can be maintained for years and even for generations. This addresses – at least within the limited space of textual data – a problem that has plagued hypertext systems since the 1970s and that still afflicts the World Wide Web. Those who read these papers years from now will surely find that many of the URLs in the citations no longer function but all of the CTS citations should be usable – whether we remain with this data model or replace it with something more expressive. Computer Scientists Jochen Tiepmar and Gerhard Heyer show how they were able to develop a CTS server that could scale to more than a billion words, thus establishing the practical nature of the CTS protocol.

If there were a Nobel Prize for Classics, my nominations would go to Blackwell and Smith for CITE/CTS and to Bruce Robertson, whose paper on Optical Character Recognition opens the section on *Data Entry, Collection, and Analysis for Classical Philology*. Robertson has worked a decade, with funding and without, on the absolutely essential problem of converting images of print Greek into machine readable text. In this effort, he has mastered a wide range of techniques drawn from areas such as computer human interaction, statistical analysis, and machine learning. We can now acquire billions of words of Ancient Greek from printed sources and not just from multiple editions of individual works (allowing us not only to trace the development of our texts over time but also to identify quotations of Greek texts in articles and books, thus allowing us to see which passages are studied by different scholarly communities at different times). He has enabled fundamental new work on Greek. Meanwhile the papers by Tauber, Burns, and Coffee are on representing characters, on a pipeline for textual analysis of Classical languages and on a system that detects where one text alludes to – without extensively quoting – another text.

At its base, philology depends upon the editions which provide information about our source texts, including variant readings, a proposed reconstruction of the original, and reasoning behind decisions made in analyzing the text. The section on *Critical Editing and Annotating Greek and Latin Sources* describes multiple aspects of this problem. Fischer addresses the challenge of representing the apparatus – the list of variants traditionally printed at the bottom of the page. Schubert and her collaborators show new ways of working with multiple versions of a text to produce an edition. Dué and Hackney present the Homeric Epics as a case where the reconstruction of a single original is not appropriate: the Homeric Epics appeared in multiple forms, each of which needs to be considered in its own right and thus a Multitext is needed. Berti concludes by showing progress made on the daunting task of representing a meta-edition: the case where works exist only as quotations in surviving works and an edition consists of an annotated hypertext pointing to – and modifying – multiple (sometimes hundreds) of editions.

We end with a glimpse into born-digital work. *Linguistic annotation and lexical databases* extends practices familiar from print culture so far that they become fundamentally new activities, with emergent properties that could not – and still cannot fully – be predicted from the print antecedents. Celano describes multiple dependency treebanks for Greek and Latin – databases that encode the morphological and syntactic function of every word in a text and that will allow us to rebuild our basic understanding of Greek, Latin, and other languages. Passarotti's paper on the Index Thomisticus Treebank also brings us into contact with Father Busa and the very beginning of Digital Humanities in the 1940s. With Boschetti we read about the application of WordNet and of semantic analysis to help us, after thousands of years of study, see systems of thought from new angles.

I began my work on (what is now called) Digital Classics in 1982 because I was then actively working with scholarship published more than a century before and because I knew that my field had a history that extended thousands of years in the past. Much has changed in the decades since, but the pace of change is only accelerating. The difference between Classics in 2019 and 2056 will surely be much greater than that between 1982 and 2019. Some of the long term transformative processes are visible in this collection.

One fundamental trend that cuts across the whole collection is the emergence of a new generation of philologists. When I began work, few of us had any technical capabilities and fewer still had any interest in developing them. What we see in this collection of essays is a collection of classical philologists who have developed their own skills and who are able to apply – and extend – advances in the wider world to the study of Greek and Latin. This addresses the existential question of sustainability of Greek and Latin in at least two ways.

First, I was very fortunate to have five years of research support – 1.000.000 EUR/year – from the Alexander von Humboldt Foundation as a Humboldt

Professor of Digital Humanities at Leipzig. I also have been able to benefit from support over many years for the Perseus Project from Tufts University. Both of those sources contributed to a number of these papers, both directly (by paying salaries) and indirectly (e.g., by paying for people to come work together). But what impresses me is how rich the network of Digital Classicists has become. We were able to help but the system is already robust and will sustain itself. We already have in the study of Greek and Latin a core community that will carry Digital Classics forward with or without funding, for love of the subject. In this, they bring life to the most basic and precious ideals of humanistic work.

Second, we can see a new philological education where our students can learn Greek and Latin even as they become computer, information or data scientists (or whatever label for computational sciences is fashionable). Our students will prepare themselves to take their place in the twenty-first century by advancing our understanding of antiquity. Our job as humanists is to make sure that we focus not only on the technologies but on the values that animate our study of the past.

Gregory R. Crane
(Perseus Project at Tufts University and Universität Leipzig)

Contents

Data Entry, Collection, and Analysis for Classical Philology

Critical Editing and Annotating Greek and Latin Sources

Linguistic Annotation and Lexical Databases for Greek and Latin

Introduction

Many recent international publications and initiatives show that *philology* is enjoying a "renaissance" within scholarship and teaching. The digital revolution of the last decades has been playing a significant role in revitalizing this traditional discipline and emphasizing its original scope, which is "making sense of texts and languages". This book describes the state of the art of digital philology with a focus on ancient Greek and Latin, the classical languages of Western culture. The invitation to publish the volume in the series *Age of Access? Grundfragen der Informationsgesellschaft* has offered the opportunity to present current trends in digital classical philology and discuss their future prospects.

The first goal of the book is to describe how Greek and Latin textual data is accessible today and how it should be linked, processed, and edited in order to produce and preserve meaningful information about classical antiquity. Contributors present and discuss many different topics: Open data of Greek and Latin sources, the role of libraries in building digital catalogs and developing machine-readable citation systems, the digitization of classical texts, computer-aided processing of classical languages, digital critical analysis and textual transmission of ancient works, and finally morpho-syntactic annotation and lexical resources of Greek and Latin data with a discussion that pertains to both philology and linguistics.

The selection of these topics has been guided by challenges and needs that concern the treatment of Greek and Latin textuality in the digital age. These challenges and needs include and go beyond the aim of traditional philology, which is the production of critical editions that reconstruct and represent the transmission of ancient sources. This is the reason why the book collects contributions about technical and practical aspects that relate not only to the digitization, representation, encoding and analysis of Greek and Latin textual data, but also to topics such as sustainability and funding that permit scholars to establish and maintain projects in this field. These aspects are now urgent and should be always addressed in order to make possible the preservation of the classical heritage. Many other topics could have been added to the discussion, but we hope that this book offers a synthesis to describe an emergent field for a new generation of scholars and students, explaining what is reachable and analyzable that was not before in terms of technology and accessibility. The book aims at bringing digital classical philology to an audience that is composed not only of Classicists, but also of researchers and students from many other fields in the humanities and computer science. Contributions in the volume are arranged in the following five sections:

https://doi.org/10.1515/9783110599572-001

Open data of Greek and Latin sources

This section presents cataloging and publishing activities of two leading open access corpora of Greek and Latin sources: the Free First Thousand Years of Greek of the Harvard's Center for Hellenic Studies that is now part of the Open Greek and Latin Project of the University of Leipzig, and the Digital Latin Library of the University of Oklahoma. The third paper describes principles and best practices for publishing and sustaining Linked Ancient World Data and its complexities.

Cataloging and citing Greek and Latin authors and works

The first paper of this section describes the history of the Perseus Catalog and its use of open metadata standards for bibliographic data. The other two papers describe digital library architectures developed for addressing citations of classical scholary editions in a digital environment. The first contribution describes CITE (Collections, Indices, Texts, and Extensions), which is a digital library architecture originally developed for the Homer Multitext Project for addressing identification, retrieval, manipulation, and integration of data by means of machine-actionable canonical citation. The second contribution presents an implementation of the Canonical Text Services (CTS) protocol developed at the University of Leipzig for citing and retrieving passages of texts in classical and other languages.

Data Entry, collection, and analysis for classical philology

The four papers of this section discuss practical issues about the creation and presentation of digital Greek and Latin text data. The first paper explains the technology behind recent improvements in optical character recognition and how it can be attuned to produce highly accurate texts of scholarly value, especially when dealing with difficult scripts like ancient Greek. The second paper presents an overview of character encoding systems for the input, interchange, processing and display of classical texts with particular reference to ancient Greek. The third paper introduces the Classical Language Toolkit that addresses the desideratum of a complete text analysis pipeline for Greek and Latin and other historical languages. The fourth paper addresses the phenomenon of viral intertextuality and demonstrates how current digital methods make its instances much easier to detect.

Critical editing and annotating Greek and Latin sources

The four papers of this section present different topics concerning critical editions and annotations of classical texts. The first paper describes current challenges and opportunities for the critical apparatus in a digital environment. The second paper gives a short description of the software tool e-Comparatio developed at the University of Leipzig and originally intended as a tool for the comparison of different text editions. The third paper describes the Homer Multitext Project and its principles of access within the long history of the Homeric epics in the centuries through the digital age. The fourth paper describes how the digital revolution is changing the way scholars access, analyze, and represent historical fragmentary texts, with a focus on traces of quotations and text reuses of ancient Greek and Latin sources.

Linguistic annotation and lexical databases for Greek and Latin

This section collects papers about morpho-syntactic annotation and lexical resources of Greek and Latin data. The first paper is an introduction to the dependency treebanks currently available for ancient Greek and Latin. The second paper is a description of the Index Thomisticus Treebank based on the corpus of the Index Thomisticus by father Roberto Busa, which is currently the largest Latin treebank available. The third paper investigates methods, resources, and tools for semantic analysis and thematic annotation of Greek and Latin with a particular focus on lexico semantic resources (Latin WordNet and Ancient Greek WordNet) and the semantic and thematic annotation of classical texts (Memorata Poetis Project and Euporia).

I would like to thank all the authors of this book who have contributed to the discussion about the current state of digital classical philology. I also want to express my warmest thanks to the editors of the series *Age of Access?* and to the editorial team of De Gruyter for their invitation to publish the volume and for their assistance. I'm finally very grateful to Knowledge Unlatched (KU) for its support to publish this book as gold open access.

Monica Berti (Universität Leipzig)

Bibliography

Apollon, D.; Bélisle, C.; Régnier, P. (eds.) (2014): Digital Critical Editions. Urbana, Chicago, and Springfield: University of Illinois Press.

Bod, R. (2013): A New History of the Humanities. The Search for Principles and Patterns from Antiquity to the Present. Oxford: Oxford University Press.

Lennon, B. (2018): Passwords. Philology, Security, Authentication. Cambridge, MA: The Belknap Press of Harvard University Press.

McGann, J. (2014): A New Republic of Letters. Memory and Scholarship in the Age of Digital Reproduction. Cambridge, MA: Harvard University Press.

Pierazzo, E. (2015): Digital Scholarly Editing. Theories, Models and Methods. Farnham: Ashgate.

Pollock, S.; Elman, B.A.; Chang, K.K. (eds.) (2015): World Philology. Cambridge, MA: Harvard University Press.

Turner, J. (2014): Philology. The Forgotten Origins of the Modern Humanities. Princeton, NJ: Princeton University Press.

Open Data of Greek and Latin Sources

Leonard Muellner

The Free First Thousand Years of Greek

Abstract: This contribution describes the ideals, the history, the current procedures, and the funding of the in-progress Free First Thousand Years of Greek (FF1KG) project, an Open Access corpus of Ancient Greek literature. The corpus includes works from the beginnings (Homeric poetry) to those produced around 300 CE, but also standard reference works that are later than 300 CE, like the Suda (10th Century CE). Led by the Open Greek and Latin project of the Universität Leipzig, institutions participating in the FF1KG include the Center for Hellenic Studies, Harvard University Libraries, and the library of the University of Virginia.

Ideals and early history of the project

The Free First Thousand Years of Greek (FF1KG), now a part of the Open Greek and Latin Project at the Universität Leipzig, was the brainchild of Neel Smith, Professor and Chair of the Department of Classics at the College of the Holy Cross, with the sponsorship and support of the Center of Hellenic Studies (CHS) in Washington, DC. It started in 2008–2009 from a set of ideals about digital classical philology that Professor Smith and the CHS have been guided by, as follows: 1) digital resources for classical philology should be free and openly-licensed and therefore accessible to all without cost and with the lowest possible technical barriers but the best technology available behind them; 2) software development flourishes long-term in an open environment that uses standardized and free tools and invites collegial participation,[1] as opposed to a closed environment that uses proprietary tools for short (or even medium-) term gain; 3) in order to survive and thrive in the future, the field of Classics requires and deserves creative, well-designed, and practical digital resources for research and teaching that rigorously implement the two previous principles; 4) rather than presenting a broad spectrum of users with tools that are ready-made without their participation or input, it is best to enable, train, and involve young people, undergraduates and graduate

1 Raymond (1999), originally an essay and then a book, was inspirational for the present author on this point.

Leonard Muellner, Center for Hellenic Studies, Harvard University

https://doi.org/10.1515/9783110599572-002

students both, in the technologies and the processes that are necessary for the conception, creation, and maintenance of digital resources for classics teaching and research; and 5) the markup of texts, whether primary or secondary, in internationally standard formats, such as TEI XML (http://tei-c.org), is the best way to guarantee their usability, interoperability, and sustainability over time.

The fundamental research and teaching tool that a field like Classics needs is as complete a corpus of open and downloadable texts as possible in each language, Greek or Latin, with a full panoply of ways to read, interpret, search, and learn from them. Building such a corpus from the bottom up is challenging in many obvious ways. Texts in Ancient Greek, which is the disciplinary focus of the Center for Hellenic Studies and the Free First 1K of Greek, present the challenging technical difficulty of an alphabet available in a wide variety of fonts (each standard for a given collection of texts, but there is no overall standard font), and with seven diacritical marks appearing singly and in combinations over and under letters (acute, grave, and circumflex accents; smooth and rough breathings; iota subscript and underdot). That makes it difficult to create machine-readable texts in Ancient Greek from printed texts using basic computational tools for optical scanning and character recognition. As a result, Neel Smith thought it would be wise to begin by making overtures on behalf of CHS to the existing but proprietary and fee-based corpus of Ancient Greek texts, the Thesaurus Linguae Graecae (TLG) in Irvine, CA, in an effort to partner with them in both improving and opening up their collection of texts.

By that time, Smith and his colleague, Christopher Blackwell, Professor of Classics at Furman University, had developed and perfected a protocol that they called CTS (Canonical Text Services, now in its 5th iteration, http://cite-architecture.org) for building, retrieving, querying, and manipulating a digital reference to an item as small as a letter or a chunk as large as anyone might need from a classical text, as long as the text in question is accessible by way of a structured, canonical reference system, and as long as the text is marked up in some form of XML that can be validated. In Smith's and Blackwell's parlance, a canonical reference system is one based on a text's *structure* (chapter and verse, or book and line, for instance) rather than on points in a physical page (like the Stephanus or Bekker page-based references that are normal for citing the works of Plato and Aristotle). They had also developed sophisticated ways of parsing and verifying machine-readable polytonic Greek against a lexicon of lemmatized forms. Both CTS and their verification tools seemed to Smith and Blackwell to offer significant advantages over the existing technologies of the TLG, but their attempt to partner with the leadership of the TLG was not well-received.

This left Smith, Blackwell, and the CHS with one option: to build a free and open corpus of texts from scratch. The initial, modest idea was to create a corpus of Ancient Greek texts that would answer to the basic needs of students and researchers of texts in the classical language and that would work with the CTS system. Such a scope implied several restrictions: 1) the corpus would include texts attested in manuscript, but not fragments (in other words, texts attested in snippets inside other texts) or inscriptions or papyri, whether literary or documentary, which do not have a canonical reference system; 2) the basic time frame would be from the beginnings of Greek literature up to the end of the Hellenistic period, around 300 CE, to include the Septuagint and the New Testament but not the Church Fathers; 3) some later texts necessary for the study of the basic corpus, such as the Suda, a 10th Century CE encyclopedia of antiquities, or the manuscript marginalia called scholia for a range of classical authors, some of which are pre- and some post 300 CE, would also be included in the collection. Hence the Free First Thousand Years of Greek is in some ways less and in some ways more than its name betokens.

First steps, then a suspension

The first requirement of the project was a catalog of the texts to be included in it, and Smith began the significant task of compiling one with funding from CHS for two student helpers in the summer of 2010; that work continued in the summer of 2011, but then other projects and obligations supervened. An overriding concern for the CHS technical team was the development of software for online commentaries on classical texts, an effort that resulted in the initial publication in 2017 of *A Homer Commentary in Progress*, an inter-generational, collaborative commentary on all the works of the Homeric corpus (more on its sequel and their consequences for the Free First Thousand Years of Greek follow). For Professor Smith, the focus of his energies became the centerpiece of the Homer Multitext Project (http://www.homermultitext.org), the interoperable publication of all of the photographs, text, and scholia of the Venetus A manuscript of the Homeric *Iliad* in machine-actionable, which took place this past spring; it will continue with the similar publication of other medieval manuscripts with scholia, such as Venetus B or the Escorial manuscripts of the Homeric *Iliad*.

Resumption of the FF1KG

But the Free First Thousand Years of Greek was never far from the concerns of either CHS or Professor Smith – in fact, both of these projects are intimately related to it – and in 2015, with the support of Professor Mark Schiefsky, then chair of the department of classics at Harvard University, we reached out in an attempt to collaborate with our long-term partner, Gregory Crane, editor-in-chief of the Perseus Project, Professor of Classics at Tufts University and Alexander von Humboldt Professor of Digital Humanities at the University of Leipzig. He and his team of colleagues and graduate students at Universität Leipzig and Tufts University had already begun a much more inclusive project that could reasonably subsume it, namely, the Open Greek and Latin (OGL) project.

OGL aims to be a complete implementation of the CTS protocols for structuring and accessing texts in XML documents; it aims to include multiple, comparable versions of a given classical text wherever possible, along with its translation into multiple languages; and it will provide *apparatus critici* (reporting textual variants) where the German copyright law allows them; in addition, it will include POS (part of speech) data for every word in the corpus, with the ultimate goal of providing syntactical treebanks of every text as well. It also will include support for fragmentary texts, such as the digital edition of K. Müller's edition of the fragments of Greek history, the DFHG, http://www.dfhg-project.org, with a digital concordance to the numbering of the fragments in the modern edition of F. Jacoby, which is still under copyright. Developing the infrastructure to include fragmentary texts of this kind has been a major achievement of Monica Berti, the editor-in-chief of the DFHG as well as of Digital Athenaeus, http://www.digitalathenaeus.org, an ancient text that presents canonical reference problems but is also a major source of fragmentary quotations of other texts from antiquity, many of them lost to us otherwise.[2]

Summer interns at CHS and the FF1KG workflow

The subsuming of the Free First Thousand Years of Greek to the Open Greek and Latin project began in earnest in March of 2016, when the CHS hired three summer interns from a pool of over 170 applicants to be trained in the technologies of the OGL and to contribute to the ongoing creation of the corpus of Greek texts. Professor Crane and his team graciously embraced the concept of the Free First Thousand Years of Greek, and because of the extraordinary work of Alison Babeu, a long-time member of the Perseus team, a catalog of works that would include it was already in place, namely, the Perseus Catalog,

2 See her contribution to this collection, entitled "Historical Fragmentary Texts in the Digital Age".

http://catalog.perseus.org. In May of 2016, Crane sent Thibault Clérice, then a doctoral candidate at Leipzig (now MA director of the Master Technologies «Numériques Appliquées à l'Histoire» at the École Nationale des Chartes in Paris) to the CHS in Washington, DC in order to train the CHS year-round publications intern, Daniel Cline, and the author of this article, L. Muellner, in the workflow of the OGL. The idea was that we, in turn, would train the summer interns, who were scheduled to arrive at the beginning of June. Thibault was the right person for the job because he had developed a suite of Python-based tools called CapiTainS (https://github.com/Capitains) to verify that any TEI XML file was valid and in particular compliant with the CTS protocols. But before discussing his tools, we need to go back one step.

The process of generating and verifying files for inclusion in the Free First Thousand Years of Greek begins with high-resolution scans of Greek texts from institutional (for example https://archive.org) and individual sources. These scans are submitted to Bruce Robertson, Head of the Classics Department at Mt. Allison University in New Brunswick, Canada, who has developed a suite of tools for Optical Character Recognition of polytonic Ancient Greek called Lace (http://heml.mta.ca/lace/index.html and for the latest source, https://github.com/brobertson/Lace2). His software is based on the open source Ocropus engine. After its first attempt to recognize the letter forms and diacritics of a Greek text, Lace is set up for humans to check and correct computer-recognized Greek, with the original scanned image on pages that face the OCR version, in order to make verification quick and straightforward.

After someone corrects a set of pages in this interface, Robertson's process uses HPC (High Performance Computing) in order to iterate and optimize the recognition of letters and diacritics to a high standard of accuracy, even for the especially difficult Greek in a so-called *apparatus criticus* "critical apparatus". A critical apparatus is the textual notes conventionally set in small type at the bottom of the page in Ancient Greek and Latin texts (or for that matter of any text that does not have a single, perfect source). It reports both textual variants in the direct (manuscripts, papyri, etc.) and indirect (citations of text in other sources) transmission of ancient texts, along with modern editors' corrections to the readings from both transmissions. Correctly recognizing the letters and diacritics of lexical items in a language is one thing, but it is altogether another thing to reproduce the sometimes incorrect or incomplete readings in the manuscripts (and not to correct them!) that populate a critical apparatus, but Robertson's software can do both. In any case, he is continually optimizing it, and the most recent version uses machine-learning technology to correct its texts. Learning how to edit an OCR text is the first task that the CHS interns learn to do.

Once a Greek text is made machine-readable by an iterated Lace process, OGL requires that it be marked up in EpiDoc TEI XML (for the EpiDoc guidelines, schema, etc., see https://sourceforge.net/p/epidoc/wiki/Home/; for TEI XML in general, see http://www.tei-c.org/). TEI XML endows the text with a suite of metadata in the TEI.header element as well as a structural map of the document (using Xpath) that is a requirement for the CTS protocol. Up to now, that encoding process has been carried out by Digital Divide Data (DDD), https://www.digi taldividedata.com, a third-world (Cambodia, Kenya, Indonesia) company employed by corporations and universities in the first world that trains and employs workers in digital technologies. This step is painstaking and not inexpensive, but by the time that the FF1KG joined them, the OGL team had already generated a large corpus of Greek and Latin texts with funds from multiple sources, including the NEH, the Mellon Foundation, the Alexander von Humboldt Stiftung, and others (see more below on new funding sources for further digitization expenses of this kind). Once an Ancient Greek text in the FF1KG has been marked up in EpiDoc by DDD, it is installed by the OGL team in the GitHub repository of the FF1KG, a subset of the OpenGreekandLatin repository, at http://opengreekandla tin.github.io/First1KGreek/.[3] The directory structure of the installations in that repository are consistent with the structure and numbering schemes of the Perseus catalog for authors and works, and the infrastructure files, such as dot-files like the .cts_xml files, are also consistent with the requirements of CTS.

These newly marked-up and installed sources were the subject of the majority of the work carried out by the CHS interns in the summers of 2016 and 2017; they also received year-round attention from members of the Leipzig team. Thibault Clérice had developed a verification tool called Hooktest (available in the previously cited CapiTainS GitHub directory) that could be run on all of the files in the repository to detect errors in them – flaws in the TEI headers within each XML file, flaws in the structural information specified for CTS compliance, and a host of other small but critical details that could go wrong in the process of generating EpiDoc XML that is CTS-compliant. In training Cline and Muellner in the spring of 2016, Clérice spent most of the time teaching us how to understand and correct and then rerun Hooktest in response to its error messages. Hooktest itself has been updated several times since then, and it now runs on a different system (originally ran on Docker, https://www.docker.com now the online server, Travis, https://travis-ci.org), and over the past three summers, the CHS interns have developed documentation that consolidates its accumulated wisdom on that

3. All files in this repository and the other OGL repositories are backed up at https://zenodo.org (last access 2019.01.31).

process. In the past summer, there was a dearth of newly digitized files from DDD for the FF1KG, so the (now) *four* interns turned to the conversion and verification, again via Hooktest, of the XML files of the Perseus collection to CTS compliance as their major task. In addition to that work and further OCR work training Lace, the CHS summer interns have learned how to contribute to the DFHG (Digital Fragmenta Historicorum Graecorum) and the Digital Athenaeus projects mentioned above. Like the FF1KG, both are openly licensed projects that benefit from hearty participation by anyone who wants to add to and learn from them.

Funding sources and in-kind contributions to the FF1KG and the OGL

As mentioned above, the OGL has been funded over its development by a broad range of sources, including the NEH, the Mellon Foundation, the IMLS, and others. In 2016, the CHS committed $50,000 to fund steps in the digitization of Ancient Greek texts for the FF1KG, with the idea that it would be matched by other funding obtained by OGL. That sum of money has been earmarked and set aside for digitization of the FF1KG since 2016, and the expectation is that it will be spent and matched in 2019 as part of a grant to the OGL by the DFG (Deutsche Forschungsgemeinschaft, or German Research Association). The CHS also earmarked funds for the development of a user interface into the texts of the FF1KG; more about that in a moment. The CHS funds were not from the CHS endowment, but from revenue generated by the CHS publications program, its printed books, in particular the so-called Hellenic Studies Series. In the Fall of 2016, when she heard about renewed progress with the FF1KG, Rhea Karabelas Lesage, the librarian for Classics and Modern Greek Studies at Harvard University Library, applied for $50,000 of funding through the Arcadia Fund, and she succeeded in her application. That sum paid for the digitization and mark-up in EpiDoc by DDD of 4,000,000 words of Greek. In addition, in 2017, Rhea used funds from her budget as Classics librarian to digitize and include in the FF1KG a series of scientific texts for a course being given at Harvard University by Professor Mark Schiefsky, the Classics chair. Another Classics librarian, Lucie Stylianopoulos of the University of Virginia (UVA), became an enthusiastic supporter of the project, and every year since 2016, she has been successful in acquiring funding from the UVA library for a group of four to six interns during the Fall and Spring terms to learn the technologies and to contribute significantly to the conversion and verification of texts in the FF1KG repository. The UVA team originally (in 2016) trained at CHS, but this past September a CHS trainer, the publications intern Angelia Hannhardt, visited Charlottesville and worked with the new interns *in situ*. The same two Classics librarians, Lucie and Rhea, worked together with members of the Tufts team, especially Lisa Cerrato and Alison Babeu, along with David Ratzan and Patrick Burns of the Institute for the Study of the Ancient World (ISAW), to set up a workshop on the OGL and the FF1KG that was held at Tufts University a day before the annual meeting of the Society for Classical Studies (SCS) in Boston in January this year (2018). A large group (over sixty) of librarians, undergraduates, graduate students, and classics professionals came early to the conference in order to attend hands-on demonstrations of the technologies in FF1KG and OGL. Our hope was that they could begin to learn how to participate and also, how to teach others. The workshop was publicized and supported by the Forum for Classics, Libraries, and Scholarly Communication (http://www.classicslibrarians.org), an SCS-affiliated group that has advocated for and worked with the FF1KG team since it resumed development in 2016. Lastly, in response to outreach from Lucie Stylianopoulos, Rhea Lesage, and the librarians at CHS, a memorandum of understanding is about to be (in November, 2018) signed between the reinvigorated National Library of Greece (NLG) in its beautiful new location (see https://transition.nlg.gr) and the OGL/FF1KG team at Leipzig, to train staff and students in Athens in the processes of the development of the corpus. We expect that training and new work will begin there in the very near future.

New developments from an Open Access corpus of texts

Building a corpus of texts takes time, money, and dedicated workers like those from Leipzig, CHS, UVA and soon the NLG, but their work is invisible until there is a way to access it. The current list of texts in the FF1KG is visible and downloadable here: http://opengreekandlatin.github.io/First1KGreek/. There are now over 18 million words of Greek, with about 8 million to come for the "complete" FF1KG. Given that all the texts in the corpus are open access, anyone can download them and build software around them. The CHS leadership, with the agreement of the Leipzig team, wished to inspire an early "proof-of-concept" access system that would highlight the existence and some of the functionality that the new corpus could eventually provide. After an RFP, in July of 2017, CHS financed a design sprint orchestrated by a team from Intrepid (https://www.intrepid.io) headed by Christine Pizzo. They spent three intense days with the OGL team in Leipzig talking with the staff and connecting in the morning with CHS personnel stateside as well. The goal was to understand the conception of the whole OGL and to develop a design template for the functionality that an access system for the corpus might use. They produced a set of designs, and that fall, after another RFP, Eldarion (http://eldarion.com), and its CEO, James Tauber, were chosen by Gregory Crane to implement the design; funding came from Crane's budget, and the result was made public in March of 2018, namely, the Scaife Viewer (https://scaife.perseus.org). Named for Ross Scaife, an early evangelist for digital classics who was a dear friend to the Perseus team and CHS and whose life was tragically cut short in 2008, the Scaife Viewer is a working prototype for accessing the Greek and Latin texts now in the corpus, along with some Hebrew and Farsi texts. The Viewer currently deploys much (but not all) of the technology that the project teams have envisioned: multiple editions and aligned multiple translations of classical texts, with tools to help learners read the original language and to understand the texts, but also tools to help researchers search within the texts in the corpus in multiple and complex ways. New texts in both languages are being added to the repository at varying rhythms, and the Scaife Viewer is set up to incorporate new sources on a weekly basis. Its software will also soon undergo further development with funding from a grant by the Andrew Mellon Foundation directed by Sayeed Choudhury, Associate Dean for Data Management and Hodson Director of the Digital Research and Curation Center at the Sheridan Libraries of the Johns Hopkins University.

Another example of the potential of an open-access corpus is not yet functional, but there is again a working prototype that makes concrete what can and will be done. This project, funded by the CHS and under development by Archimedes Digital (https://archimedes.digital), is called New Alexandria, and its purpose is to provide a platform for the development of fully-featured, collaborative online commentaries on texts in classical languages around the world – not just the Ancient Greek and Latin texts in the OGL/FF1KG, but also the 41 other languages in the corpus being developed by the Classical Language Toolkit (https://github.com/cltk; the principals of CLTK are Kyle Johnston, Luke Hollis, and Patrick Burns). Current plans are to provide a series of curated commentaries by invitation only but also an open platform for uncurated commentaries by individuals or groups that wish to try to provide insight into a text in a classical language as the CLTK defines it. The working prototype for such an online commentary is *A Homer Commentary in Progress*, https://ahcip.chs.harvard.edu, a collaborative commentary on all the works in the Homeric corpus by an intergenerational team of researchers. This project, which is permanently "in progress", is intended to provide an evergreen database of comments by a large and evolving group of like-minded specialists. The comments they produce are searchable by canonical reference, by author, and also by semantic tags that the author of a comment can provide to each comment; the reader of comments always sees the snippet of text being commented upon and can opt to see its larger context in a scrolling panel, and there are multiple translations as well as multiple texts on instant offer for any text. Every canonical reference within a comment to a Homeric text is automatically linked to the Greek texts and translations, and every comment also has a unique and stable identifier that can be pasted into an online or printed text.

As a last example of what can happen when the ideals with which this presentation began are realized, we point to one further development: the last two projects, the Scaife Viewer and the New Alexandria commentaries platform, are interoperable and will in fact be linked, because both are implemented in compliance with the CTS protocols. Even now, a reader of Homer in the Scaife Viewer can already automatically access comments from *A Homer Commentary in Progress* for the passage that is currently on view; the right-side pane of the viewer simply needs to be expanded in its lower right-hand corner to expose scrolling comments. Further linkage, such as to Pleiades geospatial data on ancient sites (https://pleiades.stoa.org) and to the *Lexicon Iconographicum Mythologiae Classicae* (*LIMC*, headquarters in Basel) encyclopedia of ancient iconography, are in the pipeline for the New Alexandria project and the Scaife Viewer as well.

Bibliography

Berti, M. (ed.): "Digital Athenaeus". http://www.digitalathenaeus.org (last access 2019.01.31).

Berti, M. (ed.): "Digital Fragmenta Historicorum Graecorum (DFHG)". http://www.dfhg-project.org (last access 2019.01.31).

Clérice, T.: "Capitains". https://github.com/Capitains (last access 2019.01.31).

Crane, G.: "First 1000 Years of Greek". http://opengreekandlatin.github.io/First1KGreek/ (last access 2019.01.31).

Elliott, T.; Bodard, G.; Cayless, H. (2006–2017): "EpiDoc: Epigraphic Documents in TEI XML. Online material". https://sourceforge.net/projects/epidoc/ (last access 2019.01.31).

Frame, D.; Muellner, L.; Nagy, G. (eds.) (2017): "A Homer Commentary in Progress". https://ahcip.chs.harvard.edu (last access 2019.01.31).

Johnston, K.; Hollis, L.; Burns, P.: "Classical Language Toolkit". https://github.com/cltk (last access 2019.01.31).

Perseus Digital Library (2018): "Scaife Viewer". https://scaife.perseus.org (last access 2019.01.31).

Raymond, E. (1999): The Cathedral and the Bazaar. Sebastopol, CA: O'Reilly Media.

Robertson, B.: "Lace: Polylingual OCR Editing". http://heml.mta.ca/lace/index.html (last access 2019.01.31).
Smith, N.; Blackwell, C. (2013): "The CITE Architecture: Technology-Independent, Machine-Actionable Citation of Scholarly Resources". http://cite-architecture.org (last access 2019.01.31).

Samuel J. Huskey

The Digital Latin Library: Cataloging and Publishing Critical Editions of Latin Texts

Abstract: The Digital Latin Library has a two-fold mission: 1) to publish and curate critical editions of Latin texts, of all types, from all eras; 2) to facilitate the finding and, where openly available and accessible online, the reading of all texts written in Latin. At first glance, it may appear that the two parts of the mission are actually two different missions, or even two different projects altogether. On the one hand, the DLL seeks to be a publisher of new critical editions, an endeavor that involves establishing guidelines, standards for peer review, workflows for production and distribution, and a variety of other tasks. On the other hand, the DLL seeks to catalog existing editions and to provide a tool for finding and reading them, an effort that involves the skills, techniques, and expertise of library and information science. But we speak of a "two-fold mission" because both parts serve the common goal of enriching and enhancing access to Latin texts, and they use the methods and practices of data science to accomplish that goal. This chapter will discuss how the DLL's cataloging and publishing activities complement each other in the effort to build a comprehensive Linked Open Data resource for scholarly editions of Latin texts.

Introduction

Although Latin texts have been available in electronic form for decades, there has never been an open, comprehensive digital resource for scholarly editions of Latin texts of all eras. In the era before the World Wide Web, collections such as the Packard Humanities Institute's (PHI) Latin Texts, Perseus, or Cetedoc made collections of texts available on CD-ROM, but those collections were limited by era (e.g., PHI and Perseus covered only Classical Latin texts) or subject (e.g., Cetedoc covered Christian Latin texts).[1] Matters improved with the wide

1 Cetedoc (sometimes known erroneously as CETADOC) was originally developed by the Centre Traditio Litterarum Occidentalium (CTLO). The full name of the database was "Cetedoc Library of Christian Latin Texts."

Samuel J. Huskey, University of Oklahoma

https://doi.org/10.1515/9783110599572-003

adoption of networked computing, but for many years collections of Latin texts were limited to a particular era (e.g., Perseus[2]), behind a paywall (e.g., Cetedoc, which became part of Brepolis' Library of Latin Texts[3]), or offline (e.g., PHI, which did not publish its texts online until 2011[4]). Sites such as The Latin Library and Corpus Scriptorum Latinorum are more expansive, but they have not kept pace with developments in technology, and since it is not always clear what the source of their texts is, they are of limited use for scholarly purposes.[5]

The Open Greek and Latin Project, however, promises to publish millions of words of Greek and Latin from all eras, along with robust resources for analyzing and reading the texts. As of this writing they have made significant progress toward that goal. Aside from the scale, what separates the Open Greek and Latin project from others is the focus on creating an open scholarly resource, with rich, citable metadata on the sources for the texts. But even the Open Greek and Latin project has established a boundary of 600 CE, which means that much of Medieval and Neo-Latin will be excluded.

But one thing that all of these resources have in common is that they omit the features that distinguish scholarly critical editions. That is, their texts lack an editorial preface that explains the history of the text and its sources, a bibliography of previous scholarship on the text, a critical apparatus with variant readings and other useful information, or any of the other items necessary for serious study. Whether the omission is because of copyright restrictions, the technical difficulty of presenting the information in a digital format, or the needs of the site's intended readership, it means that, with some exceptions, scholars must still consult printed critical editions for certain kinds of information.[6]

That is not to say that existing digital collections are useless for scholarship. After all, the goal of the Open Greek and Latin Project is not to publish critical editions, but to increase the amount of human-readable and machine-actionable Greek and Latin available online, and it promises to be an invaluable resource for a wide range of scholarship, from traditional literary and historical studies to

---

2 http://www.perseus.tufts.edu (last access 2019.01.31). It should be noted that the Perseus Digital Library expanded its Latin holdings to include authors from later eras, but on a limited basis. Its latest version (https://scaife.perseus.org, last access 2019.01.31) promises to be more expansive in terms of both texts in its library and tools available for studying them.

3 http://www.brepolis.net (last access 2019.01.31).

4 http://latin.packhum.org (last access 2019.01.31).

5 Corpus Scriptorum Latinorum: A Digital Library of Latin Literature: http://forumromanum.org/literature/index.html (last access 2019.01.31); The Latin Library: https://thelatinlibrary.com (last access 2019.01.31).

6 Kiss (2009–2013) is a notable exception. The catalog edited by Franzini et al. (2016–) contains details on other resources, but truly critical editions on the internet are still rare.

the latest developments in natural language processing. Rather, the point of this brief survey has been to define the space that the Digital Latin Library (DLL) means to fill: the collection and publication of critical editions of Latin texts from all eras, and the materials associated with them.[7]

To accomplish its objective, the DLL has two main initiatives: the DLL Catalog and the Library of Digital Latin Texts (LDLT). The purpose of the former is to collect, catalog, and provide an interface for finding Latin texts that have been digitized or published in digital form. The purpose of the latter is to publish new, born-digital critical editions of Latin texts from all eras. The rest of this paper will discuss these two wings of the DLL and their complementary goal of supporting new work in Latin textual criticism.

The DLL Catalog

As with other elements of the DLL, the "D" stands for "Digital" in a number of different ways. First and foremost, all of the items in the DLL Catalog are digital in some respect, either as digitized versions of printed materials or as digital texts.[8] Second, the catalog itself is digital, built with and operating entirely on open source technology. Most people will use the DLL Catalog via the web interface, but the datasets will be serialized in JSON-LD and available for downloading and reuse, in keeping with the best practices known as Linked Open Data.[9] Third, owing to the abundance of materials and the limited resources of the DLL, leveraging digital technology to ingest, process, and publish data is essential. Accordingly, building applications to facilitate those tasks is part of the scholarly endeavor of the DLL Catalog.[10]

Another way in which the DLL Catalog is digital is in its use of data modeling. Taking a cue from the Perseus Catalog[11] and using concepts from the

7 The Digital Latin Library project has been funded by generous grants from the Andrew W. Mellon Foundation's Scholarly Communications division from 2012 to 2018, and by ongoing institutional support from the University of Oklahoma.
8 See Sahle (2016) for an extended discussion of the difference between "digitized" and "digital." In short, a digital scan of a book may be referred to as "digitized," but not "digital," since it merely represents an object that exists in a non-digital format. To qualify as "digital," an edition must have distinct characteristics that would cease to function outside of the digital realm.
9 The repository is available at https://github.com/DigitalLatin (last access 2019.01.31).
10 See https://github.com/DigitalLatin/dllcat-automation (last access 2019.01.31).
11 http://catalog.perseus.org (last access 2019.01.31).

Functional Requirements for Bibliographic Records (FRBR)[12] model as a basis and data gathered from user studies, June Abbas and her team of researchers from the University of Oklahoma's School of Library and Information Studies designed an information behavior model to accommodate the different kinds of data to be stored in the catalog and the different ways in which users would interact with that data.[13] The following sections describe the resulting information architecture of the catalog and how it seeks to cater to the needs identified in Abbas' user studies.

Authority records

Authority records for authors and works provide the foundation for the DLL Catalog's information architecture. Each author of a Latin work has an authority record that identifies that author unambiguously and provides supporting attestations from a variety of sources to confirm the identity. In most cases, several forms of the author's name are recorded, especially the authorized name, which is usually identical to the authorized name in a major research library such as the U.S. Library of Congress, the Bibliothèque nationale de France, the Deutsche Nationalbibliothek, or others. Alpha-numerical or numerical identifiers such as the Virtual International Authority File ID or the Canonical Text Services identifier are also recorded, along with details about relevant dates and places. The purpose of an author authority record is to provide a single point of reference for individual authors. That way, searches for "Vergil", "Virgil", or "Vergilius" lead to the same information. Additionally, the cataloging process is more successful when automated matching algorithms have access to variant name forms.

Similarly, authority records for works support the vital functions of the catalog. Since dozens, if not hundreds, of works are known simply as *Carmina*, *Historiae*, or simply *fragmentum*, to take just three examples, it is important to have a means of disambiguating them. Accordingly, each work has its own authority record, with an authorized form of the title and any variant titles, along with information about its place in any collections, its author(s), and any abbreviations or other identifiers commonly in use.

Different content types for digitized editions, digitized manuscripts, and digital texts are the DLL Catalog's architectural frame. These content types

---

12 https://www.ifla.org/publications/functional-requirements-for-bibliographic-records (last access 2019.01.31).

13 See Abbas et al. (2015) for information about the methods and outcomes of the user studies.

store metadata related to specific instances of texts, each one connected to its creator and work through an entity reference so as to be discoverable in a variety of searches. Each record also contains a link to the external resource where the item can be found.

Contents

As of this writing, the DLL team has added authority records for over three thousand authors and nearly five thousand works spanning the time period from the third century BCE to the twentieth century CE. Many of those records were culled from information in standard reference works (e.g., *Clavis Patrum Latinorum*) and dictionaries (e.g., *Oxford Latin Dictionary, Thesaurus Linguae Latinae*), but records are also added nearly every time a new collection is added to the catalog, which is one of the reasons why the quest to catalog all Latin authors and works will be asymptotic.

Several collections are at different stages of being added to the catalog. With regard to digital texts, all of the items in following collections have been processed and cataloged: Perseus, PHI, Digital Library of Late-antique Latin Texts, and Biblioteca Italiana. Items on the related sites Musisque Deoque and Poeti d'Italia are in process and will be added by the end of 2019. These sites were selected because the sources of their texts are clearly identified and the texts themselves are openly available. Collections of texts behind a paywall (e.g., the Loeb Classical Library and Brepolis) are also in process, but since freedom of access is a priority, they will be added to the catalog at a later date.

As for digitized editions, efforts have focused on cataloging items in the public domain at resources such as the HathiTrust Digital Library, the Internet Archive, and Google Books.[14] Two categories in particular have received the most attention: early editions (*editiones principes*) and items in Engelmann's magisterial survey of Latin texts published between 1700 and 1878, *Bibliotheca Scriptorum Classicorum*. As of this writing, eighty-two early editions have been cataloged, including fifty-four editions of Latin texts published by Aldus Manutius. Over time, editions published by other early printers (e.g., Sweynheym and Pannartz, Jodocus Badius Ascensius), will be added to the collection. The survey of Engelmman's bibliography has so far yielded nearly three thousand

14 HathiTrust Digital Library: https://www.hathitrust.org (last access 2019.01.31); Internet Archive: https://archive.org (last access 2019.01.31); Google Books: https://books.google.com (last access 2019.01.31).

individual editions. Overlapping some of those are the records added in the effort to catalog all editions published in the history of the B.G. Teubner publishing house. To date, there are nearly nine hundred records in that collection.

The DLL Catalog also has a content type for manuscripts. Based on the guidelines of the Text Encoding Initiative's module for manuscript description, this content type is designed to be a resource for those wishing to find and view digital images of manuscripts of Latin texts. Since access to images of manuscripts varies widely among repositories, and since the metadata for manuscripts can be complex, progress on this initiative has been slower, but the catalog currently has nearly 1,300 records in process.

In sum, the DLL Catalog contained over 10,000 items when it was launched in the fall of 2018. Efforts to augment the catalog with items from other collections and library will be part of the DLL's ongoing mission to facilitate access to manuscripts, previously published critical editions, and other materials necessary for scholarly study of Latin texts.

The Library of Digital Latin Texts

Just as the DLL Catalog focuses on collecting historical editions and manuscripts of Latin texts, the Library of Digital Latin Texts (LDLT) focuses on publishing new, born-digital critical editions of Latin texts from all eras. The rest of this chapter will discuss what that means.

The subject of publishing digital scholarly editions is awash in paradoxes, some of them real, others only perceived. It is commonly assumed that younger scholars have an affinity for technology but pursue traditional modes of publication out of concern for the advancement of their careers. Conversely, it is assumed that senior scholars have more latitude for experimenting with new forms of publication, but lack the motivation or ability to learn new technologies. In both cases, the assumptions are only partly true. Although younger scholars are well-advised to publish their work in established outlets, it is not true that their age gives them any special facility with technology. Similarly, more established scholars do have some room for experimenting with publication formats, but it is ageist to assume that they necessarily have a block with respect to technology.

Leaving aside the false dichtomies of age and acumen, the LDLT aims to address the two real factors underlying those concerns. First, peer-review is essential to scholarly publications, so it is vital to have policies and procedures in place to ensure that LDLT editions meet the highest standards of the profession in that regard. Second, the digital format of the LDLT distinguishes it from traditional critical editions in print, so it is important to take advantage of computing technology; at the same time, it is crucial not to exclude scholars from working on LDLT editions for lack of technical skill. The DLL has launched two initiatives to address both of these concerns.

Policies and procedures

It is one thing to publish something online in the sense of making it publicly available; it is something else entirely to submit one's work to review and criticism by one's peers in the field as part of an independent organization's publication process. Accordingly, the DLL publishes the LDLT through its affiliation with the Society for Classical Studies (SCS), the Medieval Academy of America (MAA), and the Renaissance Society of America (RSA). Throughout the planning and implementation stages, the DLL has convened regular meetings of an advisory board composed of representatives from all three organizations. The chief goal of these meetings was to devise and agree upon policies and procedures for subjecting LDLT editions to the same level of peer-review that other publications typically receive.

Since all of the organizations publish monographs or other print publications, they have the organizational structures in place for managing the process of receiving submissions, identifying potential reviewers, making final decisions to publish or not to publish the material, and working with a press to see the project through to completion. Submissions to the LDLT are handled in the same manner. First, scholars submit proposals for LDLT editions to the publications board of the appropriate organization. Depending on the organization and the nature of the text, the proposal may include, for example, the argument for the edition, a sample of the work, a description of the strategy and timeline for completing the edition, and a statement of the editor's qualifications. Second, the board reviews the proposal, with consultation of qualified peer reviewers, if necessary, and decides whether or not to pursue it. If the outcome is favorable, the proposal is entered into a database of projects, and the organization authorizes the DLL to begin working with the editor. If the final version receives a favorable recommendation from the board, the edition is published in a version-controlled repository under the control of the DLL.

Another part of this initiative is the drafting of publishing agreements between 1) the DLL and the affiliated learned societies, and 2) the editors of LDLT editions, the DLL, and the learned society under whose imprimatur the edition will be published. These agreements state the rights and responsibilities of all parties, especially with regard to the open license under which LDLT editions are published. As of this writing, the Office of Legal Counsel at the University of Oklahoma, the DLL's host institution, is working with the DLL and the learned societies to finalize the agreements ahead of the publication of any editions.

Digital publication

Leveraging the digital nature of the LDLT means not only continuing to pursue and develop new methods for the use of technology with Latin texts, but also facilitating the participation of editors and other users of the LDLT who have varying levels of comfort with technology.

Key to this effort is clarifying what is meant by "digitial scholarly edition" in the first place, at least within the confines of the LDLT, since that term is in use elsewhere for everything from simple HTML documents to complex, multimedia databases. Indeed, a quick survey of the editions cataloged by Franzini et al. (2016–) reveals just how capacious the usage of "digital scholarly edition" is. As of this writing, the catalog has two hundred ninety-six items in general. Application of the filters for "scholarly", "digital", and "edition" reduces that number to two hundred thirty-seven. Those filters are based on the work of Sahle, who offers a useful way of thinking about the digital component (2016, 28): "Scholarly digital editions are scholarly editions that are guided by a digital paradigm in their theory, method and practice." But his discussion reveals that the "digital paradigm" is closely bound to presentational format. That is, by his definition, editors of scholarly digital editions are accountable for the quality of not only their textual scholarship, but also the design, implementation, and functionality of the interface and its accompanying technology. Although it is certainly the case that arguments about a text can be advanced through information visualization, the DLL asserts that human-computer interaction, data visualization, and user interface design should be taken seriously as scholarly disciplines unto themselves. Moreover, although some textual scholars might have the aptitude and capacity for developing mastery of these additional disciplines, they are the exceptions.

Accordingly, the LDLT aims to separate content from presentational format as much as possible. The qualification "as much as possible" is a nod to the fact that any representation of textual data, whether in plain text, encoded in Extensible Markup Language (XML), or on paper has a presentational format that influences how a reader (human or machine) interacts with it. Nevertheless, since data visualization and interface design add several layers of complexity to the traditional task of editing a text, an LDLT edition consists of the contents of a single XML file published in a version-controlled repository. As will be explained below, the DLL provides some official and experimental visualizations of the data in an LDLT edition as part of its ongoing scholarly research initiatives. Additionally, since LDLT editions are published on an open basis, anyone is free to reuse the data for other projects, including, but not limited to, the design and implementation of independent reading environments and data visualizations. But the edition file itself includes only prefatory materials, text, and scholarly apparatus; there are provisions for including expanded notes on the text, but extended commentary is outside of the scope of an LDLT edition. Additionally, editors are encouraged to include research notes, images, transcriptions of manuscripts, collation tables, and other materials in the repository that contains the edition file, for the sake of users who wish to conduct further research or who might have other uses for the research data. The option to include such materials is also in recognition of the scholarly approach that holds that a text's multiple versions in its various sources cannot be adequately conveyed to readers in a single critical edition.[15]

If the DLL left all decisions about content, encoding strategies, and presentational formats to editors, the LDLT would be just a loose collection of projects, each with its own unique approach and features, and it would be viable as a publication forum only for editors with the requisite technical skill. Although prescribing the encoding method and separating content from presentation does set some limits on what may be included in an LDLT edition, it also ensures that LDLT texts will have features in common, which means that they will be more useful as a uniform corpus of texts. It also means that they will work with the LDLT's applications.

Just as the "D" in the DLL Catalog includes the development of digital tools for processing information for the catalog, the "D" in LDLT emcompasses the digital tools and methods developed by the DLL for facilitating the creation and use of digital editions. The following tools and methods are the DLL's independent scholarly research outcomes in support of the LDLT project.

15 Such is the prevailing view of the essays collected by Apollon et al. (2014). See also Heslin (2016), who considers textual ctiticism as a "mental disorder," and who argues in favor of variorum editions instead. During a panel discussion at the 2018 annual meeting of the Society for Classical Studies, Heslin appeared to agree that the LDLT's approach of providing a canonical edition and access to transcriptions and collation materials is a good way of bridging the divide between new and traditional philology.

Encoding guidelines

Huskey and Cayless' "Guidelines for Encoding Critical Editions for the Library of Digital Latin Texts" are the foundation for the other research projects associated with the LDLT. A customization of the Text Encoding Initiative's guidelines, with strong ties to Epidoc, the LDLT's encoding guidelines provide instructions for using XML to represent the various kinds of information typically found in critical editions, including the preface, main text, the various types of scholarly apparatus, and ancillary materials.

The majority of the work in developing the guidelines involved manually encoding a model edition. Giarratano's first edition of the bucolic poetry of Calpurnius Siculus was selected for this project for several reasons. First, Calpurnius Siculus' seven *Eclogues* add up to about the length of a "book" of Classical Latin poetry or prose: 759 lines of poetry. That seemed to be a manageable and reasonable size for a model text. Second, the textual tradition involves a number of interesting problems, including lacunae and the transposition of words, lines, and whole stanzas. Third, Calpurnius' poetry has attracted the attention of many illustrious figures in the history of philology, including Boccaccio, Heinsius, Burman, Scaliger, and Wilamowitz, among others, so the bibliography is rich and interesting from a historical point of view. Finally, Giarratano's edition features an ample and detailed apparatus criticus, with plenty of edge cases for testing the limits of the data model. In consultation with Cayless, Robert Kaster, and Cynthia Damon on technical and textual matters, and with the assistance of several students at the University of Oklahoma,[16] Huskey encoded every line of poetry and every entry in the apparatus criticus, along with the preface, description of manuscripts, and the conspectus siglorum.[17] At the same time, Huskey and Cayless collaborated on compiling the encoding patterns, rules, and techniques into a document that eventually became the guidelines.

To test the applicability of the guidelines to other kinds of texts, the DLL enlisted some scholars to prepare pilot editions for the LDLT. Whether or not these editions will be published is up to the learned societies affiliated with the project to decide, but having materials for testing purposes has been invaluable. To ensure broad applicability of the guidelines, we selected a variety of texts, including books 9–12 of Servius' commentary on the *Aeneid* (edited by

---

16 Shejuti Silvia, Bharathi Asokarajan, Sudarshan Vengala, Vamshi Sunchu, Alexandra Owens, and Matthew Mitchell.

17 The current version of the model edition of Calpurnius Siculus' bucolic poetry may be found at https://github.com/sjhuskey/Calpurnius_Siculus (last access 2019.01.31).

Robert Kaster), Pseudo-Caesar's *Bellum Alexandrinum* (edited by Cynthia Damon), Peter Plaoul's Commentary on the *Sentences* of Peter Lombard (edited by Jeffrey Witt), and the Book of Genesis from the Codex Amiatinus (edited by Andrew Dunning). The encoding of each text has contributed to the evolution of the guidelines and preliminary results indicate that they will accommodate the majority of texts submitted to the LDLT.

In addition to providing uniform guidelines for producing material for the LDLT, the guidelines themselves are also a plank in the DLL's platform for promoting different forms of digital scholarship. More than just an application of existing instructions for encoding data, the guidelines are an argument about the form and function of critical editions. The addition of each new text to the LDLT will test that argument, and the guidelines will evolve to accommodate previously unforeseen scenarios.

Automated encoding

Editors have the option of encoding their editions themselves, using any of the many commercial and open source products for writing and editing XML, but they can also avail themselves of the automated encoding processes developed by the DLL. These automated processes have been developed in part as a way of testing the validity of the LDLT's data model. The argument is that if the encoding guidelines provide a sufficiently detailed structure for the various kinds of textual data, it should be possible to automate much of the standard encoding processes through algorithms based on the guidelines. For example, Felkner and Huskey have developed a series of Python scripts that automate the encoding of nearly all of a prospective LDLT edition, freeing editors to focus on textual matters instead of low-level encoding issues that do not require editorial scrutiny. Anything that cannot be encoded automatically is likely to require the editor's input regarding the precise nature of textual data in question, effectively highlighting the fundamental role that human judgment continues to play in textual criticism. Whether editors resolve those issues independently or in consultation with the DLL, the outcome is likely to influence further development of the automated encoding tools, and possibly the guidelines themselves.

LDLT viewer

The LDLT viewer, designed by Hugh Cayless, provides much of the functionality that June Abbas, co-PI on the DLL project, identified as necessary or desirable through her user studies. Based on the CETEIcean reader Cayless developed for the Text Encoding Initiative,[18] the LDLT viewer leverages HTML5 Custom Elements to avoid the need to process the XML data before displaying it in an internet browser. Instead of requiring the intermediate step of a data transformation via XSLT or some other method, the LDLT viewer application renames the elements in accordance with Custom Elements conventions. The resulting HTML preserves the structure of the original XML file, but it renders the data in a way that is more friendly to human readers.

The LDLT viewer preserves the traditional layout of a critical edition, with the text occupying the main portion of the display and the apparatus criticus appearing at the bottom of the screen, but there are also some important innovations. Chief among them is the additional dynamic apparatus display. Clickable icons appear to the right of any portion of the text that has corresponding data in the apparatus. Hovering the mouse over an icon causes the lemma in question to be highlighted in the main text. Clicking on the icon activates a dialog box that reveals the apparatus data related to that lemma. Clicking on a variant reading causes the variant to be substituted for the lemma in the main text so that it can be evaluated *in situ*. It will also cause related variants to be substituted simultaneously. For example, if a manuscript has two words or phrases transposed and that tranposition has been encoded in sufficient detail, clicking on one word or phrase will activate the other one, too, lest the viewer display a version of the text that does not exist in some source.

If an editor has tagged variant readings with terms from the taxonomy of variants included in the LDLT's encoding guidelines, other functionality is also enabled in the form of filters.[19] Users who do not wish to see apparatus entries concerned solely with orthographical variants can activate a filter to hide variants with that tag. Similar filters are available for morphological and lexical variants. A reset button restores the edition to its original state.

During development of the LDLT viewer, the DLL pooled some resources with the Open Philology Project to support the development and expansion of the Alpheios Reading Tools into Javascript libraries that can be deployed independently of specific browsers.[20] The LDLT viewer implements the Latin word parser and dictionary lookup libraries so that users can click on words to see automated lexical and morphological analyses.

18 https://github.com/TEIC/CETEIcean (last access 2019.01.31).
19 The section "Tagging Readings for Analysis" (https://digitallatin.github.io/guidelines/LDLT-Guidelines.html#apparatus-criticus-analysis, last access 2019.01.31) is the result of a collaboration between Huskey and Robert Kaster.
20 https://alpheios.net (last access 2019.01.31).

The LDLT viewer also operates on a framework compatible with Canonical Text Services, which means that users will be able to use CTS URNs to cite specific passages in texts.

Data visualization

To demonstrate the potential applications of data visualization scholarship to Latin texts, the DLL is making available a downloadable desktop application pre-loaded with a number of visualizations developed by Chris Weaver, another co-PI on the DLL project, and his students. Using the framework from his Improvise visualization application,[21] Weaver and his students have developed techniques to represent textual data in ways that will highlight the potential uses of visual data analysis for Latin textual studies. These visualizations are the most experimental of the the DLL's projects. Consequently, they should be considered candidates for further development after their initial release.

VariantFlow, developed by Shejuti Silvia, is a storyline visualization that represents manuscripts and other sources for a critical edition as individual lines that tell the story of variation in the text through their intersections and divergences. Proceeding along a horizontal plain that tracks the "story" of the critical apparatus from left to right, the lemmata serve as checkpoints. Observing how the storylines of the sources converge or separate throughout the text's overall "story" can provide a new perspective on the textual tradition.

TexTile, developed by Bharathi Asokarajan, uses pixels to represent the sources of a text and colors to indicate the degree of variance from the lemma, based on a string metric known as Levenshtein distance.[22] This tool presents the data in three different levels of focus: individual apparatus entry, line, and text chunk. Users control which level they see with a slider that brings different lemmata into focus. A spectrum of colors represents the degree to which a source varies from a given lemma or an edition's text in general.

Encodex, developed by Weaver, is a visual interface that integrates a regular text viewer with the visualizations mentioned above. As users scroll through the text, various kinds of highlighting will alert them to words or phrases with corresponding data in the apparatus. The other visualizations

21 http://www.cs.ou.edu/~weaver/improvise/index.html (last access 2019.01.31).

22 For more on Levenshtein distance, see https://en.wikipedia.org/wiki/Levenshtein_distance (last access 2019.01.31).

are synchronized with the scrolling operation in Encodex, giving readers a dynamic environment in which to explore different ways of looking at the text.

Conclusion

In some respects, this chapter has been about the future, since the various components described above will have their official launch while this book is in press. But even after their launch, there will never be a point at which the Digital Latin Library can be said to be complete. Although the DLL Catalog will launch with a large number of authority records and individual items, scouring the corners of the internet for Latin texts will be an ongoing project, both in terms of cataloging the content and developing new tools and methods for using it. Similarly, building the LDLT will be a long-term project, considering the number of Classical, Medieval, and Neo-Latin texts in need of new treatment as digital editions. But it is worth doing, especially if the availability of a sustainable outlet for publishing high quality, peer-reviewed Latin texts on an open basis encourages a new generation of scholars to continue the tradition of textual criticism.

Bibliography

Abbas, J.M.; Baker, S.R.; Huskey, S.J.; Weaver, C. (2015): "Digital Latin Library: Information Work Practices of Classics Scholars, Graduate Students, and Teachers". In: Proceedings of the Annual Meeting of the Association for Information Science and Technology. Silver Spring, MD: Association for Information Science and Technology. https://www.asist.org/files/meetings/am15/proceedings/openpage15.html (last access 2019.01.31).

Apollon, D.; Bélisle, C.; Régnier, P. (eds.) (2014): Digital Critical Editions. Urbana, Chicago, and Springfield: University of Illinois Press.

Asokarajan, B.; Etemadpour, R.; Huskey, S.J.; Abbas, J.M.; Weaver, C. (2016): "Visualization of Latin Textual Variants using a Pixel-Based Text Analysis Tool". In: Proceedings of the International Workshop on Visual Analytics. Geneva, Switzerland: The Eurographics Association. http://diglib.eg.org/handle/10.2312/eurova20161119 (last access 2019.01.31).

Crane, G.R.; Berti, M.; Geßner, A.; Munson, M.; Selle, T.: The Open Greek and Latin Project. http://www.dh.uni-leipzig.de/wo/projects/open-greek-and-latin-project (last access 2019.01.31).

Elliott, T.; Bodard, G.; Cayless, H. (2006–2017): EpiDoc: Epigraphic Documents in TEI XML. http://epidoc.sf.net (last access 2019.01.31).

Engelmann, W.; Preuss, E. (1882): Bibliotheca Scriptorum Classicorum. Volume 2: "Scriptores Latini". Leipzig: Wilhelm Engelmann.
Felkner, V.K.; Huskey, S.J.: "Digital Latin Library: Automation". https://github.com/DigitalLatin/automation (last access 2019.01.31).
Franzini, G.; Andorfer, P.; Zaytseva, K. (2016–): Catalogue of Digital Editions: The Web Application. https://dig-ed-cat.acdh.oeaw.ac.at (last access 2019.01.31).
Giarratano, C. (1910): Calpurnii et Nemesiani Bucolica. Naples: Detken et Rocholl.
Heslin, P. (2016): "The Dream of a Universal Variorum: Digitizing the Commentary Tradition". In: C.S. Kraus; C. Stray (eds.): Classical Commentaries: Explorations in a Scholarly Genre. Oxford: Oxford University Press, 494–511.
Kiss, D. (2009–2013): Catullus Online: An Online Repertory of Conjectures on Catullus. http://www.catullusonline.org (last access 2019.01.31).
Sahle, P. (2016): "What is a Scholarly Digital Edition?". In: M.J. Driscoll; E. Pierazzo (eds.): Digital Scholarly Editing. Cambridge: Open Book Publishers, 19–39.
Shejuti, S.; Etemadpour, R.; Huskey, S.J.; Abbas, J.M.; Weaver, C. (2016): "Visualizing Variation in Classical Text with Force Directed Storylines". In: Proceedings of the Workshop on Visualization for the Digital Humanities. Baltimore, MD: IEEE.

Hugh A. Cayless

Sustaining Linked Ancient World Data

Abstract: May 31st, 2018 marked the sixth anniversary of the Linked Ancient World Data Institute (LAWDI), a workshop funded by the US National Endowment For the Humanities. This makes it a good time to take stock of the Ancient World Linked Data initiatives that have been around for some time, as well as some that have foundered and some that are new. What makes for sustainable Linked Open Data? Why do some initiatives thrive while others fail? What resources do successful LOD sites need, and how may *they* be obtained? The promise of LOD is that it frees our information from the silos in which it is housed, permitting cross-system interactions that improve the quality and usefulness of the information in any single system. This article will take the broader view of the definition of Linked Data suggested by Tim Berners-Lee's foundational "Linked Data – Design Issues" paper, as encompassing more types of data than simply RDF and other "Semantic Web" technologies. This view of LOD is pragmatic and leverages the strengths of semantic technologies while avoiding their weaknesses.

Introduction

The title of this paper will require some definition before discussion of its subject matter can proceed. What is "sustainable" data? What is "Linked Data"? What counts as "Ancient World" data? May 31st, 2018 marked the sixth anniversary of the first Linked Ancient World Data Institute (LAWDI), a program funded by the US National Endowment for the Humanities (NEH).[1] A number of projects represented at LAWDI's two events, at the NYU Institute for the Study of the Ancient World in 2012, and then the following year at Drew University are still up and running, meaning they have successfully passed the startup phase. This paper will examine five of these long-running projects in the field of Ancient Studies which may be considered Linked Open Data sites and discuss how they have managed to sustain themselves and what their prospects for the future are.

1 See Elliott (2014) for follow-up articles by many of the participants.

Hugh A. Cayless, Duke University

https://doi.org/10.1515/9783110599572-004

Broadly speaking, data, and the applications that disseminate data, may be said to be sustainable when their maintenance costs do not exceed the resources available and are not likely to do so in the future. Moreover, the communities that use that data should find its continued availability important enough to contribute to its maintenance, whether monetarily or via their own labor. Data sets may be fairly static, e.g. reports of completed work, or may require periodic revision; they may grow steadily as new data are deposited and updated or remain relatively constant in size. Different types of curatorial intervention and expertise will be required depending on whether data sets change by addition or via editing, and both scholarly and technical expertise may be required in order to keep them going. Questions of survivability factor into the data sustainability question also. How hard would it be to migrate the data to a new dissemination platform? How hard are they to edit? Would they survive a period of neglect?

Sustainability boils down to questions about the nature of the data and the community's investment in its continued availability. Who is responsible for it? How available and discoverable is it? Is its maintenance funded or voluntary? What systems does it depend upon in order to remain available? What are the costs of maintaining it? As we will see, there are a number of possible answers to these questions, and making Linked Open Data sustainable requires a combination of strategies, including institutional support, collaboration agreements, keeping costs manageable, keeping user communities engaged, and keeping (or at least exporting) data in forms that can survive a loss or transition of support.

Turning to Linked Open Data, we find a similar set of questions. There is an inherent tension in the definition of Linked Data over how that data should be represented. Must it be modeled according to the Resource Description Framework (RDF)? Can Linked Data be in any format made discoverable via a set of encoded relationships? Berners-Lee's original notes on the subject in "Linked Data – Design Issues"[2] define five levels, of increasing quality:

1. Available on the web (whatever format) but with an open licence, to be Open Data.
2. Available as machine-readable structured data (e.g. excel instead of image scan of a table).
3. As (2) plus non-proprietary format (e.g. CSV instead of excel).
4. All the above plus: Use open standards from W3C (RDF and SPARQL) to identify things, so that people can point at your stuff.
5. All the above plus: Link your data to other people's data to provide context.

2 (Berners-Lee 2006).

This scheme is, on the face of it, agnostic about what data should be represented in what format (with a bias towards non-proprietary formats), but most subsequent implementations and interpretations of "Linked Data" have focused on RDF and the suite of protocols around it as the delivery mechanism (not simply the means of identification) for information, and many LOD datasets have thus been published encoded entirely in RDF formats. In this guise, the Linked Data enterprise seems clearly to be a continuation of the original Semantic Web, an idea originally popularized by an article in *Scientific American*, also by Berners-Lee. Indeed, the definition given on the W3C's site explicitly ties Linked Data to the Semantic Web.[3] For the purposes of this paper, however, I will consider sites that make an attempt to follow Berners-Lee's general principles, but do not necessarily store, nor expose *all* of their data as RDF as "Linked Open Data" projects. Further, I will argue that to do so would incur the risk of exploding the costs of already-expensive projects. The LOD sites we will examine take a pragmatic view which leverages the strengths of Linked Data architectural styles and semantic technologies while avoiding their weaknesses.

Linked Ancient World Data sites

The projects which were represented at the LAWDI meetings and which this paper will examine are Pleiades, which serves as a digital gazetteer of ancient places, Papyri.info, which publishes texts and data relating to ancient handwritten documents on surfaces such as papyrus and ostraca, Trismegistos, which aggregates data about ancient documents, people, and places, Open Context, which collects archaeological reports, and Nomisma, which provides a thesaurus of numismatic concepts with links out to coin records in a variety of numismatic datasets.

Pleiades (https://pleiades.stoa.org/) is arguably the oldest of these, having originally been conceived in 2000, as a follow-on to the printed *Barrington Atlas of the Greek and Roman World*.[4] Formal work on the project did not begin

3 W3C, *Linked Data*, passim. "Linked Data lies at the heart of what Semantic Web is all about"; "To achieve and create Linked Data, technologies should be available for a common format (RDF), to make either conversion or on-the-fly access to existing databases (relational, XML, HTML, etc)".
4 Ed. by Talbert (2000).

until 2006, however, after a successful funding bid to the National Endowment for the Humanities.

> Pleiades has received significant, periodic support from the National Endowment for the Humanities since 2006. Development hosting and other project incubation support was provided between 2000 and 2008 by Ross Scaife and the Stoa Consortium. Additional support, primarily in the form of in-kind content research and review, has been provided since 2000 by the Ancient World Mapping Center at the University of North Carolina at Chapel Hill. Web hosting and additional financial support (not least our annual hosting costs and my time as managing editor) has been provided since 2008 by the Institute for the Study of the Ancient World at New York University.[5]

Pleiades's internal data model does not rely on RDF, but it does publish its data in various forms, which include RDF (see https://pleiades.stoa.org/downloads). The system is built on top of Plone, a Content Management System based on the Zope application server, written in Python. It deals with entities in the form of Places, Locations, and Names. Places are abstractions which may be associated with zero or more Locations and Names. Each of these entities will have an HTTPS URI that identifies it. For example, https://pleiades.stoa.org/places/727070 (Alexandria) has an associated location (https://pleiades.stoa.org/places/727070/darmc-location-1090) and a set of names, e.g.

> Alexandreia ad Aegyptum: https://pleiades.stoa.org/places/727070/alexandreia-ad-aegyptum
> Alexandria: https://pleiades.stoa.org/places/727070/alexandria
> al-Iskandariya: https://pleiades.stoa.org/places/727070/al-iskandariya-1

All of these have variant spellings. Because Pleiades treats these as distinct "pages" a search for "al-Iskandarīya" on Google will turn up the name page listed above, which will in turn direct the searcher to the Place record for that Alexandria (there are many).

Parts of the Papyri.info data set began their existence much earlier.[6] The Duke Databank of Documentary Papyri (DDbDP) began work in 1982, and was issued on CD-ROM. The Advanced Papyrological Information System (APIS) and the Heidelberger Gesamtverzeichnis (HGV) began in the 1990s. The DDbDP reproduced the texts of published editions of papyrus documents; HGV holds expanded metadata about them, including bibliography, better provenance

5 Elliott, personal communication, 2018-09-21.

6 The author was the principal architect of the Papyrological Navigator – the browse and search portion of the Papyri.info site.

information, some translations, and links to images where available; APIS contains what are essentially catalog records, focusing on description of the artifact, along with images for some of the papyri and translations. Thus, the DDbDP and HGV are focused on editions, while APIS focuses on the document itself. Data from Trismegistos[7] was added on more recently.

Planning to revive the DDbDP, which was no longer being actively edited, and whose data had been hosted by the Perseus Project since the mid-1990s, began in 2006. Thanks to grant funding from the Mellon Foundation and the NEH, Papyri.info was developed as an update and replacement for the discovery facilities provided by Perseus and as a means to crowdsource the editing of the data, which the DDbDP was no longer able to sustain at Duke. Papyri.info began by following the some of the principles Berners-Lee outlined: all data would be openly available and licensed for re-use, each document would have a stable URI that both identified it and served allowed its retrieval, but it did not initially use any RDF technologies. Because the system is an amalgamation of several datasets, which do not align perfectly, deciding how to assemble the information was quite tricky. HGV might treat as many what the DDbDP considered as a single document, for example. Or HGV might rely on a different publication as the "principal edition". APIS might treat documents differently than either of the other two because of its emphasis on the artifact. An edition might assemble multiple fragments (with different curatorial histories) into a single text, for example.

All of this meant unifying the display of information about a papyrus document was not straightforward. The datasets knew about each other, and referenced each other to an extent, and after a few false starts, the project settled on using RDF to describe the links between records in the different datasets. Relationships between records are extracted from the source documents and then used to generate an aggregate view of each document. A page in Papyri.info like http://papyri.info/ddbdp/p.fay;;110 pulls together data from HGV, Trismegistos, APIS, and the DDbDP. Exploration of the Linked Data section linked at the bottom of the page will reveal that the source for the page's data is http://papyri.info/ddbdp/p.fay;;110/source, which is related to:

the TM text, https://www.trismegistos.org/text/10775,
the HGV record, http://papyri.info/hgv/10775/source,
the APIS record, http://papyri.info/apis/columbia.apis.p387/source,
the APIS images, http://papyri.info/apis/columbia.apis.p387/images.

7 Trismegistos (https://www.trismegistos.org: last access 2019.01.31) will be treated in more detail below.

These relations are stored in an RDF triple store referred to as the "Numbers Server". This keeps track of the relationships between content from the various collections, as well as information about superseded editions in the DDbDP. All of Papyri.info's textual data is also maintained in a GitHub repository.[8] An hourly sync process keeps the data current. The system uses a triple store to manage relations between documents, which are stored on disk. Text documents are stored as TEI EpiDoc files, versioned using Git. So while Papyri.info makes use of RDF, it makes no attempt to store nor expose all of its data in that form.

Trismegistos (TM) began development in 2005, when its director, Mark Depauw, received a Sofja Kovalevskaja Award from the Alexander von Humboldt-Stiftung. The project, 'Multilingualism and Multiculturalism in Graeco-Roman Egypt', was the foundation of Trismegistos, which has grown beyond its initial focus on Egypt to encompass ancient documents of all kinds. Trismegistos assigns unique URL identifiers to documents, which means it can serve as a "data hub" for identifying documents across projects, in much the same way as Pleiades functions for places. Trismegistos and Papyri.info have a close relationship, in which TM identifiers help serve to disambiguate documents for the PN, and the PN's data is used as a source for TM's research. The two sites collaborate and interlink their documents extensively. Data exchange from TM to Papyri.info remains somewhat informal, based on periodic data dumps, while TM relies on Papyri.info's GitHub repository. As we have already seen, TM URLs are in the form https://www.trismegistos.org/text/10775. Besides texts, TM collects data around Collections, Archives, (ancient) People, Places, (ancient) Authors, and (modern) Editors. TM manages its data using a FileMaker Pro database, which exports to a MySQL database that serves as the back end of the PHP-based TM website. It does not export nor expose any RDF.

Open Context began in December 2006. It provides a platform for the publication, archiving, and annotation of archeological data. The site has gone through several cycles of refactoring, from PHP and MySQL, to PHP-Zend Framework, MySQL and Solr, to its current state as a Python-Django, PostgreSQL, and Solr site. Open Context is organized around Projects, Subjects, and Media, each instance of which has its own stable URL in the following forms:

Projects: https://opencontext.org/projects/3DE4CD9C-259E-4C14-9B03-8B10454BA66E
Subjects: https://opencontext.org/subjects/0801DF9C-F9B2-4C76-0F34-93BE7123F373
Media: https://opencontext.org/media/48c1bdeb-ffb9-4fd3-84d2-20ba189a1f4a

8 https://github.com/papyri/idp.data (last access 2019.01.31).

While it does not use RDF internally, Open Context models its data in a PostgreSQL database in a graph-like fashion, and it only produces RDF for external services (e.g. Pelagios) to consume. Most consumers of its data prefer to receive it in tabular form. Eric Kansa reports that, while an internal RDF triple store is a desideratum, questions of data provenance and versioning, and the difficulties RDF has with these problems, make it a low priority.[9]

Nomisma is the youngest of the projects we will discuss, having first begun in 2010, and also adheres most closely to the standard definition of a Linked Open Data site, as it models and stores all of its data in RDF. The site provides "stable digital representations of numismatic concepts". These concepts serve as a backbone for browsing and querying across several numismatic datasets. Nomisma entities are drawn from concepts such as mints, coin types, and numismatic concepts, and these link out to datasets from sources including the American Numismatic Society (ANS), the Portable Antiquities Scheme, the British Museum, and the Staatliche Museen zu Berlin. Despite its offering the purest version of Linked Open Data that we have seen, Nomisma's RDF does not provide a complete representation of the scholarly space it represents. Data from the ANS is edited in XML form using the Numismatic Description Standard (NUDS) and then transformed to RDF for ingestion into Nomisma. Not all of the data represented in a NUDS file makes its way into Nomisma's triple store. The site plus its associated datasets thus serve as a kind of distributed database of coinage information.

All of the entities modeled by Nomisma are dealt with as Simple Knowledge Organization System (SKOS) Concepts,[10] meaning that they are essentially treated as subjects in a taxonomy. SKOS makes available several useful properties for relating Concepts to other entities. So the Nomisma identifier http://nomisma.org/id/ephesus represents the "idea" of the mint at Ephesus and http://nomisma.org/id/ephesus#this represents the "spatial location" Ephesus (which has, e.g. geocoordinates). Information about the provenance of this data is attached to the URI http://nomisma.org/id/ephesus#provenance. The Nomisma interface surfaces a list of links to the first 100 coins related to an entity from partner projects, with the opportunity to download the full set as CVS or to view and modify the SPARQL query that produced the list.

---

9 Kansa, personal communication, 2018.

10 SKOS develops "specifications and standards to support the use of knowledge organization systems (KOS) such as thesauri, classification schemes, subject heading lists and taxonomies within the framework of the Semantic Web".

Models for sustainability

The funding models for these five Linked Data resources all vary. Pleiades is led by Tom Elliott, the Associate Director for Digital Programs at the Institute for the Study of the Ancient World (ISAW). He, and occasionally other personnel at ISAW are responsible for its ongoing maintenance, while its development cycles have been funded by grants from the NEH with support from ISAW. Papyri.info was developed under the auspices of the Integrating Digital Papyrology project (IDP), led by Joshua Sosin and funded by grants from the Andrew W. Mellon Foundation, along with some funding from the NEH for APIS. Since the completion of IDP, Duke University Libraries has supported its ongoing development and maintenance. The Duke Collaboratory for Classics Computing (DC3) is the group responsible for technical maintenance and upgrades. Trismegistos is supported by Mark Depauw's position as a faculty member at Leiden, and Mark has been successful in obtaining funding from various sources to support its ongoing development. Open Context was begun and continues to be developed by Eric and Sarah Kansa, with its funding dependent on grants and consulting work. It recently received an NEH Challenge Grant, with which Open Context hopes to put its funding on more stable ground. Nomisma is a project of the American Numismatic Society (ANS). It was begun in 2010 by Andrew Meadows and Sebastian Heath. Ethan Gruber took over as lead developer in 2012 and has continued in that position since.

None of the sites employ what might be called a "lightweight" digital infrastructure. All use backend databases of different types. Papyri.info and Nomisma both use Apache Jena and Fuseki, a Java-based RDF triple store. Papyri.info and Open Context use Apache Solr, a Java-based search engine. Papyri.info and Trismegistos both employ MySQL as a database, Open Context uses PostgreSQL, and Pleiades the Zope Object Database. Most of them have a dynamic front-end, where pages are assembled upon request from data in the database. Without taking a deep dive into the technologies involved, we can still say with confidence that all of the resources under discussion have both infrastructural and maintenance requirements that demand a significant allocation of server storage, memory, and CPU to host them. Moreover, they are of sufficient complexity and scale that experienced people are needed to maintain them. If we were to place them in Vinopal and McCormick's model for levels of support in Digital Scholarship Services, they would all be at the highest tier (4, Applied R&D), and deployed at tier 3 (Enhanced Research Services).[11] None

11 See Vinopal (2013, 32, fig. 1).

of them could be simply moved into the care of, e.g. a typical university research library without additional funding (probably including additional staff) for their maintenance.

Most of the sites under discussion mitigate the risks involved in running a resource-intensive service by publishing their data in static forms and at multiple venues. Pleiades exports its data daily in a variety of formats, including JSON, KML, CSV, and RDF. Papyri.info exposes its RDF and TEI XML data alongside its web pages, and also provides a public repository on GitHub containing all of its source data. Nomisma provides downloads of its data in JSON-LD, Turtle, and RDF/XML. Open Context permits the download of project data or search results in tabular (CSV) or Geo-JSON form. Only Trismegistos does not currently provide a data export feature, but it does share its data with Papyri.info in the form of periodic database dumps. Papyri.info's data in particular provide a salutary lesson in the value of static data exports. Both the DDbDP and APIS data contained by the site were converted from older forms from previous projects. The DDbDP data is on its third iteration, having begun life as Beta Code,[12] created for the PHI CD-ROMs, then converted to TEI SGML + Beta Code for ingestion into the Perseus Project, and finally to EpiDoc XML and Unicode for import into Papyri.info. The open formats used by PHI and Perseus made these migrations an achievable, if not always simple exercise.

To varying degrees, all of these resources rely on the involvement and commitment of particular individuals. Pleiades would not exist without Tom Elliott, nor Trismegistos without Mark Depauw, nor Open Context without Eric Kansa. Were they to cease being involved, the futures of these projects might be in doubt. Pleiades is less vulnerable, as it has an institutional home at ISAW, which one hopes would decide to continue it without him. Papyri.info certainly would not exist in its current form without the director of DC3, Joshua Sosin, and its major components owe their architecture to and are still maintained by Ryan Baumann and myself, but it would likely survive the departure of any of its key personnel. It would take a withdrawal of support by its home institution to threaten it. Although Nomisma as it exists is largely the creation of Ethan Gruber, the ANS supports it, and so it would also be likely to continue if Ethan departed. All of the services under discussion have been significantly shaped by their developers, and many of these developers have been present since the inception of the project.

---

12 (TLG 2016).

Of course, reliance on individual contributors is a double-edged sword: they are hard to replace, and there is some increased risk because of their importance to the project. On the other hand, maintenance costs may be cheaper because the people with the most intimate knowledge of the services are the ones who run them. These costs might go up significantly if service maintenance were handed off to less-expert teams and the continuance of the projects themselves might be at risk. The institutions which support these projects have chosen to do so by supporting individual developers in ways that bear more similarity to faculty than technical staff. Duke University Libraries created a new Digital Classics research unit, DC3, and hired Baumann and myself to staff it. ISAW has its own Digital Programs department which Tom Elliott heads. The Curatorial Department at the ANS employs Ethan Gruber as their Director of Data Science. All of us publish, and present at conferences both in our home fields and in Digital Humanities venues, with the support of our institutions. All of us are involved in initiatives that reach well beyond the walls of those institutions.

For institutions that wish to support "Tier 4" type projects, it may be beneficial to have the ability to hire project personnel in association with those projects. Acquiring successful or promising projects along with their personnel may be a better way to grow an institution's digital portfolio than attempting to grow it from scratch. The creation of DC3 certainly followed this model. Despite being the institutional leader of the Integrating Digital Papyrology grant that produced Papyri.info, Duke University was not able to field the personnel to actually develop it. The work was contracted out to King's College London, NYU, and the University of Kentucky Center for Visualization & Virtual Environments. At the conclusion of the grant, Duke University Libraries established DC3 to maintain and continue the project, and the Papyri.info site was transferred there from NYU in 2013. Pleiades similarly followed Tom Elliott to ISAW in 2008, and one might wonder whether Open Context might achieve long-term support via a similar route.

Another important aspect of sustainability that all of these projects exemplify is community engagement. Nomisma and Papyri.info have made themselves indispensable tools for the small scholarly communities they represent (Numismatics and Papyrology). Pleiades, Trismegistos, and Open Context all have a larger purview, but they too have made themselves indispensable to the point where, if they ceased to exist, something would have to be created to replace them.

Linked Data and complexity

We have so far spent some time discussing the five projects' relationship to RDF and Semantic Web technologies without relating them to the definitions of Linked Data and its relationship to RDF. RDF works by encoding data as triples, in the form Subject, Predicate, Object, where the Subject and Predicate parts of each statement are URIs, and the Object is either a URI or a string (a "literal"). Modern triple stores further refine this scheme by adding a Graph URI, making each statement a quad. RDF data can be queried using the SPARQL query language, so once data has been structured as RDF, there is a ready-made way to extract information from it, or even to generate new information from existing statements. This makes for a powerful tool for scholarly inquiry, provided sufficient information has been encoded as RDF. Since statements can be linked (e.g. the Subject of one statement may be the Object of another), the information in a triple store may be said to form a graph. The foundation of Linked Data is the use of real, dereferenceable web URLs in RDF data sets, meaning that links to web resources are embedded in the semantic graph.

RDF is hard to criticize as a data format, because it is technically able to represent almost any more-complex data structure. But certain data formats have properties and affordances that may make them easier to work with and more suitable for representing certain types of data. XML and JSON Arrays, for example, both have intrinsic order, which RDF lacks.[13] In order to represent ordered data in RDF, it is typically necessary either to emulate a Linked List or to use a custom ontology for the purpose. RDF also has a hard time with qualified relationships. Recording the circumstances under which an assertion was made, for example, which would mean attaching extra metadata to a triple, requires rather extensive workarounds. All of this means that, while RDF can be devised that would represent something like a Text Encoding Initiative (TEI) XML document, the actual implementation might not provide any benefits over the original document beyond the ability to query it with SPARQL, and would be considerably harder to edit or even display in a usable fashion. Because RDF atomizes any data it represents into triples or quads, presenting or editing it means (re)assembling those atomic facts into a larger structure, in the correct order. Because it is a graph, the "records" therein are unbounded (i.e. the connections between

---

13 RDF does have a built in Seq container type, which defines an order to its members based on their property names, but this order must be imposed by a client reading the RDF, which is itself an un-ordered set of triples (or quads). RDF Lists are analogous to lists in various programming languages, e.g. LISP. The first item has a property linking to the content (the first) and a property linking to the next node in the list (the rest).

pieces of data may extend to any length in any "direction"), so technology has to be applied to retrieving only the sensible pieces of data for the intended purpose.

One might consider TEI documents to be an edge case where RDF is an unsatisfactory representation, but in fact the data modeling around any scholarly project is likely to be esoteric. This sets up an inherent tension, as the explicit goal of LOD is interoperability. Even when (apparently) well-defined standards are adopted for the description of a project's data model, the local interpretation of those standards and the "gray areas" they inevitably contain will make the definition of mappings between datasets a necessary precondition for interoperation. If the goal of LOD is the same as the Semantic Web, where purely machine-mediated domain exploration is possible, then it is only likely to be achievable in cases where the semantics of the data are lightweight.

The TEI has struggled over the years with questions of interoperability, for precisely the same reasons.[14] Data modeling is an interpretive act, and because of that, the more complex and extensive it is, the more individualized it necessarily becomes. It follows that there is an inverse relationship between comprehensiveness and interoperability. Since the latter is the entire goal of LOD, concentrating on simplicity in the Linked Data one exposes would seem to be a better investment than working on fully encoding one's data in a semantic format. Recent developments, notably the introduction of the JSON-LD format, would seem to represent a turn towards such simplicity. JSON-LD is the basis for Linked.art, for example, which aims to develop a more usable profile of CIDOC-CRM, one of the more complex cultural heritage RDF vocabularies. Linked.art's analysis of CIDOC-CRM classes provides an interesting insight into the ways in which attempts to be comprehensive may result in unhelpful complexity or even failure to fulfill an obvious need. For example, the discussion of E30 Right, states:

> The basic problem with E30 Right is that it is a Conceptual Object, and Conceptual Objects cannot be destroyed. While there is any carrier of the object, including the CIDOC-CRM description of it or even within someone's memory, then the concept still exists somewhere. As it cannot be written down without persisting it, it cannot be destroyed and instead it can simply pass out of all knowledge. This means that the existence of the Right is not the same as the validity of the Right: the concept of slavery in America still exists, but it is no longer legally valid. There are no terms within the CRM to express the effective dates, and the CRM-SIG clarified that the right's effectiveness would be a different sort of resource. In particular that an E30 Right "is the formulation of the right, the terms", and not whether the right had any legal standing in any jurisdiction at any point in time.[15]

---

14 (Bauman 2011).
15 From https://linked.art/model/profile/class_analysis.html#ineffective-classes (last access 2019.01.31).

That a reasonable design decision might make it hard to do something practical, like express rights that are limited in time or space doesn't invalidate the whole enterprise by any means, but it is a signal that efforts to be complete and correct in a specification may come at the expense of usability. One should not need a Ph.D. in the philosophy of law to implement a small part of a data model.

Any sufficiently expressive data model runs the risk of provoking what we might term "over-encoding" by analogy to the idea of overengineering in software development. Specifications (like CIDOC-CRM or TEI) have a tendency to address problems that don't exist yet, but plausibly might, in their quest for completeness. Users of those specifications, especially new users, may tend to encode information without thinking about whether doing so provides any benefit, responding to a theoretical imperative rather than a real-world need. Doing so may, like overengineering, incur little immediate obvious harm but may also divert resources that might be used elsewhere and make processing and interoperability more complicated, thus having a net negative effect on project usability and sustainability.[16]

Simplicity is the hallmark of one of the more successful efforts at building a cultural heritage LOD network, Pelagios,[17] which aggregates data around places published by a variety of projects. Pleiades serves as the "hub" for these datasets, which use Open Annotation (OA) RDF to associate Pleiades place URIs with whatever information the project publishes. OA merely associates the annotation body with the URI being annotated (the target) without necessarily doing anything to characterize the nature of the link. Pelagios aggregates annotation datasets published by partner projects and provides tooling to research these. Pleiades, meanwhile, can use Pelagios's API to query what projects are referring to a particular Pleiades place. This means there is a straightforward way for pages in Pleiades to provide links out to associated material via Pelagios without having to maintain those linkages itself.

In this way, on a basic and practical level, the publication of stable resources and linkages with some (even if weak) semantics promises to be a huge boon for discoverability. This is likely to matter much more in the long run than whether a particular piece of data is in a particular format because it answers a basic scholarly need: "Can I find a piece of information and get from it to potentially useful related information?" Search engines use links for purposes of

16 Sporny's (2014) discussion of the relationship between JSON-LD and the Semantic Web refers to the tendency of Semantic Web specification developers to focus on the wrong things. "Too much time is spent assuming a future that's not going to unfold in the way that we expect it to".

17 (Simon 2014).

discovery and ranking and HTML links in the browser are only weakly (if at all) characterized. Google and its competitors employ machine learning algorithms to rank their search results with a great deal of success. The real strength of LOD may then be its architectural style, which by insisting on resolvable URLs for identifiers, exposes the components of a data set and the links between them to the web instead of hiding them behind a query interface.[18]

The five LOD projects under discussion all check at least some of the boxes in Berners-Lee's 5-star scheme, and all identify the important entities in their datasets using resolvable URIs and link to related data, both internally and externally. Most of them, however, put RDF somewhat at arm's length, using it as only one of several export formats (Pleaides, Nomisma) or structuring their data as nodes in a graph without attempting to encode the data using RDF (Papyri.info, Open Context, Trismegistos). Only Nomisma fully embraces RDF as a first-class data structure, and notably, it is only part of a broader infrastructure, the external nodes in which do not encode their data directly in RDF. Arguably, it performs, in a distributed way, the same function as the "Numbers Server" in Papyri.info. As we have seen, all of these are complex projects, requiring expert maintenance and support. It is notable that none of them, with the possible exception of Nomisma, embrace the Semantic Web interpretation of LOD.

Conclusion

Having explored some of the more successful Linked Ancient World Data systems and the ecosystems around them, we can summarize the characteristics that have enabled these projects to continue for years, well past the startup phase. All of them have provided long-term support for key personnel. None of them have attempted to build a resource and then hand it off to some other entity to maintain. All of them either have institutional or other long-term support, or are actively working on developing a support framework. All of them have become an indispensable resource for their communities, so that support or pressure might be brought to bear should they become threatened. All of them have embraced LOD as a means to connect their data to the wider digital cultural heritage infrastructure, but have at the same time avoided the complexity of attempting to represent their full range of data as RDF.

18 Cf. Ogbuji (2016) on the beneficial effects for visibility on the web of recasting public library catalogs as Linked Data.

If we can attempt to derive a recipe for long-term success in cultural heritage LOD from the examples in this essay then, we might say the following:

1. Involve and provide long-term support for technical specialists who also have content expertise and interest if possible.
2. Obtain Institutional commitments to ensure #1.
3. Prioritize focus on the needs of the community or audience and the practicalities of meeting those needs over following rubrics for LOD.
4. Expose or export data in reusable formats as both a means of attracting partners and as a hedge against disaster.
5. Intentionally engage partner projects and share data with them to ensure that links endure.

It should surprise no one that there are no "silver bullets" here. LOD opens up many interesting possibilities for cross-project data reuse and for building a true ecosystem of online cultural heritage resources, but the technology does not obviate the need for human collaboration and community engagement to make these possibilities real.

Bibliography

Bauman, S. (2001): "Interchange vs. Interoperability". In: Proceedings of Balisage: The Markup Conference 2011. Balisage Series on Markup Technologies. Volume 7. Mulberry Technologies, Inc. https://doi.org/10.4242/BalisageVol7.Bauman01.

Berners-Lee, T. (2006): Linked Data. https://www.w3.org/DesignIssues/LinkedData.html (last access 2019.01.31).

Berners-Lee, T.; Hendler, J.; Lassila, O. (2001): "The Semantic Web". Scientific American, May 2001, 29–37.

Elliott, T.; Heath, S.; Muccigrosso, J. (eds.) (2014): "Current Practice in Linked Open Data for the Ancient World". ISAW Papers 7. http://doi.org/2333.1/gxd256w7.

Gruber, E. (2018): "Linked Open Data for Numismatic Library, Archive and Museum Integration". In: M. Matsumoto; E. Uleberg (eds.): CAA2016: Oceans of Data. Proceedings of the 44th Conference on Computer Applications and Quantitative Methods in Archaeology. Oxford: Archaeopress, 35–40.

Linked.art. https://linked.art/index.html (last access 2019.01.31).

Ogbuji, U.; Baker, M. (2015): "Data Transforms, Patterns and Profiles for 21st century Cultural Heritage". In: Proceedings of the Symposium on Cultural Heritage Markup. Balisage Series on Markup Technologies. Mulberry Technologies, Inc. Volume 16. https://doi.org/10.4242/BalisageVol16.Ogbuji01.

Simon, R.; Barker, E.; de Soto, P.; Isaksen, L. (2014): "Pelagios". ISAW Papers 7. http://doi.org/2333.1/gxd256w7.

Sporny, M. (2014): "JSON-LD and Why I Hate the Semantic Web". http://manu.sporny.org/2014/json-ld-origins-2/ (last access 2019.01.31).

Talbert, R.J.A. (2000): Barrington Atlas of the Greek and Roman World. Princeton, NJ: Princeton University Press.
Thesaurus Linguae Graecae (TLG) (2016): The TLG® Beta Code Manual. http://www.tlg.uci.edu/encoding/BCM.pdf (last access 2019.01.31).
Vinopal, J.; McCormick, M. (2013): "Supporting Digital Scholarship in Research Libraries: Scalability and Sustainability". Journal of Library Administration 53, 27–42.
World Wide Web Consortium: Linked Data. https://www.w3.org/standards/semanticweb/data (last access 2019.01.31).

Cataloging and Citing Greek and Latin Authors and Works

Alison Babeu

The Perseus Catalog: of FRBR, Finding Aids, Linked Data, and Open Greek and Latin

Abstract: Plans for the Perseus Catalog were first developed in 2005 and it has been the product of continuous data creation since that time. Various efforts to bring the catalog online resulted in the current Blacklight instance, first released in 2013. Currently, both the XML data behind the Perseus Catalog and the digital infrastructure used to support it are undergoing a significant revision, with a focus on finally making the bibliographic data available as Linked Open Data (LOD). In addition, work is underway to develop a digital infrastructure that is not just open source but that is more easily extensible and better supports navigating the complex relationships found in that data. This article describes the history of the Perseus Catalog, its use of open metadata standards for bibliographic data, and the different open source technologies used in building and putting it online. It also documents the challenges inherent in the creation of open bibliographic data and ends with a discussion of the move towards LOD and other planned future directions.

1 Introduction

The Perseus Catalog[1] at its beta release in 2013 declared the broad purpose of providing systematic catalog access to at least one open access edition of every Greek and Latin author from antiquity to around 600 CE. This ambitious announcement was vastly different in scope from its initial modest goals when

1 http://catalog.perseus.org (last access 2019.01.31).

Note: The Perseus Catalog, in all its iterations, owes its beginnings to David Mimno and its growth to Bridget Almas, Anna Krohn, and Greg Crane. Special thanks to Cliff Wulfman for pushing my thinking on all things metadata, to Monica Berti for finally making me write this, to Sam Huskey and Paul Dilley for providing inspiration for a broader catalog world, and to Lisa Cerrato for everything.

Alison Babeu, Perseus Project, Tufts University

https://doi.org/10.1515/9783110599572-005

the creation of metadata for collections outside of the Perseus Digital Library[2] (PDL) first began in 2006. Over its thirteen year history, the Perseus Catalog has grown from a classical text finding aid to an expanding component of the infrastructures of both its parent project the PDL and related projects such as Open Greek and Latin (OGL).

2 Overview of key standards for the Perseus Catalog

The central standard underpinning the Perseus Catalog is the FRBR (Functional Requirements for Bibliographic Records) entity-relationship model, which was designed as a conceptual framework to assist in the creation of bibliographic records independent of any one set of cataloging rules (IFLA 1998). Of particular importance to the Perseus Catalog are the FRBR model Group 1 entities (works, expressions, manifestations, and items), which were proposed as one potential means of organizing bibliographic data. While a work is defined as a "distinct intellectual or artistic creation," an expression is the "intellectual or artistic realization of a work," a manifestation physically embodies the expression of a work, and an item is a "single exemplar of a manifestation." To illustrate, Homer's *Iliad* is a work; a critical edition by Thomas Allen is an expression; a 1931 Oxford publication of that edition is a manifestation; and an individual library copy of that publication is an item.

The other key standard behind the catalog metadata and architecture is the Canonical Text Services Protocol (CTS)[3] and the related CITE (Collections, Indexes, Texts and Extensions) Architecture, both developed by the Homer Multitext project.[4] While CTS defines a network service to identify and retrieve text fragments using permanent canonical references expressed by CTS-URNs, the CITE Architecture supports discovery and retrieval of texts or collection of objects.[5] CTS has been influenced by the FRBR model and defines several key concepts utilized by the Perseus Catalog for its data architecture. To begin with, the CTS hierarchy has created *textgroups* above the work level. Textgroups support more strategic grouping of texts because they are used not just for literary

2 http://www.perseus.tufts.edu (last access 2019.01.31).

3 http://cite-architecture.org (last access 2019.01.31).

4 http://www.homermultitext.org (last access 2019.01.31).

5 For further discussion of CTS and recent implementations see Tiepmar and Heyer (2017) and their contribution in this volume.

authors but also for corpus collections, and they also require unique identifiers. While *works* are defined as in the FRBR model, CTS has defined *editions/translations* instead of *expressions*, a practice the catalog has followed to indicate a particular published version of a work.

CTS-URNs are used in the catalog to uniquely identify editions and translations and form the basis both for version identifiers and for canonical edition URIs. They utilize work identifiers from three classical canons: the Thesaurus Linguae Graecae (TLG), the Packard Humanities Institute (PHI), and the Stoa Consortium list of Latin authors.[6] For example, consider the URN: *urn:cts:greekLit:tlg0012.tlg001.perseus-grc1*,[7] "tlg0012" is the *textgroup* identifier for Homer, author 0012 in the *TLG Canon*; "tlg001" is the *work* identifier for the *Iliad* assigned by the TLG; and "perseus-grc1" is the *version* identifier for the 1920 Oxford *edition* by Thomas Allen available in the PDL.

The Perseus Catalog also currently contains two kinds of metadata: bibliographic records for editions/translations of works and authority records for its authors/textgroups. In order to increase the interoperability and extensibility of the catalog data, two standards from the Library of Congress (LC) were chosen: the MODS (Metadata Objection Description Standard)[8] XML schema was used for bibliographic metadata and MADS (Metadata Authority Description Standard)[9] was used for all authority records.

In addition, the Perseus Catalog also includes what has often been referred to internally as *linkable data*, rather than fully Linked Open Data (LOD).[10] While there was not sufficient time to implement full LOD prior to the May 2013 beta release, resources published within the catalog do use Perseus data URIs under the http://data.perseus.org URI prefix. This prefix is followed by one or more path components indicating the resource type, a unique resource identifier, and an optional path component identifying a specific output format (Almas et al. 2014). The general catalog pattern is http://data.perseus.org/catalog/<textgroup urn>[/format], with URIs for catalog records distinguished from PDL text records

6 TLG (http://stephanus.tlg.uci.edu); PHI (http://latin.packhum.org/about); STOA (https://github.com/paregorios/latin-authors/blob/master/fodder/StoaLatinTextInventory.csv) (last access 2019.01.31).

7 See http://catalog.perseus.org/catalog/urn:cts:greekLit:tlg0012.tlg001.perseus-grc1 (last access 2019.01.31).

8 http://www.loc.gov/standards/mods/ (last access 2019.01.31).

9 http://www.loc.gov/standards/mads/ (last access 2019.01.31).

10 For more on linked data, see https://www.w3.org/DesignIssues/LinkedData.html (last access 2019.01.31).

by the catalog path element.[11] There are published URIs for textgroups, works, and edition/translation level records, with full CTS-URNs used for texts in catalog record URIs. Additionally, users can also link to an ATOM feed for the catalog metadata for any textgroup, work or edition/translation by appending the format path to the URI.

3 Related work

Three research areas in particular have influenced the recent evolution of the Perseus Catalog, namely: the development of semantic bibliographic metadata/ontologies and LOD models for other catalogs; the use of CTS-URNS and other semantic identifiers in similar digital classics projects; and the development of classical text knowledge bases and online work catalogs that include similar data.

First, as the Perseus Catalog transformation work is currently using the FRBRoo ontology[12] to rethink its metadata, relevant research includes how bibliographic ontologies[13] might be used for mass conversion of legacy bibliographic records into LOD (Chen 2017), and how the use of bibliographic ontologies can move metadata workflows towards the creation of LOD (Guerrini and Possemato 2016, Clarke 2014). Other influential work (Fuller et al. 2015, Jett et al. 2016) has been conducted by the HathiTrust Digital Library affiliated Research Center (HTRC)[14] that investigated how bibliographic ontologies could be used to remodel traditional bibliographic data in their large-scale digital library so that it better supported scholars in citing and accurately referencing specific editions in the collection.

A second area of related research involves how other digital classics projects have made use of CTS-URNs or other semantic identifier systems to implement and support stable identification of digital objects within their collections. The Coptic Scriptorium[15] faced related challenges in its efforts to

11 Thus the textgroup URI for Homer's *Iliad* would be: http://data.perseus.org/catalog/urn:cts:greekLit:tlg0012.tlg001 (last access 2019.01.31).

12 http://www.cidoc-crm.org/frbroo/home-0 (last access 2019.01.31). See Le Boeuf (2012) for an overview of the ontology and its potential for bibliographic data conversion to the Semantic Web.

13 For a comprehensive overview and comparison of four major data models (FRBR, FRBRoo, BIBFRAME, Europeana Data Model) see Zapounidou et al. (2016).

14 https://www.hathitrust.org/htrc (last access 2019.01.31).

15 http://copticscriptorium.org (last access 2019.01.31).

uniquely identify the expressions of texts and other types of linguistic objects in its collection as well as in its need to expand its category of "digital expressions" to include various visualizations and annotations on objects such as manuscripts (Almas and Schroeder 2016). Similar data modeling and identifier issues have also been encountered by Syriaca.org,[16] and Michelson (2016) and Gibson et al. (2017) have discussed both this project's digital infrastructure (TEI-XML, LOD, GitHub) and its extensive work in assigning stable URIs to all the entities found in their digital reference works.

The third and most important area of related work involves two new digital classics canons/catalogs with which the PDL team is actively collaborating: the Iowa Canon of Ancient Authors and Works and the Digital Latin Library (DLL) Catalog.[17] The Iowa Canon, in development since 2015, will offer extensive metadata for Greek and Latin texts, such as genre, time and place of composition, as well as links to other canonical references.[18] It includes additional metadata on both lost and fragmentary authors and works.[19] In the summer of 2018, the DLL released a beta interface to their collection of classical author and textual metadata. The DLL Catalog[20] focuses on helping users find openly available Latin texts online from the classical era up to neo-Latin texts. Its metadata collection (including authority records for authors and works) has made use of data from both the Perseus Catalog and the Virtual International Authority File (VIAF)[21] and includes item records both to digitized books and to digital texts in numerous collections.

---

16 http://syriaca.org (last access 2019.01.31).

17 https://catalog.digitallatin.org (last access 2019.01.31).

18 Earlier relevant work in integrating data from Greek and Latin canons is that of the Classical Works Knowledge Base (http://cwkb.org/home), which is also an important component of the HuCit ontology, a domain-specific ontology and knowledge base of metadata involving ancient authors and work titles (Romanello and Pasin 2017) (last access 2019.01.31).

19 Fragmentary authors are those authors whose texts have only survived through the quotation and transmission of other authors and texts (Berti et al. 2015). And for more on the the Perseus Catalog and the Iowa Canon's complementary work, see (Babeu and Dilley, forthcoming).

20 Before releasing the catalog, the DLL team conducted two information behavior studies (Abbas et al. 2015; 2016) that helped inform its design.

21 http://viaf.org (last access 2019.01.31).

4 History of the Perseus Catalog and its development

4.1 Perseus Catalog 1.0 (2005)

The first inspiration for what became the Perseus Catalog grew out of a Perseus software developer taking a cataloging class (Mimno et al. 2005) that introduced him to the FRBR conceptual model. Mimno decided to investigate how FRBR could be used to organize the PDL classics collection since it was small in size, highly structured, and already roughly cataloged.

This initial catalog design utilized pre-existing unique identifiers available for a large majority of Perseus texts. Called abstract bibliographic objects or ABOs, these identifiers were central at the time to the PDL document management system. ABOs were designed to represent distinct "units of intellectual content in the digital library" or, in other words, works.[22] Along with ABOs, MODS were used for bibliographic records for expressions (the editions used for PDL texts) and manifestations (the TEI-XML versions) and MADS for authority records for works and authors. Since all of the PDL texts were digital and there were no physical items, the first Perseus Catalog only implemented the first three levels of the FRBR hierarchy. The experimental system also made use of the open source XML database eXist.[23]

Two key observations from this hierarchical catalog design are particularly relevant. First, this experiment illustrated the challenge of representing the part-whole relationship among different works, manifestations and expressions. Within the PDL classics collection, many manifestations of short works were part of larger volumes, such as poetic anthologies or collected Greek orations. The solution that was implemented involved automatically creating a single manifestation level record for a multi-work volume and then linking it to multiple expression-level works. While this plan worked in 2005 for the relatively small PDL collection, it presented serious scalability issues as the catalog data collection grew exponentially.

Secondly, the creation of the eXist system involved several searching and indexing problems. Searching a hierarchical catalog can require very complicated queries as it may need to draw on information from multiple levels. The solution that was employed was to maintain two parallel versions of the catalog. While each version contained the same records, the first set was

22 For more on ABOs see Smith et al. (2001).

23 http://exist-db.org/exist/apps/homepage/index.html (last access 2019.01.31).

a collection of individual records (one for each work, expression and manifestation) which served as the editable source code; the second set contained composite records and served as the compiled version, with one XML document for each work containing all its expressions and the manifestations of those expressions. This compiled version was then utilized as a "flat" catalog optimized for searching in eXist and required over 50 XSLT stylesheets to control the display in response to queries. These composite versions also made use of the custom tags <work> <expression> and <manifestation> in order to maintain the FRBR hierarchical structure, a practice that did not continue in the next stage of metadata creation.

4.2 Perseus Catalog 2.0 (2006–2012)

4.2.1 Mass book digitization, new partnerships, and new goals

The experimental system described above was only briefly online and never intended to scale beyond the PDL classics collection. Subsequent developments expanded its scope. Firstly, two massive book digitization projects, starting with Google Books[24] and soon afterwards followed by the Open Content Alliance (OCA) of the Internet Archive[25] began providing access to thousands of Greek and Latin editions in the public domain. Secondly, a grant from the Andrew W. Mellon Foundation for the Cybereditions project led the PDL team to reconsider what type and level of data to include within the Perseus Catalog. The experimental catalog of 2005 only included records and links to PDL editions, but the additional funding supported greatly expanded metadata creation. A decision was made therefore to create an extensible and growing catalog, inspired by FRBR, that would bridge the gap between the deep but narrow coverage of disciplinary bibliographies such as the TLG and the much broader but shallower metadata found within library catalogs regarding classical editions.

From 2006 to 2009, the PDL actively participated in the OCA and created a bibliography of editions to be digitized. The ultimate goal was to provide granular intellectual access to individual works by classical authors at the online page level in these editions. In creating this initial bibliography we focused on editions that were fully in the public domain because we wanted to develop an open collection of primary sources that could be utilized without any

24 http://books.google.com (last access 2019.01.31).
25 https://archive.org (last access 2019.01.31).

restrictions. Since the PDL did not expect at the time to be able to create full TEI-XML digital editions of these many authors and works, it was ultimately decided that the catalog should provide analytical level detail not only to the OCA editions but also to a comprehensive canon of Latin and Greek authors. This decision led to the creation of an extensive open access bibliography[26] of Greek and Latin authors and works with a list of standard editions that could be used to guide future digitization. The list was created by combining the standard lists of authors, works and reference editions from a number of prominent classical Greek and Latin lexicons and is still continuously updated as new authors and works are added to the catalog.

4.2.2 The Perseus Catalog metadata and authority records

Between 2006 and 2013, large amounts of metadata[27] were created for numerous digital editions found within Google Books, the OCA, and eventually the HathiTrust. Six basic types of editions were identified with slight variations as to how they were cataloged.[28] The typical cataloging practice was to create single MODS manifestation level records for each volume (rather than for an entire edition), and for those volumes that contained more than one author/work entry, <relatedItem type="constituent"> component records for the individual works were created *within* those MODS records. The constituent records included relevant work identifiers, page numbers and online page level links to digital manifestations.

Separate duplicate expression level MODS records were also created that were linked to these top-level manifestations through the use of <relatedItem type="host">. While this provided a way to both quickly gather up individual expression records for an author in one folder as they were cataloged and to add them to the spreadsheets used for collection management, it also meant that a significant amount of redundant data was created at the same time. The only type of edition with a slightly different practice were multi-volume editions for single works (e.g. a multi-volume edition of Livy's *Ab Urbe Condita*). MODS records were created for each volume with unique descriptive metadata

26 https://tinyurl.com/y86ttntv (last access 2019.01.31).

27 For a full description of the MODS/MADS records including XML examples see Babeu (2008; 2012).

28 See the catalog wiki: *The Different Types of Editions and the Addition of Analytical Cataloging Information* https://git.io/fp7CY (last access 2019.01.31).

such as volume number, extent of the work, and publication dates, but there was no collocation other then being saved in the same folder.

Whether MODS and MADS records were created from scratch using a template or downloaded from different sources, certain types of information were typically added or enhanced. For MODS records this included standard identifiers/headings from library systems for author names and work titles; unique work identifiers from standard canons; structured metadata for all author/work entries; links to online bibliographic records, digital manifestations and page level work links. For MADS records this included lists of variant names with language encoded; standard identifiers (e.g. VIAF number); lists of work identifiers for linking to MODS records; and links to online reference sources.

4.2.3 First experiments with open source system

In the fall of 2011, with a growing mass of metadata and no user interface, PDL staff began active discussions regarding the Perseus Catalog metadata and what type of interface it would require. One key challenge was that the metadata was very granular with thousands of deeply hierarchical XML records to be indexed. It was eventually decided that supporting a native XML database would require more time and resources than were available. In addition, while an open source and adaptable system was preferred, most of the open source library systems that were examined did not provide support for MODS records. Despite not having MODS support, the eXtensible Catalog (XC)[29] system was ultimately chosen as the first test interface.

After an initial test data conversion was conducted in fall 2011,[30] a first XC prototype catalog interface was made available for internal testing. This prototype utilized the Fedora Repository[31] (to store the catalog records) and made use of the XC Drupal and Metadata Services toolkits. The Metadata Services toolkit supported the XC interface and allowed it to present "FRBRIzed, faceted navigation across a range of library resources", and it was this FRBRIzed support with which we most wanted to experiment. Due to the lack of MODS support, however, all metadata had to be reverse transformed into MARCXML for

29 http://www.extensiblecatalog.org (last access 2019.01.31).
30 For more on the 2011–2012 work, see http://sites.tufts.edu/perseusupdates/beta-features/catalog-of-ancient-greek-and-latin-primary-sources/frbr-catalog-sips/ (last access 2019.01.31).
31 https://duraspace.org/fedora/ (last access 2019.01.31).

import into the XC environment.[32] Extensive internal testing of this interface revealed a number of issues, largely due to the reverse transformation, which caused significant data loss and strange duplication issues. The PDL team therefore concluded another implementation solution would need to be found.

4.3 Perseus Catalog Beta (2013–2017)

4.3.1 New metadata practices and workflows: moving to Blacklight and GitHub

In 2012, it was decided that the XC instance could not fully exploit the catalog's XML data and a digital library analyst was hired to assist in the catalog development process. Consequently, active work to get the catalog data online began in earnest. This work would involve a transition from previously closed workflows to a new open and collaborative environment, largely through the use of GitHub.

For a number of years, metadata had been managed on a restricted CVS server and Eclipse software was used for adding data and committing changes. The move of catalog metadata to GitHub was part of a larger transition from closed to open environments that the PDL had undertaken. All catalog metadata was now downloadable and all new data also became publicly viewable upon committing,[33] in addition, the source code was also made available soon after the live release.[34] The adoption of GitHub best practices thus offered a new level of transparency. Extensive documentation was also created for both the code[35] and for catalog usage.[36]

Along with the move to GitHub, it was decided to use project Blacklight[37] as an interface to the catalog's data. Blacklight is an "open source, Ruby on Rails Engine that provides a basic discovery interface for searching an Apache Solr[38] index,"[39] all of which could be customized used Rails. Out of the box, Blacklight

32 For full technical details, see http://sites.tufts.edu/perseusupdates/beta-features/catalog-of-ancient-greek-and-latin-primary-sources/frbr-catalog-sips/ (last access 2019.01.31).
33 Available at https://github.com/PerseusDL/catalog_data and https://github.com/PerseusDL/catalog_pending (last access 2019.01.31).
34 https://github.com/PerseusDL/perseus_catalog (last access 2019.01.31).
35 https://github.com/PerseusDL/perseus_catalog/blob/master/doc/PerseusCatalogDocumentation.docx (last access 2019.01.31).
36 Blog with FAQ, usage guide, and other data at http://sites.tufts.edu/perseuscatalog/ (last access 2019.01.31).
37 http://projectblacklight.org (last access 2019.01.31).
38 http://lucene.apache.org/solr/ (last access 2019.01.31).
39 https://github.com/projectblacklight/blacklight/wiki (last access 2019.01.31).

provided a standard search box, faceted searching, and stable document urls, all features which made it an excellent candidate for an interface. Over the spring of 2013, the PDL team converted the XML data into ATOM feeds for reviewing, tracked problems, and developed customized Ruby subclasses. The catalog first went live in May 2013 and included MADS records[40] for authors/textgroups with lists of works, and MODS edition/translation records that were grouped under top level work records.[41]

One major change to metadata practices after the release was that every MODS record now contained an automatically assigned and unique CTS-URN to serve as a version identifier. This new practice was unrelated to Blacklight and had to do instead with the PDL's prior decision to follow the CITE and CTS standards. In addition, where once there had been one MODS record created for each individual work/expression even if the that record also included a translation, the system automatically split these expressions into two MODS edition/translation records, each with their own URN, as required by the CTS model. While this had the positive effect of finding and splitting translations apart from editions in the browsing environment and data tables, it also had the negative effective of creating additional metadata.

At the time of the beta release, the catalog system also automatically created CTS-URNs for all the individual expressions in the data, and generated expression level records for all the author/work constituent records in the large composite MODS editions that did not have them. This system would also continue to create CTS-URNs for MODS records it ingested from catalog_pending on GitHub, the location for all newly created records. To enable collaborators to make contributions to this repository, record templates and a form to reserve a CTS URN and/or create a base level MODS record were added. In addition, now that all records and versions had published CTS-URNs, an additional data correction pass was involved using the CITE Collection tables[42] if records were deleted or if a published version was incorrect. When the first catalog data set was generated, four relevant CITE_Collection tables were created for all the data in the repository (authors, textgroups, works, versions) as was required by the CTS/CITE standard and certain types of data changes had to be registered here manually.

---

40 See the authority record for Cicero: http://catalog.perseus.org/catalog/urn:cite:perseus:author.364 (last access 2019.01.31).

41 Such as Cicero's *De Amicitia*: http://catalog.perseus.org/catalog/urn:cts:latinLit:phi0474.phi052 (last access 2019.01.31).

42 For a full explanation of the CITE Collection tables and the Perseus catalog see https://git.io/fp7W5 (last access 2019.01.31).

The only other major cataloging change involved how single work multi-volume editions were cataloged. Originally each volume had its own MODS record with a work identifier and it thus had a CTS-URN generated for it, so a seven volume edition of Livy in the beta catalog ended up with seven URNs instead of one. Hundreds of invalid CTS-URNs were thus created in the beta catalog so, from 2013 onwards, the new practice was still to create MODS records for each volume (using the ID attribute to indicate volume number) but then to save all the records (each with the same CTS-URN) in a single modsCollection file.[43]

4.3.2 OGL and new collections for metadata

In 2013, another major development would change the goals of the Perseus Catalog once again when the PDL's editor in chief, Gregory Crane, became a Humboldt professor and established the Digital Humanities Chair at the University of Leipzig (DH Leipzig) in Germany. One of the major projects begun at DH Leipzig was OGL,[44] which sought to produce at least one open source digital edition – ideally, multiple editions – of every Greek and Latin text from antiquity through approximately 600 CE.[45] In addition, DH Leipzig also worked with the Saxon State and University Library Dresden (SLUB) to digitize several hundred Greek and Latin volumes.[46] Many of these new collections grew exponentially before even basic metadata creation[47] or cataloging, other than a basic TEI header and the creation of a CTS-URN, could be accomplished. While there was some brief experimentation in the automatic creation of metadata through the use of a CSV sheet,[48] only one collection, a highly-structured Arabic language corpus, was ever imported into the catalog using this method.

43 This process also involved extensive data cleanup as a large number of records had to be manually collated and CTS-URNs redirected.
44 https://www.dh.uni-leipzig.de/wo/projects/open-greek-and-latin-project/ (last access 2019.01.31). The Humboldt Chair ended in 2018, but the OGL continues forward as part of an international collaborative partnership: http://opengreekandlatin.org (last access 2019.01.31).
45 A full list of available collections can be found here: https://github.com/OpenGreekAndLatin (last access 2019.01.31).
46 http://digital.slub-dresden.de/en/digital-collections/127/ (last access 2019.01.31).
47 For further discussion of OGL metadata and the Perseus Catalog see Crane et al. (2014).
48 https://git.io/fp7lT (last access 2019.01.31).

4.4 Current work in remodeling the data (2017–present)

Changes in staffing in 2016 coupled with the lack of dedicated funding to maintain and update the Perseus Catalog have led to the current status: a significant backlog of metadata that has not been ingested into the final data repository; corrections to metadata within the final data repository that have not been pushed to the database underlying the Blacklight instance; and numerous technical issues with the way that interface represents the catalog metadata documented and unresolved. Therefore in the fall of 2017 the PDL contracted with the Agile Humanities Agency (Agile) to thoroughly review and enhance the current catalog metadata formats and to investigate whether the Blacklight instance should be updated or if a new interface should be developed instead.

4.4.1 Blacklight interface and updating issues

After its 2013 release, three updates were made to the Blacklight instance, each with their own technical challenges and unresolved metadata issues. The time between updates led to large amounts of new and revised data being stored in catalog_pending making it difficult to keep track of the different types of metadata changes and to test whether errors had been fixed. Nonetheless, the use of Blacklight as an interface to the Perseus Catalog had been reasonably successful, and has served as the beta – and, indeed, only – interface to the data for over 5 years. As the senior Perseus software developer noted in 2016, however, the custom programming approach that adapted Blacklight to support pre-existing data creation workflows led to long-term sustainability issues and a hard to maintain idiosyncratic codebase.

This codebase had in fact made updating the catalog nearly impossible for as Agile noted in their review, previous data ingestion had required catalog developers to twice build the tool's index by hand and internal tables often had to be manually managed. Blacklight handles the indexing of MARC and other fielded bibliographic records quite well and uses the Rails framework to allow Ruby developers to write sub-classes to support other formats as had been done for MODS in the beta release. The underlying database is SQL, however, and modeling the catalog's metadata in ActiveRecord (Ruby's object front-end to SQL) had proven difficult and time consuming. Since any modification of the ActiveRecord format required a Rails developer to write new code to migrate the database, Agile staff concluded that while Blacklight could possibly be updated, this would require both a programmer with Ruby expertise and more stable and clearly defined metadata.

4.4.2 Agile assessment of current metadata

As identified by Agile's analysis, one major issue with the Perseus Catalog bibliographic records is that MODS records served as both records of bibliographic *manifestations* and as records of the abstract *works* contained within them. Further complicating matters was not just how expressions had been defined as versions/translations but also the large number of bibliographic items that could be versions (epigrams, plays, whole books, etc). Because distinctions between abstract works and their editions and translations were not well established, they had found it difficult to automatically extract different properties and relationships. In addition, Agile noted that using MODS records to encode non-bibliographic text aggregations (e.g. editions containing dozens or hundreds of works) and creating individual MODS records for expressions had also led to a number of serious problems: large amounts of data duplication, inconsistency in the records as the MODS standard evolved, increasingly complex MODS records, and the inability to specifically address many items within the catalog.

Due to all of this semantic complexity, Agile recommended utilizing the FRBRoo ontology to represent the underlying relational structures and FRBR level information found within the records. In FRBRoo, editions and translations are individual works that are members of a larger complex work, and MODS records could be recast as encodings of manifestations that carry expressions of one or more editions or translations of one work or many works. Thus the work of the Perseus Catalog began to move from more routine metadata creation into the needed – if somewhat nebulous – world of conceptual and ontological modeling of bibliographic data.

4.4.3 Agile recommendations for new metadata practices

After the suggestion was made and accepted to use FRBRoo, Perseus catalog staff also began implementing a number of Agile recommendations in terms of converting the metadata records. MODS records were still going to be used to encode traditional bibliographic information, and a plan was created to work from the existing records to generate statements about "Manifestation Product Types that carry expressions." One challenge this approach introduced was that a way was needed to address all of the MODS records as unique manifestations with identifiers that could be referenced. The current plan is to use OCLC identifiers where available with the possibility of using CITE-URNs for all top level manifestation records also being explored.

The version and expression level data found within the MODS records also needed to be better encoded. The first step was to remove all work identifiers and CTS URNs from the top-level manifestation records and the second step was to use the <relatedItem> tag to separately encode works and expressions. Thus for an edition of Herodian's *Ab Excessu Divi Marci Libri Octo*, instead of having <identifier type="cts-urn">urn:cts:greekLit:tlg0015.tlg001.opp-grc1</identifier> in the top level record, this identifier has now been relocated to a separately encoded constituent statement using "otherType="work" and "otherType"="expression".[49] This new format has also made it both quicker and easier to encode multiple language expressions (or even both Perseus and OPP[50] expressions) within the same manifestation.

The way single work *multi-volume* editions are cataloged has also been greatly changed again. Instead of creating large modsCollection files with one MODS record for each volume, Agile proposed creating one MODS record instead for the whole edition and to expand the use of the <relatedItem type="constituent"> element again. In this case <otherType= "structure"> was used to encode the physical structure of a work found *within* each volume with only unique manifestation level details given. This allowed the top level manifestation record to then represent the entire edition and the constituent records to encode unique volume level information (e.g. publication years, the section of a work it contains, online links, different editors, etc.). Encoding all of this information in a single MODS records makes it much easier to quickly determine what content of a work is in a given volume.[51]

The final type of change to MODS records impacted records for multi-work manifestations (either single or multi-volume). Previously, the catalog update system would take multi-work manifestation MODS records and automatically create edition/translation level records but would then eliminate the record of the entire manifestation. It was decided for the moment to stop this separate record creation process and the top level manifestation records that had been split apart in the beta and subsequent data creations were recompiled automatically. These newly recreated manifestations included full lists of encoded constituent works, albeit with only top level information (page numbers and page level links to online manifestations were not included). Re-inverting the data once again enabled us to quickly count how many works were within a volume

---

49 To see the full MODS record: https://git.io/fp7WE (last access 2019.01.31).

50 OPP stands for the Open Philology Project at Leipzig, a version identifier chosen to represent non-PDL editions.

51 For a sample two volume edition of Tacitus *Annales*, see https://git.io/fp7WV (last access 2019.01.31).

and to more easily answer the question of how many editions have actually been cataloged. One unresolved and important challenge introduced by this approach, however, is that of where and how to store the expression level data left behind in the separate records. This data is not currently found within the newly revised catalog data files but will be "added back in" once an appropriate format and structure is decided upon.

Another unresolved metadata challenge, in terms of adding new editions to catalog_data, was the inability to relaunch the system that automatically created CTS-URNs for MODS records. At the end of the Agile revision project, the data within catalog_pending was not ingested but only converted to the newer formats, with a number of errors due to the varying types of works found within this repository. Manual revision of these records, including correcting errors and creating CTS-URNs for new work/expressions is ongoing. On the other hand, all of the new MADS authority records within catalog_pending were successfully ingested. In addition, as a further enhancement, all of the author name files were renamed to their CITE URNs as a first step towards LOD compliance.

A number of other changes were also suggested and implemented by Agile in terms of MADS authority records. Agile suggested that the most comprehensive data listing of authors, works and expressions maintained by the PDL was not the catalog itself but was instead the open access bibliography first created in 2005. A MADS RDF database was thus created from this spreadsheet, with MADS authority records created not just for all of the works on the list but also for the many authors not yet in the Perseus Catalog (as there had been no editions cataloged for them). These MADS records contain CTS-URNs which can then be used to potentially link MODS expression constituents to expanded work level data. MADS work authority records were created again because the lack of them not only limited automatic reasoning about works but also meant there was no metadata space for work description (variant name titles, uncertain dates, contested authorship attribution), and no way to pull in data from other sources about a work. Interestingly, this practice of creating work authority records was implemented in the Perseus experimental catalog but the sheer volume of data creation made it impossible to continue manually.

4.4.4 LOD at last? Commitment to openness and future directions

Over the course of almost a year's work, it was determined that the amount of metadata revision needed and the inability to update/modify the Blacklight instance required a rethinking of what could be accomplished. While the metadata is still being actively converted and edited, work on a new interface has been put off for the time being until there are further funds for infrastructure, deployment and testing. At the same time, work is also still ongoing to represent the metadata found in the both the catalog and its related bibliographic spreadsheets and adapt it in such a way that captures the complex relationships between works, expressions, and manifestations. It has been decided that RDF due to its relational nature and its logical foundation, would make it the ideal format to which the catalog data could be transformed.[52]

An initial RDF knowledge base of statements about authors, works, expressions and manifestations has been developed and an additional knowledge base of statements relating expressions to manifestations has been generated from the converted MODS records. This RDF data can be loaded into any triple store and queried using SPARQL.[53] It is hoped that this knowledge base upon completion and release can be efficiently linked to tools or bibliographies that will allow librarians and scholars to update and correct it easily. In addition, the creation of such a knowledge base will allow for machine-readable applications to make use of the data. By encoding bibliographic knowledge as RDF, we seek to integrate our work with the semantic web and the larger global work of scholars and librarians who have already captured bibliographic information in RDF.[54]

An extensive amount of Linked Open Data about ancient authors and works has been generated within the last few years, and, ideally, partnerships with the Iowa Canon, DLL, and OGL will continue. At the same time, the Perseus Catalog RDF does provide something unique: expression and manifestation level metadata that links works to their published editions and translations. It may turn out that the need for a separate interface to the Perseus Catalog becomes redundant as its most useful part is its bibliographic data about actual works with links to their online expressions and manifestations. If that data can be packaged up and better searched through other projects' APIs and interfaces, then work will likely exclusively focus on the development of more metadata as LOD for sharing with other digital classics projects. Much of the effort of the next year will be to try to both design and implement a system that will enable Perseus catalog metadata creators to curate authority metadata about ancient authors and works and, similarly, to collect and

52 We are closely following the work of the MODS to RDF mapping group. See https://tinyurl.com/yaud3gmt (last access 2019.01.31).

53 Access to this knowledge base is currently only available through an experimental web application.

54 See for example the work of OCLC: https://www.oclc.org/research/themes/data-science/linkeddata.html (last access 2019.01.31).

curate references to both online editions and links to specific portions of them. There is a need for a new metadata management system that allows not only for efficient creation of metadata but supports collaborative workflows between the different projects.

5 Conclusion

So after thirteen years, the goal of the Perseus Catalog has evolved once again: having shifted from 1) a FRBR-based interface to the PDL classics collection, 2) to an online finding aid both for PDL texts and for all Greek and Latin works produced up until 600 CE, 3) to a metadata source for OGL and its component projects, and now 4) to the aim of producing a comprehensive, extensible and machine readable knowledge base about Greek and Latin texts.

Whatever future path the development of the Perseus Catalog takes in terms of infrastructure and data creation, the leaders of this effort remain committed to openness. This is not simply limited to the distribution of data and any code, but more importantly extends to a desire to collaborate with the growing number of digital classics projects exploring the same issues.

Bibliography

Abbas, J.; Baker, S.R.; Huskey, S.J.; Weaver, C. (2015): "Digital Latin Library: Information Work Practices of Classics Scholars, Graduate Students, And Teachers". In: Proceedings of the American Society for Information Science and Technology. Wiley Online Library. 52, 1–4.

Abbas, J.; Baker, S.R.; Huskey, S.J.; Weaver, C. (2016): "How I Learned to Love Classical Studies: Information Representation Design of The Digital Latin Library". In: Proceedings of the 79th ASIS&T Annual Meeting. Access Innovations Inc. Volume 53, 1–10.

Almas, B.; Schroeder, C. (2016): "Applying the Canonical Text Services Model to the Coptic SCRIPTORIUM". Data Science Journal 15. http://doi.org/10.5334/dsj-2016-013.

Almas, B.; Babeu, A.; Krohn, A. (2014): "LOD in the Perseus Digital Library". ISAW Papers 7: Current Practice in Linked Open Data for the Ancient World. New York, NY: Institute for the Study of the Ancient World. http://dlib.nyu.edu/awdl/isaw/isaw-papers/7/almas-babeu-krohn/ (last access 2019.01.31).

Babeu, A. (2008): "Building a "FRBR-Inspired" Catalog: The Perseus Digital Library Experience". Perseus Digital Library. http://www.perseus.tufts.edu/publications/PerseusFRBRExperiment.pdf (last access 2019.01.31).

Babeu, A. (2012): "A Continuing Plan for the "FRBR-Inspired" Catalog 2.1? (Fall 2012)". Perseus Digital Library. http://sites.tufts.edu/perseusupdates/files/2012/11/FRBRPlanFall2012.pdf (last access 2019.01.31).

Babeu, A.; Dilley, P. (forthcoming): "Linked Open Data for Greek and Latin Authors and Works." In: Linked Open Data for the Ancient World: Standards, Practices, Prospects, ISAW Papers.

Berti, M.; Almas, B.; Dubin, D.; Franzini, G.; Stoyanova, S.; Crane, G. (2015): "The Linked Fragment: TEI and the Encoding of Text Reuses of Lost Authors". Journal of the Text Encoding Initiative 8 https://jtei.revues.org/1218 (last access 2019.01.31).

Chen, Y.N. (2017): "A Review of Practices for Transforming Library Legacy Records into Linked Open Data". In: E. Garoufallou; S. Virkus; R. Siatri; D. Koutsomiha (eds): Metadata and Semantic Research. MTSR 2017. Cham: Springer, 123–133.

Clarke, R.I. (2014): "Breaking Records: The History of Bibliographic Records and their Influence in Conceptualizing Bibliographic Data". Cataloging & Classification Quarterly 53:3–4, 286–302.

Crane, G.; Almas, B.; Babeu, A.; Cerrato, L.; Krohn, A.; Baumgart, F.; Berti, M.; Franzini, G.; Stoyanova, S. (2014): "Cataloging for a Billion Word Library of Greek and Latin". In: DATeCH '14: Proceedings of the First International Conference on Digital Access to Textual Cultural Heritage. New York, NY: ACM, 83–88.

Fuller, T.N.; Page, K.R.; Willcox, P.; Jett, J.; Maden, C.; Cole, T.; Fallaw, C.; Senseney, M.; Downie, J.-S. (2015): "Building Complex Research Collections in Digital Libraries: A Survey of Ontology Implications". In: Proceedings of the 15th ACM/IEEE-CS Joint Conference on Digital Libraries. New York, NY: ACM, 169–172.

Gibson, N.P.; Michelson, D.A.; Schwartz, D.L. (2017): "From Manuscript Catalogues to A Handbook of Syriac Literature: Modeling An Infrastructure For Syriaca.Org". Journal of Data Mining & Digital Humanities. Special Issue on Computer-Aided Processing of Intertextuality in Ancient Languages (May 30, 2017). http://arXiv:1603.01207 [cs.DL].

Guerrini, M.; Possemato, T. (2016): "From Record Management to Data Management: RDA and New Application Models BIBFRAME, RIMMF, and OliSuite/WeCat". Cataloging & Classification Quarterly 54:3, 179–199.

IFLA. (1998): Functional Requirements for Bibliographic Records. Final Report. Volume 19 of UBCIM Publications-New Series. München: K.G. Saur. https://www.ifla.org/publications/functional-requirements-for-bibliographic-records (last access 2019.01.31).

Jett, J.; Fuller, T.N.; Cole, T.W.; Page, K.R.; Downie, J.S. (2016): "Enhancing Scholarly Use of Digital Libraries: A Comparative Survey and Review of Bibliographic Metadata Ontologies". In: Proceedings of the 16th ACM/IEEE-CS on Joint Conference on Digital Libraries, JCDL '16. New York, NY: ACM, 35–44.

Le Boeuf, P. (2012): "A Strange Model Named FRBRoo". Cataloging & Classification Quarterly 50:5–7, 422–438.

Michelson, D.A. (2016). "Syriaca.org as a Test Case for Digitally Re-Sorting the Ancient World". In: C. Clivaz; P. Dilley; D. Hamidović (eds.): Ancient Worlds in Digital Culture. Leiden and Boston: Brill, 59–85. http://dx.doi.org/10.1163/9789004325234_005.

Mimno, D.; Crane, G; Jones, A. (2005): "Hierarchical Catalog Records Implementing a FRBR Catalog". D-Lib Magazine 11:10. http://www.dlib.org/dlib/october05/crane/10crane.html (last access 2019.01.31).

Romanello, M.; Pasin, M. (2017): "Using Linked Open Data to Bootstrap a Knowledge Base of Classical Texts". In: Second Workshop on Humanities in the Semantic Web (WHiSe II) co-located with 16th International Semantic Web Conference (ISWC 2017). CEUR, 3–14.

Smith, D.A.; Mahoney, A.; Rydberg-Cox, J. (2001): "Management of XML Documents in an Integrated Digital Library". Extreme Markup Language 2000. https://people.cs.umass.edu/~dasmith/hopper.pdf (last access 2019.01.31).

Tiepmar, J.; Heyer, G. (2017): "An Overview of Canonical Text Services". Linguistics and Literature Studies 5, 132–148.

Zapounidou, S.; Sfakakis, M.; Papatheodorou, C. (2016): "Representing and Integrating Bibliographic Information into the Semantic Web: A Comparison of Four Conceptual Models". Journal of Information Science 43:4, 525–553.

Christopher W. Blackwell and Neel Smith

The CITE Architecture: a Conceptual and Practical Overview

Abstract: CITE, originally developed for the Homer Multitext, is a digital library architecture for identification, retrieval, manipulation, and integration of data by means of machine-actionable canonical citation. CITE stands for "Collections, Indices, Texts, and Extensions", and the acronym invokes the long history of citation as the basis for scholarly publication. Each of the four parts of CITE is based on abstract data models. Two parallel standards for citation identify data that implement those models: the CTS URN, for identifying texts and passages of text, and the CITE2 URN for identifying other data. Both of these URN citation schemes capture the necessary semantics of the data they identify, in context. In this paper we will describe the theoretical foundations of CITE, explain CTS and CITE2 URNs, describe the current state of the models for scholarly data that CITE defines, and introduce the current data formats, code libraries, utilities, and end-user applications that implement CITE.

Introduction

The very articulate Astronomer Royal Martin Rees has described the goal of science in this way:

> The aim of science is to unify disparate ideas, so we don't need to remember them all. I mean we don't need to recognize the fall of every apple, because Newton told us they all fall the same way.[1]

This remark captures a quintessential difference between the natural sciences and the humanities. Humanists, like scientists, unify disparate ideas, but we must record each unique phenomenon that we study. If we develop a unified view of ancient Greek poetry, for example, we will never conclude that "Because I am familiar with the *Iliad*, I do not have to remember the *Odyssey*," or "I have studied Greek poetry so I do not need to know about the tradition of

1 (Tippett and Rees 2013).

Christopher W. Blackwell, Furman University
Neel Smith, College of the Holy Cross

https://doi.org/10.1515/9783110599572-006

Serbo-Croatian epic." Humanists care about apples generically because of their marvelous, specific, variety.

Christopher Blackwell and Neel Smith, as Project Architects of the Homer Multitext project (HMT), originally developed the CITE[2] architecture to meet the needs of that project.[3] Together with the Editors, Casey Dué and Mary Ebbott, we recognized the need for an architecture that would outlive specific, rapidly changing technologies, while at the same time thoroughly capturing the semantics of our work in a format that both humans and machines could work with.

We were surprised to find that, despite the centuries-long tradition in disciplines like classical studies of citing texts by canonical reference, this experience had not been generalized in the digital humanities community. Even the most forward-looking digital projects a decade ago were relying on textual references that failed to represent the semantics implicit in conventional canonical citation, and were instead expressed in notations such as URLs that, while machine-actionable today, were closely tied to specific ephemeral technologies. We began work on the Canonical Text Services protocol (CTS), and eventually devised the CTS URN notation for citing texts. We subsequently applied this scheme – URN notation for citation, a service for retrieval of material identified by URN, and client software that talks to the service – to all the material in the HMT project: texts, physical artifacts like manuscripts, documentary objects like photographs, and analytical objects such as morphological analyses and syntactical graphs of texts.

CITE allows us to name the things we are studying in a very precise and flexible way. We can identify "Book 2 of the *Iliad* in any version," or "The third letter *iota* in the Greek text of *Iliad* Book 1, line 1, as it appears on Manuscript *Marcianus Graecus* Z.454 [=822]". We can identify a physical page of a manuscript as a physical page, as easily as we can identify an image of that page, and we can easily associate any number of images with a single physical artifact. We can identify smaller regions of an image with citations that can identify the part of an image that depicts a single character, while retaining the context of the larger image. With CITE we can cite abstractions as easily as concrete objects. For example, we can use CTS URNs to identify a passage of text in an edition; this is concrete data. But two readers might disagree on the syntax of that passage; that is,

2 CITE stands for "Collections, Indices, Texts, and Extensions".

3 The Homer Multitext (http://www.homermultitext.org) is a project of the Center for Hellenic Studies of Harvard University (last access 2019.01.31). It aims to document the history, tradition, and language of Greek epic poetry. Casey Dué and Mary Ebbott are its editors; Christopher Blackwell and Neel Smith are its architects.

these readers might assert two competing graphs, abstract data-objects that organize the (concrete and agreed upon) text differently. In the CITE architecture, we can work with the concrete text (identified by a CTS URN) and both of those abstract graph-objects, identified by CITE2 URNs.

CITE identifiers can capture and align versioned collections of data. For example, in the *HMT* project, we cite manuscript folios, but we do not have much to say about the physical objects beyond the fact that certain lines of the *Iliad* and certain commentary texts appear on a given folio. So our citation to "MS A, folio 12-recto [HMT edition]" points to a data record that has relatively little information: This is the 24th folio-side; it is a "recto". A codicologist might make a collection of data about this manuscript in which each object has much more data: sequence number, recto/verso, degree of gelatinization, repairs, quality of ink, etc. That collection would be "MS A, folio 12-recto [Codicology edition]". The structure of CITE URN citations allows us to have these two collections, each recording different data, but not losing the fact that "MS A, folio 12-recto" is in fact the same thing in both. Thus, in a CITE environment, a machine or human can discover "everything anyone says about MS A, folio 12-recto."

CITE is a framework independent of any particular technology. The principles of CITE would work on paper and ink as easily as in a digital computer. Its principles can be implemented in different languages, for different hardware and software. Since 2001, Blackwell and Smith have implemented CITE in Perl, XSLT, Java, Groovy, Javascript (now ECMAScript), using data stored in SQL Databases, Google BigTable, eXist XML Databases, and Fuseki RDF databases.

As of 2018, the reference implementation of CITE consists of specific libraries of code (written in the Scala language[4]). These are dedicated to specific tasks: one library is for creating and manipulating URN citations; one is for working with passages of text and textual corpora; one is for objects in collections. The "tier 1" libraries give us control over specific objects of study, "scholarly primitives". When these primitives are citable in a way that machines can work with, the "tier 2" libraries allow composition and analysis of those objects: additional code libraries are concerned with relations among objects, or more specific compositions, such as the three-way relationship among a "text-bearing artifact" (*e.g.* and inscription), a digital transcription of the text, and documentary evidence (a digital photograph).

Finally, there is CEX, the CITE Exchange format. This is a way to capture complex digital library content in a flexible, plain-text format.[5] CEX can capture

4 https://www.scala-lang.org (last access 2019.01.31).
5 https://cite-architecture.github.io/citedx/CEX-spec-3.0.1/ (last access 2019.01.31).

texts, collections of objects, and relations among citable resources. It serves large projects and small ones. A single CEX file might contain a Greek text and English translation of a single poem. But the entire Homer Multitext dataset is currently published as a single CEX file of 13.5 megabytes.

Working with texts: OHCO2, CTS URNs

The CITE Architecture evolved from initial work that was concerned with organizing editions and translations of the Homeric *Iliad* for the Homer Multitext. "Canonical Text Services" (CTS) is the set of specifications and libraries in CITE for working with texts.

CTS is based on an abstract model of "text"; it makes sense and works only in terms of that abstract model. This model defines a text as "An ordered hierarchy of citable objects."[6] It is called "OHCO2", with the '2' distinguishing it from an earlier proposed definition of text as "an ordered hierarchy of *content* objects."[7]

Citable texts are modeled as a set of citable nodes, each with four properties:

1. Each node belongs to a work hierarchy.
2. Each node is uniquely identified in a citation hierarchy.
3. Nodes are ordered within a single text.
4. Nodes may have richly structured textual content.

The CTS URN captures both the work hierarchy and the citation hierarchy.[8] It is a standard for machine-actionable canonical citation.

The work hierarchy represents texts as they are cited by scholars. Conceptually, the work hierarchy partially overlaps with the Functional Requirements for Bibliographic Records (FRBR),[9] but since FRBR aims to model bibliographic entries as they are cataloged by librarians, there are also noteworthy differences. The roof of the work hierarchy identifies any group of texts that are conventionally cited together in the naming authority's tradition. Examples could be based on concepts such as "author" (e.g., the works of Mark Twain), "geographic origin" (e.g., papyri from Oxyrhynchus), "subject

6 (Smith and Weaver 2009).
7 (DeRose et al. 1990).
8 The formal specification for CTS URNs is at http://cite-architecture.github.io/ctsurn_spec/ (last access 2019.01.31).
9 For FRBR, see the publications listed by the International Federation of Library Associations https://www.ifla.org (last access 2019.01.31).

matter" (e.g., Latin curse tablets), or any other grouping (e.g., a group of texts named the "Federalist Papers").

A CTS URN begins with namespace declarations, followed by the text-group identifier. This identifier may be followed by an identifier for a specific notional work within that group, corresponding to the work level of FRBR. This in turn may be followed with an identifier for a specific version of that work, either a translation or an edition, corresponding to the expression level of FRBR. A version identifier may be followed by an identifier for a specific exemplar of the version, corresponding to the item level of FRBR. (Note that there is no level of a CTS URN corresponding to the FRBR "manifestation.")

The passage component is a hierarchy of one or more levels expressing a logical citation scheme applying to all versions of a text. A poem might be cited by the single unit of "poetic line." A prose work might be cited by a hierarchy such as "book/chapter/section/subsection." Passage references at any level of the text's citation hierarchy may identify either a single citable node or a range indicated by the first and last nodes of the range.

If the work component of the CTS URN is at the version or exemplar level, reference to a single citable node may be extended with indexed occurrences of a substring or a range of substrings; in a reference to a range of nodes, either or both of the first and last nodes may be extended in the same way. Indexed substring references are permitted only with URNs at the version or exemplar level because they are inherently language-specific.

CTS URNs by example

`urn:cts:greekLit:tlg0012.tlg001.msA:10.1` This CTS URN has five fields, separated by a colon. The first three are namespace declarations: `urn:cts:greekLit:`, declaring that it is a URN according to the CTS specification, and that any subsequent values are guaranteed to be unique within the `greekLit` namespace.[10] The fourth field is the work hiearchy. `tlg0012` is an essentially arbitrary identifier defined, in the `greekLit` namespace, as referring to "Homer Epic". `tlg0012.tlg001` is the arbitrary identifier for "Homeric Epic, *Iliad*". `msA` identifies a specific edition of the *Iliad*, the Homer Multitext's diplomatic

10 `greekLit` is a namespace controlled by the Center for Hellenic Studies of Harvard University's "First Thousand Years of Greek" project.

transcription of the poetic text of the Venetus A manuscript (*Marcianus Graecus* Z.454 [=822]). The fifth and final field is the citation hierarchy. This URN identifies Book 10, line 1, of that particular version of the Homeric *Iliad*.

`urn:cts:greekLit:tlg0012.tlg001:10.1` In this CTS URN, there is no version identifier specified. This URN refers to every passage identified as "10.1" in any version of the *Iliad*, in any medium and in any language. Some versions of the *Iliad* do not have a passage "10.1". For example, the Bankes Papyrus in the British Library (BM Papyrus 114) contains only some verses from *Iliad* Book 24; this papyrus, then, is not included in the texts this URN identifies.

`urn:cts:greekLit:tlg0012.tlg001.villoison:10.1` This URN identifies Book 10, line 1, in the print edition published by Jean-Baptiste-Gaspard d'Ansse de Villoison in 1788. CTS URNs are not limited to identifying digital texts.

`urn:cts:greekLit:tlg0012.tlg001.villoison.tj4265:10.1` The work hierarchy of this CTS URN has an additional record after the version identifier. This identifies an *exemplar*, a specific instance of a version of the text. In this case, the URN identifies Book 10, line 1 in Thomas Jefferson's personal copy of Villoison's 1788 edition of the Homeric *Iliad*.[11]

In any CTS URN, the citation component is optional. `urn:cts:greekLit:tlg0012.tlg001.villoison.tj4265:` identifies Jefferson's copy of this edition in its entirety (note the final colon, required by the specification). `urn:cts:greekLit:tlg0012.tlg001:` accordingly refers to the *Iliad* in general, any and all versions of it.

Analytical exemplars

With physical books, an exemplar is a specific copy, such as Thomas Jefferson's personal copy of Villoison's edition of the *Iliad*, mentioned above. In the digital realm the CTS definition of "exemplar" is "a text derived from an identified version according to some defined analytical process." The Homer Multitext has published a diplomatic edition of the Iliadic text of the Venetus A, identified as `urn:cts:greekLit:tlg0012.tlg001.msA:`. The project also plans to publish

11 (d'Ansse de Villoison 1788). See *The Papers of Thomas Jefferson: Volume 28 1 January 1794 to 29 February 1796* (Princeton University: 2000) index: https://jeffersonpapers.princeton.edu/alpha-glossary/64/v (last access 2019.01.31).

a transformation of that digital edition with all abbreviations expanded and the Byzantine orthography normalized to the modern orthography for ancient Greek. This derivation would be an exemplar, identified by the URN: `urn:cts:greekLit:tlg0012.tlg001.msA.normal:`.

An exemplar may also extend the citation hierarchy of the version from which it is derived. This creates a *citable tokenization*. For many kinds of analysis, it is necessary to address parts of the Iliadic text more specifically than Book + Line, tokenizing the text. An exemplar might be a specific tokenization of a version. If we were to tokenize the *Iliad* in the service of syntactic analysis, we might create an exemplar where each lexical word has a unique citation: `urn:cts:greekLit:tlg0012.tlg001.msA.syntax-tokens:1.1.1` would identify Book 1, Line 1, *token 1* of an exemplar derived from the HMT's diplomatic edition of the *Iliad*; in this tokenization, the first token (1.1.1) would be μῆνιν, the first word of the poem. 1.1.2 would be "ἄειδε", the second word.

This allows multiple, independent analyses of a version of the text to coexist. A metrical analysis of the *Iliad* might result in a citable text, of which `urn:cts:greekLit:tlg0012.tlg001.msA.metrical-feet:1.1.1` would identify the text: "μηνιν α", the first metrical foot of the *Iliad*. Note that in this exemplar, the editors might omit diacritical marks as unnecessary for this particular analysis. Both a "syntax token" and "metrical foot" exemplar can exists, uniquely an unambiguously citable, offering text-content suited to specific kinds of analysis, explicitly aligned to the edition from which they were derived, and thus implicitly aligned to each other.

Digital humanities projects have long offered tools for transforming texts. The CTS hierarchy, expressed in the CTS URN, allows us to turn those analytical transformations from *procedural methods* to *declarative objects of study* by making them subject to specific citation.

The contents of CTS texts

CTS, following the OHCO2 model, sees a "text" as, essentially, the ordered list of unique citations; the textual-content of each citation can be plain-text or text and markup of any kind. CTS is entirely agnostic of matters of language, formatting, or markup of texts. The CITE Architecture provides a mechanism for "discoverable data models", described below, which is the means by which a project can identify for automated processes, applications, or services any specifics about the text contents of a particular CTS version or exemplar.

Canonical citation vs. traditional citation

CTS URNs provide machine-actionable canonical citations that capture the semantics of a text according to the OHCO2 model. It is important to emphasize that *canonical* citation is not, here, synonymous with *traditional* citation. Canonical, here, means “unique and persistent”. For some texts, the traditional scheme of citation translates well to OCHO2: the New Testament’s chapter/verse, poetic line for epic poetry, book/section/subsection for the Greek historians. For other texts, the traditional scheme of citation will not work for canonical citation according to OHCO2 and CTS. The works of Plato and Aristotle, for example, traditionally cited according to pages of specific early printed editions, require an editor to define and apply a different scheme of citation. More modern works often have no citation scheme beyond “chapter” and pages in specific editions. For these, a digital editor interested in using CTS must assert a new citation scheme, such as chapter/paragraph.[12]

Working with objects: CITE Collections and CITE2 URNs

In the CITE2 model, citable objects are modeled as unique objects in versioned collections. A version of a collection is defined by its properties and their values; a versioned collection is a list of citable object properties. The CITE2 URN captures these semantics.

The values of properties in a CITE Collection are typed, but the possible types are constrained to:

- `StringType`
- `NumberType`
- `BooleanType`
- `CtsUrnType`
- `Cite2UrnType`

12 For an example of modern texts implemented as CTS texts, and published via CEX, see the CTS implementation of the novels of Jane Austen published at https://github.com/cite-architecture/citedx (last access 2019.01.31). For these, the traditional citation scheme of novel/chapter is extended by the editorial assertion of the paragraph as the leaf-node.

Properties of StringType can, optionally, specify a controlled vocabulary. A collection of manuscript folios, for example, might have a side property of type StringType, but constrained to values of either "recto" or "verso".

The type of a property value, and in the case of StringType with a controlled vocabulary, is enforced by the CITE code libraries, which will throw an exception and refuse to build a CITE Collection object with invalid data.

As an example of a Cite Collection, we represent a papyrus fragment as a collection of text-bearing surfaces. The notional collection's URN is: urn:cite2:fufolio:poxy2099:. In this URN, fufolio is a namespace, and poxy2099 is the collection's identifier. To create a real collection, we create a citable version of this notional collection:

```
urn:cite2:fufolio:poxy2099.v1:.
```

This versioned collection has three properties: sequence, rv, label. Each of these is citable by URN:

```
urn:cite2:fufolio:poxy2099.v1.sequence:
urn:cite2:fufolio:poxy2099.v1.rv:
urn:cite2:fufolio:poxy2099.v1.label:
```

There are only two objects in this version of this collection:

```
urn:cite2:fufolio:poxy2099.v1:f1
urn:cite2:fufolio:poxy2099.v1:f2
```

f1 and f2 are arbitrary identifiers. Each of the above URNs identifies an object in the versioned collection, that is, each URN identifies all of the properties or an object with their values. Each property of an object is uniquely citable:

```
urn:cite2:fufolio:poxy2099.v1.sequence:f1
urn:cite2:fufolio:poxy2099.v1.rv:f1
urn:cite2:fufolio:poxy2099.v1.label:f1
```

Distinct objects may have identical contents, but within a collection each object is uniquely identified. Object f1 in Version v1 of this collection might have these citable property values:

```
urn:cite2:fufolio:poxy2099.v1.sequence:f1=1
urn:cite2:fufolio:poxy2099.v1.rv:f1="recto"
urn:cite2:fufolio:poxy2099.v1.label:f1="Papyrus POxy 2099, recto"
```

A collection may be referred either in the abstract as a notional collection, or concretely as a specific version of a notional collection. Each version of a collection defines a set of properties which may or may not be identical across versions, but apply to all objects within a given version. For this reason, individual objects may be canonically cited either as part of a notional or concrete collection, but individual properties can only be cited as part of a specific version of a collection.

We might have a Collection of geographical places mentioned in Herodotus: `urn:cite2:fufolio:hdtPlaces:`. We could cite one of its members with `urn:cite2:fufolio:hdtPlaces:1`. To attach actual data to this citation, we need a version of the Collection, which is defined by its properties. A very basic version of the collection might have only two properties for each object, a label and a citation to one passage of Herodotus that mentions the place:

```
urn:cite2:fufolio:hdtPlaces.v1.label:1="Halicarnassus"
urn:cite2:fufolio:hdtPlaces.v1.attestation:1=urn:cts:greekLit:tlg0016.
tlg001:1.0
```

Another version of the collection might offer richer data, or even different values for the same named property:

```
urn:cite2:fufolio:hdtPlaces.v2.label:1="Halikarnassos"
urn:cite2:fufolio:hdtPlaces.v2.attestation:1=urn:cts:greekLit:tlg0016.
tlg001:1.0
urn:cite2:fufolio:hdtPlaces.v2.pleiadesId:1="599636"
urn:cite2:fufolio:hdtPlaces.v2.latlong:1 = "37.0382205, 27.423765"
```

Here, object `1` in `v2` of this collection records a different spelling for the `label` property,[13] and adds to additional properties. The specific property values for each version can be addressed by their specific URNs, while the notional URN `urn:cite2:fufolio:hdtPlaces:1` identifies, and could be resolved to, all the values associated with that object in any version of the collection.

Collections may or may not be intrinsically ordered. The relation of citable objects in an ordered collection is analogous to the relation of citable passages in a citable text: it is possible to make statements about ordered relations at the notional level, but the ordering of citable units in individual versions are not

13 CITE is an exercise in separation of concerns, beginning with the important distinction between a *label* and an *identifier*. In our experience, it is always a mistake to try to conflate the functions of the two.

guaranteed to agree with a notional ordering. For example, in the same way that lines of a Greek tragedy might appear in a different order in different versions of the text, pages of a manuscript might have different orderings in a version recording the current bound form of a codex and a version reconstructing a different, original page sequence.

Compositions of scholarly primitives I: CITE relations

The foundation of CITE are these two categories of primitives – OHCO2 texts, and objects in collections – and the corresponding two types of URN citations that capture their semantics, CTS URNs and CITE2 URNs. This is a solid basis for documenting more complex structures as *compositions* of those primitives.

The most straightforward compositions are CITE Relations. (These are the "I" in "CITE", the "indices".) A CITE Relation has three parts: a subject, a relation, and an object.[14] Each of the three is expressed as a URN. The Subject and Object may be a CITE2 URN or a CTS URN. The Relation is a CITE2 URN, identifying an object in a collection of relation-types (or "verbs"), whose contents may be specific to a dataset or broadly applicable.

The Homer Multitext includes a collection `urn:cite2:hmt:verbs.v1:`, some of whose members include:

- `urn:cite2:hmt:verbs.v1:appearsIn` Identifying the relationship of a named person (a CITE2 URN, the subject of a relation) and the passage of the *Iliad* that mentions that person (a CTS URN, the object of the relation).
- `urn:cite2:hmt:verbs.v1:commentsOn` Identifying the relationship of a commentary text (a CTS URN, the subject of the relation) and a passage of the *Iliad* that it comments on (a CTS URN, the object of the relation).

Both of these types of relations, a character named in the text or a text that comments on another text, are potentially many-to-many relations. A passage of text might mention several characters, and a character will appear in many passage of text. Documenting these many-to-many relations is

14 CITE Relations are semantically identical to RDF Triples, and can easily be expressed as such: "Resource Description Framework (RDF): Concepts and Abstract Syntax": https://www.w3.org/TR/rdf-concepts/ (last access 2019.01.31).

simply a matter of multiplying the CITE Relations triples. So in the *HMT* 2018e data release, Achilles (`urn:cite2:hmt:pers.v1:pers1`) is mentioned in (`urn:cite2:hmt:verbs.v1:appearsIn`) 217 passages of the scholia. These 217 relations can be expressed like:

```
urn:cite2:hmt:pers.v1:pers1 # urn:cite2:hmt:verbs.v1:appearsIn # urn:
cts:greekLit:tlg5026.msA.dipl:13.A47.comment
urn:cts:greekLit:tlg5026.msA.dipl:22.36.comment
urn:cite2:hmt:pers.v1:pers1 # urn:cite2:hmt:verbs.v1:appearsIn # urn:
cts:greekLit:tlg5026.msA.dipl:13.A47.comment
...
```

By insisting that each of the three components of a relation be URNs, a body of relations can be filtered or queried according to all of the semantics captured by those URNs: all persons appearing mentioned in the intra-marginal scholia of MS A of the *Iliad*, or in Book 9 of any version of the *Iliad*; all intra-linear comments on Book 2 of the *Iliad*; all main-scholia comments on *Iliad* 1.1–1.25; etc.

Compositions of scholarly primitives II: CITE extensions

The 'E' in CITE is "Extensions", additional discoverable information providing richer composition and description of the basic scholarly primitives.

Extensions I: categorizing collections

A CITE Collection can describe a collection of images. A very basic image collection might have the properties `label`, `license`, and `caption`. (Obviously, these are collections of metadata about images, expressed as plain text; we will address actual binary image data below.) In a library where there are several different collections of images, we can distinguish them as a special category by defining an Extension. This is nothing more than another CITE Collection.

If in a library there are three collections of images:

1. `urn:cite2:hmt:venAimg.v1:`
2. `urn:cite2:hmt:venBimg.v1:`
3. `urn:cite2:hmt:e3img.v1:`

We can formally identify these three collections as belonging to a certain type by asserting a *data model* in a collection of Data Models: `urn:cite2:cite:datamodels.v1:imagemodel`, and associating each of the three image collections with that data model.

The data model itself is documented in human-readable prose online; its definition includes a link to documentation. Any user or application that is aware of the `imagemodel` data model can discover which collections in a library implement that datamodel, and (in this case) know that these collections will include at least a `label`, `license`, and `caption` property.

A user or application can ignore this association, and those collections will behave as generic CITE Collections.

Extensions II: connecting to the physical world

With collections of images in CITE, we can serialize metadata for images easily, since it is plain-text in CEX. Resolving a URN to binary image data – so the user can actually see an image – requires a connection to the physical world. A notional "image" might be resolved to a JPG file, to data delivered by the IIIF API, to a DeepZoom file, or to any combination of these.

CITE handles this by means of another "discoverable data model", additional data (itself expressed as generic CITE collections) that can identify specific collections of images as being served by one or more binary image services. By associating a CITE Collection of Images with a `binaryimg` data model, we can then publish the information necessary to resolve the image specified by URN in a CITE Collection with one or more methods for resolving that URN to a digital image:

- A type of image service (JPG file, IIIF-API, DeepZoom).
- A URL to a service hosting images from the collection.
- Filepath information necessary to resolve an image's URN to files on the server.

A working example of this is the Homer Multitext's interactive web-application.[15] The CEX of the HMT's data release identifies image collections as being exposed both as DeepZoom files and via the IIIF-API.[16] The web-application takes advantage of both of these to provide thumbnail views and interactive zooming views.

15 http://www.homermultitext.org/hmt-digital/?urn=urn:cite2:hmt:vaimg.2017a:VA304VN_0806 (last access 2019.01.31).

16 https://github.com/homermultitext/hmt-archive/blob/master/releases-cex/hmt-2018e.cex (last access 2019.01.31).

Extensions III: extension-specific predicates to URNs

In the CITE architecture we can identify passages of text at the "leaf node" level, and the CTS URN provides access to the larger context – "New Testament, John, Chapter 3, verse 16" expressed as a URN identifies a particular passage of text, but provides access to "Chapter 3" as well, or the whole "Gospel According to John", and the whole "New Testament". A CITE2 URN, likewise, can identify the value of a particular property in a particular object, or that object generically, or all objects in a particular collection. This is sound citation-practice: identifying the specific object of study in its context.

For certain kinds of data, the relationship between "object of study" and "context" requires a specifically defined notation. So a defined data model can document a model-specific *URN extension.*

In the case of the CITE `binaryimg` data model, a defined URN extension can identify a rectangular region-of-interest (ROI) on the image. The format is `URN@left,top,width,height`. A URN identifying an image of Folio 12-recto of the Venetus A manuscript is `urn:cite2:hmt:vaimg.2017a:VA012RN_0013`. To identify the ROI on that image that includes *Iliad* 1.5, we extend the URN with top, left, width, and height values, expressed as percentages of the whole image:

```
urn:cite2:hmt:vaimg.2017a:VA012RN_0013@0.1619,0.3112,0.3345,0.02451
```

This ability to extend a CITE2 URN for a specific type of object was a key to the early development of the CITE Architecture, and is the basis for the DSE Model that has become the focus of the data published by the Homer Multitext.

Extensions IV: defined compositions

DSE stands for "Documented Scholarly Editions". It is a defined data-model that can be expressed as a CITE Collection with the following properties:

- `urn` The identifiers for a DSE `Object (Cite2UrnType)`
- `label` A human-readable label `(StringType)`
- `text` A passage of text `(CtsUrnType)`
- `surface` A physical artifact that has the text on it `(Cite2UrnType)`
- `image` A ROI on a citable digital image `(Cite2UrnType)`

This implements a collection of citable objects, each consisting of a text, the physical artifact on which the text appears, and specific documentary evidence that a scholar can access to see the text as it appears on the artifact. The text, artifact, and image-evidence are each individually subject to citation. But the graph that associates them is also uniquely citable.

By virtue of the CITE URNs, for each vertex in each DSE object, we have access to the larger context. One DSE Object (that is, a single 3-way graph) from the Homer Multitext is:

- URN = `urn:cite2:hmt:va_dse.v1:il10`
- Label = "`urn:cite2:hmt:va_dse.v1:il10`"
- Text = `urn:cts:greekLit:tlg0012.tlg001.msA:1.1`
- Surface = `urn:cite2:hmt:msA.v1:12r`
- Image = `urn:cite2:hmt:vaimg.2017a:VA012RN_0013.v1@0.0611,0.225,0.467,0.09`

This object, identified as `urn:cite2:hmt:va_dse.v1:il10`, is the three-way association of *Iliad* 1.1 (as it appears on the Venetus A manuscript), with folio 12 recto of the Venetus A manuscript, as evinced by image `VA012RN_0013` in version `2017a` of the collection `urn:cite2:hmt:vaimg:`, specifically in the rectangle starting at 6.11% from the top of that image, 22.5% from the left, extending to 46.7% of its width, and 9% of its height.

Extensions V: different expressions of textual data

An object in a version of a collection might have a property of type `StringType`, and that is easily discoverable with the basic CITE tools. But of course, a `StringType` might be plain text, Markdown, some form of XML, or some other encoding. It is easy to imagine a project publishing a version of a collection of comments as plain-text, and subsequently publishing a new version that adds some markup to those comments.

Because the CITE2 URN allows identification of notional collections, versioned collections, individual properties in versioned collections, in each case across the collection or filtered by an object's identifier, we can expose additional information about the nature of a property of type `StringType`.

By means of a discoverable data model, just as we associated whole collections of images with different binary image services, we can associate properties with different encodings, without losing scholarly identity.

A CITE microservice (about which see below) at http://folio2.furman.edu/lex/collections serves a transformation of the Liddell, Scott, Jones Greek Lexicon

(*LSJ*)[17] as a CITE Collection, a collection of lexical-entities. Each object in this collection has three properties:

1. `urn:cite2:hmt:lsj.chicago_md.seq:` The sequence of an entry, because this is an ordered collection.
2. `urn:cite2:hmt:lsj.chicago_md.key:` The headword, or *lemma*, of the lexicon entry.
3. `urn:cite2:hmt:lsj.chicago_md.entry:` The entry itself.

Other projects have encoded the *LSJ* with elaborate markup in TEI-XML, but this collection aims simply to present the lexicon's entries to human readers in a clear and attractive manner. So the data in the `urn:cite2:hmt:lsj.chicago_md.entry:` property, defined as `StringType`, includes Markdown formatting.[18]

For the object identified as `urn:cite2:hmt:lsj.chicago_md:n2389`, the entry property (`urn:cite2:hmt:lsj.chicago_md.entry:n2389`) has this value:

```
**αἴλουρος**, Arist. *HA* 540a10, *Phgn.* 811b9, or αἰέλουρος, ὁ, ἡ, Hdt. and
Comici ll. cc., S. *Ichn.* 296:- `A` **cat, Felis domesticus**, Hdt. 2.66,
Ar. *Ach.* 879, Anaxandr. 39.12, Timocl. 1, LXX *Ep.Je.* 22, Plu. 2.144c.
`A.II`= ἀναγαλλὶς ἡ κυανῆ, Ps.- Dsc. 2.178; also αἰλούρου ὀφθαλμός, ὁ, ibid.
```

But the CITE publication of this data includes a *discoverable data model* identified as `urn:cite2:fufolio:extended_text_properties.v1:`. In the Collection of extended text properties, the property `urn:cite2:hmt:lsj.chicago_md.entry:n2389` is defined as being of the extended-type: `markdown`.

Any application working with this CITE data can ignore that, and will thus render the entry as above, in plain-text. But an application can discover that this property contains Markdown content, and use that information to render the entry with the Markdown transformed:

αἴλουρος, Arist. *HA* 540a10, *Phgn.* 811b9, or αἰέλουρος, ὁ, ἡ, Hdt. and Comici ll. cc., S. *Ichn.* 296:- A **cat, Felis domesticus**, Hdt. 2.66, Ar. *Ach.* 879, Anaxandr. 39.12, Timocl. 1, LXX *Ep.Je.* 22, Plu. 2.144c. A.II = ἀναγαλλὶς ἡ κυανῆ, Ps.- Dsc. 2.178; also αἰλούρου ὀφθαλμός, ὁ, ibid.

---

17 (Liddell and Scott 1940). For a discussion of this republication of a digital *LSJ*, see C. Blackwell, "Publishing the Liddell & Scott Lexicon via CITE": https://eumaeus.github.io/2018/10/30/lsj.html (last access 2019.01.31).

18 Markdown is a simple standard for applying basic typesetting (emphasis, links, list-formatting) to plain-text documents. See Ovadia (2014) and Voegler et al. (2014).

Other Extended String Text Property types currently in use include `geoJson`, and `teiXml`, but any project is free to identify others. This allows a CITE dataset to include an open-ended number of domain-specific encodings to serve specific needs, but which will all degrade gracefully to plain-text for applications, processes, or readers unaware of those extensions.

The CITE Exchange Format (CEX): plain text serialization of diverse scholarly data

CITE makes no requirements for how these objects, relations, and extensions are captured and stored. Since its origins, CITE data has been stored and served by relational database systems, the Google BigTable database, TEI-XML, RDF in `.ttl` format.[19]

In 2016, Christopher Blackwell, Thomas Köntges, and Neel Smith defined the CITE Exchange Format (CEX), a plain-text, line-oriented data format for serializing citable content following the models of the CITE Architecture. What follows here is a brief overview; the full specification is at https://cite-architecture.github.io/citedx/CEX-spec-3.0.1/.

In a CEX file, distinct types of content are grouped in separate labelled blocks, so that a single CEX source can integrate any content citable in the CITE Architecture.

Blocks are optional (although some blocks may require the presence of one or more other blocks). Authors may limit a CEX serialization to include only those kinds of citable content they choose. A null string or empty text file is a syntactically valid, although empty, CEX data serialization.

1. **Blocks** in a CEX data source are introduced by a line beginning with one of nine **block labels** listed below.
2. Blocks terminate when a new block is introduced or the end of the data source is reached.
3. Content preceding the first labelled block is ignored.
4. Blocks may occur in any sequence in a single CEX serialization.

Valid block labels are:
- `#!cexversion`
- `#!citelibrary`

19 (Chang et al. 2008). "RDF 1.1 Turtle": https://www.w3.org/TR/turtle/ (last access 2019.01.31).

- `#!ctsdata`
- `#!ctscatalog`
- `#!citecollections`
- `#!citeproperties`
- `#!citedata`
- `#!imagedata`
- `#!relations`
- `#!datamodels`

Within a block, the block label is followed by an ordered sequence of lines. That is, while the appearance of blocks in a CEX source is not ordered, line are ordered within each block.

Empty (zero-length) lines are allowed but are ignored. Lines beginning with the string // are comments and are ignored. Other lines are treated as the **block contents.**

The syntax of block contents is specific to the type of the block.

CEX affords the ability to share a potentially complex digital library as a single file, independent of any implementing technology. It also allows an expression of an integrated digital library to contain portions of datasets. A teaching edition of a Greek poem might include the poem (as a CTS text), some commentary (as a CITE Collection), and lexical information for the language of the poem. A CEX file could include only those entries from the *LSJ* lexicon that are relevant for the poem, rather than the whole dictionary. By virtue of the CITE2 URNs, those entries would not be separated from their context in the whole lexicon.

A set of demonstration CEX files is published at https://github.com/cite-architecture/citedx.

Code libraries

As of 2018, the definitive implementation of the CITE Architecture is in the code libraries published in the Cite Architecture organization on GitHub.[20] Each of these is written in the Scala[21] language, which allows them to be compiled to `.jar` files for use in the Java virtual machine, or to `.js` files for use in JavaScript/ECMAScript environments.

20 https://github.com/cite-architecture (last access 2019.01.31).
21 https://www.scala-lang.org (last access 2019.01.31).

Each of these libraries depends on SBT, the Scala Build Tool,[22] which allows the library to be compiled and tested, and to have its API documentation generated. That API documentation serves as a definitive definition of the service.

Each library's `README.md` file on GitHub provides instructions for including the library in another project.

Each of these libraries includes tests, which can be run using the Scala Build Tool. These tests constitute a body of documentation complementary to the `scaladoc` API documentation that can (also) be generated using SBT.

The current published libraries are:

Tier 1 Libraries: identification and retrieval

- `xcite`: CTS and CITE2 URN validation and manipulation
- `ohco2`: CTS Texts and corpora thereof
- `citeobj`: CITE Objects and Collections

Tier 2 Libraries: composition

- `cex`: Serializing CITE data to plain-text; generating CITE objects from plain-text serializations.
- `scm`: Scala CITE Manager
- `citerelations`: Subject-Verb-Object relations expressed with 3 URNs.
  `dse`: Documented Scholarly Editions
- `citebinaryimage`: Resolving CITE URNs to images and regions-of-interest on images
- `citejson`: De-marshaling JSON expressions of CITE data into memory representations

Services and applications

- `scs-akka`: A microservice accepting requests via HTTP and returning CITE data marshalled as JSON strings. A page of working examples, drawing on *HMT* data is at http://beta.hpcc.uh.edu/hmt/hmt-microservice/.

22 https://github.com/cite-architecture (last access 2019.01.31).

- `CITE-App`: A ScalaJS web-application that reads data from a CEX file and affords interaction with CITE texts, collections, images, and relations. Because all data is processed in-memory in the browser, this application is suitable only for relatively small and focused libraries. See a working example at http://folio.furman.edu/cite.html.
- `Server-CITE-App`: A version of CITE-App that draws its data from the Akka microservice, and is thus able to work with much larger datasets. The *HMT*'s data is exposed with this application at http://www.homermultitext.org/hmt-digital/.
- `facsimile`: http://www.homermultitext.org/facsimile/index.html. A lightweight application that uses CEX to access a static representation of the *HMT* data. The static representation is a series of Markdown files generated from a CEX library that show citable passages of Iliadic and commentary texts as transcriptions and as ROIs on images of manuscript folios.
- `LSJ Lexicon`: A bespoke application providing access to a CITE representation of *A Greek-English Lexicon*, Henry George Liddell, Robert Scott, revised and augmented throughout by Sir Henry Stuart Jones with the assistance of Roderick McKenzie (Oxford: Clarendon Press. 1940). The lexicon is captured as a CEX file, and served from an instance of the Akka microservice.

Final thoughts

The CITE Architecture arose from the earliest work on the Homer Multitext. In 2000, Gregory Nagy, Casey Dué, and Mary Ebbott began to discuss what a 21st Century edition of the *Iliad* might look like. Their interest was in preserving the tradition of transmission of the text, on the assumption that the details of that transmission hold clues to understanding the nature of Greek epic poetry as the product of an oral tradition of composition in performance. Those details lie in the variations in the text that we find from one manuscript to another, and in particular in Iliadic language quoted in scholarly commentaries from antiquity, and in other authors from antiquity. The editors of the project call these "multiforms" rather than "variants" to emphasize their conviction that these are not divergences from an original, canonical text, but equally legitimate epic expressions.

The edition they proposed would require documenting and aligning many different versions of Iliadic texts, at a fine level of granularity, and aligning those versions to other texts in prose and poetry, to lexical and morphological data, to digital images, and working with this material in ways that they knew they did not yet imagine.

In 2003, at a conference at the Center for Hellenic Studies of Harvard University, Neel Smith presented a talk entitled "Toward a 'Text Server'," in which he described some of the necessities for rigorous identification and retrieval of texts in a networked digital environment. That was the origin of Canonical Text Services, which was the first component of the CITE Architecture to reach the point of usability. Since 2003, while Neel Smith and Christopher Blackwell have been the main authors of CITE, many others have provided valuable insights, encouragement, wholesome skepticism, and intelligent criticism. An incomplete list of these scholars would include Leonard Muellner, Thomas Martin, Hugh Cayless, Ryan Baumann, Gabriel Weaver, Bridget Almas, Bruce Robertson, Monica Berti, Matteo Romanello, Francesco Mambrini, and Gregory Crane. We would like to recognize the support and inspiration of our late friend, Professor Ross Scaife of the University of Kentucky.

Bibliography

d'Ansse de Villoison, J.-B.-G. (1788): Homeri Ilias. Venetiis: Typis et sumptibus fratrum Coleti.

Chang, F.; Dean, J.; Ghemawat, S.; Hsieh, W.C.; Wallach, D.A.; Burrows, M.; Chandra, T.; Fikes, A.; Gruber, R.E. (2008): "Bigtable: A Distributed Storage System for Structured Data". ACM Transactions on Computer Systems (TOCS) 26:2, 4.

DeRose, S.; Durand, D.; Mylonas, E.; Renear, A. (1990): "What Is Text, Really?". Journal of Computing in Higher Education 1:2, 3–26.

Liddell, H.G.; Scott, R. (eds.) (1940): A Greek-English Lexicon. Revised and augmented throughout by Sir Henry Stuart Jones with the assistance of Roderick McKenzie. Oxford: Clarendon Press.

Ovadia, S. (2014): "Markdown for Librarians and Academics". Behavioral & Social Sciences Librarian 33:2, 120–124.

Smith, D.N.; Weaver, G. (2009): "Applying Domain Knowledge from Structured Citation Formats to Text and Data Mining: Examples Using the CITE Architecture". In: G. Heyer (ed.): Text Mining Services: Building and Applying Text Mining Based Service Infrastructures in Research and Industry. Leipziger Beiträge zur Informatik, Band XIV. Leipzig (reprinted in Dartmouth College Computer Science Technical Report series, TR2009–649, June 2009), 129–139.

Tippett, K.; Rees, M. (2013): "Martin Rees – Cosmic Origami and What We Don't Know". On Being. November 21, 2013. https://onbeing.org/programs/martin-rees-cosmic-origami-and-what-we-dont-know/ (last access 2019.01.31).

Voegler, J.; Bornschein, J.; Weber, G. (2014): "Markdown – A Simple Syntax for Transcription of Accessible Study Materials". In: K. Miesenberger; D. Fels; D. Archambault; P. Peňáz; W. Zagler (eds.): Computers Helping People with Special Needs. ICCHP 2014. Lecture Notes in Computer Science. Volume 8547. Cham: Springer, 545–548.

Jochen Tiepmar and Gerhard Heyer

The Canonical Text Services in Classics and Beyond

Abstract: Starting with the project A Library of a Billion Words (ESF 100146395) and ongoing in the Big Data related project Scalable Data Solutions (BMBF 01IS14014B), the NLP group in Leipzig was tasked to develop a feature complete and generic implementation of the Canonical Text Services (CTS) protocol that is able to handle billions of words. This paper describes how this goal was achieved and why this is a significant step forward for the communities of humanists and computer scientists who work with text data.

1 Introduction

With the ongoing digitization of text data and the general trend for digital publications, the ability to persistently reference text snippets as digital resources across projects becomes increasingly important. For this purpose the Canonical Text Services (CTS) protocol was developed for the Homer Multitext project supported by the Center for Hellenic Studies of Harvard University.[1] CTS incorporates the idea that annotations can naturally be based on an inherent ontology of text passages such as chapters, paragraphs, sentences, words, and letters. It allows researchers to identify precise words and phrases in particular versions of a work without having to rely on particular editions. A Canonical Text Service can be characterized as a complex text retrieval webservice that provides persistent reference (CTS) URNs for hierarchical text elements (e.g. chapter, sentence, down to character) and request functions to retrieve text content and structural meta information for each of the references as well as each span between them. As such it provides citable reference points for every

1 https://www.homermultitext.org (last access 2019.01.31). See Smith (2009).

Note: Part of this work was funded by the German Federal Ministry of Education and Research within the project ScaDS Dresden/Leipzig (BMBF 01IS14014B) and by the European Social Fund in the project The Library of a Billion Words (ESF 100146395).

Jochen Tiepmar, Gerhard Heyer, Universität Leipzig

https://doi.org/10.1515/9783110599572-007

possible text passage in a document, making it a very valuable tool for (digital) humanists.[2]

A graph based and an XML based implementation provided the basic functionalities of the protocol but the more advanced functionalities like sub references and text spans proved to be problematic for these solutions. They were additionally developed around specific data sets and hard to adapt to external resources. Therefore and in order to expand the usefulness of CTS beyond the Classical languages (i.e. Greek and Latin), it seemed reasonable to develop a third implementation based on the documented learned lessons with a specific focus on efficient scalability and generic applicability.

2 The relevance of CTS in computer science

Tiepmar (2018) shows that CTS can be technically seen as a RESTFul webservice[3] that integrates well with existing technical solutions as they are for instance used in CLARIN[4] or more recently in projects like Das Digitale Archiv NRW.[5] Instead of being in competition with used systems, it provides huge potential for technical improvements as described in the following pages.

2.1 Normalized text access across data sources

Even though they are all modern and ongoing projects, examples like Deutsches Textarchiv, Perseus, Eur Lex (EU 2017) and Project Gutenberg show that each requires individual ways to access data.[6] Perseus offers a public GitHub repository and the other three projects specific websites. There is no obvious way to collect a dump of the data, which means that in order to work with the data sets locally, an individual web crawler has to be implemented or the data has to be requested via one of the contact possibilities.

Another problem is that digitized documents are often published in varying formats. Each of the four examples uses a specific markup to structure their

2 For a more detailed explanation about Canonical Text Services, see Smith (2009), Blackwell et al. (2017), Tiepmar et al. (2014) and Tiepmar (2018).
3 (Fielding 2000).
4 (Hinrichs and Krauwer 2014).
5 (Thaller 2013).
6 (Geyken et al. 2011); (Smith et al. 2000); (Hart 2017).

documents. DTA and Perseus offer texts in TEI/XML but the metadata markup is varying. Generally, to access individual text units it is required to know in which way the structure is marked in each document before being able to access it. For instance, to access individual lines it may be required to look for <l> or </lb> and paragraphs may be marked as <p> or <div type ="paragraph">. It may even be problematic to find out how or if the document is structured in the first place. This is a problem because it prevents the implementation of tools that can be reused without adaptation effort.

Because of the strict design of CTS, tools can be developed to work in such a generic way that they are able to work with any CTS endpoint. This makes it possible to exchange and access text data without having to learn how a certain data set should be accessed.

2.2 Separate structural meta information

Documents can be divided into a hierarchical system of text parts like for example chapters that consist of sentences or songs that consist of stanzas that consist of verses. This structural meta information is part of the metadata markup possibilities that are provided by TEI/XML or DocBook but, since this information is technically not different from any other meta information, it is hard to use it as input for tools.

Yet it showed that this information can be very useful and tools would benefit from a reliable generic way of accessing it. Since CTS URNs are built from this structural meta information, they also indirectly encode it as it is illustrated in the following example. The URNs have been shortened for better readability:

:1:1.1:1.1.1 O Christmas tree, O Christmas tree !
:1.1.2 How are thy leaves so verdant !
:1.1.5 O Christmas tree, O Christmas tree,
:1.1.6 How are thy leaves so verdant !
:1.2:1.2.1 O Christmas tree, O Christmas tree,
:1.2.2 Much pleasure doth thou bring me !
:1.2.5 O Christmas tree, O Christmas tree,
:1.2.6 Much pleasure doth thou bring me !

This problem could also be solved by agreeing on what is considered as a structural metadata tag, but this solution would still have the potential to create ambiguity as it is illustrated in the following example:

<chapter> This is a chapter that references chapter <chapter>1</chapter> </chapter>.

In this constructed example, a reference to another chapter is marked with the same tag that is used for the text passage. <chapter> is a reasonable (and the only) choice for a tag that describes structural information. But doing so means that its use as meta information in <chapter>1</chapter> would be interpreted as structural information, resulting in an additional sub chapter with the text content 1:

> <chapter> This is a chapter that references chapter <chapter> 1 </chapter> </chapter>.

While it can be discussed, which of the interpretations is "more right" and whether or not this example should be considered as realistic, it is obviously true that the technical interpretation can be ambiguous if meta information and document structure use the same markup.

With CTS URNs, this encoding of the hierarchical information in documents can be accessed separately from the meta information encoded in the metadata markup and can serve as the basis for new generic algorithmic approaches to text mining.

2.3 Granularity

Current text reference systems like for instance the PID handles that are used in CLARIN or the URNs that are used in Das Digitale Archive NRW allow to reference electronic resources.[7] In the context of text data such references mostly correlate to individual text files. CTS URNs additionally enable researchers to reference structural elements of digitized documents like chapters or sentences in a unified way.

This fine granular reference system is for instance one of the advantages that justified the inclusion of the CTS protocol in CLARIN as it is described by Tiepmar et al. (2017) and Grallert et al. (2017), because it allows text research infrastructures to provide persistent identifiers for the structural elements of a text with varying granularities.

2.4 Text streaming

The work described by Smith (2009) indirectly points out another advantage of the usage of CTS:

7 (van Uytvanck 2014); (Thaller 2013).

> "These Canonical Text Services URNs make it possible to reduce the complexity of a reference like First occurrence of the string 'cano' in line 1 of book 1 of Vergil's Aeneid to a short string that can then be used by any application that understands CTS URNs".

This also implies that it is possible to reduce long texts to CTS URNs and request them as they are needed. In this way the memory needed for software that handles texts or text parts can be reduced because the software does not have to memorize the text passages but instead memorizes the relative short CTS URNs and requests text information as it is needed.

Because of the hierarchical properties of CTS URNs, they may also allow specific caching techniques. Generally, books tend to include more text than can be shown on a monitor in a reasonable way. If a text passage is too big to be visualized as a whole, it may be more memory efficient to use a sliding window that spans some of the smaller text parts on a lower depth that correlates to the amount of text that is visible in one moment. This streaming technique can be especially valuable when working with systems that do not have access to vast amounts of access memory like smart devices or small notebooks. Figure 1 illustrates this by showing how sets of ten sentences are processed at one moment instead of the complete text.

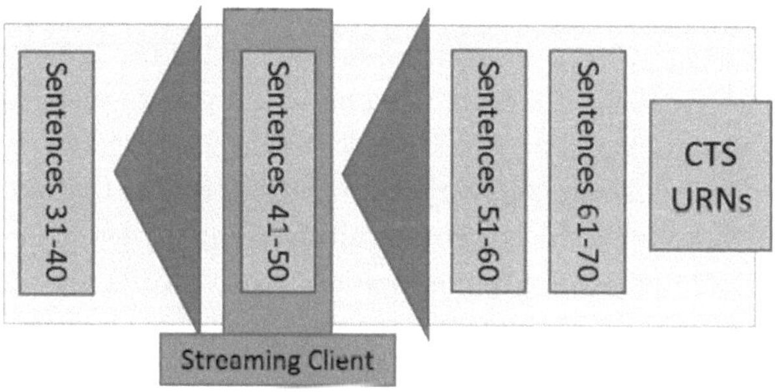

Figure 1: CTS URN based text streaming.

This technique is for example used in CTRaCE to limit the amount of cached content to a reasonable amount instead of handling the full document at any given time.[8]

8 (Reckziegel et al. 2016).

3 Index implementation

A detailed analysis by Tiepmar (2018) concludes that the following requirements must be met for the technical basis of a CTS implementation:

- (At least) UTF-8 support.
- Capability of online – especially multi user – handling.
- Established & Accessible (Usability).
- Independence from a specific input data type.
- Prefix string search or a similarly fitting implicit hierarchy retrieval mechanism.
- Support for sequential order index and range queries.

The implementation of the index itself is most efficiently done using a trie or prefix search tree[9] using prefix search based hierarchy retrieval that can be programmed using standard server SQL techniques.

3.1 Prefix search based hierarchy retrieval

Hierarchical information based on CTS URNs can be requested similar to how prefix based search is done in a trie. For instance, to find out which of the CTS URNs belong to *urn:cts:perseus(. . .):1.*, it is sufficient to traverse the trie according to the given URN. Any (recursive) child node is one of the structural child elements of the URN that was provided as input. Resolving the hierarchical information in CTS URNs can be done by applying the same algorithms that are used for string prefix search because the structural information in them is encoded by the continuation of their string representation. Parent URNs are always prefix sub strings and the set of child URNs is exactly the same as the result set of a string prefix search.

The result of this mapping of seemingly unrelated tasks is that the hierarchy retrieval in this context is technically not a task of data architecture but of information retrieval. String based methods can be used to extract the hierarchy information that is encoded in the CTS URNs. This especially means that the hierarchy information does not have to be modelled explicitly in the data set but is implicitly known to the system as soon as CTS URNs are added. The consequence is that the optimal hierarchy index for a Canonical Text Service is not

9 (Brass 2008).

necessarily a hierarchical data structure but a data structure that is optimised for prefix string search.[10]

An additional benefit of this approach is that it is very flexible. Prefix sub string search works with strings of any length and therefore this approach theoretically supports any possible citation depth. It also does not depend on the URN syntax or any kind of fixed formula and could also extract the hierarchical information from the following example that is far from a valid CTS URN notation[11]:

axl_cts_greekLit(tlg0003.tlg001<perseus_eng1)
axl_cts_greekLit(tlg0003.tlg001<perseus_eng1)buch1
axl_cts_greekLit(tlg0003.tlg001<perseus_eng1)buch1_3
axl_cts_greekLit(tlg0003.tlg001<perseus_eng1)buch1_3the5thverse

This approach is flexible enough that changes in the URN syntax or related future schemas can be supported. This especially means that this method can be applied to similar systems like the CITE[12] protocol – which uses references similar to CTS URNs for discrete objects and images – without significant effort.

3.2 Proposed index implementation

The proposed index implementation is based on MySQL Version 5 (Oracle 2018), or similar systems like MariaDB.[13] UTF-8 is supported, along with a vast number of other character sets. It is an established data storage technique in the context of online services that is often part of the pre-installed software packages for servers.[14] MySQL does not have a required input data format, the data has to be added and requested by the software that uses it. Responses are generally formatted into or from specific formats by the application software.

---

10 Which is more specific than *tree*, but would also include potential non tree prefix search methods.

11 *axl_cts_greekLit(tlg0003.tlg001<perseus_eng1)buch1* is the parent node of *axl_cts_greekLit (tlg0003.tlg001<perseus_eng1)buch1_3* and so on.

12 http://www.homermultitext.org/hmt-docs/cite/cite-overview.html (last access 2019.01.31).

13 https://mariadb.org (last access 2019.01.31).

14 SQL is included in software like Xampp, hosting services like Strato and Host Europe and requirement for Wordpress – one of the most established Blog/Website backends.

Sequential order indices as the basis for range queries can be implemented using an incrementing integer, that can simultaneously act as the primary key for the data rows. In order for this index to be useful to find left and right neighbour entries, it should be made sure, that the incrementing integer value is free of gaps.[15]

Prefix based string search can be implemented using the *LIKE* command with wildcard symbol % that matches any number of characters. *LIKE BINARY* makes sure that the search is done with case sensitivity. *LIKE BINARY* queries are significantly slower than *LIKE* queries because SQL does a complete scan for *BINARY*. Therefore every *BINARY* query is applied using a syntax similar to *LIKE AND LIKE BINARY*,[16] which means that SQL only does the expensive case sensitive lookup after the search room is limited to the case insensitive matches.

The following example illustrates the used prefix based string search:

urn:cts:greekLit:tlg0003.tlg001.perseus_eng1:3.116
urn:cts:greekLit:tlg0003.tlg001.perseus_eng1:4
urn:cts:greekLit:tlg0003.tlg001.perseus_eng1:4.1
urn:cts:greekLit:tlg0003.tlg001.perseus_eng1:4.2
(. . .)
urn:cts:greekLit:tlg0003.tlg001.perseus_eng1:40
urn:cts:greekLit:tlg0003.tlg001.perseus_eng1:40.1

The LIKE BINARY query for urn:cts:greekLit:tlg0003.tlg001.perseus_eng1:4. returns the following result set[17]:

urn:cts:greekLit:tlg0003.tlg001.perseus_eng1:4.1
urn:cts:greekLit:tlg0003.tlg001.perseus_eng1:4.2

Both results are child URNs of the input CTS URN. Any child URN of the input CTS URN must be part of the result set because all of them start with the input CTS URN. It is important to append the delimiting characters to the request parameter.[18] If the prefix search would be done using *urn:cts:greekLit:tlg0003.*

15 The result from MySQL's *AUTO_INCREMENT* is not necessarily gap free.
16 SELECT urn WHERE urn LIKE "urn:cts:pbc:bible.parallel.eng.kingjames:2.1.%" AND urn LIKE BINARY "urn:cts:pbc:bible.parallel.eng.kingjames:2.1%".
17 SELECT urn WHERE urn LIKE BINARY "urn:cts:greekLit:tlg0003.tlg001.perseus_eng1:4.%".
18 The dot "." and the colon ":".

tlg001.perseus_eng1:4 as the input parameter instead of *urn:cts:greekLit:tlg0003.tlg001.perseus_eng1:4.*, the result would include the correct CTS URNs

urn:cts:greekLit:tlg0003.tlg001.perseus_eng1:4.1
urn:cts:greekLit:tlg0003.tlg001.perseus_eng1:4.2

as well as the incorrect CTS URNs

urn:cts:greekLit:tlg0003.tlg001.perseus_eng1:40
urn:cts:greekLit:tlg0003.tlg001.perseus_eng1:40.1

MySQL provides a B-Tree index that can be applied to text data and is used for LIKE comparisons if the input string does not start with the wildcard character. This results in a database table as shown in Table 1.

Table 1: CTS URN database table.

ID	URN	text
22	urn:cts:greekLit:tlg0003.tlg001.perseus_eng1:3.116	The same (...)
23	urn:cts:greekLit:tlg0003.tlg001.perseus_eng1:4	NULL
24	urn:cts:greekLit:tlg0003.tlg001.perseus_eng1:4 .1	The spring (...)
25	urn:cts:greekLit:tlg0003.tlg001.perseus_eng1:4 .2	About the (...)

Using this schema, every table row corresponds to exactly one structural element of the input document. The column *ID* is indexed as the primary key of the database and serves as the sequential index that is required for the range queries and the neighbour requests. The column *URN* is indexed using MySQL's B-Tree implementation and is used for the prefix based string search that serves as the hierarchical index. The column *text* is not indexed as it is not used for any kind of request.[19] Additional columns can for example be added to store language information or the type of each structural element.

19 The text column has been indexed due to the implementation of the fulltext search described in section 3.2, but this additional index is not required for the CTS index.

The text is only stored on the lowest hierarchical level because the text on higher levels is generated dynamically.

The advantage of this index implementation is that it naturally supports the data specific requirements without requiring a remarkably sophisticated technical setup to work. Since CTS requires server software by definition and some variant or version of (My)SQL is generally part of the package that is included in server software, this approach does not add any significant technical requirement for the average user. SQL databases are also not limited to any specific programming language. While this implementation is based on JAVA,[20] the basic programming logic of the index is handled using SQL queries. This means that it could be reimplemented in any other programming language without the need for a newly developed index technique.

The disadvantage of this approach as it is currently implemented is that the length of CTS URNs is restricted to 255, the maximum length of MySQL's *VARCHAR* data type. Since these references are supposed to be used as citations in human readable documents, this disadvantage should not be problematic.[21] Because CTS URNs are separated by namespaces, it can also be expected that this is not a future problem. Even if the allowed characters are arbitrarily limited to English letters, the potential combinations of delimiting namespace names – and therefore the set of supported text corpora – already include 26^n elements with n being the length of the namespace string.[22] If the number of possible namespaces is eventually too low, it could be multiplied by the use of a different URN namespace like *urn:cts2:*.

It is important to emphasize that this work does not propose that a CTS implementation must be done using SQL. SQL merely serves as the tool that is used to implement a B-Tree based trie data structure[23] and is especially fitting because of how established it is as part of server software packages. The hierarchical information is not necessarily stored in the B-Tree but in the way it is processed.

A detailed technical comparison by Tiepmar (2018) shows that this approach is a significant improvement over the graph and XML based CTS solutions.

---

20 JAVA was chosen because of its widespread support and its uncomplicated use as web applications (Servlets).

21 The CTS URN *urn:cts:pbc:bible.parallel.eng.kingjames:2.1.2* is 46 characters long.

22 456976 for $n = 4$.

23 A balanced tree that is processed in such a way that input and output is equal to that of a trie.

4 Unique features

4.1 Additional request functions

Since most of the additional features are not covered by CTS, it was necessary to implement the possibility for additional requests that do not interfere with future iterations of the CTS protocol. This is assured by using a different URL path than any of the CTS requests. Any of the official requests starts with the URL path http://cts.informatik.uni-leipzig.de/perseus/cts/.

The path for any of the additional requests starts with http://cts.informatik.uni-leipzig.de/perseus/plain/.

The added requests use a different optional URL branch than the official requests and therefore can not contradict the current and future CTS specifications.

The following (incomplete)[24] list of requests provide more convenient or efficient request possibilities compared to what would be necessary if only CTS requests are used:

- *editions, authors, titles* and *titlesandurns* provide a list similar to the content of the text inventory from the CTS request *GetCapabilities*. For text collections that contain several hundreds of thousands of documents, the text inventory file is a relatively large XML document.[25] This can create performance problems when the inventory is processed, especially because CTS does not provide any paging mechanism. The added features do allow paging and do not require XML parsing. The result is that data can be processed in chunks and the full data set can be requested faster and with less memory impact.[26]
- *metaforkey* provides a URN specific request possibility for any kind of document level meta information that is part of the CTS data set. Without this function, this information is only served as part of the text inventory file, which means that the full text inventory has to be

24 Requests like *getPassage* or *childList* are not considered because they work exactly like their official CTS counterparts.

25 At least the title, author, publication date and URN of each document.

26 Requesting the full *GetCapabilities* for the 62281 documents of the TextGrid data set using Firefox 52.0.2 (32-Bit) on a Intel(R) Core(TM) i5-4200U CPU @ 1.60GHz with 4 GB RAM (Windows 8 64 bit) resulted in an application crash after 1 minute and 50 seconds. Requesting *plain/editions* resulted in the full URN list after 21 seconds. *GetCapabilities* is the only specified source for document level CTS URNs.

processed any time a specific part of meta information for a document is required.
- Requests like *urncount* and *doccount* are added to provide useful statistics about the size of the text collection.
- Requests like *urnstypes*, and *urnstypestextlength* provide fine grained technical views on the data that might be more useful in a development environment. For instance, *urnstypestextlength* provides the structural markup of the document and the length of every text part as illustrated in the following example:

  urn:cts:greekLit:tlg0003.tlg001.perseus_eng1: edition -
  urn:cts:greekLit:tlg0003.tlg001.perseus_eng1:1 book -
  urn:cts:greekLit:tlg0003.tlg001.perseus_eng1:1.1 chapter 1335
  urn:cts:greekLit:tlg0003.tlg001.perseus_eng1:1.2 chapter 2608
  urn:cts:greekLit:tlg0003.tlg001.perseus_eng1:1.3 chapter 2304

This enables tool implementers for example to know beforehand how much more text parts can fit on a screen.

4.2 Configuration parameter

Since most the post processing features are additional – and therefore optional – functions, a configuration parameter is required to enable users to specify if an option should be activated or deactivated. The specifications specifically highlight

http://myhost/mycts?configuration=default request=GetCapabilities

as a valid URL and it can be assumed that this implies that additional parameters may be added to a request. If this interpretation is not correct, then the parameter has to be considered as an optional extension of the protocol.

Table 2 provides an overview about the parameters that are available.

Each of the parameters can be configured with the boolean values *true* or *false*. Multiple parameters can be combined using the underscore character as it is done in the following example:

configuration=seperatecontext=true_deletexml=false_usectsnamespace=false

An exemplary use of the parameter is described in section 4.3.

Table 2: Configuration parameters.

Parameter	Effect
divs	Document structuring using numbered <div*>s
epidoc	Document structuring using Epidoc (Bodard 2010)
newlines	Document structuring using newlines
maxlevelexception	Return *error* for unsupported citation level requests
escapePassage	XML-escape the text content
seperatecontext	Add (the optional) text context to a passage or separate it
smallinventory	Text inventory reduced to a URN list
xmlformatting	Pretty print XML
deletexml	XML markup deleted for increased readability
usectsnamespace	Use the CTS namespace for CTS specific XML tags

4.3 Text passage post processing

Since the text passage that is requested is generated dynamically, it is technically possible to influence the generation process in various ways. Therefore it is possible to implement different views on the same text data sample. The result of such a post processing mechanism can be considered as an additional automatically edited variant that is available without any need for individually edited documents. While the examples in this section only include basic post processing steps, it is possible to extend this feature as part of future work to provide automatically generated transcriptions into other lexical alphabets, complementary information like named entities or citation links and many other useful mechanisms.

The different views on the text passages are requested using the configuration parameter described in section 4.2.

Figure 2 shows an example text passage from the Perseus data set as it is requested using the configuration parameter

configuration=divs=true_deletexml=false_escapepassage=false

This combination of parameters structures the text passage using numbered <div*>s and includes the text content without escaping the XML characters or

```
- <passage>
  - <div1 n="1" type="card">
      <stage TEIform="stage">Enter the Chorus of Trojan guards.</stage>
    - <sp TEIform="sp">
        <speaker TEIform="speaker">Chorus</speaker>
      - <p TEIform="p">
          Go to Hector's couch. Which of you squires that tend the prince, or
          <milestone ed="p" n="5" unit="line" TEIform="milestone"/>
          from the warriors who were set to guard the assembled army durin
          <stage TEIform="stage">Calls to Hector in the tent.</stage>
          Lift up your head! Prop your arm beneath it! Unseal that fierce eye
          <milestone ed="p" n="10" unit="line" TEIform="milestone"/>
          Hector! It is time to hearken.
        </p>
      </sp>
    - <sp TEIform="sp">
        <speaker TEIform="speaker">Hector</speaker>
      - <p TEIform="p">
          Who is this? Is it a friend who calls? Who are you? Your password?
        </p>
      </sp>
    - <sp TEIform="sp">
        <speaker TEIform="speaker">Chorus</speaker>
```

Figure 2: Configuration parameter Example 1.

deleting the XML content. If this configuration is used, it is possible to request invalid XML which would result in client and server side parsing errors. To avoid this problem, requests that include sub passage notation or spans of CTS URNs will ignore the *escapepassage* parameter and set it to *true*. This also happens if text content that could not be parsed as XML is part of the text of the source document. If static CTS URNs based in valid XML source files are requested, this problem cannot happen because every static text part is based on a valid XML node in the source file.

Figures 3 and 4 show the same text passage using different configurations and especially illustrate the difference in the handling of the structural markup and the meta information markup. Figure 3 uses the configuration parameter

configuration=divs=true_deletexml=false_escapepassage=true

This parameter configuration also uses numbered <div*>s to communicate the document structure but makes sure that any XML reserved character in the text content is escaped. This view illustrates the difference between the structural and the meta information markup especially well.

```
- <passage>
  - <div1 n="1" type="card">
      <stage TEIform="stage">Enter the Chorus of Trojan guards.</stage> <s|
      Hector's couch. Which of you squires that tend the prince, or you armor-
      TEIform="milestone" /> from the warriors who were set to guard the ass
      the tent.</stage> Lift up your head! Prop your arm beneath it! Unseal th
      unit="line" TEIform="milestone" /> Hector! It is time to hearken.</p> </
      is this? Is it a friend who calls? Who are you? Your password? Speak! W
      TEIform="sp"> <speaker TEIform="speaker">Chorus</speaker> <p TE
      army.</p> </sp> <sp TEIform="sp"> <speaker TEIform="speaker">Hec
      <speaker TEIform="speaker">Chorus</speaker> <p TEIform="p">Be o
      <p TEIform="p">I am. Is there some midnight ambush?</p> </sp> <sp
      </sp> <sp TEIform="sp"> <speaker TEIform="speaker">Hector.]</spea
      tidings of the night? <milestone ed="p" n="20" unit="line" TEIform="mi
      TEIform="placeName">Argive</placeName> army we take our night's r
    </div1>
  - <div1 n="23" type="card">
      <milestone unit="strophe" TEIform="milestone" /> <sp TEIform="sp">
      allies' sleeping camp!<milestone ed="p" n="25" unit="line" TEIform="m
      friend to your own company, bridle the horses.</p> <p TEIform="p">W
      TEIform="p"> <milestone ed="p" n="30" unit="line" TEIform="milesto
      leaders of the light-armed troops and the Phrygian archers?</p> <p TEIf
    </div1>
```

Figure 3: Configuration parameter Example 2.

Figure 4 uses the configuration parameter

configuration=epidoc=true_deletexml=true_escapepassage=false

This combination of parameters uses a notation similar to the Epidoc format (Bodard 2010) to provide the document structure. XML characters in the text content are not escaped. Instead anything that resembles an XML notation is deleted.[27] Depending on the structural markup quality, this configuration can already provide a relatively reader friendly way to serve the data. Yet, since there is no technical way to differentiate XML markup from text snippets like *1<3. 3>2.*, this view may delete text content that it should not. Deleting the XML from the text requires *escapepassage* to be *false*. This implies that *deletexml* does not work in cases that are problematic for *escapepassage*.

27 Anything that matches <*>.

```
- <passage>
  - <tei:TEI>
    - <tei:text>
      - <tei:body>
        - <tei:div n="1" type="card">
            Enter the Chorus of Trojan guards. Chorus Go to Hector's couch.
            receive fresh tidings from the warriors who were set to guard the
            head! Prop your arm beneath it! Unseal that fierce eye from its re
            Is it a friend who calls? Who are you? Your password? Speak! W
            army. Hector Why this tumultuous haste? Chorus Be of good co
            your post and rouse the army, unless you have some tidings of th
            armor?
          </tei:div>
        - <tei:div n="23" type="card">
            Chorus To arms! Hector, seek your allies' sleeping camp! Stir the
            Who will go to the son of Panthus? Who to Europa's son, captain
            the light-armed troops and the Phrygian archers? String your hor
          </tei:div>
        - <tei:div n="34" type="card">
            Hector Your tidings inspire now fear, now confidence; nothing is
            [Leaving your watch you rouse the army.] What does your noisy
            statement have you made.
          </tei:div>
```

Figure 4: Configuration parameter Example 3.

4.4 Licensing

Content licenses often require that a specific license text and the source of a document are disclaimed if parts of the content are re-used or published.[28] This is not considered in the specification of the CTS protocol, even though serving text passages has to be considered as a re-use or publication, especially when it is possible to request the text passage that is the complete document. Consequentially, many publicly available text corpora are excluded from being served by a Canonical Text Service.[29]

This implementation of CTS provides the possibility to serve a license- and a source text on document- and corpus level. The license text on corpus level is manually configured by the administrator of the CTS instance. The text on document level is extracted from the input files and therefore based on the information that was added by the document editors. The configured address of the CTS instance is added to the source text by the system as illustrated in the following example:

28 For instance CC-BY (Creative Commons 2018).

29 For example Das Deutsche Textarchiv (Geyken et al. 2011).

<reply>
<urn> urn:cts:dta:moritz.reiser02.de.norm:654 </urn>
<passage> Der Rektor hatte darin sehr Recht – denn der Vorfall wurde bald bekannt, und es hie"s nun: wie! </passage>
<license> Distributed under the Creative Commons Attribution-NonCommercial 3.0 Unported License. </license>
<source> http://www.deutschestextarchiv.de/moritz_reiser02_1786 (...) retrieved via Canonical Text Service www.urncts.de/dta/cts with CTS URN urn:cts:dta:moritz.reiser02.de.norm:654 </source>
</reply>

The server address has to be configured manually because certain network configurations include proxy mechanisms that make it difficult to detect the external server address automatically from within a network application.

4.5 CTS cloning

One of the benefits of a system like a Canonical Text Service is its potential use as an application independent archival tool that supports more spontaneous project specific archives and seamlessly connects them to organised central archival projects. In order to achieve this, it is required that the data can be moved from one physical address to another without reference changes. Since CTS URNs are application independent per definition,[30] the problem of reference changes is solved.

Using the possibility to request the structural information of a document along with the text content of each structural element[31] and the meta information from the text inventory, any document that is served by this implementation of CTS can be reconstructed in another CTS instance. This process is called CTS Cloning.

It is possible to implement such a system without the use of the combined structural and textual information and only by the means that the specifications provide. Yet this would require a relatively large number of requests because the text content of each structural element would have to be requested

30 And therefore service independent.

31 See the div-View described in section 4.3.

individually.[32] For this reason, CTS Cloning in its current form only works with CTS instances that are based on this implementation.

It is possible to filter the documents that are supposed to be cloned based on the information that is encoded in the document level CTS URNs. Text inventory based meta information filters are not implemented because they can be specified as a list of document level CTS URNs and therefore the ability to filter the documents by a specific piece of optional meta information is not required.

Document clones can be added to an existing CTS instance. Duplicates can only happen if one of the source data sets did not respect the already reserved CTS namespaces.[33] Duplicate CTS URNs are ignored.

Since document sets can be filtered and combined, it is easily possible to create subsets of text corpora that share a research question specific set of properties that was not considered as part of the originally created text corpora. For instance, it is possible to combine the texts from a specific time frame based on the TextGrid and Deutsches Textarchiv corpora or to compile a data set based on a specific set of topics, languages or genres. This compilation of documents can be used to investigate research question specific effects and provide the compiled data set along with the results.

The possibility to clone the documents enables users to manually change the text content of an established CTS URN. This corrupted data set can be used as a text reference if the corresponding CTS request is sent to the corrupted clone instead of the original CTS instance. For instance, the CTS request

> http://cts.informatik.uni-leipzig.de/perseus/cts/?request=GetPassage&urn=urn:cts:greekLit:tlg0003.tlg001.perseus_eng1:1.1

could be redirected to another CTS request

> http://mysserver.de/pbc/cts/?request=GetPassage&urn=urn:cts:greekLit:tlg0003.tlg001.perseus_eng1:1.1

that might resolve the CTS URN based on manually changed text content. The response would be equal[34] except for the manually changed bits of information. Since URLs are often hidden behind a label to improve readability, it is possible

32 21'911'559 requests to recreate the structural information of the CTS instance containing the texts from the Deutsches Text Archiv. Using the combined information reduces this number to 8'190, the number of document level CTS URNs.

33 Like *urn:cts:dta:* or *urn:cts:perseus:*.

34 Potentially including the manually configured server address in the source text.

to hide corrupted CTS requests. This issue can be partly solved by making sure that CTS URNs are always requested from trusted sources that can be managed by a central service like the Namespace Resolver.[35] It is also advised to check the trustworthiness of any URL before clicking on it as it should be general practise for users of internet resources.

5 Conclusions

This paper describes the technical basis for the first feature-complete implementation of the Canonical Text Services protocol. During the course of this work it was possible to extend the protocol with useful features such as a licensing mechanism and more efficient request features that circumvent the disadvantages of the use of XML. As shown at the beginning of this paper, CTS is a helpful tool for software developers that can be the basis for numerous innovations, especially since it is now agreed on both by researchers in computer science and the humanities. Future work may include improvements in individual features, integration in existing infrastructures and application in similar work as for instance the aforementioned CITE protocol.

Bibliography

Blackwell, C.; Roughan, C.; Smith, D. (2017): "Citation and Alignment: Scholarship Outside and Inside the Codex". Manuscript Studies 1: 1. http://repository.upenn.edu/mss_sims/vol1/iss1/2 (last access 2019.01.31).

Bodard, G. (2010): "Epigraphic Documents in XML for Publication and Interchange". In: F. Feraudi-Gruénais (ed.): Latin on Stone: Epigraphic research and electronic archives. Lanham: Lexington Books, 1–17.

Brass, P. (2008): Advanced Data Structures. Cambridge: Cambridge University Press.

Creative Commons (2018): Attribution 4.0 International (CC BY 4.0). https://creativecommons.org (last access 2019.01.31).

EU (14.05.2017). EUR-Lex. http://eur-lex.europa.eu/homepage.html (last access 2019.01.31).

Fielding, T. (2000): Architectural Styles and the Design of Network-based Software Architectures. PhD Thesis. Irvine: University of California.

Geyken, A.; Haaf, S.; Jurish, B.; Schulz, M.; Steinmann, J.; Thomas, C.; Wiegand, F. (2011): Das Deutsche Textarchiv: Vom historischen Korpus zum aktiven Archiv. Cologne: Digitale Wissenschaft Stand und Entwicklung digital vernetzter Forschung in Deutschland.

35 (Tiepmar 2018).

Grallert, T.; Tiepmar, J.; Eckart, T.; Goldhahn, D.; Kuras, C. (2017): "Digital Muqtabas CTS Integration in CLARIN". CLARIN Annual Conference 2017. CLARIN ERIC.
Hart, M. (2017): Project Gutenberg. http://www.gutenberg.org (last access 2019.01.31).
Hinrichs, E.; Krauwer, S. (2014): "The CLARIN Research Infrastructure: Resources and Tools for E-Humanities Scholars". In: Proceedings of the Ninth International Conference on Language Resources and Evaluation, LREC 2014. European Language Resources Association, 1525–1531.
Oracle (2018): MySQL Reference Manual 5.7. https://dev.mysql.com/doc/ (last access 2019.01.31).
Reckziegel, M.; Jaenicke, S.; Scheuermann, G. (2016): "CTRaCE: Canonical Text Reader and Citation Exporter". In: Digital Humanities 2016. Kraków: Jagiellonian University. http://dh2016.adho.org/static/data/485.html (last access 2019.01.31).
Smith, D. (2009): "Citation in Classical Studies". Digital Humanities Quarterly 3: 1. http://www.digitalhumanities.org/dhq/vol/3/1/000028/000028.html (last access 2019.01.31).
Smith, D.; Rydberg-Cox, J.; Crane, G. (2000): "The Perseus Project: A Digital Library for the Humanities". Literary and Linguistic Computing 15:1, 15–25. https://doi.org/10.1093/llc/15.1.15.
Thaller, M. (2013): Das Digitale Archiv NRW in der Praxis. Eine Softwarelösung zur digitalen Langzeitarchivierung. Kölner Beiträge zu einer geisteswissenschaftlichen Fachinformatik 5. Hamburg: Verlag Dr. Kovač.
Tiepmar, J. (2018): Implementation and Evaluation of the Canonical Text Service Protocol as Part of a Research Infrastructure in the Digital Humanities. PhD Thesis. Leipzig: Universität Leipzig.
Tiepmar, J.; Eckart, T.; Goldhahn, D.; Kuras, C. (2017): "Integrating Canonical Text Services into CLARIN's Search Infrastructure". Linguistic and Literature Studies 5:2, 99–104. http://www.hrpub.org/journals/article_info.php?aid=5844 (last access 2019.01.31).
Tiepmar, J.; Teichmann, C.; Heyer, G.; Berti, M.; Crane, G. (2014): "A New Implementation for Canonical Text Services". In: Proceedings of the 8th Workshop on Language Technology for Cultural Heritage, Social Sciences, and Humanities (LaTeCH). EACL, 1–8. https://aclweb.org/anthology/W/W14/W14-0601.pdf (last access 2019.01.31).
van Uytvanck, D. (2014): PID policy summary. CLARIN. Utrecht: SCCTC.

Data Entry, Collection, and Analysis for Classical Philology

Bruce Robertson

Optical Character Recognition for Classical Philology

Abstract: This paper explains the technology behind recent improvements in optical character recognition and how it can be attuned to produce highly accurate texts of scholarly value, especially when dealing with difficult scripts like ancient Greek. Drawing upon several practical experiments using the Ciaconna OCR system (itself based on OCRopus), it shows: the impact of Unicode normalized forms on recognition accuracy; the importance of removing ambiguously encoded characters from training material; the advantage of using separate classifiers for different scripts; the helpful effects of image augmentation; and the effects of binarization levels. It also describes how Ciaconna embeds information about spell-check and dehyphenation within its output.

Introduction

Classical philologists may have noticed in the past years a remarkable expansion of texts, especially Greek ones, available online as open data. Throughout much of the 1990s and 2000s, the venerable Perseus collection may have offered an excellent foundational collection of canonical texts in history, poetry and philosophy; but open texts pertaining to the history of science, scholia, and minor philosophical works were lacking. Today, in contrast, the First Thousand Years of Greek project, whose data can be viewed and visualized within the Scaife Digital Reader, offers a far more extensive corpus of open texts, adding at latest count 22 million new words of Greek. New optical character recognition (OCR) techniques have made some of this expansion possible: whereas almost all Greek in the original Perseus collection was generated through expensive manual double-key entry, much of the new data in the Scaife Viewer began as high-quality OCR output whose errors were manually corrected, a far more affordable prospect if the OCR is accurate enough. The latter approach opens new avenues for digitizing scholarly works, including journal articles, monographs and ancient texts for which open editions are not available.

This chapter aims to explain to the digital philologist the conceptual and computational foundations of OCR, especially as it pertains to scholarly

Bruce Robertson, Mount Allison University

https://doi.org/10.1515/9783110599572-008

materials. It is based in my eight years of working on Greek and Latin-script OCR, most recently within the First Thousand Years of Greek project. In this consortium, I wrote all the specialized OCR code, supervised the high performance computing environment in which the OCR took place and provided web-based editing environment to improve the correction task. The following guide should help today's philologist understand the leading edge of OCR, whether she or he merely wants to make use of these data knowledgeably or perhaps wants to participate in an extensive OCR-based project.

Scholarly OCR

The term "Optical Character Recognition" is commonly used to denote the process of transforming a computer image of text into a digital text file, usually so that the latter can be subjected to all the digital tools that manipulate and analyze text. The words in a page image cannot, in isolation, be treebanked, searched, sorted or subjected to n-gram analysis; OCR makes this possible. As a term OCR is, at best, synecdoche, since recognizing characters *per se* is only one small step in a much broader sequence of processes necessary to complete this transformation. (Indeed, as we will see, the best algorithms today do not really even perform 'character recognition' but rather something more like 'line recognition'.)

The approach one takes to each of these steps depends in large part on the intended use of the textual output. It might be surprising to know that for many purposes, even academic ones, relatively low quality OCR output has many uses: often such output can be corrected or subjected to sufficiently clever fuzzy search algorithms so that the corresponding page images can be shown. Services such as JSTOR use this 'image-fronted' search technique. With this approach, also, the exact reading order of the words on the page image need not be accurately determined. It is also clear that a highly useful service like Google n-grams can be developed without perfect OCR.

In contrast, the OCR results for projects that are preparing complete renderings of texts, what I am calling here 'OCR for scholars', must be highly accurate, since scholars have a very low tolerance for errors in their texts. For this reason, the First Thousand Years of Greek project paid commercial editors to correct our OCR to 99.95% character accuracy, or no more than 5 mistakes per every 10,000 characters. Every correction adds to the labour cost and therefore, within a fixed budget, reduces the number of words produced by the project. For example, output with 95% accuracy will need 495 changes per 10,000 characters; whereas output with 97% accuracy requires only 295, a reduction by 40.4%. This two percent improvement in OCR accuracy allows for 40% more material to be generated with the same budget! In fact, if the reading order of the page is even slightly misrepresented or if more than, say, 5 characters per 100 are incorrectly recognized, then the time it takes to correct such results becomes greater than the time it would take to transcribe the text manually. Thus, scholarly OCR is far more demanding than many other of its uses, but there is one mitigating aspect: OCR for scholarly use usually involves a relatively limited corpus of texts, perhaps thousands of texts, but nothing like the volume of commercial applications. In this context, it is worthwhile carefully to optimize each possible aspect of the process.

Initial steps in OCR

Corpus OCR begins by acquiring or taking digital images of pages that share similar (ideally, identical) fonts and layouts, so that when we have trained the OCR engine to recognize a small set of these pages, it can operate on a great number at once. Of course, the best results come from the best images. If lower quality images are available, for instance on Google Books, it is tempting to begin with them; but this is often a bad decision because the labour required to correct these results might be much more than the relatively short amount of time it takes to simply re-scan the books, ensuring better, and therefore less time-consuming, raw output. A flat-bed scanner ensures the images are in-focus and evenly illuminated.

These images are then 'cleaned' either manually or automatically, using a program like ScanTailor, which separates two-up scans into separate pages, straightens the images, dewarps them and removes minor artefacts and blank margins. Following this, the page is (usually) binarized – that is, made into a black-and-white image. The operator should inspect the output of the binarization stage, ensuring that the binarization level produces a human-readable output.[1] The next computational step divides the page into separate lines while attempting to follow the proper reading order of the document. The algorithms that do this processing are often devised for modern texts and for Latin script. A layout of ancient Greek with little space between lines may

1 If one begins with black-and-white images, binarization is not necessary, but this is usually a poorer approach because it allows the scanner or camera effectively to decide upon the binarization level, and these are rarely optimized for character recognition.

require that the algorithm's parameters be altered. At times a complex page layout might require a separate computational pre-process, as in Robertson, Dalitz, and Schmitt (2014).

Recognizing characters

The next step, recognition of the characters in these lines, is the most critical in OCR, and it is here that the greatest advances have taken place in the past years. For these reasons, the limitations and potential of character recognition algorithms must be comprehended in order to achieve high-quality results.

To understand these, imagine a writing system comprising only two glyphs: one, like Latin 'O' or Greek majuscule omicron, is a black circle on a white background; the other, like Latin 'I' or Greek majuscule iota, is a black vertical line on a white background. The computer recognizes as a possible glyph every blob of black pixels that is surrounded by white. How could a computer be programmed to tell the difference between these two types of blobs? One obvious approach would be to find the rectangle or 'bounding box' around them. If this box's profile is, say four times taller than it is wide, then we say it has the 'is-tall' *feature*. We can apply this feature to have a robust way of choosing between, or *classifying*, glyphs in this imaginary writing system. A blob that has the 'is-tall' feature is classified as an 'I'; otherwise, it is classified as an 'O'.

Unfortunately, someone adds a third character to this writing system, one that looks like Latin 'M' or Greek majuscule mu. If we use the feature and classifier we described above, we can be certain that this new character won't be classified as 'M', of course, since the classifier knows nothing of that character. It will probably be classified as 'O', since its bounding box is squarish. To make an engine that recognizes all three characters we need to extract at least one more feature from all our blobs and then make a new classifier that is based on it and the old one. Let us say this new feature will be horizontal symmetry: 'I' and 'O' will have this feature, but 'M' will not because its top half is not symmetrical with its bottom half. Our new classifier might work like this: if a blob has the is-tall feature and the horizontal symmetry feature, it is an 'I'; if doesn't have the is-tall feature and has the horizontal symmetry feature, it is an 'O'; and if it doesn't have the is-tall feature and doesn't have the horizontal symmetry feature, it is an 'M'. This leaves one other possibility, that a blob has the is-tall feature but isn't horizontally symmetrical. We might want to indicate that this is a result that confounds our classifier.

This example illustrates the fundamental elements of all OCR engines: they test for features, and they somehow integrate the results of those tests to make a classifier. But as we add more characters say 'E', 'H', 'N' and 'P', it's clear that many more features will be needed and that the classifier's means of integrating these becomes more complex.

Adding code that tests for features – such as the volume of black space in various regions, or vertical symmetry – is a one-off challenge, and such code can automatically be applied to every dark region. In contrast, as the number of glyphs and feature tests increase, the classifier becomes very hard to produce by hand, especially one that is optimized for the best results. OCR engines like Tesseract 3 and Gamera therefore test connected components for features that are defined by human-created code, and they then use a class of machine learning algorithms called 'supervised learning algorithms' to discover the best classifier. This is the one that best matches the results of the feature tests with a set of human-verified corresponding characters known as 'ground truth.' These algorithms scores the output for one certain weighting of the importance of the features. They then move on to a slightly different weighting compare the score and, based on this information, try to come up with an even better setting, and so on.

This optimization can only do so much: it seeks to get the best possible result given the features extracted, where *best* is defined by the given ground truth. If the ground truth is not representative of the images eventually to be processed, the optimized classifier could be worse at OCR'ing those images than another classifier using the same features and glyphs! For instance, if the volume to be OCR'd is a critical edition, and the classifier is optimized only using the body of the text and not the apparatus criticus, the optimization will never take into account the high frequency of the usual letters and sigla that appear in the apparatus. (In fact, it probably would never get the chance to test itself on symbols like '‖'.) Similarly, if some pages use different fonts or stylistic variations (bold, italics, etc.), then these will be well processed only if their features are extracted and they are included in the ground truth used to generate the optimized classifier. Therefore one cannot omit training for certain parts and then 'ignore' the resulting bad output because to ignore something, you first have to classify it; otherwise, because the classifier has been trained only on the desirable parts, it will tend to produce output that resembles those parts, and distinguishing them as 'to be ignored' is a new problem, and solving these problems in sequence is no easier.[2]

2 This is a corollary of the so-called 'no free lunch theorem' in optimization (Wolpert and Macready 1997).

This simplified overview makes clear one of the reasons that OCR for Greek texts is particularly challenging. We noted that when a new glyph was added, the task of the classifier became more complicated. Now since it is almost always the case that predominantly Greek pages still include some Latin glyphs, we cannot ignore these, or we will get lines of Greek output and have a difficult time knowing what is useless. Thus, whereas a Latin critical edition might be require a classifier to distinguish between 120 glyphs, Greek editions usually double this number, and thereby they make a much greater demand of the classifier. Additionally, each human writing system provides a set of characters that are easily distinguishable amongst themselves; but Latin script and Greek comprise many characters, especially upper-case ones, that are nearly identical. If our initial writing system contained Latin 'O' *and* Greek majuscule omicron along with Latin 'I' *and* Greek majuscule iota, the feature extraction would need to be much more subtle, and even with all that the results would depend on the typeface involved.

Assuming careful selection of the ground truth characters, the approach described so far has a number of advantages. It requires little training – maybe only three pages' worth – to become adept. Secondly, it performs well with rarely occurring glyphs because each glyph is subject to the same feature tests and then becomes part of the classifier. Finally, with this system it is possible for a programer to modify the code, noting the position and ascribed characters of each connected component. For this reason, previous Greek OCR systems were built using supervised learning systems, such as Rigaudon,[3] based on the Gamera OCR library,[4] and White (2013), based on the Tesseract 3 engine. Both of these use the k-NN supervised learning algorithm.[5]

But there are also obvious problems with this approach. First, although it is based in a one-to-one correspondence between connected components and glyphs, in practice the situation often is messier. The letter 'i' ideally comprises two connected components, but often the letter's superscript dot is not separated from its vertical stroke. Also, imperfect scanning sometimes causes two characters to join together into a single connected component. Even more common for classical philologists is the situation where diacritical accents join with each other or with their combining letter. Two solutions are possible:

3 (Robertson and Boschetti 2017).
4 (Droettboom et al. 2003).
5 (Kononenko and Kukar 2013).

either the system can recognize these combined glyphs are representing a sequence of characters, or it can recognize them as a class of characters that should be divided (or 'cut'), allowing the resulting two connected components to be further recognized. Both solutions are imperfect, since the first greatly increases the number of glyphs to be identified and the second results in strangely shaped glyphs which are hard to identify as their own connected components.

For these reasons, a new approach to character recognition has become increasingly popular. In a recent presentation on scholarly OCR, an audience member asked presciently, "if the computer is so smart, why doesn't *it* figure out the best features for character recognition?" In fact, that is exactly what happens in this new approach, which is based on so-called Recurrent Neural Networks, a class of artificial neural networks that can take credit for the expanding role of Machine Learning in everyday life, from the ever-improving voice recognition of smart speakers in the home to facial recognition. RNN-based OCR engines (like Ocropus or Tesseract 4) replace the supervised learning algorithms described above with a kind of learning algorithm that has no need of human-determined features: its classifier takes as input *simply lines of the characters*, not a set of feature scores, and as it trains over a great number of iterations it forms a neural net classifier that can transform the image of a line of text into the corresponding characters. Strictly speaking, then, they do not perform optical *character* recognition, but rather optical *line* recognition: the context of a character in its line becomes pertinent information. (Although there are now many RNN-based open source OCR projects to chose from, this paper will explore this technology using the longstanding Ocropus engine.[6])

Thus overall these classifiers usually perform better than those based on supervised learning algorithms. They are also typically more robust and agile when handling poorer data: their results degrade more slowly when confronted with characters or diacritics that are combined. Furthermore, they automatically manage the reordering of characters that diacritics sometimes make necessary. Their only drawback is that they require copious, accurate training data.

6 (Breuel 2008). Tesseract's version 4 offers an RNN mode, while Calamari (Wick 2019), Kraken (Kiessling 2019) and Ocropus3 (Breuel 2019) offer much speedier line recognition and classifier generation. Calamari notably integrates an image augmentation process as discussed below.

Choosing ground truth

OCR ground truth is unicode plain text: no sort of markup can be used to indicate italicized text, superscripts or text layout. Despite this, there is a trade-off to be made here between the number of different characters in the training set and the accuracy of the output. It should be understood that for training purposes not every separate glyph must be represented with a different code point: all methods of training can learn, for instance, to represent both italicized and upright ‘a’ with the same output. Nevertheless, special attention must be paid to each and every character’s encoding in the ground truth, with consideration for how it might be used in the future. For instance, quotation marks: should left and right variants be encoded differently? The same is true for various glyphs that can be used in Greek texts: if a single glyph in the page images is represented in ground truth by two different Unicode characters, the classifier optimizes for an illusory distinction, in the process very likely becoming somewhat worse at distinguishing between actual characters.

The effect of data ambiguity

This can be demonstrated if we note the degraded performance caused by intentionally confusing a set of ground truth that otherwise produces well-performing classifier. Classifier performance is measured through character accuracy, the percentage of characters that are ‘right’.[7] For example, a classifier was trained on 1113 lines of Loeb text that comprised 82 unique Greek characters. When tested against a different page of Loeb Greek – proper procedure dictates that the test document not be used for training purposes – this classifier scored a 99.1% character accuracy after 19600 lines of training. Half of these lines were then altered: the “middle dot” (U+00B7) character replaced the “Greek ano teleia” (U+0387) character; “double quotation mark” was substituted for the characters that had been carefully encoded as either “right double quotation mark” or “left double quotation mark”; and the text’s interrogative punctuation, previously indicated with the “semicolon” character, was swapped with the “Greek question mark” (U+037E) character. The result is a slightly confused ground truth, in which a small number of glyphs were

7 More formally, this is calculated as $(n - e) / n$, where n equals the number of characters in the ground truth and e equals the number of errors as determined by Levenshtein distance (Rice et al. 1993).

represented in two different ways, a common situation when more than one editor provides the training text.[8] This classifier could only muster a far poorer maximum character accuracy of 95.5% after 26700 lines of training, a drop of 3.6%. It is important to note that the additional errors did not in fact pertain to the characters that our experiment altered: many other letters and diacritics were mis-identified or not produced in the output. So automated search-and-replace should be used to disambiguate the ground truth to one or the other, always with the goal of reducing the number of characters in the training set to a minimum necessary number.

This is not to say that every aspect of character encoding should be simplified. Distinctions between glyphs certainly should be preserved if they will matter to the text's users. Superscript letters and numbers, for example, might be omitted or normalized as plain letters or numbers in a business context, but in scholarly works they often play a crucial role in understanding the reading order of a text by linking footnotes with the pertinent section of the text's body. Similarly, where Gothic letters are used as sigla, for example, the 𝔓 (Gothic 'P') used for New Testament papyrus numbers, it is worthwhile to use a separate code point for this character, such as the "Fraktur P" designated by the Unicode consortium for mathematical use (U+1D513).

It is important to check that the OCR engine does not normalize the various styles of quotation marks, apostrophes, etc. in a manner that undoes this careful decision-making. Indeed, unless one tests the character accuracy herself, transformations like these will give the appearance of higher-scoring results, since they simplify the training and testing material. Grepping the source code for the string 'normal' or for the "right double quotation mark" character is a good way to search for and, if necessary, remove or alter these parts of the OCR engine.

Unicode normalization

An even more pervasive problem arises with the so-called normalization forms of Unicode text. Unicode offers four normalized forms, 'decomposed', 'composed' and the 'compatibility' variants of both of these. 'Composed' normalization uses the smallest number of characters to represent a set of glyphs; decomposed uses the maximum, and it orders them according to a set of rules. For instance, the grapheme ā can be represented as a single character, U+0101, or as a sequence of 'a' (U+0061) plus 'macron above' (U+0304), though it cannot be represented with

---

8 In total 342 characters were changed, 1.4% of all the ground truth characters.

sequence 'macron above' followed by 'a'. The former is the 'composed' form; the latter, 'decomposed'. A great number of Greek letters with their diacritics can be represented in either form. Therefore mixing composed and decomposed forms result in ground truth subject to the problem of ambiguity described above. To avoid this, OCR programs will apply normalization. However the form of normalization might not be best for our purposes, and often it is preferable to change the OCR code to use normalization that is to our advantage.

First we might wonder if there is a difference in performance between decomposed and composed forms, especially in ancient Greek texts, where this issue frequently arises. To study this and other questions, ground truth for OCRing Loeb editions was produced, comprising 3428 lines of text, both Greek and English, drawn from a variety of sources.[9] Its ground truth comprised 254 unique characters when using the Unicode composed normalized form ('NFC'), but this reduced to unique 155 characters when that ground truth was represented with the decomposed normalized form ('NFD'). (This is because each combination of a vowel and sequence of diacritics is represented by a different character in the composed form, multiplying the number of characters.) According to our reasoning above, it seems likely that the smaller character set will give better results; but perhaps in this instance the odd positioning of the characters, superimposed as they are, will make it more difficult for an RNN-based classifier to recognize them.

We can visualize the results with the chart in Figure 1. For the two training sets described above (differing only in their the normalization forms), classifiers were saved after each 100 steps, or iterations, of training. These 300 classifiers were used to generate results on two test pages: one that mainly contained Greek lines and another that mainly contained Latin-script (English) lines. The chart plots the character accuracy of these results on the y axis with the training iteration on the x axis, showing the difference in training progress between the two training sets for each image.[10] It can be seen that the decomposed form caused the training to progress more rapidly and reached a higher point of accuracy overall for both page images. It can also be seen that the composed form ground truth caused the training algorithm to twice dip down to a very poor

9 The page images, taken from the Internet Archive, Google Books and scanned by hand, varied in resolution from 300 to 600 pixels per inch.

10 This and the following charts use the logit scale on the vertical axis, where logit(a) = log(a/(1-a)). This is chosen to represent the greater challenge and importance of improvements as results increase towards 100%.

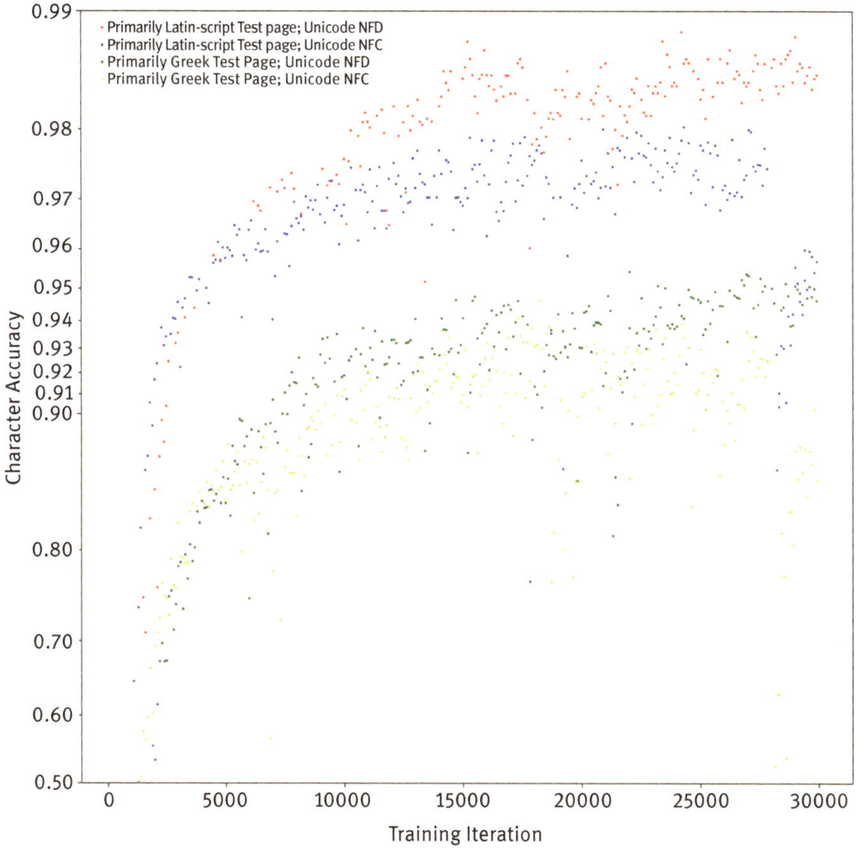

Figure 1: Scatter plots of training progress for ground truth in Unicode composed and decomposed normalized forms, tested against predominantly Latin-script and Greek-script pages. Progress is represented by character recognition accuracy versus training iteration.

score and consequently climb back from these. It also had greater volatility, with a standard deviation of accuracy at 0.25 compared 0.13 for the decomposed dataset. Finally, and most importantly, the highest character accuracy score of the decomposed training data operating on the primarily Greek page was 96.3%; the composed dataset only reached 94.7%. With the primarily English page, the decomposed training data reached a score of 99.3%, while the composed training data was 1.3% worse at 98%. (The relative improvement matters here, and these scores should not be compared to those mentioned earlier, since those used a far smaller character set.) Clearly, in all respects the decomposed normalization form is preferable, yet most OCR engines will normalize to the composed form and their code needs to be rewritten to do decomposed normalization instead. Because of the already very high scores of the Latin-script results, the remainder of the paper will concentrate on pages that primarily contain Greek characters, though the observations should be understood as pertaining to both.

The Unicode 'compatibility' forms pose a different problem. These are intended to simplify processes like indexing and search, and so they convert unusual characters to ones that are similar but more familiar. For instance, all superscript numbers and letters are converted into their ordinary Arabic equivalents and the Gothic 'P' used for New Testament papyrus numbers becomes a plain Latin-script one. This can easily erase the decisions made regarding ground truth and its careful editing as discussed above. It can be difficult to detect this problem because one might assume that the errors are caused by misrecognition, not altered training data. Once again it is worthwhile to scan OCR source code for the pertinent keywords, in this case "NFKC" or "NFKD", to ensure that the engine does not perform this transformation at a low level.[11]

Improving training images

So far, we have considered the effect that ground truth has on our training results. But training involves both lines of text and images of those lines, and the proper manipulation of the latter can also improve recognition results. RNN approaches to OCR make the neural network responsible for choosing as well as integrating the features employed effectively to detect the characters. One effect of this is that the neural net can easily rely on features that are incidentally specific to the input images but not truly dispositive for other images.[12] The best way to avoid this is to increase the amount of training data, but generating ground truth is costly. Another approach is to slightly alter the training images, matching these to the already-produced ground truth. Among people working on image analysis and classification this is known as 'data augmentation' and a widely studied practice.[13] Many programming libraries exist for augmentation; I used the Python Augmentor library.[14] Because augmentation is particularly used in

---

11 As of this writing, the Ocropus engine performs a NFKC transformation on all training data and Tesseract 4 strongly defaults to the NFC form.

12 For example, if, by sheer coincidence, every line with an 'e' in the third position had a black pixel in the top left of the line image, a neural net's classifier might heavily weight this feature even though it will not prove effective.

13 (Mikołajczyk and Grochowski 2018).

14 (Bloice et al. 2017).

image analysis, it is important to use these libraries carefully, since many of their capabilities pertain to image recognition, but not to OCR. When training a neural net to recognize a car or a cat, for example, they rotate or crop the image drastically, since these objects should still be recognized despite these distortions. The line images for OCR training should not, of course, be changed these ways, but it can help training to add fuzzier or slightly sheared copies to the training set. I have found the `random_distortion` function of Augmentor to be effective.

Image augmentation is particularly effective when working with a small set of training data, but it can help in all circumstances. Figure 2 shows two scatterplots of character accuracy for each training iteration. Both use the best ground truth from Figure 1, namely the decomposed unicode normalization form, The series labeled 'without augmentation' matches each line of this

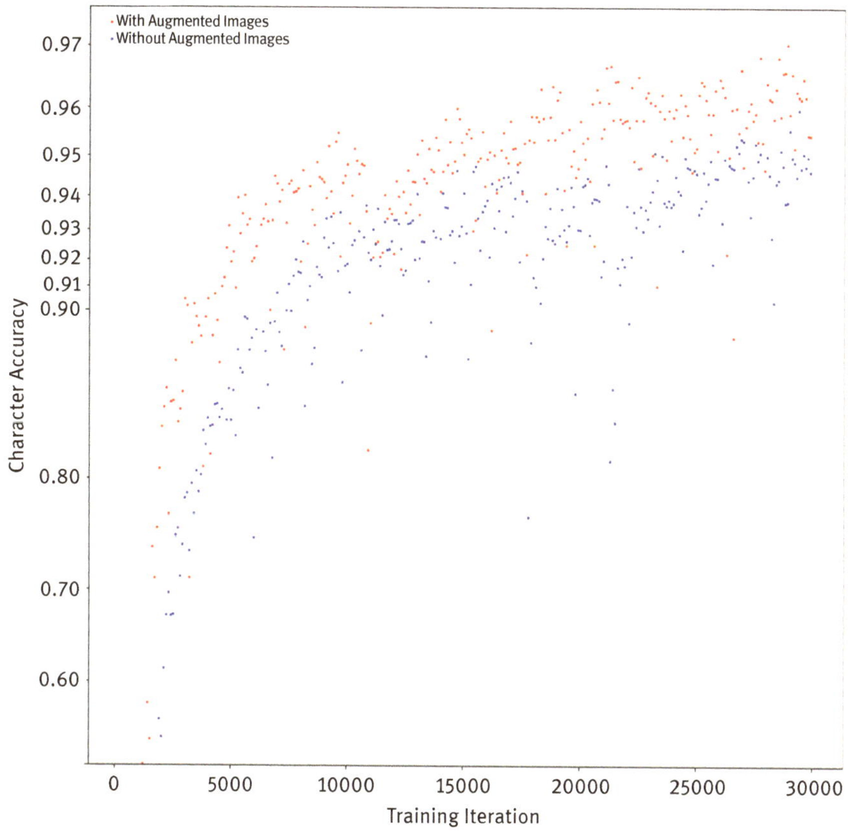

Figure 2: Scatter plots of training progress using unaugmented and augmented training images. Progress is represented by character recognition accuracy versus training iteration.

ground truth with a single image; that labelled 'with augmentation' matches each line with an additional three images, each randomly distorted copies of the original. The improves the maximum character accuracy score from the previous 96.2% to 97.0%.

Image augmentation takes place after binarization, the first step in an OCR process, which converts a grayscale or colour image into a binary, or black-and-white, one. In this step, a threshold of image darkness is set, beyond which a pixel is represented as black, not white. Because one part of a page can be more illuminated than another, a good binarization algorithm, such as `ocropus-nlbin` (a component of the Ocropus system), will vary this threshold depending on the general darkness of separate regions within the page image. Nevertheless, it is still possible to set an over-all binarization level, and this has an important impact on the appearance of glyphs. Darker binarization will cause glyphs to take up more space and possibly cause adjacent ones to join together into one connected component. This is especially true with Greek diacritics and their combining characters. Lighter binarization will make the strokes of glyphs thinner, eventually causing them to break into multiple connected components. Training should be performed at a binarization level that ensures easy reading and reasonable separation of glyphs. In the examples shown here, a level of 0.7 (70%) was used.

However, as Figure 3 shows, the result of this training did not perform optimally when evaluated against a test document binarized at the same 0.7 threshold! Instead, the three lighter steps, 0.4–0.6 all performed slightly better, with the 0.4 threshold yielding an improved maximum character accuracy of 98.2%, an improvement over the 0.7 threshold of 0.8%.

By comparing the binarized images and the resulting documents, we can see why. Figure 4 shows one accented character as it appears at the 0.4 and 0.7 binarization levels. The smooth breathing mark failed to be identified at the latter level. It appears that the significantly greater definition between the acute accent and the smooth breathing mark at the 0.4 level was an aid to the classifier, even though it had been trained at a higher binarization level.

It was noted above that neural networks require large volumes of training material, but we might wonder how much is enough. Figure 5 shows the results of four rounds of training 151 Greek and English characters, all subject to 30,000 rounds of training and evaluated against the same (primarily Greek-text) test document. In the first round, though, only ten pages of training data were used.[15] In this case the maximum character accuracy is 94.6%, and it can be seen that on four occasions the training accuracy dropped out. With three times as

15 Each page in this set comprises about 30 lines, or 1900 characters, of ground truth.

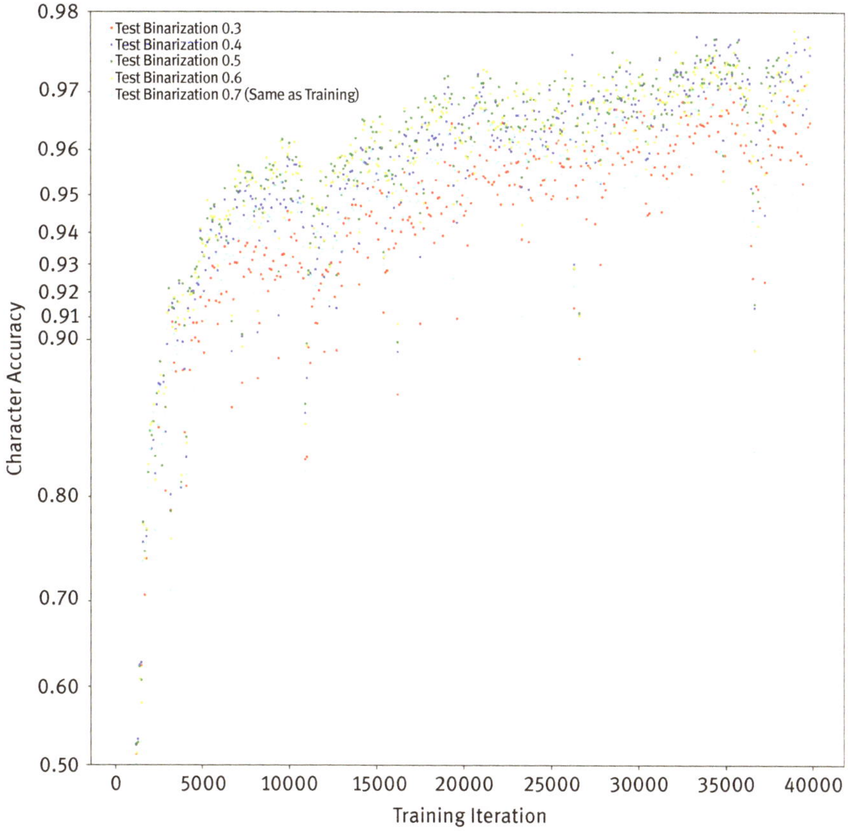

Figure 3: Scatter plots of training results using test images of varying binarization (darkness) and classifiers trained on images at a 0.7 level. Progress is represented by character recognition accuracy versus training iteration.

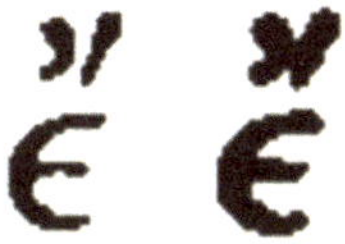

Figure 4: An accented Greek character at the 0.4 (left) and 0.7 (right) binarization level.

many pages of training material, the results improve considerably, up to 97% accuracy. Interestingly, the next increase, to fifty pages, does not provide a corresponding increase in accuracy: this session's maximum accuracy is 95.4%. Finally, with seventy pages of training material, an excellent training session occurs and the accuracy peaks at 98.8%. Considering that 96% accuracy is our benchmark for profitable editing, it seems that one should seek out minimally around twenty to twenty-five pages of training material. (Data augmentation, as described above, might help improve results with minimal training material.)

A practical approach to amass large volumes of training material is as follows: begin with a few pages of transcribed ground truth and with its resulting classifier generate additional pages which can be corrected by editing. Iterating in this way often means that the last thirty pages of new training material is easier to come by than the first five. However, as Figure 5 shows, any arbitrary increase in training volume does not always guarantee improved results with any given page.

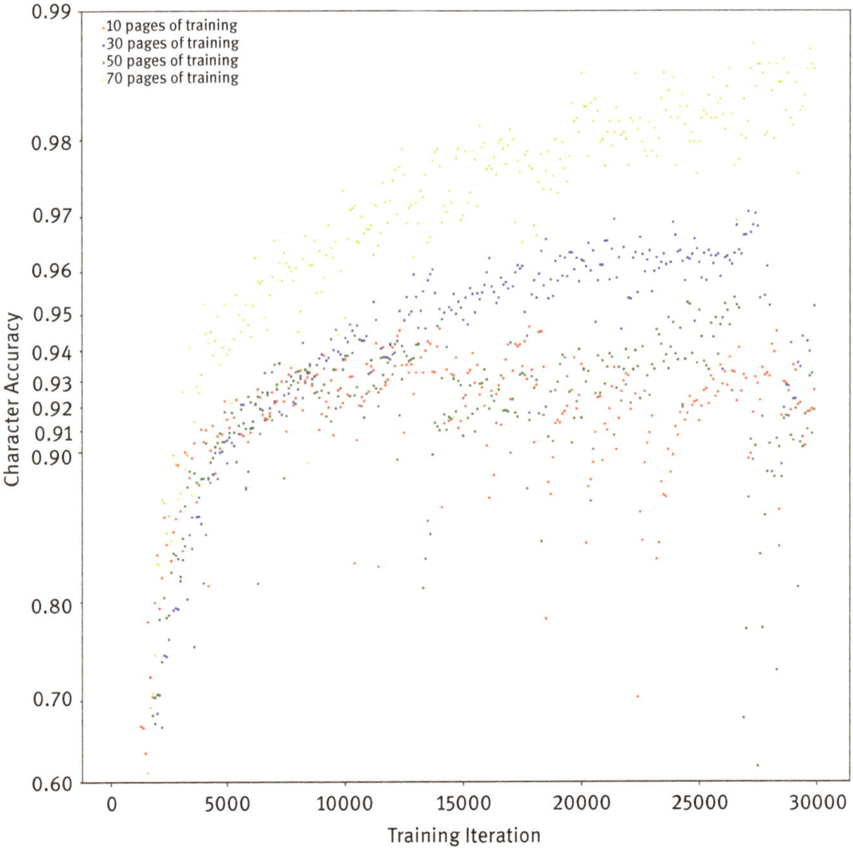

Figure 5: Scatter plots of training results using different volumes of training material. Progress is represented by character recognition accuracy versus training iteration.

Post-processing

Ocropus, like other OCR engines, outputs its text in a format identifying the region of the page image corresponding to the text's words and lines. In this case, the hOCR format is used, a variant of HTML.[16] The first two 'span' elements in Example 1 show how this format uses the HTML 'class' and 'title' attributes to indicate the type of text range and the coordinates of the corresponding rectangle on the page image. I have programmed a sequence of further post-processing steps as part of the Ciaconna OCR system that attempts to make OCR output as useful as possible for scholarly purposes.[17] These steps further modify the hOCR output, embedding additional information in HTML5-compliant custom data attributes. These begin with the string `data-` ("HTML 5.2" n.d.).

Often scholarly editions, like other texts, are laid out in a compact justified format, requiring the use of hyphens to split words between lines. Such hyphenation impedes some uses of a resulting digital text, such as indexing and search, as well as the production of new marked-up texts, the purpose of the First Thousand Years of Greek project. The first step of post-processing, then, in the Ciaconna system aims to reassemble hyphenated forms, adding information about the hyphenation as attributes on the two pertinent words' <span> elements. The program, named `dehyphenate.py` identifies hyphenated pairs in hOCR output even if the first word of the second line is preceded by a line number, a common event in scholarly editions.[18] As shown in Example 1, the `data-dehyphenatedform` attribute on the first of the two words provides the reassembled form, and the `data-hyphenendpair` and `data-hyphenstartpair` provide a unique and matching number for this hyphenation instance on the page. Finally, the `data-hyphenposition` attribute indicates after which character the hyphen appears. This information is useful because if the word is automatically corrected by a later process, the corrected parts can be applied properly to the two halves of the hyphenation.

Example 1: Output from dehyphenation and spellcheck routines of Ciaconna. Spellcheck output is indicated in bold face. This is generated from Herodotus et al. ([1908]). *Herodoti Historiae, recognovit breviqve adnotatione critica instrvxit Carolus Hu.* 2, V.86.2

```
<span class="ocr_line" title="bbox 89 1230 1815 1302">
    ...
    <span class="ocr_word" title="bbox 1296 1235 1815 1297" id="_47100321129176"
```

16 (Breuel and Kaiserslautern 2007).

17 (Robertson 2019).

18 At present, however, it does not properly handle the case where marginal text follows the last, hyphenated word of the first line.

```
        data-manually-confirmed="false" data-dehyphenatedform="ἀπαλλάχθησαν·" data-
        hyphenposition="7" data-hyphenendpair="2" data-spellcheck-mode="True"
        data-selected-form="ἀπαλλά-">
            Ἀπαλλά-
        </span>
</span>
<br />
<span class="ocr_line" title="bbox 150 1314 1818 1388">
    <span class="ocr_word" title="bbox 150 1319 412 1383"
    id="_47100321131408" data-manually-confirmed="false" data-
    dehyphenatedform="" data-hyphenstartpair="2" data-spellcheck-
    mode="True">
        χθησαν·
    </span>
    ....
</span><!-- end of 'ocr_line' →
```

Despite all efforts to improve raw OCR results, errors inevitably occur. In the examples above, the mixed-language classifiers dealing with around 155 glyphs produced a maximum accuracy of slightly above 98%, which means that nearly two out of every characters is misidentified. Often these are substitutions of similarly-shaped upper-case Latin-script and Greek letters or they are substitutions of one combination of diacritics for a slightly different combination, given how small these are printed. Some sort of post-processing, therefore, can be a very powerful tool to correct these obvious errors. In all cases this involves applying a so-called language model to the raw OCR output, and that output is made to conform to the model in some way. However, this is yet another step in the OCR process where we must be careful to attune our tools to the nature of the materials we are processing.

Imagine the case where we were certain that every word in the raw output was represented in a 'dictionary' file that comprised hundreds of thousands of unique words. With that certainty, we could produce extraordinarily effective post-processing with the following simple algorithm: output every input word that is in this dictionary, and for every input word that isn't, output the dictionary word that is 'closest' to it. This might be suitable for certain OCR proposes, but for ours, the digitization of textual editions, it would be very inappropriate. This is because editions include important forms that do *not* conform to such a dictionary but must not be corrected, such as words in obelized regions or in the apparatus criticus. Not only would such an algorithm increase the error rate in such instances, once a word has been erroneously 'corrected' to a form permitted in the language, it is much harder for an editor who knows the language to identify and correct the error manually. Accordingly, our OCR process applies spellcheck with a very light touch, applying a list of common substitutions, such as the Latin-for-Greek errors described above, and it records the status of the spellcheck in the `data-spellcheck-mode` attribute shown in Example 1. The data encoded in this augmented hOCR format informs our OCR editing webapp, called Lace, a detailed description of which is beyond the scope of this paper. Lace assists the editor by colour-coding the spell-check status of each word, and most importantly it stores the manually corrected results so that these can be repurposed as training data.

The future

Thus far this system has generated 52,938,168 editable words of ancient texts, of which 10,237,171 are manually verified, providing an excellent basis for further classifier training. This paper suggests two approaches that will improve results further. The first is to train three classifiers for every font: one that recognizes Latin script and Greek together, and one each for only the Latin and only the Greek words in the ground truth. (We have the advantage here that in most scholarly material Greek and Latin letters are not combined in the same word. The exception is certain symbols in apparatus critici.) Each line would be recognized first with classifier trained with both scripts. Then the "Greek" words that don't pass spellcheck would be re-recognized by the Greek-only classifier, and the dubious "Latin" words re-recognized by the Latin-script-only one. We have seen that since each of these classifiers has to contend with only half as many glyphs as the comprehensive one, they are more accurate, with even the Greek classifier rising above 99% accuracy. Of course, it is essential that the algorithm distinguishing Greek words from Latin ones be very accurate; one mistake at this level will probably add many additional erroneous characters. The second improvement will come from OCRing each line at a variety of binarization levels and selecting the best results from each, a technique that was applied even more aggressively in the Rigaudon OCR suite described in Robertson and Boschetti (2017).

These improvements and others will be necessary if the texts of the so-called *second* thousand years of Greek are to be digitized satisfactorily. The much greater quantity of these texts makes it unlikely that commercial manual editing will be financially possible. Instead, we hope that interested scholars will undertake to correct this material manually, thereby establishing a corrected text for others and providing additional training material for improved classifiers. One hopes that a character accuracy of better than 99% will encourage philologists to participate in such a project.

Bibliography

Bloice, M.D.; Stocker, C.; Holzinger, A. (2017): "Augmentor: An Image Augmentation Library for Machine Learning". arXiv [cs.CV]. http://arxiv.org/abs/1708.04680.
Breuel, T.M. (2008): "The OCRopus Open Source OCR System". Electronic Imaging 2008, 68150F – 68150F – 15. International Society for Optics and Photonics.
Breuel, T.M. (2019): Ocropus3. GitHub. https://github.com/NVlabs/ocropus3 (last access 2019.01.31).
Breuel, T.M.; Kaiserslautern, U. (2007): "The hOCR Microformat for OCR Workflow and Results". In: ICDAR 2007. Proceedings of the Ninth International Conference on Document Analysis and Recognition. Volume 2. Washington DC: IEEE Computer Society, 1063–1067.
Droettboom, M.; MacMillan, K.; Fujinaga, I. (2003): "The Gamera Framework for Building Custom Recognition Systems". JScholarship. Sheridan Libraries Staff Research. https://jscholarship.library.jhu.edu/handle/1774.2/44378 (last access 2019.01.31).
"HTML 5.2." n.d. https://www.w3.org/TR/html52/ (last access 2019.01.31).
Kiessling, B. (2019): Kraken. GitHub. https://github.com/mittagessen/kraken (last access 2019.01.31).
Kononenko, I.; Kukar, M. (2013): Machine Learning and Data Mining Introduction to Principles and Algorithms. Oxford: Woodhead Publ.
Mark, D.; Whistler, K. (2018): "UAX #15: Unicode Normalization Forms". May 10, 2018. http://unicode.org/reports/tr15/ (last access 2019.01.31).
Mikołajczyk, A.; Grochowski, M. (2018): "Data Augmentation for Improving Deep Learning in Image Classification Problem." In: 2018 International Interdisciplinary PhD Workshop (IIPhDW). Institute of Electrical and Electronics Engineers (IEEE), 117–122.
Rice, S.V.; Kanai, J.; Nartker, T.A. (1993): "An Evaluation of OCR Accuracy". Information Science Research Institute. http://citeseerx.ist.psu.edu/viewdoc/download?doi=10.1.1.80.7878&rep=rep1&type=pdf#page=9 (last access 2019.01.31).
Robertson, B. (2019): Ciaconna. GitHub. https://github.com/brobertson/ciaconna (last access 2019.01.31).
Robertson, B.; Boschetti, F. (2017): "Large-Scale Optical Character Recognition of Ancient Greek". Mouseion 14:3, 341–359.
White, N. (2013): "Training Tesseract for Ancient Greek OCR." The Eutypon 28–29, 1–11.
Wick, C. (2019): Calamari. GitHub. https://github.com/Calamari-OCR/calamari (last access 2019.01.31).
Wolpert, D.H.; Macready, W.G. (1997): "No Free Lunch Theorems for Optimization". In: IEEE Transactions on Evolutionary Computation 1:1, 67–82.

James K. Tauber
Character Encoding of Classical Languages

Abstract: Underlying any processing and analysis of texts is the need to represent the individual characters that make up those texts. For the first few decades, scholars pioneering digital classical philology had to adopt various workaround for dealing with the various scripts of historical languages on systems that were never intended for anything but English. The Unicode Standard addresses many of the issues with character encoding across the world's writing systems, including those used by historical languages, but its practical use in digital classical philology is not without challenges. This chapter will start with a conceptual overview of character coding systems and the Unicode Standard in particular but will discuss practical issues relating to the input, interchange, processing and display of classical texts. As well as providing guidelines for interoperability in text representation, various aspects of text processing at the character level will be covered including normalisation, search, regular expressions, collation, and alignment.

Introduction

The representation of texts electronically must be grounded in the representation of individual characters in those texts and it is for this reason that character encoding is a foundational part of digital philology.

In this chapter we will look at the character encoding of classical texts with an emphasis on Unicode. I will provide a conceptual introduction and brief history to illustrate the development of those concepts. To avoid being too abstract, however, I will give examples relevant to Ancient Greek as well as demonstrate certain processing characteristics of Unicode via snippets of Python. I include discussion of things to watch out for and common pitfalls.

Preliminaries and history

The idea of encoding the letters of the alphabet using combinations of a much smaller set of symbols goes back centuries. Francis Bacon developed a secret

James K. Tauber, Eldarion

https://doi.org/10.1515/9783110599572-009

code that represented each letter as a sequence of just two symbols. This approach foreshadowed both the telegraph and the computer where letters, numbers, and other characters are encoded as sequences of 1s and 0s.

In 1870, Émile Baudot developed a code whose descendants became the standard for the telegraph, used right up until the introduction of ASCII. Baudot's code, which had some similarities to Bacon's handwritten cipher, was a fixed-length encoding where each letter was represented by a sequence of five binary digits – 1s and 0s or "bits" – enabling the encoding of 32 different characters at a time. In fact, Baudot's code supported 64 different characters, by having two sets of 32 characters and reserving one character in each set to mean "switch to the other set".

In 1963, the 7-bit American Standard Code for Information Interchange (ASCII) was released and quickly became widely adopted. The extra codes that seven bits afforded meant a certain number of codes could be used, not for printable characters but as control codes for printers to indicate line breaks, page breaks, tabs, and so on.

As computers increasingly adopted ASCII, however, there was a problem. The set of characters supported was fine for the US but was inadequate for languages in Western Europe, to say nothing of scripts such as Greek or Cyrillic. The East Asian languages, with their large inventories of ideographs were out of the question.

The first work around, where only a handful of necessary characters were missing, was to replace lesser-used characters. Some French-speaking countries used a variant of ASCII that replaced { and } with é and è respectively. Countries like Greece replaced the entire repertoire of letters with their own (forming the ELOT 927 standard). These work arounds meant you always had to be aware of what particular character set was being used.

Over time, as more computer systems adopted the 8-bit "byte", it became helpful to use all 256 codes that this enabled. Various character sets were developed that kept the first 128 codes identical to ASCII with the other 128 available for extra characters. This meant ASCII characters (including the control characters) could be transmitted without worrying about the particular variant being used. It also meant a full 128 extra characters were possible.

A number of variants adopting this approach were standardised as the ISO-8859 family. Each was compatible with ASCII for the first 128 codes but specified a different set of additional 128 characters. ISO 8859-1 (also known as Latin-1) extended ASCII with most of the characters needed for the languages of Western Europe. ISO 8859-2 did the same for Central and Eastern European countries using a Latin alphabet. ISO 8859-5 provided Cyrillic, ISO 8859-7 provided monotonic Greek, and ISO 8859-8 provided modern Hebrew.

As well as those ratified by standards organisations, additional character encodings were introduced by various operating system vendors. Still used to this day is Microsoft Windows CP-1252, a variant of Latin-1.

Alongside this explosion of 8-bit character encodings, countries such as China, Japan and Korea developed their own character encodings that used two bytes to support the larger set of characters they required.

Unicode history

In late 1987, developers at Apple and Xerox started working on a single "Unicode" to rule them all. The name was intended to evoke the idea of being universal in coverage of the world's writing system, uniform in structure, and with each character assigned a unique code position.

It was determined a fixed-width 16-bit encoding (allowing up to 65,536 characters) would be sufficient for unifying existing character encoding standards.

Unicode 1.0 was published in 1991. There was a competing international standard being developed at the same time but it was eventually agreed that the international standard, ISO 10646, would synchronise their character codes with Unicode and this synchronisation continues to this day.

In 1996, Unicode 2.0 was released and, through the use of surrogate pairs (see below) it expanded the available codespace 17-fold from 65,536 positions to 1,114,112, largely to accommodate archaic and historical writing systems that were not originally envisaged to need encoding.

Since then there have been regular releases of Unicode and, at the time of writing, Unicode 12.0 is being prepared.

Other non-Unicode approaches

Although Unicode is the only reasonable choice for digital philology nowadays, other approaches to the representation of characters in historical languages were used before the widespread adoption of Unicode. As they may still be encountered in legacy data, it is worth mentioning two.

Custom fonts

One approach common before the broad adoption of Unicode and still seen in older online resources is the use of custom fonts that place non-standard glyphs in place of those assumed by the character encoding. This approach relied on the recipient having the necessary font and it being used at the appropriate time.

While this was a usable workaround for display purposes, the conflation between character encoding and font choice made processing much more difficult, particularly due to the inconsistent reuse of codes between fonts.

BetaCode

Pioneering work in digital classical philology was already taking place at a time when computers were only capable of encoding Latin characters, numerals, and some basic punctuation.

BetaCode was developed by David Packard in the late 1970s to enable the representation of Greek characters with this limited character set.

BetaCode is not a character encoding system in the way we mean here as it is not about assigning numerical codes to characters and then encoding them as bits. Instead, BetaCode is essentially a transliteration scheme that maps Greek characters and diacritic marks to the available Latin characters (which may then be represented using any number of character encoding systems). For example, an omega with rough breathing, a circumflex and iota subscript would be transliterated `W(=|`.

In practice, some resources are inconsistent in their ordering of diacritics in BetaCode and care must be taken, particularly when converting to Unicode.

Unicode fundamentals

In any digital processing of text, we are potentially interested in a variety of textual elements. We may care about words, sentences, paragraphs, chapters, or entire works. We may care about elements smaller than a word: syllables, and individual letters (with or without diacritic marks such as accents).

Which elements we care about, how we demarcate them, how we determine their equivalence to one another will depend on not only the specific language but the particular task at hand. A search may want to ignore any distinction between uppercase and lowercase letters, or the accentuation but those are important in running text. Running text may not display vowel length but a dictionary might.

The goal of a character encoding system is to provide a set of fundamental units on top of which larger text elements can be built. These fundamental units, called *characters* are assigned numerical *character codes*. Any text element then becomes representable as a sequence of these character codes.

The first step of any character encoding system is to select which characters need to represented. This collection of characters is referred to as the *character repertoire*. Some space of numbered code positions (or *code points*) is then defined and characters are assigned to these points. This effectively assigns each character a numerical code. There are then a number of ways of encoding this numerical code as a string of one or more bytes.

Beyond all this, Unicode provides data about each character, necessary for its rendering and processing, as well as various algorithms for text processing that make use of these data.

Character repertoires and code spaces

As of version 12.0, Unicode has a repertoire of 137,929 characters. This covers not only characters from scripts in modern use but also many archaic and historic scripts. Ongoing work ensures increasing coverage.

The original Unicode specification only had a codespace of 65,536 points (representable with 16-bit numbers) but since 2.0, Unicode has supported 1,114,112 (17 × 65,536) points to which characters may be assigned.

A code position (also known as a *code point*) is really just an integer and the Unicode codespace consists of the range of integers from 0 to 1,114,111 (10FFFF in hex).

Some are reserved for future use, private use, or use in surrogate pairs (see below). A few are marked as never to be used. The majority of code points, however, are intended for *graphic characters*, that is characters to be displayed. A small number are for control codes (mostly due to legacy from ASCII).

Once a character from the repertoire is assigned a code point in the codespace, it is called an *encoded character* or *coded character*. We can refer to a particular character at a code point with `U+XXXX` where `XXXX` is the code point in hexadecimal.

In Python 3, the built-in `ord()` function will return the code-point of a one-character string.

```
>>> ord('α')
945
```

or as a hex string:

```
>>> hex(ord('α'))
'0x3b1'
```

Given an integer, `chr()` will return the character at that code-point.

```
>>> chr(0x3B1)
'α'
```

Outside of a specific programming language, we would say that 'α' is U+03B1. Within a Python string, characters may be referred to by their (hexadecimal) code point using `\uXXXX`.

```
>>> 'alpha is \u03b1'
'alpha is α'
```

Characters versus glyphs

Selecting a character repertoire means deciding what counts as a distinct "character".

A key design principle of the Unicode Standard is that characters are not the same as glyphs. A *character* is an abstract element in a writing system whereas a *glyph* is a specific shape rendered on screen or in print. The shape of a lowercase 'a' in a particular font is a glyph but the abstract idea of a "lowercase a" is a character.

Unicode is fundamentally concerned with characters, not glyphs, and while the Unicode code charts give example glyphs to provide guidance on what is meant by a particular character, there is nothing in Unicode that describes the precise shape, size, or orientation of glyphs.

The reasons for why Unicode draws the distinctions it does with certain characters, while conflating others, are complex and there are notions of equivalence and compatibility between characters that will be discussed later. Both purity and practicality have a part to play and it must be remembered that a major goal of Unicode was to unify existing character encoding systems which may or may not have had exactly the same design philosophy of Unicode.

But to give some flavour of the challenges, consider the following.

A Latin capital A and Greek capital Alpha might look identical in a font, but are they the same character? Is the μ used for the unit prefix micro- the same as the Greek letter? Is a superscript digit the same character as the subscript version? Is a final sigma in Greek just a variant glyph or a different character from the normal sigma? What about the differing initial, medial and final forms of Arabic letters? Is 'é' a single character or is the acute accent a separate character added to the 'e'? If the latter, is that acute the same acute used in the Greek 'έ' ?

The answers Unicode has for these questions will depend on legacy encoding, whether characters are used in the same writing system or not, whether there would be visual confusion between two characters, whether the characters behave differently in case folding or text segmentation or sorting, and so on.

The structure of the Unicode codespace

There is a structure to the space of code points to which characters are assigned and we provide a brief overview of that structure here.

Planes and blocks

As mentioned earlier, in 1996, Unicode extended the codespace with an additional 16 x 65,536 code points on top of the original 65,536. Each chunk of 65,536 points is called a *plane*. The original space of code points, representable with just a single 16-bit number, is now referred to as the *Basic Multilingual Plane* (BMP) or Plane 0. The other 16 planes are collectively referred to as the *Supplementary Planes*.

Within a plane, code positions are grouped into blocks. Blocks are just an organisational device and not necessarily an indication of language, script, or any specific character properties. A sample of the blocks most relevant to classical philology include:

Basic Latin (ASCII)	0000–007F
Latin-1 Supplement	0080–00FF
Spacing Modifier Letters	02B0–02FF
Combining Diacritical Marks	0300–036F
Greek	0370–03FF
Greek Extended	1F00–1FFF
General Punctuation	2000–206F

although many others exist for the other scripts of historical languages.

Private use area

To accommodate the encoding of characters not currently (or ever to be) represented in Unicode, there are a number of code points designated as a *Private Use Area* (PUA).

The area from U+E000 to U+F8FF (consisting of 6,400 code points) as well as the entirety of Planes 15 and 16 are designated as Private Use Areas.

Communities can assign otherwise unsupported characters to points in the private use area by agreement among themselves without fear of clashing with any official assignments.

Private use areas are used by everything from scholars working on obscure writing systems or transcriptions of manuscripts with rare symbols to conlangers wanting to exchange electronic texts in their favourite constructed language.

Surrogate pairs

The area from U+D800 to U+DFFF is designated for use in surrogate pairs which is a mechanism used by the UTF-16 encoding form to address the supplementary planes with two 16-bit code units while still only using a single 16-bit code unit for characters in the BMP. This is described in the section below on UTF-16.

Diacritics and modifying marks

Many writing systems involve marks that, in some way, modify a base character. For example, the grave accent in è, the diaeresis in ï, the ogonek in ǫ, the macron in ā, or the rough breathing and acute accent in ἅ.

The combinatorial possibilities quickly explode, especially when one considers that modifying marks may combine (as in the case with the alpha above). If each combination was assigned to its own code point, thousands of code points would be necessary. So the approach taken by Unicode is to separately assign each base character and modifying mark to their own code point and a sequence of two or more characters is used to convey a base with its diacritics.

Now there are some exceptions to this. Some combinations, for legacy reasons, have a dedicated code point. This is true for Greek because of existing character encoding systems that Unicode was incorporating. It's important to recognise this an exception, though, and even in the case of Greek, not all combinations are expressed in this way.

This does, though, lead to different sequences of Unicode character essentially meaning the same thing. For this reason, and as will be discussed below, Unicode has notions of equivalency and character sequences can be normalised for comparison purposes.

Unicode character database

The *Unicode Character Database* provides a wide range of properties for each character useful in various processing and rendering applications. The database gives a name for the character, the block the character is in and, in many cases, the script the character is part of.

In addition, the database provides information on case mappings, directionality, decompositions, and more. This information is vital to many of the algorithms that accompany the Unicode Standard and help define how to divide words and break lines, sort text, format numbers, fold cases, handle bidirectional text, optionally ignore diacritics when searching and so on.

The Unicode Character Database is provided in a machine readable form for download. Some of the more commonly used information is also directly available from Python via the `unicodedata` standard library module.

The `name()` function in the `unicodedata` module returns the name of the given character:

```
>>>import unicodedata
>>> unicodedata.name('α')
'GREEK SMALL LETTER ALPHA'
```

General character categories

Every assigned character in Unicode has a *general category*. This is one of the properties defined for each character in the Unicode Character Database.

The top-level general categories are Letter (L), Mark (M), Number (N), Punctuation (P), Symbol (S), Separator (Z), and Other (C). Each general category is split into further subcategories.

Characters in the M category represent diacritics and are also referred to as *combining characters*. Any graphic character that is not a combining character is said to be a *base character*. Multiple combining characters may be used with a single base character, but the base character always comes first.

Nonspacing marks

Within the combining characters, there is a subset referred to as the *nonspacing marks*. These are marks like smooth breathing, the acute or the macron that wouldn't normally take up any extra width with a fixed-width font. Nonspacing marks have a general category of Mn unless they fully enclose their base character, in which case they have a general category of Me.

An example of general categories

Consider the following text:

Il 1.1 μῆνιν

Here is each character's code point (in hexadecimal) and category:

I	l		1	.	1		μ	η̃		ν	ι	ν
49	6C	20	31	2E	31	20	03BC	03B6	0342	03BD	03B9	03BD
Lu	Ll	Zs	Nd	Po	Nd	Zs	Ll	Ll	Mn	Ll	Ll	Ll

Where Lu = uppercase letter, Ll = lowercase letter, Zs = space separator, Nd = decimal digit, and Mn = nonspacing mark. Note that the *η̃* is represented by two characters: *η*, a lowercase letter (Ll) and the circumflex, a nonspacing mark (Mn).

The function `category()` in unicodedata will return the category of the given character.

```
>>> unicodedata.category(",")
'Po'
```

Encoding forms

At the core of Unicode is the assignment of characters to code points, which effectively assigns each character in the repertoire a unique integer representation. But our ultimate goal, at least in terms of storage and transmission, is how to represent characters in terms of bits.

There are three primary mappings-to-bits, called *encoding forms*, that Unicode provides: UTF-32, UTF-16, and UTF-8. These respectively use sequences of 32-bit, 16-bit, and 8-bit *code units* to represent character sequences.

All three encoding forms are capable of representing all code points in Unicode but have different advantages in different contexts. The follow table demonstrates the different encoding forms applied to characters from different parts of the code space:

		UTF-32	UTF-16	UTF-8
a	U+0061	00000061	0061	61
æ	U+00E6	000000E6	00E6	C3 A6
α	U+03B1	000003B1	03B1	CE B1
ἄ (pre-composed)	U+1F04	00001F04	1F04	E1 BC 84
(Linear B 'A')	U+10000	00010000	D800 DC00	F0 90 80 80

One may occasionally encounter references to UCS-2 or UCS-4. UCS-4 is functionally equivalent to UTF-32 and UCS-2 is a obsolete subset of UTF-16.

UTF-32

UTF-32 is the simplest encoding form for Unicode as it is a fixed-width, 32-bit representation of a code point with no conversion necessary.

UTF-16

UTF-16 is optimised for the BMP and will use a single 16-bit code unit (that is, two bytes) for all characters in that plane. Other planes are still accessible using pairs of 16-bit units (that is, four bytes) known as surrogate pairs.

UTF-16 is at most the same size as UTF-32 and, in the vast majority of cases (namely with characters on the BMP), is half the size. For this reason, UTF-16 is almost always to be preferred over UTF-32.

Surrogate pairs are a pair of code units that, if treated as code points in isolation, are never used. But as a pair, they can be converted to a code point outside the basic plane.

The first in the pair (the *high-surrogate*) must be in the range U+D800 to U+DBFF and the second in the pair (the *low-surrogate*) must be in the range U+DC00 to U+DFFF.

A choice of one of the 1,024 numbers in the high-surrogate range and one of the 1,024 numbers in the low-surrogate range gives 1,024 x 1,024 = 1,048,576 addressable code points, which is the size of the code space in the supplementary planes.

UTF-8

UTF-8 is a variable-width encoding which, although capable of representing the entire Unicode codespace, is optimised for ASCII. A text containing just 7-bit ASCII characters will take one byte per character under UTF-8. This is at the expense of some characters (those from U+800 on up), taking more bytes than UTF-16.

Not only are code points from U+0000 to U+007F represented as one byte in UTF-8, but they are done so in a way that is identical to ASCII. This makes UTF-8 backwards compatible with ASCII. Any valid ASCII sequence is valid UTF-8.

Code points from U+0080 through U+07FF are representable with two bytes, U+0800 through U+FFFF with three bytes, and the supplementary planes with four bytes.

Endianness and the byte order mark

When dealing with code units of more than one byte, there is always the question of whether the individual bytes are big-endian or little-endian (the so-called "endianness"). This means that UTF-16 and UTF-32 encoding forms actually come in two variants. Unicode has a helpful way to give an internal hint as to the endianness used in a sequence.

The code point U+FEFF is assigned a zero width, no-break space. This is a character which basically has no effect. If a system decoding, say, UTF-16 got the endianness wrong, a U+FEFF would come across (incorrectly) as U+FFFE. The latter is a Unicode noncharacter. In other words, the code point is not assigned a character and never will be. That effectively means that if a decoding system encounters a U+FFFE, it must be assuming the wrong endianness.

By putting the U+FEFF character at the start of a UTF-16 or UTF-32 file, you effectively are letting the decoder whether the byte sequence is big or little ending. For this reason, the character is also known as the Byte Order Mark (BOM).

Equivalence, compatibility, and normalization

As mentioned earlier, there is a certain amount of complexity to the question of whether two things should be considered the same character (or sequence of characters) or not. The Unicode Standard has the notion of *equivalence* to formally define that, at least in certain contexts, some sequences of code points should be treated as representing the same abstract character.

Unicode distinguishes two types of equivalence: *canonical* and *compatibility*. Canonical equivalence means that two (sequences of) code points should essentially be considered the same. That is, they should render the same, be processed the same, and be substitutable for one another. Compatibility equivalent means that there may be differences in appearance and in how they should be processed in some situations, but that there are other situations where they could be considered equivalent.

Canonical equivalence

One relevant example of canonical equivalence in sequences with a base character and one or more combining characters. If a pre-composed character exists, it is canonically equivalent to the decomposition into a combining sequence.

For example ἄ, in its pre-composed form, is assigned to U+1F04 and given the name, "GREEK SMALL LETTER ALPHA WITH PSILI AND OXIA". It is canonically equivalent to:

U+03B1 GREEK SMALL LETTER ALPHA	U+0313 COMBINING COMMA ABOVE	U+0301 COMBINING ACUTE ACCENT

The latter is referred to as the *canonical decomposition* of U+1F04.

Note that, in this case, order matters. The sequence U+03B1 U+0301 U+0313 is not equivalent to U+03B1 U+0313 U+301 (and hence not equivalent to U+1F04). The order of the two combining characters matters because they attach to the same place on the base character. The place of attachment is indicated by the *combining class* property.

With something like ᾷ, though, the sequence U+03B1 U+0342 U+0345 is equivalent to U+03B1 U+0345 U+0342 because the two combining characters attach in different places.

Compatibility equivalence

Compatibility equivalence is a weaker condition. Ligatures are generally compatibility equivalent to their separate-letter versions but not canonically equivalent. U+00B5, the code point for the unit prefix micro-, has a *compatibility decomposition* to U+03BC, the Greek mu, but not a canonical decomposition. Superscript and subscript digits (which have their own code points) also have a compatibility decomposition to the corresponding plain digits.

Normalization

If character sequences are canonically equivalent then, in almost all cases you want them to be considered equal when processing. If character sequences are compatibility equivalent, you may also want them to be considered equal. The Unicode Normalization Algorithm transforms strings into a form, called a *normalization form*, such that equivalent strings will have the same form. Once in a normalization form, testing equivalence is therefore just a matter of binary comparison.

There are four Unicode Normalization Forms:

Normalization Form D	NFD	do a canonical decomposition
Normalization Form C	NFC	do a canonical decomposition followed by a canonical composition
Normalization Form KD	NFKD	do a compatibility decomposition
Normalization Form KC	NFKC	do a compatibility decomposition followed by a canonical composition

Normalization can also be used to fully decompose a string or fully compose it.

The NFD form of ἄ U+1F04 "GREEK SMALL LETTER ALPHA WITH PSILI AND OXIA" is, for example, U+03B1 U+0313 U+0301, the base alpha with the smooth breathing and acute as separate combining characters.

The NFC form of U+03B1 U+0313 U+0301 is likewise U+1F04.

The `normalize()` function on `unicodedata` converts Unicode strings to one of the four normalization forms.

```
>>> for character in unicodedata.normalize('NFD', '\u1F04'):
... print(hex(ord(character)), unicodedata.name(character))
...
0x3b1 GREEK SMALL LETTER ALPHA
0x313 COMBINING COMMA ABOVE
0x301 COMBINING ACUTE ACCENT
>>> unicodedata.normalize('NFC','\u03b1\u0313\u0301') == '\u1F04'
True
```

Whether two strings are canonically equivalent can be determined by comparing either their NFC or NFD normalizations. Whether two strings are compatibility equivalent can be determined by comparing either their NFKC or NFKD normalizations.

Common pitfalls in character encoding

Unknown encoding and mojibake

If a text is interpreted (that is, decoded) assuming a different character encoding from that used to produce it, unexpected characters can result. These unintended characters are referred by the Japanese term *mojibake* which literally means “character changing”.

Here is the first line of the *Iliad* when encoded as UTF-8 but treated as Latin-1:

Î¼á¿†Î½Î¹Î½ á¼„ÎµÎ¹Î´Îµ Î¸Îµá½° Î Î·Î»Î·ÏŠÎ¬Î´ÎµÏ‰ á¼ˆÏ‡Î¹Î»á¿†Î¿Ï‚

One solution is to manually set the character encoding on the receiving side (in, for example, the browser or text editor) to that used by the sender. But given this requires action on the part of the recipient, this is nothing more than a workaround. In many cases, the better solution is to make sure the correct character encoding has been transmitted along with the text. For example, in HTML a `meta charset="utf-8"` element can ensure the correct browser interpretation. XML and JSON can use UTF-8 without any need for explicit declaration.

Missing characters in a font (fall back)

Systems, if asked to render a particular character using a font that does not have a glyph for that character will either display some dummy character or fallback to another font that does have a glyph for the character. If no fonts exist on the system with such a glyph, the system has no choice but to display a dummy character. In the case where a dummy character is used, it is obvious that the font is missing support for the character but in the fallback case, it might not be so clear at first glance but the display will be uneven.

Where this is quite common is the display of Greek and there are two types of problems that can arise if the first font choice does not support all the characters being used.

Firstly there is the case where the first font choice doesn’t have the full set of Greek letters but has some subset (often pi, mu, etc). The subset will be displayed in the first font choice with other letters being displayed in the fallback font.

Secondly the first font choice may have Greek support but not the precomposed polytonic Greek characters. In this case, Greek characters without diacritic will use one font and those with another.

Stray look-alikes from another script

This issue is particular pernicious because the text can look fine but process incorrectly. Various Greek characters look similar or identical to Latin characters and it can be visually impossible to pick up when the two have been mixed.

Greek in Unicode

The encoding of Greek in Unicode was initially based on ISO 8859–7 (equivalent to the Greek national standard ELOT 928) which was designed for monotonic Greek with a single "tonos" accent.

The Greek block from U+0370 to U+03FF consists of the letters (both uppercase and lowercase), the vowels with tonos and, where appropriate, with dialytika (diaeresis) and with both tonos and dialytika, punctuation and the numeral signs (keraia).

The block at U+0370 in fact provides all the letterforms for polytonic Greek, just not the breathing, accents (other than tonos), or iota subscript (ypogegrammeni). However, these are all possible via the use of combining characters from the Combining Diacritical Marks block.

The relevant Combining Diacritical Marks in the 0300–036F range are:

Code	Char	Unicode Name	Notes
U+0300	̀	COMBINING GRAVE ACCENT	Greek varia
U+0301	́	COMBINING ACUTE ACCENT	Greek oxia, tonos
U+0304	̄	COMBINING MACRON	long vowel
U+0306	̆	COMBINING BREVE	short vowel, Greek vrachy
U+0308	̈	COMBINING DIAERESIS	Greek dialytika
U+0313	̓	COMBINING COMMA ABOVE	Greek psili, smooth breathing mark
U+0314	̔	COMBINING REVERSED COMMA ABOVE	Greek dasia, rough breathing mark
U+0342	͂	COMBINING GREEK PERISPOMENI	Greek-specific form of circumflex (whether the glyph looks like tilde or inverted breve)
U+0345	ͅ	COMBINING GREEK YPOGEGRAMMENI	

Note that there is a COMBINING CIRCUMFLEX ACCENT at U+0302 but that's not what we think of as a circumflex. In Greek we use U+0342, the COMBINING GREEK PERISPOMENI.

There is a COMBINING GREEK DIALYTIKA TONOS at U+0344 but use of this is discouraged in favour of an explicit sequence of U+0308 U+301 (which is the canonical decomposition for U+0344 anyway).

There is a COMBINING GREEK KORONIS at U+0343 but this is canonically equivalent to U+0313 which is preferred.

The Greek Extended block from U+1F00 to U+1FFF exists to provide precomposed polytonic Greek characters. Note, however, that it is entirely possible to do polytonic Greek without this block, using base characters from the "Greek" block at U+0370 along with combining characters outlined above.

The following are the code points preferred for punctuation and the numeral sign commonly found in Greek texts:

Code	Char	Unicode Name	Notes
U+002C	,	COMMA	
U+002E	.	FULL STOP	
U+003B	;	SEMICOLON	preferred over U+037E "GREEK QUESTION MARK"
U+00B7	·	MIDDLE DOT	preferred over U+0387 "GREEK ANO TELEIA"
U+02B9	ʹ	MODIFIER LETTER PRIME	preferred over U+0374 "GREEK NUMERAL SIGN"
U+2019	’	RIGHT SINGLE QUOTATION MARK	preferred over U+02BC "MODIFIER LETTER APOSTROPHE"

Other issues with Unicode Greek

Precomposed vs decomposed characters

Given that almost (but not) all useful combinations of Greek base character with combining characters also have a precomposed equivalent, the question arises: is one preferred over the other?

It should be again noted that the existence of the precomposed characters is for legacy reasons. Without the constraints of existing ELOT standards, Unicode almost certainly would have done away with the precomposed characters.

Many processing tasks (collation, accent-stripping, etc) are more easily done with decomposed characters. Keyboard input can also be easier with decomposed characters. This does place extra burden on fonts and rendering systems but ultimately this is where the burden should lie.

All this said, the storage and transmission of precomposed Greek text is not particularly problematic given decomposition is easily achievable via normalization forms. Many electronic Greek texts normalize to NFC for storage.

Combining accents and vowel length

Running Greek text rarely indicates vowel length but dictionaries may do so. There are no adequate precomposed characters for representing things like the imperfect ῑ̔́στημι. Unicode is perfectly capable of representing it with combining characters but input and rendering systems, including the fonts themselves, sometimes lack support.

Tonos vs oxia

During the monotonic reform of the Greek language in the 1980, the number of accents was reduced from three to just one, the tonos. Although the tonos resembled the acute, reformers were keen to distance themselves from the older system and encouraged type designers to make it visually distinct from the acute.

In 1986, the Greek government officially equated the tonos with the acute. Unfortunately, this equivalency did not make it into Unicode until version 3.0 and so we are left with TONOS pre-compositions in the Greek block alongside OXIA pre-composition in the Greek Extended block, both of which decompose to a combining acute.

Since Unicode 3.0, the normalization of OXIA to TONOS should be harmless and from the point of view of processing, it is. Unfortunately there are a number of otherwise excellent fonts that render tonos and acute distinctly. In the eyes of Unicode and the Greek government, however, they are equivalent.

Which phi and which theta?

U+03C6 "GREEK SMALL LETTER PHI" and U+03B8 "GREEK SMALL LETTER THETA" should be used for Greek text (regardless of whether straight or looped style). U+03D5 "GREEK PHI SYMBOL" and U+03D1 "GREEK THETA SYMBOL" are only intended for mathematical symbols.

Apostrophe marking elision

Besides the straight apostrophe at U+0027 (which really only exists for compatibility with ASCII) the characters U+2019 and U+02BC are also apostrophe-like characters.

Despite the name "RIGHT SINGLE QUOTATION MARK", U+2019 is intended for both the quotation mark and an apostrophe when used as punctuation (in English, for example, to mark contractions or the possessive).

U+02BC "MODIFIER LETTER APOSTROPHE" is intended when either a distinct letter (in many languages representing a glottal stop) or when modifying a base character (often to represent an ejective).

The apostrophe marking elision in Greek (for example, in γένοιτ' ἄν) falls into the former category and so the Unicode Standard prefers U+2019 for that purpose.

There are some resources, however, that use U+02BC. The primary reason for this choice seems to be that some systems doing text segmentation assume U+2019 is a quotation mark and not part of the preceding word. This is a limitation of the text segmentation being used.

The use of U+02BC is therefore a workaround to deal with incorrect word-breaking by tools. From a character coding, perspective, U+2019 is the correct code point to use.

Keyboard input

Operating systems support virtual keyboards or input sources that map the keys pressed on a physical keyboard to alternative code points for entering a particular script.

There are multiple ways these virtual keyboards / input sources support the entry of characters with diacritics.

The first approach involves pressing the key for the base character, followed by a key for the non-spacing combining character.

The second approach involves a *dead key* for the desired diacritic first which puts the keyboard in a state waiting for a legal base character to be entered second. This may result in a precomposed character rather than a combining character sequence.

Different virtual keyboard layouts may offer one or both of these approaches.

Processing Unicode

Stripping diacritics

With a decomposition it is easy to strip diacritics by filtering out particular characters either by exact match (if you want to strip specific diacritics such as accents while keeping, say, breathing intact) or by general category to strip all.

Sorting and collation

Without additional character data, the sorting of text is usually purely on the basis of code points. In other words, if a character's code point is earlier in the codespace, the character sorts earlier. This is rarely appropriate for at least three reasons. Firstly, the layout of characters in the codespace is based on many factors besides what their collation order should be. Secondly, culturally expected collation order is often language-specific. Language communities sharing the same script still may not sort words the same way. Thirdly, sorting often cannot be done by treating characters in isolation. Sorting in many languages involves treating certain sequences of characters as a single unit.

Fortunately, Unicode specifies the Unicode Collation Algorithm (UCA) for this purpose. Information about how characters are to be sorted are represented in a *collation element table*. Particular locales may require a custom collation element table, although Unicode does provide a default, the Default Unicode Collation Element Table (DUCET) which, out-of-the-box, enables the correct sorting of Ancient Greek.

Many tools such as databases and text editors support the UCA via the International Components for Unicode (ICU) C++ library. Wrappers for ICU exist for many programming languages (including Python) but this author has also implemented a pure-Python version of the UCA called PyUCA.

Regular expressions

Regular expressions in most languages have a certain amount of support for Unicode. In Python (and many other languages) a `\d` in a regex will match all digits (category Nd) not just 0–9 and `\w` will match non-Latin characters just as well as Latin.

There is also an external Python library `regex` which provides richer support including matching by properties such as block, script, and general category.

With all processing, it is important to be aware of equivalency issues and using a normalization form is recommendation for most processing.

The future of Unicode

Through the efforts of projects such as the Script Encoding Initiative, the world's remaining uncoded minority scripts have a good chance of eventual representation in the Standard. Since the expansion of the codespace to the supplementary planes, there is opportunity for encoding the historical scripts not yet included. And, in the meantime, the private use areas are available.

Support for Unicode in operating systems, programming languages, text editors, and fonts is widespread with only occasional shortcomings. For the foreseeable future, the Unicode Standard provides the single most stable representation for the characters in digital texts whether modern or historical.

References

Author's Unicode Resources. https://jktauber.com/unicode/ (last access 2019.01.31).
ICU – International Components for Unicode. http://site.icu-project.org/ (last access 2019.01.31).
Nick Nicholas's Greek Unicode Issues. http://www.opoudjis.net/unicode/unicode.html (last access 2019.01.31).
Python Library unicodedata. https://docs.python.org/3/library/unicodedata.html (last access 2019.01.31).
Python Library regex. https://pypi.org/project/regex (last access 2019.01.31).
Python Library pyuca. https://pypi.org/project/pyuca (last access 2019.01.31).
Script Encoding Initiative. http://www.linguistics.berkeley.edu/sei/ (last access 2019.01.31).
The Unicode Standard. http://www.unicode.org/versions/latest/ (last access 2019.01.31).
Unicode FAQ on Greek Language and Script. https://www.unicode.org/faq/greek.html (last access 2019.01.31).

Patrick J. Burns

Building a Text Analysis Pipeline for Classical Languages

Abstract: With large text collections for Ancient Greek and Latin now widely available, classicists are increasingly interested in extracting information systematically from these texts. The fields of information retrieval and natural language processing offer tools and methods to address this, but classical-language support can be limited and researchers must often cobble together separate, sometimes incompatible tools to accomplish basic text analysis tasks. In this chapter, I review the tools currently available for digital philological work on Ancient Greek and Latin and introduce the Classical Language Toolkit, an open-source Python framework that addresses the desideratum of a complete text analysis pipeline for historical languages.

1 Introduction

With large text collections for Ancient Greek and Latin now widely available, classicists are increasingly interested in extracting information systematically from these texts and constructing derivative datasets. Digital philologists have been able to turn to the fields of information retrieval and natural language processing (NLP) for tools and methods to accomplish these goals, but classical-language support can be limited and, as a result, researchers must often cobble together separate, sometimes incompatible tools to accomplish basic text analysis tasks and approximate the kinds of integrated solutions available for work in modern languages.

In the first part of this chapter, I review examples of text analysis frameworks that are available for work in modern languages (such as Stanford CoreNLP and the Natural Language Toolkit), highlighting in particular one of the defining features of these frameworks – the pipeline, a sequential workflow of transformation and annotation. Each of the frameworks listed above offer a complete pipeline of text analysis tasks, including tokenization, lemmatization, part-of-speech and morphological tagging, and named entity extraction, among other tasks. Pipelines, considered the "standard approach to realize text

Patrick J. Burns, Quantitative Criticism Lab, University of Texas at Austin

https://doi.org/10.1515/9783110599572-010

analysis processes,"[1] are an orderly and efficient way to proceed through a series of analysis tasks, especially in cases where it is useful or necessary for the results of certain tasks to be used as the starting point for processing subsequent tasks. In the second part of the chapter, I review examples of solutions to each task along the Greek and Latin text analysis pipeline and discuss briefly how they could be patched together into a makeshift pipeline if necessary.

By way of conclusion, I introduce the Classical Language Toolkit (CLTK), an open-source Python framework dedicated to natural language processing support for historical languages. CLTK has made progress in the past three years in collecting corpora for a wide variety of historical languages covering ancient, classical, and medieval Eurasia and building out the basic language resources to support these languages across the text analysis pipeline. CLTK shows promise of addressing the desideratum of a complete text analysis pipeline for Greek and Latin, as well as a large number of other less-resourced historical languages.[2]

2 Text analysis pipelines

In text analysis, transformation and annotation tasks are often processed in such a way that new annotations build on previous transformations and annotations of a given text. This sequence is commonly referred to as a pipeline, as in this definition from Henning Wachsmuth:

> "Text mining deals with tasks that often entail complex text analysis processes, consisting of several interdependent steps that aim to infer sophisticated information types from collections and streams of natural language input texts. [. . .] Because of the interdependencies between analyses, the standard way to realize a text analysis process is in the form of a text analysis pipeline, which sequentially applies each employed text analysis algorithm to its input."[3]

1 (Wachsmuth 2015, 37).
2 This chapter limits its scope to Ancient Greek and Latin, but it is important to point out that the development of NLP pipelines is an area of ongoing work for several historical languages. See, for example, Chiarcos et al. (2018) for Sumerian or Zeldes and Schroeder (2016) for Coptic.
3 (Wachsmuth 2015, 4). For a formal definition of text analysis pipelines, see Wachsmuth (2015, 37). For a clear explanation of the terminology involved in describing pipelines, specifically the use of the terms "tool" and "component," see de Castilho and Gurevych (2014, 2). In this chapter, I use "tool" to refer to a piece of software, a web application, or a web service that performs a text analysis task; I use "component" to refer to a tool that is included as a discrete step in a text analysis pipeline.

So, for example, the input sentence

Quo usque tandem abutere, Catilina, patientia nostra?

may be first transformed into a list of words (and punctuation marks) by a tokenizer to yield

['Quo', 'usque', 'tandem', 'abutere', ',', 'Catilina', ',', 'patientia', 'nostra', '?']

which in turn may be annotated by a part-of-speech (POS) tagger into a parallel list of POS tags to yield

['ADV', 'ADV', 'ADV', 'VERB', 'PUNCT', 'NOUN', 'PUNCT', 'NOUN', 'ADJ'][4]

and so on. In this configuration, the POS tagger depends not directly on the plaintext that was originally fed into the pipeline, but rather uses as its input the output of the preceding tokenizer. These kinds of relations between the constituent parts, or components, of a pipeline are illustrated in Figure 1.

Even this system can grow quite complex as the number of components is increased. An advantage to working with pipelines is that this complexity is managed by the sequential workflow as well as the storage of annotations in parallel data structures. Another advantage of using well-defined pipelines in text analysis work is that this practice promotes shareability and reproducibility in research workflows.[5] Because of these advantages in managing and supporting task analysis processes, pipelines are considered the "standard approach" for this kind of work.[6]

---

4 There are several annotation schemes for POS tagging; this example uses the Universal POS tagset; cf. https://universaldependencies.org/u/pos/ (last access 2019.01.31).

5 (de Castilho and Gurevych 2014): "It is essential that [. . .] pipelines can easily be shared between researchers, to reproduce results, to evolve experiments, and to allow for a better understanding of the exact details of an experiment."

6 (Wachsmuth 2015, 37). There are disadvantages in working with pipelines as well. For example, they can be inefficient. Assigning each annotation task, for example, its own space in a pipeline adds certain processing overhead and can introduce redundancies where tasks are strongly correlated, such as (as we will see in greater detail below) lemmatization and POS tagging. In addition, pipelines can be subject to error propagation, since errors introduced early in the execution flow can have downstream consequences. See Marciniak and Strube (2005) and Clarke et al. (2012, 1–2) for potential areas of improvement in pipeline design.

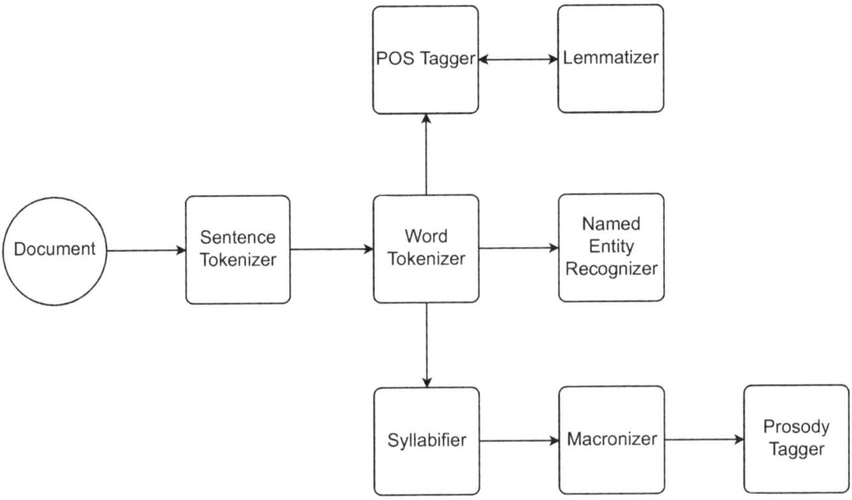

Figure 1: Here is a sample text analysis pipeline, proceeding left-to-right from a plaintext Latin document to a collection of derivative annotations.

3 Text analysis frameworks

The two most prominent frameworks for building pipelines have been GATE (General Architecture for Text Engineering) and UIMA (Unstructured Information Management Architecture), both of which are Java-based and use XML to define instructions for processing components.[7] Both GATE and UIMA offer robust systems for the sequential processing of unstructured text and allow for a great deal of flexibility and extensibility in design, either through rules-based annotations (for example, the JAPE annotation language for GATE) or through the development of Java annotation scripts.

These frameworks may prove useful for large, production-ready applications, but for many researchers in digital philology a more "batteries-included" framework is likely suitable enough. Options abound at present: OpenNLP, DKPro-Core,[8] ClearNLP, LingPipe, spaCy, Argo, Weblicht, to name

7 Gate: (Cunningham 2002); UIMA: (Ferrucci and Lally 2004).

8 Note that OpenNLP and DKPro are implementations of UIMA for which a collection of NLP components has been included by default.

just a few.[9] In the remainder of this section, I would like to concentrate on two frameworks with widespread adoption and active development that highlight, as I see it, two different philosophies toward the use of pipelines: Stanford CoreNLP and the Natural Language Toolkit.

Stanford CoreNLP is a self-described Java "annotation pipeline framework," with robust support for common tasks.[10] Pipelines in CoreNLP are conceived of as an "Annotation" object, that is a list of instructions of which components should be run in which order.[11] Text is added to the Annotation and then, as each component is run, either the transformed text or the annotated text is stored in the object. While specific components can be called at runtime, by default, the full pipeline is applied to a given text. The components are pre-defined such that a specific algorithm is used for each task in order to take advantage of state-of-the-art speed and accuracy. The presentation of a "core" pipeline with a set of "core" components is not an accident. As originally conceived, developers valued ease of use: "Most users benefit greatly from the provision of a set of stable, high quality linguistic analysis components, which can be easily invoked for common scenarios."[12] Accordingly, users are presented with a fully functional pipeline from the outset. It can be customized, but it does not need to be. Given no intervention from the user, a complete pipeline from tokenization to coreference resolution is ready to be run.[13]

---

9 OpenNLP: https://opennlp.apache.org/; DKPro-Core: https://dkpro.github.io/dkpro-core/; ClearNLP: https://github.com/clearnlp; LingPipe: http://alias-i.com/lingpipe/; spaCy: https://spacy.io/; Argo: http://argo.nactem.ac.uk/; Weblicht: https://weblicht.sfs.uni-tuebingen.de/weblichtwiki/index.php/Main_Page (last access 2019.01.31). Language-specific options may prove useful depending on the research project; see, for example, FudanNLP for Chinese text (https://github.com/FudanNLP/fnlp) or IceNLP for Icelandic text (https://github.com/hrafnl/icenlp) (last access 2019.01.31). NLP, including its application to classical languages, is a quickly developing and ever evolving area. For digital philologists, one development worth watching is the integration of NLP datasets and models with web services, as for example with META-SHARE (Piperidis 2012) and Language Application Grid (LAPPS) (Verhagen et al. 2016).
10 (Manning et al. 2014); available online at https://stanfordnlp.github.io/CoreNLP/ (last access 2019.01.31). Note that since the writing of this chapter, a Python implementation of the Stanford tools has been released (StanfordNLP, available online at https://stanfordnlp.github.io/stanfordnlp/) with some out-of-the-box support for Greek and Latin. As it has just been released, it is too early to evaluate fully its impact of digital classical philology.
11 This process is described in detail at https://stanfordnlp.github.io/CoreNLP/pipelines.html (last access 2019.01.31).
12 (Manning et al. 2014, 56).
13 It is interesting to note, in the context of this chapter, that the developers of CoreNLP started the project from a desire to move away from what I have called makeshift pipelines; (Manning et al. 2014, 55): "Previously, when combining multiple natural language analysis

The Natural Language Toolkit, on the other hand, has a different philosophical orientation and as such a different approach to text analysis pipelines. NLTK is an open-source Python NLP framework with origins in a pedagogical approach to NLP.[14] From its inception, it promoted a set of "requirements," namely consistency, extensibility, documentation, simplicity, and modularity, alongside a set of "non-requirements," namely comprehensiveness, efficiency, and cleverness. The goal was to support a complete pipeline of text analysis tasks, while allowing users to "augment and replace existing components, learn structured programming by example, and manipulate models."[15] Considering its pedagogical focus, it is unsurprising that the framework has become so closely associated with what amounts to a user guide-as-textbook, *Natural Language Processing with Python*, or the "NLTK Book."[16] The structure of the book promotes a pipeline-centered take on text analysis as readers are guided from tokenization to tagging to other advanced tasks over the course of twelve chapters. Since the focus is on learning NLP basics and best practices, for each task, users are offered a number of options and are presented with the advantages and disadvantages of working with various interfaces, algorithms, and so on. For example, in chapter 5, users are introduced to several different POS taggers offered by NLTK (including default tagging, regular expression tagging, n-gram tagging, transformation-based tagging, and so on).[17] By working one's way through the NLTK book, it becomes possible to write basic Python scripts that function as pipelines.

These frameworks cover two different approaches to the problem of supporting end-to-end pipelines. CoreNLP, not unlike Gate or UIMA, works by specifying a set of instructions for defining the execution flow of different components. NLTK, on the other hand, at least in its original conception, has a pedagogical focus and so the creation of a pipeline, that is the decision about which components to use and how best to connect their inputs and outputs, is left to the user. Again, with respect to its pedagogical orientation, the focus is on the user understanding the function of each component and, just as importantly, understanding the relationship between each component, rather than simply setting a series of instructions in motion.

---

components, each with their own ad hoc APIs, we had tied them together with custom code glue. The initial version of the annotation pipeline was developed in 2006 in order to replace this jumble with something better."

14 (Loper and Bird 2002): "NLTK provides a simple, extensible, uniform framework for assignments, projects, and class demonstrations. [...] It was deliberately designed as courseware and gives pedagogical goals primary status." The project is available online at https://www.nltk.org (last access 2019.01.31).

15 (Loper and Bird 2002, 1).

16 (Bird et al. 2015).

17 (Bird et al. 2015, Ch. 5.4).

With their different philosophical orientations, CoreNLP and NLTK each offer pros and cons for how we should think about building pipelines for use with Greek and Latin texts. Before we can do this, however, it is necessary to look first at what is currently available with respect to "pipelines" for classical languages.

4 "Pipelines" for classical languages

4.1 Coverage of classical languages in text analysis frameworks

For all of the progress in text analysis frameworks for modern-language research, the fact remains that classical-language support still lags behind. This is particularly apparent with respect to the development of pipelines. Neither CoreNLP nor NLTK support Greek and Latin out of the box. As such, digital philologists working with these languages must forge an alternative path.

In the section that follows, I review the available "components" for classical languages, that is standalone tools that perform the kinds of transformations or yield the kinds of annotations we would expect in a fully implemented pipeline.

4.2 Available "components" for classical languages

This section highlights tools that digital philologists have been able to avail themselves of in the absence of dedicated, well-resourced frameworks like CoreNLP or NLTK.[18]

4.2.1 Tokenization

In most text analysis pipelines, tokenization – whether the division of a text into paragraphs, sentences, words, or some other meaningful unit – is the first

---

18 This discussion of specific pipeline tasks in the following sections as well as the selection of tools and resources mentioned for supporting digital philological work on Greek and Latin is meant to be representative rather than comprehensive. I work here from the premise, "If I wanted to emulate a CoreNLP-style pipeline, what standalone tools could I use to get the job done."

step. Since the vast majority of Greek and Latin text collections are derived from modern editions in which sentences are punctuated and words are delimited by spaces, most tokenization tasks for these languages do not require a customized solution. Accordingly, there tend not to be standalone tools for tokenization, but rather this step tends to be built into the preprocessing stage of other components.

4.2.2 Lemmatization

Lemmatization (and the closely related areas of part-of-speech tagging and morphological tagging) has a long tradition of computational work in Greek and Latin and continues to be a particularly active area of research.[19] Unsurprisingly, then, it is perhaps the pipeline task best supported by standalone tools. There are both command line tools available for Greek and Latin lemmatization as well as web applications and services, allowing for great flexibility in how these tasks can be performed and how results can be obtained for use elsewhere in a makeshift pipeline.

Morpheus, developed for use in the Perseus Digital Library, is perhaps the best known lemmatizer for both languages.[20] A rules-based lemmatizer drawing on data from lexica available in Perseus, Morpheus returns lemmas alongside POS identifications and morphological parses on the site's Greek Word Study Tool and Latin Word Study Tool.[21] It can also be compiled locally and run from the command line. In either case, it is possible for users to extract annotations for use in a makeshift pipeline by either cutting-and-pasting Word Study Tool results or – the more direct and efficient method – by capturing the standard output from running the command-line scripts. This is more or less the pattern for another popular Latin lemmatizer, Whitaker's Words, which can also be run either through a web application or a command-line interface.[22] Another option for extracting lemmas from texts, and a good option for working with blocks of

19 See Bodson and Evrard (1966) for an example of early work in Latin lemmatization. Eger et al. (2015, 2016) offer two recent reviews and comparisons of lemmatizers.

20 (Crane 1991).

21 The Word Study Tools are available online at http://www.perseus.tufts.edu/hopper/morph (last access 2019.01.31). Morpheus is also available as web service through the Perseids Project; the documentation for this project is available online at https://github.com/perseids-project/perseids_docs/wiki/Morphology-Service-Setup (last access 2019.01.31).

22 (Whitaker 1993); available online at http://www.archives.nd.edu/cgi-bin/words.exe (last access 2019.01.31). The documentation for command-line operation of Words is available online at http://archives.nd.edu/whitaker/wordsdoc.htm (last access 2019.01.31).

text, comes from Biblissima through their Collatinus and Eulexis lemmatizers, for work in Latin and Greek respectively.[23] Lastly, at least with respect for Latin, tools have emerged to push lemmatization forward in terms of coverage, speed, and accuracy. Lemlat stands out for having widely expanded the lexical base for assisting lemmatization; already supporting a large lexicon drawn from Georges's *Handwörterbuch*, Gradenwitz's *Laterculi vocum Latinarum*, and the *Oxford Latin Dictionary*, Lemlat has also added a large amount of onomastic data to increase coverage significantly.[24] In addition to Lemlat, another lemmatizer that has more than held its own in a crowded field is LatMor, which compares favorably to the competition in coverage and accuracy, but with processing speeds that are up to 1200 times faster.[25]

Lemmatization is well supported by standalone tools, though perhaps somewhat better for Latin than for Greek. Digital philologists should have little trouble building lexical annotations of this sort for text analysis work. Disambiguation remains a concern (so, for example, correctly tagging the Latin preposition *cum* versus the conjunction *cum*), but advances in computational approaches to lemmatization combined with advances in related annotation tasks like POS tagging are helping to solve this problem.

4.2.3 Part-of-speech (and morphological) tagging

All of the lemmatization tools noted in the previous section also provide some manner of part-of-speech and morphological tagging. This make sense as there is a close relationship between these tasks. Accordingly, POS and morphological annotations from these tools can be captured alongside lexical annotations and used in a pipeline.

Nonetheless, one tool worth calling attention to is TreeTagger, a probabilistic POS tagger written by Helmut Schmid in the mid 1990s.[26] TreeTagger has extensive language support, including classical languages. Latin is supported by two parameter files, one based on selected data from PROIEL, Perseus, and the Index

23 (Ouvard 2010). Collatinus is available online at https://outils.biblissima.fr/fr/collatinus/; Eulexis at https://outils.biblissima.fr/fr/eulexis/ (last access 2019.01.31).

24 (Passarotti et al. 2017); (Budassi and Passarotti 2016); available online at http://www.ilc.cnr.it/lemlat/ (last access 2019.01.31).

25 (Springmann et al. 2016); available online at http://www.cis.uni-muenchen.de/~schmid/tools/LatMor/ (last access 2019.01.31).

26 (Schmid 1994); available online at http://www.cis.uni-muenchen.de/~schmid/tools/TreeTagger/ (last access 2019.01.31).

Thomisticus and another much larger file based only on the Index Thomisticus; Ancient Greek with a parameter file based on PROIEL and Perseus data.[27] If one were designing a text analysis pipeline, one could easily capture its output on the command line, as with lemmatizers like Lemlat or LatMor. That said, wrappers (or programming interfaces that let you use code from one domain or language inside another) have been written so that TreeTagger can be used easily in Python, R, and JavaScript, among other languages, thus making it even easier to incorporate in custom-built pipelines.

4.2.4 Named Entity Recognition

Unlike lemmatization and POS tagging, named entity recognition (NER), or the systematic tagging of words in texts by category (so, *Roma* as a "location" or Σωκράτης as a "person") is not well-supported by standalone tools. With respect to Greek and Latin, a lack of annotated texts and robust language models underlies the problem.[28] All is not lost though as there is at least one (albeit longhand) way to retrieve annotations from Greek and Latin texts. Recogito is an online platform supporting the annotation of places, persons, and events through linked data.[29] While Recogito can provide automatic NER tagging (using Stanford CoreNLP), at present this feature is limited to English, French, German, and Spanish. That said, users can upload texts and annotate them by hand on the platform, and, with geographic entities in particular, the linked-data-enhanced advanced search does a good job with validating Greek and Latin annotations against online gazetteers.[30] These annotations can then be exported in a wide variety of data for integration into a makeshift pipeline.

---

27 Latin: (Brandolini n.d.; Passarotti n.d.); Ancient Greek: (Vatri and McGillivray n.d.). A complete list of parameter files for all supported languages can be found at http://www.cis.uni-muenchen.de/~schmid/tools/TreeTagger/#parfiles (last access 2019.01.31).

28 Erdmann et al. (2016) review the challenges of named entity recognition on Latin texts and suggest directions forward.

29 (Simon et al. 2017); available online at https://recogito.pelagios.org/ (last access 2019.01.31).

30 For example, Ὀλύμπια does not match a location entity automatically in the Recogito annotation interface, but the advanced search feature yields matches from the following gazetteers: GeoNames, the Digital Atlas of the Roman Empire, and Pleiades. Since the writing of this chapter, Recogito has introduced beta support for Latin NER.

4.2.5 Miscellaneous pipeline components

Digital philological work on Greek and Latin text raises the need for components that are encountered rarely, if ever, in pipelines for modern languages. So, for example, macronization and prosody tagging may be useful tasks for analyzing Latin literature and should be considered in the construction of a pipeline for this domain.[31] Accordingly, sites like Pede Certo, which allows users to upload a block of Latin poetry and return a fully scanned version, or Macronizer, which will add macrons algorithmically to a Latin text, should also be considered as potential components depending on the research question at hand.[32]

5 Introducing the Classical Language Toolkit

Chaining together a number of incompatible tools may prove useful for some digital philological work, but it can hardly be considered a permanent, robust solution for Greek and Latin text analysis. Extensively modifying the source code and developing resources for one of the existing frameworks is also a possibility. That said, the degree of customization that would be necessary for these languages also favors a new solution. This is where the Classical Language Toolkit (CLTK) fits into the digital philological landscape, addressing the desideratum of a complete text analysis pipeline for less-resourced historical languages such as Greek and Latin.[33]

CLTK is an open-source Python framework founded in 2014 by Kyle P. Johnson dedicated to NLP support for historical languages.[34] CLTK has

31 See Kirby (2016, 21–25) for a recent overview of this work. Prosody tagging is also an area of interest in Greek text analysis; see Papakitsos (2010).

32 Pede Certo: (Colombi 2011); available online at http://www.pedecerto.eu (last access 2019.01.31). Macronizer: (Winge 2015); available online at http://alatius.com/macronizer/ (last access 2019.01.31). Winge (2015) deserves special attention here. In addition to its primary discussion of vowel length and macronization, his thesis is also noteworthy as a review of available text analysis components for Latin. In order to complete his thesis work, Winge had to, as I write in the introduction, "cobble together separate, sometimes incompatible tools." His methodology section reveals the substantial challenges he encountered, even if his results demonstrate the excellent work that can be done, once challenges are overcome, with this sort of makeshift pipeline.

33 On less-resourced historical languages, see Piotrowski (2012, 85–86).

34 (Johnson et al. 2019). I have been a contributor to the project, in particular the Latin tools, since 2015.

made progress in recent years collecting corpora for a wide variety of historical languages covering ancient, classical, and medieval Eurasia and building out the basic resources to support these languages across the entire text analysis pipeline. Current offerings include all of the components described in Section 4 with the significant advantage that the components are all available within the same suite of NLP tools. Accordingly, starting from a plaintext file, researchers can tokenize, lemmatize, perform part-of-speech tagging and related morphological analysis, and so on without having to resort to external tools, web applications, or web services. In this respect, CLTK supports Greek and Latin in ways similar to how CoreNLP and NLTK support modern languages.

CLTK aims to meet the criteria of what Steven Krauwer calls the basic language toolkit, or BLARK.[35] The BLARK, according to Krauwer, consists of the "minimal set of language resources that is necessary to do any precompetitive research and education at all" in a given language. This includes but is not limited to 1. a collection of corpora, 2. lexical and grammatical resources, and 3. processing tools. CLTK offers all three:

1. CLTK has Ancient Greek corpora available based on the Perseus Digital Library, the First 1000 Years of Greek, and Lacus Curtius and Latin corpora available based on Perseus, The Latin Library, Lacus Curtius, and the Corpus Grammaticorum Latinorum among others, and has collected related resources such as treebanks from The Ancient Greek and Latin Dependency Treebank.[36]
2. CLTK has developed language models and lexical resources for probabilistic sentence tokenization, part-of-speech tagging, named entity recognition, and more for both languages.
3. As noted above, CLTK currently supports the following "processing tools": sentence tokenization, word tokenization, lemmatization, POS tagging, morphological tagging, basic named entity recognition, prosody tagging, and macronization. There are also modules available for other text analysis and NLP tasks such as syllabification, stemming, and phonological transcription, as well as experimental support for word embeddings using word2vec models trained on large collections of Greek and Latin text.[37]

35 (Krauwer 2003). See also, for Latin specifically, Passarotti (2010).
36 CLTK Corpora can be found in the main project GitHub repository at https://github.com/cltk (last access 2019.01.31). For The Ancient Greek and Latin Dependency Treebank, see Celano et al. (2014).
37 On word2vec and word embeddings, see Mikolov et al. (2013), and for their application to Latin-language text, see Bjerva and Praet (2015).

Development of the project is active; current offerings are continually being refined and new features are being added regularly.[38]

By establishing guidelines for a minimal toolkit, Krauwer hoped to "create better starting conditions for research, education and development in language [...] technology" and "facilitate porting of insights and expertise between languages, [...] ensuring interoperability and interconnectivity,"[39] all goals of CLTK.

One avenue of CLTK development currently under discussion with project administrators is the implementation of a data structure not unlike CoreNLP's "Annotation" object that would instantiate a complete text analysis pipeline for users upon initialization. With respect to the framework philosophies described in Section 3, CLTK has since its beginning more or less followed the NLTK's "pedagogical" approach; that is, a variety of potential components for each text processing task is made available to users and they learn which is best for their project. But the idea of getting users up and running quickly with a pre-defined pipeline of tried-and-true components, that is something closer to the CoreNLP approach, is certainly attractive, especially for lowering the barrier to entry for digital philological research and encouraging the adoption of CLTK as a general solution for text analysis on classical languages.

Another avenue of CLTK future development concerns the development, where possible, of wrappers for the tools mentioned in Section 4. Wrappers are a type of programming interface that allows you use code from one domain or language inside another without exposing the inner workings of the wrapped code. For example, I can write a Python wrapper for LatMor that uses Python commands to call this lemmatizer without users having to run LatMor themselves. The Python code sends inputs to LatMor (which is not written in Python), runs it as a background process, and stores the lemmatizer's output in a Python data structure for later use in a Python program. In this example, by including a CLTK wrapper for LatMor, we could enable its use as the lemmatization component in an otherwise CLTK-based pipeline. The advantage to users is clear. There is excellent work being done outside of CLTK in Greek and Latin

38 Krauwer also calls for BLARKs to include a "collection of skills" relating to effective use of the corpora and tools; CLTK provides extensive documentation and tutorials to support users in this way.

39 (Krauwer 2003, 1).

digital philology and users should be able to incorporate advances elsewhere in the field with as little friction as possible. As demonstrated in Section 4, a pipeline can always be assembled from disparate, incompatible components, but this is not the optimal situation. Wrappers can provide an intermediate solution through which effective pipelines can be constructed within the CLTK framework with a productive combination of both CLTK components and external components.

5.1 Access to the Classical Language Toolkit

CLTK is freely available and open source, published under the MIT license and hosted at https://github.com/cltk/cltk. More information about the project can be found at https://cltk.org/ and more information about the tools themselves, itemized by language, in the project's documentation at https://docs.cltk.org/en/latest/. Figure 2 shows the project's "pipeline" coverage at the time of writing.

6 Conclusion

Pipelines are an effective way to manage text analysis transformations and annotations and as such they are a defining feature of many NLP frameworks. Yet pipelines are only as good as the components (and the resources that components are based on, such as treebanks, lexica, grammars, and so on) that are available for a given language. At present, leading NLP frameworks like CoreNLP and NLTK support pipelines for a wide array of modern-language research, but options for classical-language research remain limited. This may change over time as Greek and Latin tools are incrementally developed for these frameworks. In the meantime, the Classical Language Toolkit fills the need for a comprehensive text analysis pipeline for these languages.

	Akkadian	Arabic	Bengali	Chinese	Classical Hindi	Coptic	Egyptian	Greek	Gujarati	Hebrew	Javanese	Latin	Malayalam	Marathi	Middle English	Middle High German	Middle Low German	Odia	Old Church Slavonic	Old English	Old French	Old Norse	Old Swedish	Pali	Persian	Prakrit	Punjabi	Sanskrit	Telugu	Tibetan	Urdu
Corpora	•	•	•	•	•	•	•	•	•	•	•	•	•	•	•	•	•	•	•	•	•	•	•	•	•	•	•	•	•	•	•
Stoplist	•	•			•			•				•		•	•	•				•	•	•					•	•			
Sentence Tokenizer								•				•									•										
Word Tokenizer	•	•						•				•			•	•					•	•						•			
Stemmer	•											•			•	•					•							•			
Lemmatizer								•				•									•										
POS Tagger								•				•					•			•		•									
Prosody Tagger								•				•				•						•									
NER								•				•									•										

Figure 2: This grid shows the current coverage of the Classical Language Toolkit's basic language resource kit. Included here are all of the historical languages for which CLTK has corpora available. With respect to coverage for text analysis tasks, note that Greek and Latin are the best supported, though there is ongoing, active development across the full range of historical languages.

Bibliography

Bird, S.; Klein, E.; Loper, E. (2015): Natural Language Processing with Python: Analyzing Text with the Natural Language Toolkit. https://www.nltk.org/book/ (last access 2019.01.31).

Bjerva, J.; Praet, R. (2015): "Word Embeddings Pointing the Way for Late Antiquity". In: Proceedings of the 9th SIGHUM Workshop on Language Technology for Cultural Heritage, Social Sciences, and Humanities (LaTeCH). Association for Computational Linguistics, 53–57.

Bodson, A.; Evrard, É. (1966): "Le programme d'analyse automatique du latin". Revue Informatique et Statistique dans les Sciences Humaines 1966:2, 17–46.

Brandolini, G. (n.d.): Latin Parameter File (TreeTagger). http://www.cis.uni-muenchen.de/~schmid/tools/TreeTagger/data/latin.par.gz (last access 2019.01.31).

Budassi, M.; Passarotti, M. (2016): "Nomen Omen. Enhancing the Latin Morphological Analyser Lemlat with an Onomasticon." In: Proceedings of the 10th SIGHUM Workshop on Language Technology for Cultural Heritage, Social Sciences, and Humanities (LaTeCH). Association for Computational Linguistics, 90–94.

Celano, G.G.A.; Crane, G.; Almas, B. (2014): The Ancient Greek and Latin Dependency Treebank. XML. https://perseusdl.github.io/treebank_data/ (last access 2019.01.31).

Chiarcos, C.; Khait, I.; Pagé-Perron, É.; Schenk, N.; Kandukuri, J.; Fäth, C.; Steuer, J.; McGrath, W.; Wang, J. (2018): "Annotating a Low-Resource Language with LLOD Technology: Sumerian Morphology and Syntax". Information 9:11, 1–16.

Clarke, J.; Srikumar, V.; Sammons, M.; Roth, D. (2012): "An NLP Curator (or: How I Learned to Stop Worrying and Love NLP Pipelines)". In: Proceedings of the 8th International Conference on Language Resources and Evaluation (LREC). European Language Resources Association, 3276–3283.

Colombi, E. (2011): Pede Certo. http://www.pedecerto.eu (last access 2019.01.31).

Crane, G. (1991): "Generating and Parsing Classical Greek". Literary and Linguistic Computing 6:4, 243–245.

Cunningham, H. (2002): "GATE, A General Architecture for Text Engineering". Computers and the Humanities 36:2, 223–254.

de Castilho, R.E.; Gurevych, I. (2014): "A Broad-coverage Collection of Portable NLP Components for Building Shareable Analysis Pipelines". In: Proceedings of the Workshop on Open Infrastructures and Analysis Frameworks for HLT. Association for Computational Linguistics and Dublin City University, 1–11.

Eger, S.; Gleim, R.; Mehler, A. (2016): "Lemmatization and Morphological Tagging in German and Latin: A Comparison and a Survey of the State-of-the-art". In: Proceedings of the 10th International Conference on Language Resources and Evaluation (LREC). European Language Resources Association, 23–28.

Eger, S.; Vor der Brück, T.; Mehler, A. (2015): "Lexicon-assisted Tagging and Lemmatization in Latin: A Comparison of Six Taggers and Two Lemmatization Methods". In: Proceedings of the 9th SIGHUM Workshop on Language Technology for Cultural Heritage, Social Sciences, and Humanities (LaTeCH). Association for Computational Linguistics, 105–113.

Erdmann, A.; Brown, C.; Joseph, B.; Janse, M.; Ajaka, P.; Elsner, M.; de Marneffe, M.-C. (2016): "Challenges and Solutions for Latin Named Entity Recognition." In: Proceedings of the Workshop on Language Technology Resources and Tools for Digital Humanities (LTD4DH). The COLING 2016 Organizing Committee, 85–93.

Ferrucci, D.; Lally, A. (2004): "UIMA: An Architectural Approach to Unstructured Information Processing in the Corporate Research Environment". Natural Language Engineering 10, 327–348.
Johnson, K.P.; Hollis, L.; Burns, PJ.; CLTK Development Community (2019): CLTK: The Classical Language Toolkit. Python. https://cltk.org (last access 2019.01.31).
Kirby, T. (2016): A Computational Method for Comparative Greek and Latin Prosimetrics. Thesis. Sarasota, FL: New College of Florida.
Krauwer, S. (2003): "The Basic Language Resource Kit (BLARK) as the First Milestone for the Language Resources Roadmap". In Proceedings of International Conference on Speech and Computer (SPECOM 2003). Moscow State Linguistic University, 8–15.
Loper, E.; Bird, S. (2002): "NLTK: The Natural Language Toolkit". In: Proceedings of the ACL-02 Workshop on Effective Tools and Methodologies for Teaching Natural Language Processing and Computational Linguistics, Volume 1. Stroudsburg, PA: Association for Computational Linguistics, 63–70.
Manning, C.; Surdeanu, M.; Bauer, J.; Finkel, J.; Bethard, S.; McClosky, D. (2014): "The Stanford CoreNLP Natural Language Processing Toolkit". In: Proceedings of 52nd Annual Meeting of the Association for Computational Linguistics: System Demonstrations. Association for Computational Linguistics, 55–60.
Marciniak, T.; Strube, M. (2005): "Beyond the Pipeline: Discrete Optimization in NLP". In: Proceedings of the Ninth Conference on Computational Natural Language Learning. Stroudsburg, PA: Association for Computational Linguistics, 136–143.
Mikolov, T.; Chen, K.; Corrado, G.; Dean, J. (2013): "Efficient Estimation of Word Representations in Vector Space". arXiv preprint arXiv:1301.3781.
Ouvrard, Y. (2010): "Collatinus, lemmatiseur et analyseur morphologique de la langue latine." Études de linguistique appliquée 158:2, 223–230.
Papakitsos, E.C. (2010): "Computerized Scansion of Ancient Greek Hexameter". Literary and Linguistic Computing 26:1, 57–69.
Passarotti, M. (n.d.): Latin IT Parameter File (TreeTagger). http://www.cis.uni-muenchen.de/~schmid/tools/TreeTagger/data/latinIT.par.gz (last access 2019.01.31).
Passarotti, M. (2010): "Leaving Behind the Less-Resourced Status. The Case of Latin through the Experience of the Index Thomisticus Treebank". In: 7th SaLTMiL Workshop on Creation and Use of Basic Lexical Resources for Less-Resourced Languages (LREC). European Language Resources Association, 27–32.
Passarotti, M.; Litta, E.; Budassi, M.; Ruffolo, P. (2017): "The Lemlat 3.0 Package for Morphological Analysis of Latin". In: Proceedings of the NoDaLiDa 2017 Workshop on Processing Historical Language. Linköping University Electronic Press, 24–31.
Piotrowski, M. (2012): Natural Language Processing for Historical Texts. San Rafael, CA: Morgan and Claypool.
Piperidis, S. (2012): "The META-SHARE Language Resources Sharing Infrastructure: Principles, Challenges, Solutions". In: Proceedings of the 8th International Conference on Language Resources and Evaluation. European Languages Resources Association (ELRA), 36–42.
Schmid, H. (1994): "Probabilistic Part-of-Speech Tagging Using Decision Trees". In: International Conference on New Methods in Language Processing. Stroudsburg, PA: Association for Computational Linguistics, 44–49.
Simon, R.; Barker, E.; Isaksen, L.; de Soto Cañamares, P. (2017): "Linked Data Annotation Without the Pointy Brackets: Introducing Recogito 2". Journal of Map & Geography Libraries 13:1, 111–132.

Springmann, U.; Schmid, H.; Najock, D. (2016): "LatMor: A Latin Finite-State Morphology Encoding Vowel Quantity". Open Linguistics 2:1.
Vatri, A.; McGillivray, B. (n.d.): Ancient Greek Parameter File (TreeTagger). http://www.cis.uni-muenchen.de/~schmid/tools/TreeTagger/data/ancient-greek.par.gz (last access 2019.01.31).
Verhagen, M.; Suderman, K.; Wang, D.; Ide, N.; Shi, C.; Wright, J.; Pustejovsky, J. (2016): "The LAPPS Interchange Format". In: Revised Selected Papers of the Second International Workshop on Worldwide Language Service Infrastructure. Cham: Springer, 33–47.
Wachsmuth, H. (2015): Text Analysis Pipelines: Towards Ad-hoc Large-Scale Text Mining. New York: Springer.
Whitaker, W. (1993): Words. http://archives.nd.edu/whitaker/wordsdoc.htm (last access 2019.01.31).
Winge, J. (2015): Automatic Annotation of Latin Vowel Length. Bachelor's Thesis in Language Technology. Uppsala University: Department of Linguistics and Philology.
Zeldes, A.; Schroeder, C.T. (2016): "An NLP Pipeline for Coptic". In: Proceedings of the 10th SIGHUM Workshop on Language Technology for Cultural Heritage, Social Sciences, and Humanities. Association for Computational Linguistics, 146–155.

Neil Coffee

Intertextuality as Viral Phrases: Roses and Lilies

Abstract: This article addresses the phenomenon of "viral intertextuality," or instances of distinct language that appear serially over multiple literary works. It demonstrates how current digital methods make instances of viral intertextuality much easier to detect. It argues for the value of reading such chains of similar phrases together. And it points toward possible improvements in digital detection and analysis methods that would further facilitate this kind of reading. The illustrative example is Vergil's description of Lavinia's blush at *Aeneid* 12.67–69, along with its predecessor and successor passages.

Introduction

Classicists often regard intertextuality as a relationship between two short pieces of text in two different works, following from the tradition of finding *loci similes*.[1] But not always. The study of window references, for one, considers a receiving text that borrows from another one, which itself borrows from a previous one.[2] The question this article poses is: what happens if we extend our consideration from the short span studied in a window reference to the long, varied life of a piece of language? Scholars of reception studies have proposed developing reception histories for individual texts.[3] Can we possibly, and profitably, develop long histories of short sections of text?

A simple answer would be, "yes," since scholars have already done it. Consider Sergio Audano's 2012 book, *Classici lettori di classici: da Virgilio a Marguerite Yourcenar*.[4] Audano traces the legacy of two Vergilian phrases. The first is Vergil's praise of a civilized life, with the phrase *inventas aut qui*

1 For an annotated bibliography on the study of classical intertextuality, see Coffee (2012). I would like to thank Cari Haas for her assistance in preparing this article. This work has been made possible in part by a major grant from the National Endowment for the Humanities Office of Digital Humanities for the Tesserae Intertext Service project.
2 (Thomas 1986, 188).
3 (Martindale 2006, 5). This whole volume (Martindale and Thomas 2006), along with Brockliss, Chaudhuri et al. (2012), provides good surveys of recent work on classical reception.
4 (Audano 2012).

Neil Coffee, State University of New York at Buffalo

https://doi.org/10.1515/9783110599572-011

vitam excoluere per artis (*Aen.* 6.663). Audano follows this phrase all the way down to the (non-hexametrical) motto on Nobel prize medals in medicine, sciences, and literature: *inventas vitam iuvat excoluisse per artas*. The second regards patriotism and the desire for glory: *vincet amor patriae laudumque inmensa cupido* (*Aen.* 6.823). Audano's study shows, among other things, the continuing influence and adaptation of Vergilian thought, as well as the elements of the Roman and classical traditions Vergil's thought conveys.

Can we undertake the sort of reading Audano performs with phrases less celebrated than those that appear on Nobel prize medals, where the imitation is more subtle? Can we do it on a still larger scale, ensuring that we capture (nearly) every instance, in a way that illuminates each of the contexts in which it appears? This article will argue "yes" here as well.

To demonstrate how we can readily find the recurrence of echoing phrases over many texts, this article will show how a suite of digital methods were employed that make such detection possible. Information about these methods can enable scholars who want to carry out such investigations, or at least provide a starting point for the discussion of best practices.

To demonstrate that this way of studying intertextuality can be enlightening, this article offers the case study of one echoing phrase, emanating again from the *Aeneid*. Here we will see a familiar type of influence, where subsequent poets are plainly borrowing from Vergil with nods to and variations on their predecessor. We will also consider the raw poetic materials from which Vergil forged his phrase. And we will discover instances where the phrase seems to pass beyond the realm of poetic imitation, or even generic language, to become a constellation of ideas and images that float free into the thought-world drawn on by later poets and even prose authors. In these last cases, the conceptual cluster remains distinctive, but the link to the *Aeneid* fades all but entirely.

Considering this wide swath of textual relationships together brings us to a model of intertextuality different from the common one mentioned above. It is a conception that does not always privilege the source text as generative of meaning, since the language at times breaks free from the source. What remains distinctive are some of the essential components of the phrase that, in this case, a canonical author forged, but carry on living, as it were, beyond a discernible relationship with that author's text, to become what we might call a viral phrase.[5]

5 In referring to these phrases as "viral" and in my section titles I use a biological metaphor to express the apparent vitality and adaptability of bits of language that persist. For a deeper exploration of the analogies and overlaps between biology, bioinformatics, and classical literature see Chaudhuri and Dexter (2017).

The successful genotype: *Aeneid* 12.67–69

In the closing book of Vergil's *Aeneid*, facing the defeat of the Latin forces at the hands of Aeneas and his Trojans, Turnus proposes to meet Aeneas in single combat to decide the conflict. Turnus's potential mother-in-law Amata bemoans his plan, implying that Turnus might lose by saying that she does not want to see Aeneas as her son-in-law. Standing nearby, Turnus's intended bride, Lavinia, blushes:

> Indum sanguineo veluti violaverit ostro
> siquis ebur, aut mixta rubent ubi lilia multa
> alba rosa, talis virgo dabat ore colores.
> *Aeneid* 12.67–69

> As when someone stains Indian ivory with crimson dye, or white lilies blush when mingled with many a rose – such hues her maiden features showed.[6]

Just what this blush means has been much debated. Lavinia could be a modest maiden blushing at the thought of marriage, especially to an enemy of her supposed betrothed. She could feel self-conscious because Turnus gazed at her, she believes she is causing strife, or she is in love with Turnus.[7] My focus in this article will not be on these causes, but rather on the imagery Vergil employs to describe Lavinia's blush, in particular the white and red flowers.[8]

This passage came to my attention through an exploratory search comparing Vergil's *Aeneid* and Prudentius' *Psychomachy* using the Tesserae multi-text tool. Tesserae provides a website that allows for various forms of intertextual search in Greek, Latin, and English.[9] The multi-text tool allows users to find similar phrases in two works, and then find *other* locations in a selected corpus where the common language from the first two texts also occurs. My search found that this passage of the *Aeneid* resembled one in the *Psychomachy*, as well as numerous others. To complement the Tesserae findings, I also searched the Packard Humanities Institute Latin corpus for similar words, employed the "Cited Loci of the Aeneid" tool published by Matteo Romanello, searched

6 Fairclough and Goold (2000) Loeb translation. All subsequent translations are from the Loeb series unless otherwise noted.

7 See Tarrant (2012, 105) *ad* 12.64–69.

8 There is a large and overlapping poetic tradition of contrasting the colors white and red (see references at Cairns (2005, 211 n. 33)). This piece will focus more closely on images with Vergil's two flowers.

9 For an overview of Tesserae and the related tools Fīlum, Musisque Deoque, and TRACER, see Coffee (2018).

Google Books, and consulted the 2012 commentary on *Aeneid* 12 by Richard Tarrant.[10] In the readings below, I will indicate in the notes where I found each parallel in order to demonstrate how search methods can be combined to develop readings of viral intertexts.

DNA fragments: Ennius and Propertius

In Latin literature prior to Vergil, we find disparate elements of his Lavinia image. Ennius had compared a blush (whose we don't know) to milk mixed with purple dye.[11]

> et simul erubuit ceu lacte et purpura mixta.
> *Annales* 361 Sk.
>
> And she blushed then like milk and crimson mingled.[12]

As in this case, sources prior to Vergil contrast the colors white and red, but do not connect lilies and roses with blushing.[13] This seems to be true of Greek literature as well. The two most common Greek words for lily (κρίνον) and rose (ῥόδον) appear together in only three passages prior to Ennius, two from Herodotus and one from Aristophanes. None of them describe love, blushing, or a maiden, but give the two flowers as undistinguished members of longer lists.[14]

Vergil therefore seems to have acted under his own inspiration when he took Ennius's description of a blush as contrasting red and white and rendered it as white lilies reflecting the red glow of roses. The flowers of course brought their

10 PHI: http://latin.packhum.org/browse: last access 2019.01.31. Cited Loci of the Aeneid: http://aeneid.citedloci.org: last access 2019.01.31. Google Books: https://books.google.com: last access 2019.01.31. Tarrant (2012, 106–107) *ad* 12.67–69. Tarrant naturally does not list all these parallels in his printed commentary: "citation of parallel passages [...] is confined to those that seemed most relevant or illuminating" (44).

11 Parallel noted by Tarrant (2012).

12 Translation adapted from Warmington (1988, frag. 352). Skutsch (1985, 526) *ad* Enn. *Ann.* 361 notes the *Aeneid* parallel.

13 As observed by Tarrant, who also notes another potential strand of influence. The Greek novelist Achilles Tatius describes a woman's reddened white cheek, alludes to the Homeric passage upon which the first part of Vergil's simile is based (*Iliad* 4.141–147), and then mentions roses (*Leucippe and Clitophon* 1.4.3). Cairns (2005, 204–205) suggests that the common elements in Vergil and Achilles Tatius stem from the Acontius and Cydippe episode of Callimachus's *Aetia*.

14 Herodotus's *Histories* 1.195.2, 2.92.4. Aristophanes *Clouds* 910–911. Passages found through a search for κρίν- and ῥόδ- in the Thesaurus Linguae Graecae.

own associations. Flowers had been used as an image to portray women's complexions, if not blushes. Catullus had described a bride as shining like a white chamomile or yellow poppy.[15] Lilies were associated with short lives: Horace, while drinking with his friends, muses on the *breve lilium* (*Carm.* 1.36.16).[16]

Vergil provides his own precedents for his use of lilies. In their two other appearances in the *Aeneid*, lilies are associated with death and passion. Other than in book 12, lilies appear only in the underworld in book 6. The souls on the banks of the Lethe are compared to bees on shining lilies (6.709). Then Anchises wishes to scatter lilies on the grave of Marcellus, though these lilies are purple (6.882–884). Elsewhere in Vergil's works, lilies are associated with love (*Bucolics* 2.45; 10.26, on Silvanus, approaching the forlorn Gallus) and prosperous farming (the Cilician farmer in Tarentum of *Georgics* 4.131).[17] The lilies used to describe Lavinia's blush might therefore bring connotations of fatality from the underworld that are appropriate for the fortunes of Turnus and the Latins, and, more distantly, erotic connotations from the *Bucolics*.

Vergil's other flower, the rose, is associated with youth, and with youthful love and death.[18] Philostratus writes that the rose is the garland of youth, a sentiment previously voiced by Anacreon, but, as Philostratus continues, neither love nor the rose last long.[19]

Another poet writing prior to Vergil does bring together lilies and reddish flowers in phrasing similar to Vergil's, though not in the context of blushing. Of Propertius's four books of elegies, the first seems to have been published around the year 30 BCE, eleven years before the publication of the *Aeneid* at Vergil's death in 19 BCE, and before Vergil had even completed his *Georgics*, in 29 BCE.[20] It seems likely then that Propertius composed the following passage of *Elegies* 1 before Vergil crafted the Lavinia description in the *Aeneid*.[21]

15 Catullus 61.185–188. Catullus's word for the white flower is *parthenice*, the meaning of which is not entirely clear. "Chamomile" is the suggestion offered by Quinn (1973, 274) ad 61.187.

16 Compare also Valerius Flaccus, *lilia per vernos lucent velut alba colores / praecipue, quis vita brevis totusque parumper / florent honor fuscis et iam Notus imminet alis* (6. 492–494). This and the words of Horace are cited by Allen (1956, 108).

17 (Tarrant 2012, 108) *ad* 12.68.

18 This paragraph is adapted from Allen (1956, 108).

19 Philostratus 55.34, Anacreon 44.9–11. On the brevity of life associated with roses, Allen gives further references to Horace *Odes* 2.3.13–14 and for Ausonius, Peiper (1886, 411).

20 Camps (1961, 5–7) puts the dates of the four books of elegies in order as 30, 26, 23, and 16 BCE.

21 Propertius passages from Books 1 and 3 discovered through the Tesserae search.

hic erat Arganthi Pege sub vertice montis,
grata domus Nymphis umida Thyniasin,
quam supra nulli pendebant debita curae
roscida desertis poma sub arboribus,
et circum irriguo surgebant lilia prato
candida purpureis mixta papaveribus.
Elegies 1.20.33–38

Here beneath the peak of the mountain Arganthus lay the well of Pege, the watery haunt so dear to Bithynia's nymphs, over which from lovely trees there hung dewy apples that owed nothing to the hand of man, and round about in a water-meadow sprang snowy lilies mingled with purple poppies.[22]

Propertius is describing the pond where Hylas will be abducted by the nymphs. He mentions white lilies and reddish flowers (here purple/red poppies) in an erotic context of loss (of Hylas by Hercules). He uses the word *mixta* that Vergil will later use and an equivalent for Vergil's *alba* – *candida*. The main differences are the absence of roses and blushing.

Propertius includes the roses, at least, in a poem in Book 2 of his *Elegies*.[23]

nec me tam facies, quamvis sit candida, cepit
(lilia non domina sint magis alba mea;
ut Maeotica nix minio si certet Hibero,
utque rosae puro lacte natant folia).
Elegies 2.3.9–12

Lilies would not surpass my mistress for whiteness; 'tis as though Maeotic snows were to strive with Spanish vermilion, or rose leaves floated amid stainless milk.

Book 2 was published around 25 BCE, six years before the posthumous publication of the *Aeneid* in 19 BCE, so Propertius could not have known the final form of Vergil's epic. Yet he goes on in Book 2 to show his awareness of the *Aeneid*, famously predicting that "something greater than the *Iliad* was being born."[24] We cannot say for certain, then, if Propertius knew the *Aeneid* 12 scene with Lavinia or, if so, in what form. What we can say is that his arrangement of floral imagery, though highly similar, does not have the elements and structure that many others would later imitate in Vergil. Propertius describes not the blush of his mistress, but only her complexion. He uses both flowers, but does not

22 Translations of Propertius adapted from Butler (1912).
23 Parallel between *Elegies* 2.3.9–12 taken from Enk (1962, 58) on Propertius *Elegies* 2.3.11–12.
24 *nescio quid maius nascitur Iliade*, 2.34.66.

combine them directly, instead picturing rose leaves floating in milk, borrowing the milk, it would seem, from Ennius.

To summarize the genesis of Vergil's floral metaphor for Lavinia's blush, then, we might say, with some simplification, that he took from Ennius the contrast between red and white to describe a blush and combined it with the contrast between red and white flowers from Propertius. Depending upon the order of influence, he may also have borrowed the rose from Propertius's Book 2.

By substituting lilies and roses to describe a blush for Ennius's milk and dye, Vergil fashioned a more compelling image. Not only does he capture the mingling of the colors, as Ennius had. In their beauty and fragility, the flowers convey the beauty and fragility of the maiden Lavinia. They also carry connotations of eroticism and mortality appropriate to a war over, among other things, a bride.

The first (non-) variation: Propertius

Book 3 of the *Elegies* appeared some four years prior to the full publication of the *Aeneid*. In this context, it is interesting to note that his mention of mixed flowers in *Elegies* 3 is diffuse in comparison with *Elegies* 1 and 2.

> illis munus erat decussa Cydonia ramo,
> et dare puniceis plena canistra rubis,
> nunc violas tondere manu, nunc mixta referre
> lilia vimineos lucida per calathos,
> et porter suis vestitas frondibus uvas
> aut variam plumae versicoloris avem.
> his tum blanditiis furtiva per antra puellae
> oscula silvicolis empta dedere viris.
>
> *Elegies* 3.13.27–32

Their offerings were Cydonian apples shaken from the bough; they gave baskets filled with purple brambles, now with their hands plucked violets, now brought home shining lilies mingled together in the maidens' paniers, and carried grapes clad in their own leaves or some dappled bird of rainbow plumage. Bought by such wooing were the kisses that girls gave their sylvan lovers in secret caves.

Here again we find, within an erotic context (wooing maidens in the Golden Age), *mixta* lilies that are (shining, *lucida*, therefore) white. Yet still there is no blush, the flowers joined with lilies are violets rather than roses, and there is no reflection, as in the description of Lavinia, of a surrounding context of blood (*sanguineo*) and loss. If Propertius was aware of Vergil's Lavinia passage, he does nothing to show it here, but seems to be just varying his own descriptions from *Elegies* 1 and 2.

Minor to major mutations I: Ovid

The complex potency of Vergil's image – a combination of beauty, eroticism, honor, shame, blood, and loss, conveyed at a critical moment within an instantly classic poem – made it irresistible to his successors. Subsequent authors at times created minor mutations, varying Vergil's language only slightly, inviting recollection of the *Aeneid.* They also created major mutations, where elements of Vergil's image remain, but the language is considerably more diffuse, to the point of obscuring any connection with the Augustan epic.

Ovid provides the earliest minor variation in his first set of published poems, the *Amores.*[25]

> at illi
> conscia purpureus venit in ora pudor,
> quale coloratum Tithoni coniuge caelum
> subrubet, aut sponso visa puella novo;
> quale rosae fulgent inter sua lilia mixtae,
> aut ubi cantatis Luna laborat equis,
> aut quod, ne longis flavescere possit ab annis,
> Maeonis Assyrium femina tinxit ebur.
> hic erat aut alicui color ille simillimus horum,
> et numquam visu pulchrior illa fuit.
> *Amores* 2.5.35–42

> But she – her guilty face mantled with ruddy shame, like the sky grown red with the tint of Tithonus's bride, or maid gazed on by her newly betrothed; like roses gleaming among the lilies where they mingle, or the moon in labor with enchanted steeds, or Assyrian ivory Maeonia's daughter tinctures to keep long years from yellowing it. Like one of these, or very like, was the color she displayed, and she was never fairer to look upon.[26]

Ovid is being characteristically subversive, taking Vergil's illustration of a chaste royal maiden's blush during a crucial council scene to describe his girlfriend's blush when he walks in on her cheating on him with another man. To achieve his humorous bathos, Ovid's passage must recall the *Aeneid.* He duly includes nearly every element of Vergil's floral image including the blush. He also includes the notion of dyeing from other half of Vergil's comparison.[27] To make the connection clearer still, Ovid includes the words *sponso* [...] *novo*, recalling the problem of Aeneas (or Turnus, if you like) as "new husband" for Lavinia.

25 Parallel discovered by the Tesserae search and noted by Boyd (1997, 113–114) and Tarrant (2012).

26 Showerman and Goold (1977) translation.

27 Which, again, Vergil drew from the description of a wounded Menelaus at *Iliad* 4.141–147.

In a subsequent work, his *Ars Amatoria*, Ovid switches to a Major Mutation. Using some of the same distinctive vocabulary, he simply revisits the topos of flowers as short-lived, applying it to the transience of beauty.[28]

> forma bonum fragile est, quantumque accedit ad annos
> fit minor, et spatio carpitur ipsa suo.
> nec violae semper nec hiantia lilia florent,
> et riget amissa spina relicta rosa.
>
> *Ars Amatoria* 2.113–116

> A frail advantage is beauty, that grows less as time draws on, and is devoured by its own years. Violets do not bloom forever, no lilies open-mouthed; when the rose is perished, the hard thorn is left behind.[29]

In contrast to the *Amores* passage, there is no blush, no whiteness to the lilies, a different placement of *rosa*, and an additional flower, *violae*. Yet the core DNA of Vergil's image remains: roses, lilies, and their association with loss. It seems less likely that Ovid is intentionally alluding to *Aeneid* 12.67–69 here than was the case in the *Amores*. Instead, it seems that the constellation of images and ideas has passed over into becoming poetic material that, while remaining distinctive, is a malleable formation that can be employed for other purposes even outside the genre of epic.

Ovid gives the material a final reworking in his *Metamorphoses*, in a eulogy for the centaur Cyllarus during the battle with the Lapiths. Ovid tells us that Hylonome, beloved of Cyllarus, used to adorn herself with rosemary, violets, roses, lilies.

> haec et blanditiis et amando et amare fatendo
> Cyllaron una tenet; cultus quoque, quantus in illis
> esse potest membris, ut sit coma pectine levis,
> ut modo rore maris, modo se violave rosave
> inplicet, interdum candentia lilia gestet.
>
> *Metamorphoses* 12.408–411

> She, by her coaxing ways, by loving and confessing love, alone possessed Cyllarus; and by her toilet, too, so far as such a thing was possible to such a form; for now she smoothed her long locks with a comb, now twined rosemary, now violets or roses in her hair, and sometimes she wore white lilies.[30]

28 Parallel found by the Tesserae search.

29 Mozley (1939) translation.

30 Miller and Gould (1984) translation.

Again in a context of loss, Ovid seems to be picking up his own formulation from the *Ars Amatoria* – he keeps the violets he added there and now further includes rosemary – but retains an additional Vergilian element by describing the lilies as "white" (*candentia*). Ovid's use again seems less a conscious allusion than a craftsman's repurposing of elements at the edge of the common stock of language.

Jumping species: Seneca's *Epistles*

The next possible echo is arguably the least connected to Vergil and so conversely the most interesting test case. It is the least connected in part because it is our only instance of a potential similarity with the *Aeneid* imagery in prose. It comes from Seneca's *Epistles*, when the philosopher is discussing the problems of luxury and decay.[31] Seneca objects that the ultra-wealthy of Rome work out elaborate tricks to grow roses and lilies in the winter, rather than waiting for them to grow naturally in the spring. He calls this practice *contra naturam*, a damning condemnation from a Stoic, signifying a practice both unnatural and morally wrong.

> non vivunt contra naturam qui hieme concupiscunt rosam fomentoque aquarum calentium et calorum apta mutatione bruma lilium, florem vernum, exprimunt?
>
> *Epistles* 122.8

> Do not people live contrary to Nature who crave roses in winter, or seek to raise a spring flower like the lily by means of hot-water heaters and artificial changes in temperature?[32]

At first sight, it strains belief that Seneca's condemnation of luxurious living has anything to do with Vergil's Lavinia description. He may mention the canonical botanical pairing, but the context seems entirely different. Not only is there no love, desire, or marriage. This is not even a poetic narrative, but a philosophical prose diatribe against decadence. Yet it is precisely the note of decadence, added to the mention of flowers, that this passage *does* share with the *Aeneid*. Roses, lilies, and loss were the core features of the image we identified in Ovid. All are here as well. For Seneca, the loss lies in the wasteful cultivating of flowers out of season and the decline of morality that leads to such extravagance.

31 Parallel found by the Tesserae search.
32 Gummere (1925) translation.

In all likelihood, so far from trying to reference the *Aeneid*, Seneca was not even thinking about the poem in composing this passage. Of course, Seneca was deeply conversant with the Roman poetic tradition and gladly reused elements of Augustan poetry, notably in his tragedies. In this case, that familiarity seems to have resulted in the unconscious employment of a template Vergil constructed, loosely presented in prose and in another thematic context. Vergil's poetic image has, as it were, jumped species from poetry, appearing now in literary prose.

Minor and major variations II: Statius's *Silvae*

In his *Silvae*, the Flavian poet Statius follows the same progression from allusion to conceptual reuse as Ovid, offering first a Minor and then a Major variation. The Minor Variation is found in *Silvae* 1.2, a wedding poem (*epithalamion*) in honor of Statius's patron Stella and his bride Violentilla.[33]

> tu modo fronte rosas, violis modo lilia mixta
> excipis et dominae nitidis a vultibus obstas.
> [...]
> non talis niveos tinxit Lavinia vultus
> cum Turno spectante rubet.
> *Silvae* 1.2.22–23, 244–245

> On your brow you receive now roses, now lilies mingled with violets, shielding your mistress's shining face.
> [...]
> Not so did Lavinia tinge her snow-white cheeks, blushing before Turnus's gaze.[34]

In this instance, Statius makes the connection with the *Aeneid* even more explicit than Ovid did in the *Amores*. Statius had already mentioned Aeneas's mother Venus at opening of poem (*genetrix Aeneia*, 11) among the goddesses who come to attend the wedding. Then at lines 22–23 he uses Vergil's exact words *lilia* and *mixta*, with the first in the same line position where it appeared in the *Aeneid*, and he slightly alters Vergil's *rosa* to *rosas*. In a parallel to Vergil's mention of the "white" (*alba*) rose, Statius just before these lines

33 Statius parallels found by the Tesserae search.
34 All Statius translations from Shackleton Bailey (2004).

mentions the "snowy limbs" (*niveos* [...] *artus*, 20) of the bride.[35] If the poetic debt were not clear enough, later in the poem Statius contrasts Violentilla explicitly with Lavinia blushing under the gaze of Turnus (244–245).

Statius nevertheless creatively reorients Vergil's imagery. Rather than describe the blush of the bride Violentilla, lilies and roses are woven into the garland worn by the bridegroom, Stella. Rather than present Violentilla as blushing red like Lavinia, Statius only refers to her as fair-skinned.

Why this reshuffling, apart from mere variation? While nodding to Vergil, Statius omits one core component of his predecessor's image, the notion of loss. This is because, in this celebratory poem, Statius must avoid summoning the shadow that hangs over Lavinia. He instead deploys Vergil's flowers to convey youth, beauty, and possibly fragility, all in a hopeful direction. Hence his dissociation of Violentilla from Lavinia's blush and the flowers. Unlike Lavinia, Violentilla is caught in no shameful or harrowing situation, but celebrates a joyful occasion. Although Statius must alter elements of Vergil's image, if he is to create a contrast between Violentilla and Lavinia, he must still evoke the image clearly. Hence his direct verbal reminiscences and explicit mention of Lavinia and Turnus.

In his second use of Vergil's image, Statius takes the exact opposite tack. His poem 3.3 is a consolation to his patron Claudius Etruscus for the death of his father. In the poem, Statius touches on the death of Etruscus's mother when Etruscus was still a very young child, and describes her passing in familiar terms.

> sed media cecidere abrupta iuventa
> gaudia florentesque manu scidit Atropos annos,
> qualia pallentes declinant <u>lilia</u> culmos
> pubentesque <u>rosae</u> primos moriuntur ad austros,
> aut ubi venia novis exspirat purpura pratis.
> *Silvae* 3.3.126–130

> But your joys fell earthwards, broken off in mid youth, and Atropos's hand severed your blooming years, as <u>lilies</u> droop their paling stems and <u>roses</u> die at the first sirocco or as when vernal purple expires in fresh meadows.

The verbal reminiscences here are limited to the mention of lilies and roses, with no supplementary words regarding mixing or whiteness, nor mention of *Aeneid* characters. The context of marriage and desire is also absent. What

35 The manuscript also has *niveis* in place of the *nitidis* printed here, another possible parallel, but I follow the Loeb of Shackleton Bailey (2004), who finds *niveis* after *niveos* just above implausible and so emends to *nitidis*.

remains again is the core conceptual cluster: lilies, roses, and the concept of loss. The death of a young mother is compared to flowers drooping in the heat of summer. As in Ovid's second two uses of Vergil's image, this hardly seems an instance of allusion, but rather the reappearance of the conceptual complex. Like Ovid, once he had used Vergil's image explicitly, Statius seems to have absorbed it and redeployed its core, perhaps unconsciously, out of a feeling for its existing resonances.[36]

Crossing the language barrier? Heliodorus's *Aethiopica*

As Vergil's image spread, it eventually crossed from Latin into other languages, including eventually, as we will see, 17th-century English poetry. Much closer to Vergil's day, we find a possible effect of his image in the work of a Greek novelist, Heliodorus, who seems to have published his *Aethiopica* sometime around 230 CE.[37] Any use Heliodorus makes of Vergil's Lavinia metaphor is necessarily a Major Mutation, since it is rendered in Greek.

The *Aethiopica* tells the story of two young lovers, Theagenes and Chariclea, and the long series of tribulations they suffered in Greece, Egypt, and Ethiopia before their eventual marriage. According to Tarrant, who himself cites Ewen Bowie, there are two passages in the *Aethiopica* that "interweave [...] V[ergil]'s simile with its main Iliadic model."[38] The first is a description of the beauty of Theagenes, despite his having been wounded.

---

36 Statius's contemporary Martial employs the motif as well. Martial writes of a new bride named Cleopatra, who flees from her over-eager husband to a pool: *lucebat, totis cum tegeretur aquis: condita sic puro numerantur lilia vitro, sic prohibet tenuis gemma latere rosas, Epigrams* 4.22.4–6 ("Brightly she showed, though covered by the o'erlapping water. So, shut in pellucid glass, lilies may be counted, so crystal forbids tender roses to lurk hidden." (Ker 1968) Loeb translation.). Here again we find the associations of eroticism, innocence (fleeing the marriage bed), purity (new bride, water), and violation. Herrick picks up Martial's image in his "Lily in a Crystal": "You have beheld the smiling rose / When virgins' hands have drawn / O'er it a cobweb-lawn / And here you see this lily shows, / Tomb'd in a crystal stone, / More fair in this transparent case / Than when it grew alone / And had but single grace" (I owe the Herrick reference to Prof. A.E.B. Coldiron.)

37 See *Oxford Classical Dictionary* vol. 4 under "Heliodorus," 654.

38 Tarrant (2012) *ad Aen.* 12.67–69, 107. The *Iliad* 4 parallel with Menelaus noted above seems to be in play as well.

> ἤνθει δὲ καὶ ἐν τούτοις ἀνδρείῳ τῷ κάλλει, καὶ ἡ παρειὰ καταρρέοντι τῷ αἵματι φοινιττομένη λευκότητι πλέον ἀντέλαμπεν.
>
> Even in this wounded condition he bloomed with a manly beauty, and his cheek, growing crimson from the blood flowing down it, gleamed by contrast with a greater whiteness.[39]
>
> *Aethiopica* 1.2.3

Here we have the contrast between red and white, representing blood and white skin of a lover with thoughts of marriage, and also the sense of possible loss through death, though Theagenes is not in fact killed. Yet loss is the only one of the canonical core elements Vergil's image to appear. There is no mention of flowers, much less lilies, roses, or their mixture.

The second passage mentioned by Tarrant describes the reaction of the nephew of the Ethiopian king Hydaspes to the king's decision to marry him to Chariclea.

> ὁ δὲ Μερόηβος πρὸς τὴν ἀκοὴν τῆς νύμφης ὑφ᾽ ἡδονῆς τε ἅμα καὶ αἰδοῦς οὐδὲ ἐν μελαίνῃ τῇ χροιᾷ διέλαθε φοινιχθείς, οἱονεὶ πρὸς αἰθάλην τοῦ ἐρυθήματος ἐπιδραμόντος.
>
> At the mention of the 'bride' Meroebos, at once from pleasure and embarrassment, went visibly crimson even with his black skin, the blush running over his face like a flame running over ash.
>
> *Aethiopica* 10.24.2

Here again, we have elements of Vergil's image, in this case including an actual blush and red skin. Lacking still is any mention of flowers, or, in this case, even of loss.

Of all of the instances considered so far, these seem least indebted to Vergil's Lavinia image, rather than just to Homer or generic descriptions of bleeding or blushing. If nothing else, however, the judgment of Tarrant and Bowie that there was a genetic line from Vergil to Heliodorus makes these passages worth keeping under consideration.

Missing genomes: Claudian's *De raptu Proserpinae*

Back in the world of Roman poetry, Claudian, a poet of the late 4th and early 5th centuries CE, makes much more explicit use of Vergil's image, but

39 Translations of Heliodorus from Tarrant (2012, 107) *ad Aen.* 12.67–69.

nevertheless leaves a curious gap. In his poem on the rape of Persephone, Claudian describes how Zeus gives Venus the task of luring the divine maiden out into the fields so Pluto can abduct her. Persephone is alone at home weaving when Venus appears, along with Pallas and Diana, and the maiden blushes at the sight of the goddesses.[40]

> niveos infecit purpura vultus
> per liquidas succensa genas castaeque pudoris
> inluxere faces: non sic decus ardet eburnum,
> Lydia Sidonio quod femina tinxerit ostro.
> *De raptu Proserpinae* 1.272–275

> A glowing blush that mantled to her clear cheeks suffused her fair countenance and lit the torches of stainless purity. Not so beautiful even the glow of ivory which a Lydian maid has stained with Sidon's scarlet dye.[41]

Claudian draws from Vergil, and Homer before him (*Il.* 4.141–147), for his mention of ivory (*decus* [...] *eburnum* for Vergil's *ebur*) and dye (*ostro*). He adds a woman performing the dyeing, an element borrowed either from Ovid's *Amores* passage or the original Homeric context. We also have a blush, here that of Persephone. And there is a looming sense of loss from the imminent rape and abduction of Persephone comparable to the cloud of uncertainty hanging over Lavinia. Absent, however, is any mention of lilies and roses; Claudian brings together nearly every element *but* the canonical flowers. Why?

It is possible that, with the appearance of numerous versions of Vergil's image in the intervening centuries, Claudian felt the roses and lilies motif could only be refreshed with a major variation, in this case omitting the flowers. He may simply have preferred the dyeing metaphor to the floral one. Or he may have wanted to preserve the effect of flower imagery for the scene of Persephone's abduction. In that scene, the fields are bright with flowers as Persephone and the other goddess race to gather them (2.88–150). And we do indeed find lilies and roses there (*lilia* [...] *rosis*, 2.128–130), though in a landscape also filled with violets, marjoram, privet, and hyacinth. Despite the missing flowers, the elements Claudian employs in his description of Persephone's blush sufficed to make his image vivid and signal his awareness of the tradition.

---

40 This passage is noted by Skutsch (1985, 526) *ad* Enn. *Ann.* 361 and Tarrant (2012, 107) *ad Aen.* 12.67–69.
41 Platnauer (1922) translation.

Blending species: Prudentius's *Psychomachy*

Around the same time Claudian was writing *De raptu Proserpinae*, the Christian poet Prudentius created his *Psychomachy*, a poem in hexameters describing the clash between virtues and vices within the soul. These battles consume the bulk of his 915-line poem, but once the various virtues defeat their vicious counterparts, they work together to build a temple that Christ can visit when he visits to earth. Ruling in that temple is Wisdom (*Sapientia*), who presides over humanity and creates laws to keep it safe. In ten lines toward the end of the poem, Prudentius describes the scepter Wisdom holds.[42]

> in manibus dominae [Sapientiae] sceptrum non arte politum
> sed ligno vivum viridi est, quod stirpe reciso,
> quamuis nullus alat terreni caespitis umor,
> fronde tamen viret incolumi, tum sanguine tinctis
> intertexta rosis candentia lilia miscet
> nescia marcenti florem submittere collo.
> huius forma fuit sceptri gestamen Aaron
> floriferum, sicco quod germina cortice trudens
> explicuit tenerum spe pubescente decorem
> inque novos subito tumuit virga arida fetus.
> reddimus aeternas, indulgentissime doctor,
> grates, Christe, tibi, meritosque sacramus honores
> ore pio; nam cor vitiorum stercore sordet.
>
> Prudentius, *Psychomachy* 879–890

> In the hands of the sovereign [Wisdom] is a scepter, not finished with craftsman's skill but a living rod of green wood; severed from its stock, it draws no nurture from moist earthly soil, yet puts forth perfect foliage and with blooms of blood-red roses intermingles white lilies that never droop on withering stem. This is the sceptre that was prefigured by the flowering rod that Aaron carried, which, pushing buds out of its dry bark, unfolded a tender grace with burgeoning hope, and the parched twig suddenly swelled into new fruits. We give to Thee, O Christ, Thou tenderest of teachers, unending thanks and offer to Thee the honour that is thy due with loyal lips – for our heart is foul with the filth of sin.[43]

Prudentius's word *intertexta* tempts the modern reader as a possible hint at his borrowings, but we hardly need the invitation, since the Christian poet uses words nearly identical to Vergil's to describe mixed roses and white lilies as well as blood. Prudentius draws further attention to his intertextuality – or, rather, biblical precedent – by simply telling us that Wisdom's flowering

---

42 Parallel found by the Tesserae search.

43 Thompson (1949) translation.

scepter was prefigured by the staff of Aaron, signifying burgeoning hope, a reference to *Numbers* 17.8. For the classical reader, the blooming scepter also recalls the scene in the *Iliad* when Achilles swore he would not fight for the Achaeans until the scepter he was holding came alive and began to grow new shoots (*Il.* 1.234–239).

The new Christian context gives Prudentius the opportunity to take the canonical image in a wholly new direction. As part of his program of repurposing classical conceptions and classical hexameter poetry to convey the messages of Christianity, Prudentius reverses the associations of loss in Vergil's image to make roses and lilies a sign of resurgence. The sprouting flowers illustrate the establishment and perpetual vigor of the reign of Wisdom and the virtues under the eye of Christ on earth. More broadly, they allude to the resurrection of Christ, the rebirth he offers to his followers, and, especially for Prudentius the poet, the rebirth of elements of classical culture into the new Christian tradition.

Prudentius's project of poetic conversion extends to the details of the image he lays claim to. In the *Aeneid*, beyond describing a blush, the red and white of the roses and lilies connotes the innocence of Lavinia, the blood of her blush, and, combined with the word "blood-colored" (*sanguineo*), the past and future bloodshed caused by her suitors. For Prudentius, the roses and lilies also evoke the innocence and blood – those of Christ, as two central elements of his story. Prudentius in fact uses the word "blood" (*sanguine*) just before his mention of the flowers, and just after the description of Wisdom concludes his poem with praise of Christ, beginning with lines 888–890 quoted here. Vergil's flowers are used not just to convey the loss of innocence and blood, but their redemption.[44]

An isolated atavistic strain: Anonymous

In his *Ars Grammatica*, the 4th-century CE grammarian Marius Victorinus, quotes the following unattributed line as an example of the formation of the pentameter:

---

44 Martha Malamud points out to me a further, intratextual reversal as well. Earlier in the poem, the vice Luxuria leaves a banquet for war with the Virtues, stepping on flowers (*ebria calcatis ad bellum floribus ibat*, 320, "trampling on the flowers, she was making her drunken way to the war," Thomson (1949) trans., adapted) and then attacks the Virtues with violets and rose petals (*uiolas lasciua iacit foliisque rosarum / dimicat et calathos inimica per agmina fundit*, 326–327, "she throws violets and fights with rose-leaves, scattering baskets of flowers over her adversaries."). The appearance of roses and lilies on the staff of Wisdom therefore also reclaims for Christianity flora previously associated in the *Psychomachy* with decadence.

> [...] lactea sanguineis lilia mixta rosis.[45]
>
> [...] milk-white lilies mixed with blood-red roses.

Unfortunately, lacking the author and the rest of the poem, we know nothing about the context of the fragment, including whether it involved love or loss. What we can say is that the author was clearly attempting to out-Vergil Vergil. The poet packed as many of the by-then-canonical words into one line as possible. Vergil put his roses and lilies on different lines. In the *Amores*, Ovid put the flowers on the same line, together with the word *mixta*, but didn't use Vergil's word for "bloody" or his concept of whiteness. In a tour-de-force distillation, our poet manages to fit "lilies," "roses," "mixed," "milky-white," and "blood-red" all into one line, even giving up one hexameter foot to jam them into a pentameter. In so doing, the poet stylishly mints a hyper-canonical version of Vergil's own canonical image.

Autochthonous blooms among the Church Fathers

At this point, it might be useful to consider an example that seems, as much as possible, unrelated to Vergil's image while still containing some of its elements, so that we can get a sense of where the boundary of connection might lie. The church father John Chrysostom, writing in Greek, shows a fondness for the pairing of roses and lilies. In describing a reading from the New Testament, Chrysostom says it seems to him like a great variety of flowers, roses, violets, and lilies (Καθάπερ γὰρ ἐν λειμῶνι πολλὰ καὶ ποικίλα ὁρῶ τῆς ἀναγνώσεως τὰ ἄνθη, καὶ πολλὴν μὲν τὴν ῥοδωνιὰν, πολλὰ δὲ τὰ ἴα, καὶ οὐκ ἐλάττω τὰ κρίνα).[46] Likewise, in writing in praise of the martyr St. Ignatius, Chrysostom says that it is hard to know where to begin in praising the great and manifold works of the saint, because it is as if we were in a meadow, seeing roses, violets, lilies, and various other flowers, and we don't know where to look first (καὶ πολλὴν μὲν τὴν ῥοδωνιὰν ἰδὼν, πολὺ δὲ τὸ ἴον, καὶ τὸ κρίνον τοσοῦτον, καὶ ἕτερα δὲ ἠρινὰ ἄνθη ποικίλα τε καὶ διάφορα).[47] The one link with Vergil is in the appearance of the two canonical flowers. Beyond that, even apart from the different language, there is no discernible verbal or thematic similarity. At most, there is the remote

45 (Keil 1961, 105 Vol. 6). This line was found with a PHI search for "ros" near "lili."
46 *Scr. Eccl. Ad populum Antiochenum*, Migne (1857) Vol. 49, 17 lines 22–23.
47 *Scr. Eccl. In sanctum Ignatium martyrem*, Migne (1857) Vol. 50, 587, line 46–48.

possibility that Vergil's influence is felt just in mention of the two flowers together. If so, it is the diminution of a wave at one end of the sea into one of countless ripples at the other end.

Medieval mutation: Carmina Burana

Among the vast corpus of medieval Latin, we find an echo indebted to Statius's optimistic version of the trope. Within the *Carmina Burana* collection, a short poem recalls the *Pervergilium Veneris* in its celebration of the springtime renewal of nature and stirring of erotic passion. The poem contains the lines:

> dulcius est carpere
> iam lilium cum rosa,
> dulcissimum est ludere
> cum virgine formosa.[48]
>
> It is sweeter still to pluck
> The lily with the rose,
> Yet sweetest to play
> With a shapely maiden.[49]

The lily and the rose are paired as an expression of untroubled joy connected with nature and erotic delights, with no trace of a blush, much less overtones of loss. This author has essentially crossed Vergil's image with the natural wonder and vigor expressed not only in the *Pervigilium Veneris* but also in the opening of Lucretius's *De rerum natura*.

Renaissance rebirth: Vida's *Christiad*

From this free, medieval adaptation of the erotic strain in Vergil's image, it is not surprising that a Renaissance poet would return quite deliberately *ad fontes*. In his *Christiad*, published in 1535, Marcus Hieronymus Vida produced an epic poem in six books narrating the passion of Christ. In his Christian answer to the great Roman epic, Vida borrowed substantially from the *Aeneid*.[50]

---

48 (Schmeller 1847, 181). I came upon this passage in Allen (1956, 93–111), which I discovered through a JSTOR search for "rose" and "lil."

49 My translation.

50 Di Cesare (1964, 114) writes that "the style [of the poem] seems almost cento," though he also notes (145) that "there is no example in the entire *Christiad* of a line, or even a half-line, lifted bodily out of the *Aeneid*."

In his epic, Vida uses Vergil's description of Lavinia daringly to portray the blush of none other than the Virgin Mary. Joseph, pleading with Pilate to spare Christ, tells the story of Christ's origins, including how he himself was once a suitor to Mary, who blushed before him and the other assembled suitors: *pudor ora pererrans / cana rosis veluti miscebat lilia rubris* (3.179–180, "a blush flashed across her pale face like red roses among lilies").[51] As with Prudentius, there is no immediate connotation of loss or violence, though the story is told by Joseph, who will fail in his efforts to keep Christ from torture and crucifixion. But Vida's language and the context of proposed marriage unmistakably recall Vergil's scene together with its long legacy.

Like Prudentius, Vida used classical poetic materials to enact a move from pagan confusion to Christian enlightenment.[52] By Vida's day, however, Christianity had left far behind its conflicts with classical culture. Christian culture could securely appropriate the products of earlier Greek and Roman civilizations with no fear that such valorization would abet a reversion to paganism. In light of *Eclogue* 4, to which Vida elsewhere alludes, Vergil himself had long been rehabilitated as an enlightened pagan precursor of Christianity.[53]

In this context, Vida's daring move seems not that daring at all. In the time of Prudentius, implicitly comparing the mother of god to the mythical wife of the founder of pagan Rome, Lavinia, could have been a touchy gesture, because of greater familiarity with the pre-Christian literary tradition and its continued cultural weight. But Vida fears no charge of blasphemy. His association of Mary with Lavinia only adds resonance and authority to his portrayal of the mother of Christ.[54]

---

51 I discovered this passage in Bruére (1966, 39) via the JSTOR search for "rose" and "lil." Translation from Gardner (2009).

52 Warner (2005, 134) writes that "the Aeneid supplies the means for the *Christiad's* readers to mark their progress from Vergilian falsehoods to Christian Truth."

53 (Kallendorf 1995, 59–62).

54 In addition to this example from Renaissance epic in Latin, Pramit Chaudhuri points out to me *per litteras* several instances of the roses and lilies topos in vernacular Italian epic of the period. In Boiardo's *Orlando furioso*, the poet uses the phrase "Tra le purpuree rose e i bianchi gigli" (6.22) to describe a locus amoenus. He uses it as well to describe female beauty (7.28, 10.95, 10.96), in the last case with the lily changed for the white privet, as it is also in 7.11, which resembles Vergil's lines most closely. Cf. 27.121, 32.13. Tasso in his *Gerusalemme liberata* has related phrases at 4.30 and 19.67.

Metaphysical metamorphosis: Marvell "The Nymph Complaining for the Death of Her Fawn"

The 17th-century English metaphysical poet Andrew Marvell is perhaps most famous for his poem "To His Coy Mistress." He was also well-versed in classical literature, writing some of his earliest poems in Greek and Latin and even publishing "A Horatian Ode upon Cromwell's Return from Ireland."[55]

Among Marvell's better-known poems is his "Nymph Complaining for the Death of Her Fawn."[56] In 122 lines, a nymph laments the death of a fawn given to her by her beloved, a hunter named Sylvio who has abandoned her. She vows to bury her fawn and die soon after, having first constructed a marble tomb with a statue of herself weeping with the fawn at her feet.

In the springtime, the nymph tells us, the fawn stayed only in her garden, which was "so with roses overgrown, / And lilies, that you would it guess / To be a little wilderness" (71–74). The small white deer would nearly disappear in the white lily beds, and it would eat the roses "until its lips e'en seem to bleed" (84), after which it would again lay "its pure virgin limbs" in "whitest sheets of lilies cold" (89–90). "Had it lived long," she imagines, "it would have been / lilies without, roses within" (91–92).

Marvell does not use Vergil's Latin words, nor even his hexameter. Nor does he make any mention of a blush. Nevertheless, his scene belongs within the tradition Vergil began, not only because Marvell surely encountered it in his Latin reading. The English poet uses the marked pairing of roses and lilies along with mention of blood. And he joins these terms to the key themes of love and loss: the nymph's love for Sylvio and her fawn, and the (symbolically related) loss of both. The death of the fawn separately parallels the loss of the nymph's chastity and innocence, not least because of the imagery of the arrow piercing of the "virgin" fawn and drawing blood.

In the context of Lavinia's blush, despite the toll of the war to that point, the threat of blood and loss hang imminent. In Marvell's poem they are realized: the

55 On his Latin poetry, see Haan (2003). In his *Faerie Queene*, the first three books of which were published in 1590, Spenser had already taken over Vergil's imagery for blushing more than once: "And in her cheekes the vermeill red did shew / Like roses in a bed of lillies shed" (Book 2 Canto 3); "A great increase in her faire blushing face; As roses did with lillies interlace" (Book 5 Canto 3) (I owe these references to Prof. A. E. B. Coldiron).

56 Vergilian connection discovered by the JSTOR search, which led to Allen (1956), who discusses the theme of flowers and loss that Marvell draws from antiquity.

bloodshed of the fawn's death is described, that of the nymph foreshadowed in her contemplated suicide. From all appearances, it would seem that Marvell had thoroughly absorbed, from Vergil or others, the associations of the two flowers, love, and loss, which he then translated from Latin epic into a romantic English idyll, further sharpening their symbolic associations.[57]

Conclusions: poetics

With his description of Lavinia's blush, Vergil created a lasting image that many other poets and authors took up for their own. Beauty, fragility, hope, loss, shame: all were combined into a powerful, flexible, and reusable formula. Some poets kept the core ideas. Ovid treated them with levity in his *Amores*. Marvell extended them for his own romanticizing purposes. Others retained the poignancy of the image but made it drive a positive message, as in Statius's celebration of marriage or the redemption of humanity and the classical tradition celebrated by Christian authors.

Among another set of authors, distinctive features of Vergil's image remain, but seem to derive from a larger conceptual and poetic vocabulary independent of Vergil or even to epic genre. In the *Carmina Burana*, the core concept of loss is simply deleted and the flowers used to express an erotic, blooming context that is fully joyful. In the case of Seneca's letters, we have simply the two flowers associated with loss through decadence. The image has lost its tie with the tradition and moved out in the wider world of writing where authors have found it.

Conclusions: methods

This study illustrates how we can use modern digital search tools to delineate a full, if not necessarily comprehensive, tradition of literary inheritance at the level of individual images and phrases. If we want to pursue this kind of research, we may hope in the future to streamline the process, so that rather than cobbling together passages with all the tools and sources employed here, scholars can more quickly map out a micro-tradition.[58]

57 Marvell's contemporary John Ford, in his 1633 play *'Tis Pity She's a Whore*, Act 1 Scene 3 writes of a blush "The lily and the rose, most sweetly strange, / upon your dimpled cheeks do strive for change" (Enk (1962, 58) on Propertius *Elegies* 2.3.11–12).

58 See Coffee (2018, 205–223) for ideas about how this work might proceed.

But do we want to pursue this kind of research? I would again answer "yes." It offers significant advantages to understanding our texts: we can read any point in the micro-tradition relative to its predecessors and successors. To take the case of Prudentius, we find he was not only drawing his image of roses and lilies from Vergil, but also incorporating a long tradition of the reworking of Vergil's image. By reinterpreting a whole strand of literary inheritance, however small, Prudentius created an even more powerful gesture of subsuming and appropriating the classical tradition than had he only reworked a Vergilian passage. Looking forward, we find Prudentius disseminating a positive version of the motif later taken up by the Christian author Vida and possibly behind the secular celebrations of love of the *Carmina Burana*.

Another possibility opened up is to take the viral intertext itself as an object of study. What was it about Vergil's image that made it so durable and adaptable? Was its persistence predicated on the canonicity of Vergil's epic, or could language from less canonical works become similarly pervasive? How far out into the wider world of Latin, and other languages, can we productively trace the movement of a viral intertext? Somewhere around the border between figured and ordinary language, as we saw with Seneca? Answers to questions like these could give us a more concrete understanding of the functional dynamics of intertextuality. That would in turn allow us to measure the artistry of individual authors against better-articulated standards of what was possible within a genre or language.

Bibliography

Allen, D.C. (1956): "Marvell's 'Nymph'". English Literary History 23:2, 93–111.
Audano, S. (2012): Classici lettori di classici: Da Virgilio a Marguerite Yourcenar. Foggia: Il Castello.
Boyd, B.W. (1997): Ovid's Literary Loves: Influence and Innovation in the Amores. Ann Arbor: University of Michigan Press.
Brockliss, W.; Chaudhuri, P.; Lushkov, A.H.; Wasdin, K. (eds.) (2012): Reception and the Classics. An Interdisciplinary Approach to the Classical Tradition. Yale Classical Studies 36. Cambridge: Cambridge University Press.
Bruére, R.T. (1966): "Review Article: Virgil and Vida." Classical Philology 61:1, 21–43.
Butler, H.E. (ed.) (1912): Propertius. London: Heinemann.
Cairns, F. (2005): "'Lavinia's Blush' (Virgil Aeneid 12.64–70)". In: D.L. Cairns (ed.): Body Language in the Greek and Roman Worlds. Swansea: Classical Press of Wales, 195–213.
Camps, W.A. (ed.) (1961): Propertius Elegies: Book I. Cambridge: Cambridge University Press.
Chaudhuri, P.; Dexter, J.P. (2017): "Bioinformatics and Classical Literary Study". Journal of Data Mining and Digital Humanities. arXiv:1602.08844 [cs.CL].

Coffee, N. (2012): "Intertextuality in Latin Poetry." In: D. Clayman (ed.): Oxford Bibliographies in Classics. New York: Oxford University Press.
Coffee, N. (2018): "An Agenda for the Study of Intertextuality". TAPA 148:1, 205–223.
Di Cesare, M.A. (1964): Vida's Christiad and Vergilian Epic. New York: Columbia University Press.
Enk, P.J. (ed.) (1962): Sex. Propertii elegiarum, liber secundus. Lugduni Batavorum: A.W. Sijthoff.
Fairclough, H.R.; Goold, G.P. (eds.) (2000): Aeneid. Books 7-12. Appendix Vergiliana. Cambridge, MA: Harvard University Press.
Gardner, J. (ed.) (2009): Marco Girolamo Vida: Christiad. I Tatti Renaissance Library. Cambridge, MA: Harvard University Press.
Gummere, R.M. (1925): Seneca. Epistles 93–124. Volume 6. Cambridge, MA: Harvard University Press.
Haan, E. (2003): Andrew Marvell's Latin Poetry: From Text to Context. Bruxelles: Latomus.
Kallendorf, C. (1995): "From Virgil to Vida: The Poeta Theologus in Italian Renaissance Commentary". Journal of the History of Ideas 56:1, 41–62.
Keil, H. (1961): Grammatici latini ex recensione Henrici Keilii. Hildesheim: G. Olms.
Ker, W.C.A. (1968): Martial Epigrams. Volume 1. Cambridge, MA: Harvard University Press.
Martindale, C. (2006): "Thinking through Reception". In: C. Martindale; R.F. Thomas (eds.): Classics and the Uses of Reception. Oxford: Blackwell, 1–13.
Martindale, C.; Thomas, R.F. (eds.) (2006): Classics and the Uses of Reception. Oxford: Blackwell.
Migne, J.P. (1857): Patrologia Graeca. Paris: Migne.
Miller, F.J.; Goold, G.P. (eds.) (1984): Ovid Metamorphoses Books IX-XV. Cambridge, MA: Harvard University Press.
Mozley, J.H. (ed.) (1939): Ovid II: The Art of Love and Other Poems. Cambridge, MA: Harvard University Press.
Peiper, R. (ed.) (1886): Decimi Magni Ausonii Burdigalensis Opuscula. Leipzig: Teubner.
Platnauer, M. (ed.) (1922): Claudianus. London: Heinemann.
Quinn, K. (ed.) (1973): Catullus: The Poems. London: Macmillan.
Schmeller, J.A. (1847): Carmina burana. Lateinische und deutsche Lieder und Gedichte einer Handschrift des XIII. Jahrhunderts aus Benedictbeuern auf der K. Bibliothek zu München. Stuttgart: Literarischer Verein.
Shackleton Bailey, D.R. (ed.) (2004): Statius. Thebaid. Books 1-7. Cambridge, MA: Harvard University Press.
Showerman, G.; Goold, G.P. (eds.) (1977): Ovid. Heroides and Amores. Cambridge, MA: Harvard University Press.
Skutsch, O. (ed.) (1985): The Annals of Quintus Ennius. Oxford: Oxford University Press.
Tarrant, R.J. (ed.) (2012): Aeneid. Book XII. Cambridge Greek and Latin Classics. Cambridge: Cambridge University Press.
Thomas, R.F. (1986): "Virgil's Georgics and the Art of Reference". HSCP 90, 171–198.
Thompson, H.J. (ed.) (1949): Prudentius. Volume 1. Cambridge, MA: Harvard University Press.
Warmington, E.H. (1988): Remains of Old Latin. Volume 1. Ennius and Caecilius. Cambridge, MA: Harvard University Press.
Warner, J.C. (2005): The Augustinian Epic, Petrarch to Milton. Ann Arbor: University of Michigan Press.

Critical Editing and Annotating Greek and Latin Sources

Franz Fischer

Digital Classical Philology and the Critical Apparatus

Abstract: The critical apparatus has been trade mark for classical philology ever since the development of the genealogical method and the establishment of the historical-critical edition. Its purpose is to justify the *textus constitutus* by displaying all significant variations in the history of a classical text and thus making editorial decisions transparent. Within digital scholarship, the critical apparatus tends to be perceived as a sign of methodological inadequacy and technological backwardness. Conceptual achievements of digital textual scholarship and their prototypical implementation into digital scholarly editions and library projects – even if mostly concerned with Medieval Latin, vernacular or modern literature – have developed a range of innovative practices, formats and features. These may help not only to transpose and vindicate the role of the critical apparatus in a digital environment but also to enhance its original core functionalities.

Introduction

In the past decade, several excellent studies have been published on the nature and appearance of digital scholarly editions, providing a broad overview and an in-depth analysis of the current state of the art regarding practices and theories in digital textual scholarship.[1] On the other hand, there is a century to look back on that produced highly instructive introductions into textual criticism and the art of critical editing.[2] This essay has nothing to share but some observations on the critical apparatus in a digital setting. It draws examples from my personal background that is informed by digital Medieval Latin critical editions, for the most part, due to the fact that there are still very few editions in digital classical philology that are both digital and critical. In doing so, this article

1 E.g. Sahle (2013), Pierazzo (2015a), and here especially, Apollon et al. (2014).
2 From Stählin (1914, first ed. 1909), Havet (1911), Maas (1927) and Pasquali (1934); over Bieler (1947), West (1973), Huygens (2000); Bourgain and Vielliard (2002); up to Reeve (2011), Tarrant (2016) and Trovato (2017) – to name just a few. For a concise description of the most prominent concepts and protagonists, see, e.g., Driscoll (2010, 87–95); Greetham (2007).

Franz Fischer, Cologne Center for eHumanities (CCeH) and Università Ca' Foscari Venezia

https://doi.org/10.1515/9783110599572-012

wants to address the question of what it means to be digital and critical. What is actually critical about a digital critical apparatus? And what is digital about it? What could be its use?

"Oh, you read Aristophanes without a critical apparatus." – What is textual scholarship, really?

The anecdote about Eduard Fraenkel's revelatory encounter with his university teacher Friedrich Leo is often recalled as a prime example for illustrating the fundamental importance of what seems to be just some negligible textual feature to the common reader:[3] Invited for a Sunday lunch to his future mentor's home in Göttingen around 1910, the young and enthusiastic Fraenkel had to confess that he read Aristophanes in the uncritical Teubner edition. Leo's genuinely surprised reaction made Fraenkel feel deeply ashamed: "Oh, you read Aristophanes without a critical apparatus", and it was at that moment that he realized "what textual scholarship really is".

The critical apparatus is an essential part of any scholarly edition, philology's most notorious feature, a manifestation of textual criticism itself. It provides the aura of a scientific, scholarly, reliable and authoritative text. The apparatus makes any text distinct to just ordinary texts, randomly published or passed on. In a way, the apparatus is to philology what the halo is to Christian iconography: an element to distinguish the saint from the sinner.

And just like the halo is vanishing in a secularized world, so does the critical apparatus seem to disappear in digital scholarship. While other areas within the domain of classical philology have taken advantage of new possibilities offered by the digital medium and even turned out to prosper (as demonstrated by the other contributions in this volume), the fate of the critical apparatus in digital classical philology has been mostly unfortunate so far.

A child of the print culture, the critical apparatus has been abandoned in digital corpora, regrettably removing all critical features of the original print publications (including introductions, *apparatus fontium* and indices), providing the plain text only, which, to make things even worse, is often not taken from the most recent scholarly edition for restrictive copyright reasons. As for those critical editions (of mostly vernacular works) that have been published in

3 "[. . .] was ordentliche Philologenarbeit bedeutet". Recalled by Fraenkel himself in his introduction to the collection of Leo's articles (1960, XL–XLI), retold by his pupil Martin Litchfield West (1973, 7) and again recently by Richard Tarrant (2016, 124–125).

a digital format, they seem to have turned the Holy Grail of textual criticism into some uncritical bag of variants, according to traditional philologists, automatically produced by collation software, incapable of adding any critical value. Yet from the other perspective, in the eyes of many digital and non-digital readers, the critical apparatus appears to be a graveyard of variants, with no bearing on the conditions of the living. Some have even gone so far as to express their contempt (or ignorance) by calling it outright "crapparatus" (as reported by Keeline 2017, 349).

Lachmann, lost in the digital world

The birth of the critical apparatus has been dated to the mid 17th century: The notes on Lucretius by the Dutch Renaissance philologist Daniel Heinsius seemed to have had that typical format which then was going to be adopted by the mid 18th century grammarians.[4] The apparatus was then further developed as a means to enable the reader to retrace and verify all editorial decisions for the reconstruction of a historical text that is extant in various witnesses, tracing back its history of transmission down the pedigree of manuscript copies as closely as possible to a lost archetype (which philologists must never get tired to stress is not necessarily the author's intended version). Notoriously, this genealogical or stemmatological method was established by the philologist Karl Lachmann (1793–1851) and spelled out by later philologists. In 1927, most influentially, Paul Maas defined a small set of rules for the reconstruction of the original and for the subsequent presentation of the critical text comprising the preface, the text itself and the apparatus criticus underneath.[5]

The stemmatological method has been criticized by scholars who did not share the idea of textual reconstruction, most notably the French scholar Joseph Bédier (1864–1934) and other philologists working with medieval vernacular text traditions such as the advocates of a Material or New Philology that gained traction with the publication of Bernard Cerquilini's polemic essay *Éloge de la variante* (1989). That criticism eventually resulted in what has been

4 Flores and Tomasco (2002). The term itself, *apparatus criticus*, "may have been used for the first time in Bengel's book title *D. Io. Alberti Bengelii Apparatus criticus ad Novum Testamentum, Tubingae 1763*" (Conti and Roelli 2015). On the genesis of Lachmann's method, see Timpanaro (2005) (first ed. 1961); on its fate in the age of post-structuralism, see Trovato (2017).

5 Maas already noted that the critical apparatus "is placed underneath the text simply on account of bookprinting conditions and in particular of the format of modern books" (§23).

called "Bédier's schism" (Trovato 2017, 77) between those scholars abiding the genealogical analysis for establishing a critical text and those scholars giving priority to a single text that actually existed. As a consequence, the whole field of textual scholarship has been further advanced and diversified while classical philology seems to have remained completely unimpressed. Combining methodological efficiency with scholarly rigour, the general appropriateness of the genealogical approach to classical works has never been questioned although it has been contrasted and refined through the work of Giorgio Pasquali (1934) and other, mostly Italian, philologists in his succession who have focused on the history of transmission and taken contaminated traditions into account.

At the same time, in the digital humanities world, a wide range of new methods and formats for editing and analysing historical texts and documents has been developed in the past decades, taking advantage of the possibilities offered by digital technology and online publication that can provide digital facsimiles of manuscripts witnesses, overcome space restrictions and restrictions of accessibility. Other achievements seem too obvious to even warrant mention: search functionalities, copy & paste, and, most importantly, the whole world of hyperlinks and inter-linkage, internally, within the edition as a complex scholarly resource, and externally, to the wide and open field of linked open data, authority files, digital libraries and other knowledge resources.[6] Still, there are only very few critical editions of classical works available on the internet. The actual research of a classicist today is carried out more and more in the digital realm: mining digital text collections and corpora, databases and other resources, using search engines, tools and software applications. Meanwhile, the most important sources for the classicist's work, critical editions of primary texts, are kept in libraries, on bookshelves, between the covers of costly print editions. Or, at the height of innovation, as PDF documents behind a pay wall of a publisher or illegally on some arcane server in no-man's land.

This is nothing new. And many a time the question has been raised: Why are there no digital editions of classical texts? Several explanations have been brought forward such as computer illiteracy among philologists, the lack of time and money, the lack of tools, or the lack of career perspectives in classics departments. But first and foremost, the reason seems to be that there is no need (Monella 2018): Classical philologists do not focus on documents and they

6 Suitable starting points for a systematic overview of the ever-growing field of digital scholarly editions might be the two online catalogues by Sahle (2008–) and Franzini (2012–); for critical reviews, the review journal for digital scholarly edition RIDE; and for a colourful snapshot, the volume on *Advances in Digital Scholarly Editing* edited by Boot et al. (2017).

do not focus on variance – both of which areas where digital philology is particularly strong. Instead, classical philologists are interested in canonical regularised text versions: in one text, in one language. Besides, they are not willing or able "to see, and embrace, the real potential of digital media", for the fear of losing control "over the way in which 'their' texts are presented".[7]

It does not take a prophet to realize that, eventually, even editors of classical works will have to go digital. But going digital, which editorial model should they follow? What are philologists today supposed to do? Paolo Monella (2018, 152–153) suggested to widen their research agenda, to embrace a plural and fluid concept of text, to join forces with post-classical philologists and historical linguists and to create comprehensively digital editions that provide transcriptions of all witnesses and apply digital tools for an automated creation of critical text versions – because only this, as has been proclaimed, would produce "truly digital editions".[8] However, while broadening the agenda and embarking on truly digital edition projects, classical philologists must not give up on the ideal of a critical text and the ideal of some uniform editorial format for authoritative, critical text editions. In fact, in recent years a rather proactive international research group has reinforced the field of stemmatology as an integral part of digital textual scholarship resulting in the publication of the *Parvum Lexicon Stemmatologicum* and a handbook on *Stemmatology in the Digital Age*.[9] This brings us back to a very practical question.

What to put in the critical apparatus?

Underneath the text, according to Maas (1927 §§ 23–24), deviations from the archetype should be noted: rejected variants, sub-variants and groups of variants from lower down in the stemma may or may not be indicated, as well as uncertainties, changes of witnesses and brief justifications of editorial decisions. The discussion about what exactly to put in the apparatus has always been vital among philologists ever since. Variance according to the Lachmannian approach is considered as merely instrumental to the goal of reconstructing the original text; minor and immaterial variants and mistakes of later scribes are considered insignificant and distracting. Historical evidence of textual transmission is seen

7 (Driscoll 2010, 104).
8 (Andrews 2012).
9 (Roelli and Macé 2015); (Roelli, forthcoming).

as a tool – or a hindrance – in the business of textual criticism to produce a *textus constitutus*. In this regard, it has no meaning in itself.

Nowadays, the selection of variant readings for the critical apparatus can be categorized as two opposing editorial practices, the maximalist and the minimalist approach.[10] The minimalist approach aims at the establishment of a clear and legible apparatus as an elegant result of the editor's judgement and craftsmanship, often at the cost of transparency. The maximalist approach seeks to include a much wider range of variants and varying textual flavours from a multitude of manuscript witnesses and previous editors, thus creating an expansive, at times overcrowded apparatus. In practice, most publications series and textual scholars develop an individual "editorial style" that is somewhere in between those competing ideologies which has led Gilbert Murray to come up with his famously infamous dictum:

> "An *apparatus criticus* [...] is a list of the MS. variations, with occasional remarks thereon. Only men of the highest moral character, religion, and social grace can produce one satisfactorily."[11]

This may or may not remain true. The distinctive properties of a good editor may be replaced by labels more adequate to present-day terminology. Without doubt, Murray's statement needs to be rephrased to gender-equitable language. Manliness as a supposedly scholarly virtue has long been abolished (even if gender-related biases and inequalities remain[12]). However, the problem of choosing remains. And for this all those handbooks and introductions by distinguished scholars and experienced editors are full of masterly advice how to avoid arbitrary choices about what information to include or exclude and how to balance accountability with readability, comprehensiveness with conciseness.

The reconciliation of Bédier's schism

In digital philology, for one thing, the question of what to put in the apparatus has become less existential. Digital editions are able to combine both approaches, the maximalist and the minimalist. From the ability to combine the two contradictory convictions an obligation arises because the mutually excluding justification is no more valid. Digital editors should give both a record

10 (Bourgain and Vielliard 2002, 79–86); (Tarrant 2016, 129–140).
11 (Archer 1936, 37).
12 Cf. Warren (2013).

of textual variance that is as full and complete as possible – or at least, if that burden is too high, provide the means that allow for a progressive completion of that record – and a critical assessment of it. How so?

In 2007, I published the online edition *Summa de officiis ecclesiasticis* of the Parisian Master William of Auxerre (†1231). This was not only the first-ever edition of William's so-called "small *Summa*" (his big one is the widely acclaimed *Summa aurea*). It has also been considered the first-ever born-digital critical edition created of a Latin work, albeit Medieval Latin and even though the method is not strictly genealogical.[13] Full transcripts of all 15 manuscript witnesses (comprising some 75,000 words each) for full-automated collation were no option. Instead, three manuscript witnesses were chosen based on a preceding stemmatological analysis: two witnesses representing the two main branches of the textual transmission to be collated against the transcript of one principal manuscript witness, in this case a copy made by an especially distinguished scribe. An odd editorial decision in favour of the "maverick" one, owed to the spirit of Bédier and Cerquilini. Nevertheless, this transcript was only the starting point for establishing a critical text; a corrected and slightly normalised text version furnished with a threefold apparatus, presenting (a) all substantial variants of the three manuscripts, (b) all biblical references and other sources, and (c) references to the works of William Durandus of Mende's *Rationale* and Jacobus de Voragine's *Legenda aurea*, both of which borrowed passages from William's *Summa*, and quite extensively so in the case of William Durandus. In addition, every chapter gives hyperlinked references to digital facsimiles of each manuscript page witnessing the present text passage.

The critical text including apparatus notes and references is generated from large data set of the critically enriched and marked up transcript of the principal manuscript. The set of variant readings in the chosen manuscripts is complete. Each variant is marked up as insignificant, significant or as the preferable lemma for the critical text. A pipeline of rule-based transformations then creates the intended presentation of a normalized, corrected and emended critical text and respective apparatus notes. All rule-based transformations draw upon the editor's critical assessment of the variant readings.

Despite any methodological flaw one might observe, the key aspect here is that the editorial task of recording variance, its assessment and the decision if and how it should be displayed in the critical apparatus of the critical text to

13 See Fischer (2008; 2013). For a more complete picture of digital critical editions preceding the *Summa* (deliberately refraining from the constitution of a critical text), see my chapter on "The presentation of the critical text" in Roelli, forthcoming (ch. 7.3).

be, are encapsulated in distinct units of information. They can, in principle, be modified and reassessed according to the editor's preference and presented in different ways for different purposes. Conceived almost two decades ago, revised almost ten years ago, this digital edition lacks many widgets and functionalities, not least dynamic features for user interaction and progressive enrichment. Its prototypical chain of transformational scripts may not be reused in any other editorial enterprise. However, it marks an ontological shift of the critical edition and the critical apparatus in particular towards what has been coined "transmedialisation" (Sahle 2010). The current change from print to digital editions is not primarily a change in publication formats. Printed critical editions provide a text that is characterized by the unity of content and form. Usability and readability of the actual text and the apparatus are based on static presentation. The very essence of the critical text is set in print with a conventional and clearly designed page layout. In contrast, digital scholarly editions are characterized by the *separation of content and form*. Content is captured and maintained as data and metadata, that is, in the form of digital image files and encoded text. It is *re*presented in data models and formats that are agnostic to and independent from any presentational format or medium. In that sense, they transcend mediality. Any publication of the content data as a fully-fledged and fully-functional edition accessible for the common reader or scholarly user is but an optional realization of an editorial perspective, a selective spin-off and visualization from the complete data set.

And even further, the actual critical text (as presented in the digital edition of William of Auxerre) does not exist in the code, nor do the entries of the critical apparatus exist in the code as such but only potentially, *in potentia, potentialiter*.

Apparatus amplificatus

A very different digital approach has been taken for the digital edition of Saint Patrick's *Confessio*, an open apologetic Latin letter from the 5th century and the oldest text written in Ireland – in any language – that has survived. The text of the *Confessio* already existed in a "well crafted" edition of "canonical" status with a "balanced" apparatus (to use the words of traditional philologists) reflecting all variants of a conveniently small set of only eight extant manuscript witnesses, provided by the "distinguished" philologist Ludwig Bieler in 1950. The digital edition was conceived as a digital stack of textual layers of manuscript facsimiles, relevant prints and facsimile editions, translations, paratexts and other additional content. *At the centre* of the stack is the critical text with the threefold apparatus, closely connecting all textual layers passage by passage via extensive use of hyperlinks, hence the term *HyperStack* in the project's title. Hovering over an apparatus entry, for example, will highlight the referenced lemma in the base text. In the apparatus entry itself, all sigla of individual witnesses are linked to the digital facsimile of the relevant page; abbreviations and sigla of witness families are resolved by a mouseover effect. All keys and symbols are linked to a list of definitions and descriptions; bibliographical references are linked to a comprehensive bibliography; biblical references are linked to external, online versions of biblical books; and testimonia are linked to the texts of Patrick's two earliest biographies which are also included in the edition.

All these features have been implemented by means of a deeply encoded text and apparatus, making explicit to the machine what otherwise, in print editions, gets implicitly understood (or not) by readers (in effect a small number of peer scholars) through their interpretation of the (often idiosyncratic) conventions of such editions. One idea behind these efforts is to draw readers (scholars and laypersons alike) into what Patrick actually wrote, from translation to original Latin to manuscript and back again. Continuously evaluated user statistics – not least around Saint Patrick's Day each year – seem to indicate that this intention has actually succeeded.

Readability and usability of the apparatus have been significantly increased by digital amplification, encouraging readers to immerse themselves in the history of the texts. This development would be welcomed by philologists even as distant as Paul Maas, who claimed: "Our *apparatus critici* have too little life in them" (1927, §24) and Richard Tarrant, stating that "the apparatus should be an invitation to the reader to engage in a dialogue with the editor", and encouraging editors to give their critical notes "a more personal voice" (2016, 141). Tom Keeline envisages an even more dynamic apparatus that allows readers to take an active role in constituting their own texts: "The dream for a digital apparatus is to record everything, but to tag each piece of the material with metadata so that all available information is placed on permanent record, but the user can pick what is actually displayed" (2017, 351).

In addition, mark-up of critical notes can include information about types and categories of each apparatus entry.[14] With textual annotation it can be specified whether it is about variant readings and if variance is substantive or just orthographical; other textual categories could indicate if they concern conjectures, deletions, corruptness, transpositions, lacunae, marginal or interlinear additions, punctuation, speaker attribution or structural differences regarding

14 In a couple of editorial projects it does; for references see Fischer (2017, 278–279).

boundaries between books, chapters, paragraphs, poems, stanzas, verses etc. Intertextual annotation could make explicit if it refers to sources, parallels, testimonia, later usage, or *nachleben*, i.e. modern allusions and imitations. Other type attributions for critical annotation can be exegetical, metrical, and rhetorical, or even more specifically, figure of speech, trope or style. Options and possibilities are endless. The actual benefit of the explicitness of such categories in the mark-up depends on the analytical potential of the data and functional presentation formats – besides the encoder's technical and philological ability.

The primacy of the data model

The few digital editions of classical texts that exist are meritorious for being both scholarly and online. However, they are based on a flat data model[15] or, rather, on a print-oriented data model, such as those exported from the widely used Classical Text Editor.[16] This is why they cannot yet live up to the great expectations of content and feature rich, truly digital editions. In fact, these editions would fall short of Sahle's restrictive definition of being digital: "A digital edition cannot be given in print without a significant loss of content and functionality" (2016, 27). Because they can.

The creation of intuitive and powerful interfaces for reading digital critical editions and their integration into larger collections and publication frameworks mainly depends on a suitable data model that is maintained and accepted by a wider community of digital philologists. For this, Hugh Cayless (2018) advocated the primacy of the data model in connection with the efforts by the Digital Latin Library (DLL; cf. Samuel J. Huskey in this volume) to create a practical editing environment and publication venue for digital critical editions of Latin texts that are supposed to combine intelligent design with a wide range of features and functionalities. Cayless and with him many other digital textual scholars even go so far as to maintain that the data is the "actual" edition – beyond any presentation or user interface.

This assertion goes hand in hand with the other reason for privileging the data model over any presentational format: the sobering awareness that every presentation will pass. Any digital edition published on CD-ROM or on the internet will break at some point. All software *is grass*, so to speak, *and all its beauty is like*

15 E.g. the editions published on the Curculio portal by Michael Hendry (cf. Monella 2018, 142, fn. 4) or the Euripides Scholia edited by Donald Mastronarde.

16 E.g. the digital edition of *Kleine und fragmentarische Historiker der Spätantike*; cf. Fischer (2017, S267–S268).

the flower of the field: The grass withers, the flower fades (Isaiah 40, 6–7). If anything, only the data will survive, or has a potentially long half-life at least, and only from the data any scholarly edition can be brought to new life. The guidelines of the Text Encoding Initiative are a most impressive testimony of that belief.[17] As of today, almost two thousand printable PDF pages are the result of four decades of an intense and continuous scholarly discourse about a data model capable of creating a record of textual information that is as accurate and complete as possible, and at the same time machine-readable, interoperable and reusable in other contexts or formats. The TEI offers a full arsenal of tags, attributes and tools for a consistent encoding of all of those above stated phenomena. The guidelines dedicate a full chapter (ch. 12) to the encoding of the critical apparatus, suggesting three different methods how to link the apparatus to the text. Symptomatically, as it seems for the relationship of classical and digital philology, the chapter is not the TEI's favourite child. The proposed data model owes its design to the traditional apparatus and can be seen as a physical embodiment of traditional textual criticism more so than a coherently formulized abstraction of textual criticism itself – if there is such thing. So far, several attempts of a dedicated working group to revise the chapter have faded without notable effect.

More innovative aspects

The development of a standard data model is also the basis for another innovative concept of digital scholarly editions: the idea of a distributed architecture. Most recently, Joris van Zundert made a case for digital editions that are conceived as a network of resources as opposed "to the architectural nature of the majority of current digital scholarly editions, which are still mostly monolithic data silos" (2018). The critical edition of Petrus Plaoul by Jeffrey C. Witt (2011) can be seen as a prototypical implementation of that concept. The edition queries facsimiles of manuscript witnesses from external databases and repositories. The technical framework operates on the reference standard IIIF (International Image Interoperability Framework) adopted by a growing number of archives and libraries that provide digital surrogates of their manuscript collections online. That way, editions or any dedicated software applications are able to retrieve and embed the image data.[18]

17 Maybe, or maybe not fatefully ensnared by XML technology; cf. Pierazzo (2015b); Cummings (2018).
18 (Witt 2018).

One can easily imagine that such distributed architectures could be further complemented by other types of external or outsourced repositories: those collecting and analysing variants from a defined set of manuscripts (e.g. from the three copies of Dante's *Commedia* written by Boccaccio; see Tempestini and Spadini 2015–2018) or those compiling conjectures on the work of a given author (e.g. on the work of Catullus; see Kiss 2013–2017) or those collectively accumulating transcripts, collations and other data related to a massive manuscript tradition (e.g. of the Greek New Testament as gathered in New Testament Virtual Manuscript Room) – always provided that the relevant data is accessible in a predictable way to the edition as a "data consuming application".[19] Feeding distributed data into networked resources, the work of a critical editor – *Philologenarbeit* (according to Fraenkel), grammarian's craft (according to Bieler), *ars edendi* (according to Huygens) – might become the work of a critical synthesizer.

Witt's edition is pioneering in two further respects. First, the edition is "progressive" which means that it was published in a pre-critical stage. Text and apparatus are a draft. Readers are invited to register and improve the text by leaving comments or by suggesting additions or corrections of variant readings from relevant witnesses. Second, in order to facilitate the critical engagement with the text, a collation tool has been implemented into the edition: As soon as transcripts of the witnesses for a particular passage are available, they can be automatically compared against each other and textual differences can be highlighted.

Concluding remarks

Despite a somewhat troubled relationship, digital philology has wrought a number of technical and methodological innovations concerning the critical apparatus that may help to overcome some of the shortcomings of printed critical editions. Integrated into an array of further critical features of a digital edition,[20] the critical apparatus can become a powerful tool connecting the *textus constitutus* to the evidence of the manuscript witnesses, thus enabling readers to verify editorial decisions or otherwise make their own hypotheses – which are, in fact, core functions and *raison d'être* of any critical apparatus.

19 (Witt 2018).
20 Cf. Fischer (2017, S278–S280).

It has been demonstrated by some prototypical realisations of digital critical apparatuses that a major achievement of digital philology is the separation of content and form, data and presentation. As a consequence, large amounts of visual and textual data can be included: manuscript facsimiles, transcripts, collations and further exhaustive documentation. On the content side, this data can be categorized and qualified by the critical encoder-editor in order to create a critical representation of the textual transmission. In the code, all critical assessments and editorial decisions can be made explicit and formalized with the goal of creating consistency and ultimately – the philologist's dread or dream – of automatizing the editorial process, at least in parts.[21] On the presentational side, this data can be made accessible through digital editions providing the critical text and apparatus in alternative, readable and functional formats. Advanced digital publication frameworks may integrate dedicated tools and features to search, visualize, analyse and progressively enrich this data and to enable various other forms of user interaction.

There are many ways, rules and tools for critically assessing textual evidence in order to create and provide a critical representation of historical text. With the digital transformation of the critical edition and with the emergence of novel features and manifestations in a digital setting, does the nature of textual criticism change? – If we loosely define textual criticism as making sense of textual transmission by applying a methodology that transparently and consistently assesses textual evidence as documented by textual witnesses and by the whole complex of textual transmission – what, then, is *digital* textual criticism? Digital textual criticism is (or should be) just the same – the same, but better. It is (or should be) about making sense of textual transmission by applying a methodology that is to a certain degree computer-assisted and therefore *more* transparent, *more* consistent and *better* documented. However, the critical assessment itself, as for now, is still in the domain of the editor[22] – but grounded, ideally, in a better understanding of textual transmission which, ideally, can be better or more effectively shared with other scholars.

---

21 (Barabucci and Fischer 2017).

22 This seems to be the point Barbara Bordalejo (2018) is making against any revolutionary fuss, supposedly propagated by Peter Robinson and other digital humanists, claiming instead that "the revolution is only in the title" and that nothing has really changed – disregarding, however, the ontological implications of applying digital methods, and mistaking the concept of transmediality (as a central component of the digital paradigm shift proclaimed by Sahle 2016, 28) for multimediality.

Epilogue: the swords of textual criticism

One more time, what is digital philology, really? An extreme form of textual criticism can be physical, even. The most extreme physical method of textual criticism is probably sword fighting – as applied by a community of enthusiasts of historical martial arts in order to create digital variorum editions of fencing books from the 15th century. Using an easy-to-use editor based on Wiki technologies they transcribe the various and variant versions of the works of the old fencing masters. The developer of the Wiki software, Ben Brumfield, calls them "accidental editors" (2017). They never planned or decided to become editors. They just wanted to exercise martial arts according to the instructions of the old masters. And for this reason, as a matter of fact, these "editors by accident" have become critical editors. They create critical texts tracing the textual transmission to an archetype and going beyond, emending the text if necessary according to the original intention of the master and the original practice taught some 700 years ago. The re-enactment of that practice informs their reading of the text. They fight, and the physicality of trying out moves is their method of textual criticism: If a reading or interpretation concerning the instructions how to wield your weapon is wrong the fighter will immediately experience the mistake.[23]

There are two conclusions to be drawn from this curious and rather unusual case. First, digital philology is about enabling people – scholars, philologists or sword fighting enthusiasts. Digital philology has the capacity to record, structure and present textual data and information in ways that empower the reader or rather user to critically engage with the material, impossible to achieve in print. It can thus respond to a natural need, because, and that is the other conclusion, textual criticism is in our human nature. In the pursuit of knowledge and truth, people will always adapt and refine efficient methods and tools to comply with their desire for a reliable text.

Bibliography

Andrews, T.L. (2012): "The Third Way: Philology and Critical Edition in the Digital Age". Variants 10, 61–76. Postprint online version: http://boris.unibe.ch/43071/ (last access 2019.01.31).

23 Brumfield gave an inspiring pub lecture on the topic in Cologne in 2016 (see https://youtu.be/7X6rj35rE1k: last access 2019.01.31) followed by a frightening demonstration by a group of sword fighters (https://youtu.be/rupktpz0Xrg: last access 2019.01.31).

Apollon, D.; Bélisle, C.; Régnier, Ph. (eds.) (2014): Digital Critical Editions. Urbana: University of Illinois Press.

Archer, Ch. (1936): "G.M. – W.A. 1895–1924". In: H.A.L. Fisher; G. Murray (eds.): Essays in Honour of Gilbert Murray. London: Allen & Unwin, 31–48.

Barabucci, G.; Fischer, F. (2017): "The Formalization of Textual Criticism: Bridging the Gap between Automated Collation and Edited Critical Texts". In: P. Boot; A. Cappellotto; W. Dillen; F. Fischer; A. Kelly; A. Mertgens; A.-M. Sichani; E. Spadini; D. van Hulle (eds.): Advances in Digital Scholarly Editing. Leiden: Sidestones Press, 47–54. https://www.sidestone.com/books/advances-in-digital-scholarly-editing (last access 2019.01.31).

Bieler, L. (1958): "The Grammarian's Craft. A Professional Talk". Folia. Studies in the Christian Perpetuation of the Classics 10:2, 3–42. (First published as an offprint from Folia, October 1947, January 1948, May 1948).

Boot, P.; Cappellotto, A.; Dillen, W.; Fischer, F.; Kelly, A.; Mertgens, A.; Sichani, A.-M.; Spadini, E.; van Hulle. D. (eds.) (2017): Advances in Digital Scholarly Editing. Leiden: Sidestones Press. https://www.sidestone.com/books/advances-in-digital-scholarly-editing (last access 2019.01.31).

Bordalejo, B. (2018): "Digital versus Analogue Textual Scholarship or The Revolution is Just in the Title". Digital Philology: A Journal of Medieval Cultures 7:1, 7–28.

Bourgain, P.; Vielliard, F. (2002): Conseils pour l'édition des textes médiévaux. Vol. III: Textes littéraires. Paris: École nationale des chartes.

Brumfield, B. (2017): "Accidental editors". In: P. Boot; A. Cappellotto; W. Dillen; F. Fischer; A. Kelly; A. Mertgens; A.-M. Sichani; E. Spadini; D. van Hulle (eds.): Advances in Digital Scholarly Editing. Leiden: Sidestones Press, 69–83. https://www.sidestone.com/books/advances-in-digital-scholarly-editing (last access 2019.01.31).

Cayless, H. (2018): "Critical Editions and the Data Model as Interface." In: R. Bleier; M. Bürgermeister; H.W. Klug; F. Neuber; G. Schneider (eds.): Digital Scholarly Editions as Interfaces. Norderstedt: BoD, 249–263. https://kups.ub.uni-koeln.de/9119/ (last access 2019.01.31).

Cerquiglini, B. (1989): Éloge de la variante: Histoire critique de la philologie. Des travaux. Paris: Seuil.

Classical Text Editor, version 9.3 (2019): http://cte.oeaw.ac.at/?id0=main (last access 2019.01.31).

Conti, A.; Roelli, Ph. (2015): "Apparatus". In: Ph. Roelli; C. Macé (eds.): Parvum lexicon stemmatologicum. University of Helsinki. https://wiki.helsinki.fi/display/stemmatology/Apparatus (last access 2019.01.31).

Cummings, J. (2018): "A World of Difference: Myths and Misconceptions about the TEI". Digital Scholarship in the Humanities, fqy071. https://doi.org/10.1093/llc/fqy071.

Driscoll, M.J. (2010): "The Words on the Page. Thoughts on Philology, Old and New". In: J. Quinn; E. Lethbridge (eds.): Creating the Medieval Saga: Versions, Variability, and Editorial Interpretations of Old Norse Saga Literature. Odense: Syddansk Universitetsforlag, 85–102. http://www.driscoll.dk/docs/words.html (last access 2019.01.31).

Fischer, F. (ed.) (2007–2013): Guillelmus Autissiodorensis. Summa de officiis ecclesiasticis. Köln: Universität zu Köln. http://guillelmus.uni-koeln.de (last access 2019.01.31).

Fischer, F. (2008): "The Pluralistic Approach – The First Scholarly Edition of William of Auxerre's Treatise on Liturgy". Jahrbuch für Computerphilologie 10, 151–168. http://computerphilologie.tu-darmstadt.de/jg08/fischer.html (last access 2019.01.31).

Fischer, F.; Harvey, A. (eds.) (2011): Saint Patrick's Confessio. Dublin: Royal Irish Academy. https://confessio.ie (last access 2019.01.31).
Fischer, F. (2013): "All Texts Are Equal, but... Textual Plurality and the Critical Text in Digital Scholarly Editions". Variants 10, 77–92. https://kups.ub.uni-koeln.de/5056/ (last access 2019.01.31).
Fischer, F. (2017): "Digital Corpora and Scholarly Editions of Latin Texts: Features and Requirements of Textual Criticism". Speculum 92, Suppl. 1, S265–S287. https://doi.org/10.1086/693823.
Flores, E.; Tomasco, D. (2002): "Nascita dell'apparato critico". Vichiana 4:1, 3–6.
Franzini, G. (2012–): A Catalogue of Digital Editions. https://dig-ed-cat.acdh.oeaw.ac.at (last access 2019.01.31).
Greetham, D. (2007): "What is Textual Scholarship?". In: S. Eliot; J. Rose (eds.): A Companion to the History of the Book. Oxford: Blackwell, 21–32. DOI: 10.1002/9780470690949.ch2.
Havet, L. (1911): "Manuel de critique verbale appliquée aux textes latins". Paris: Hachette.
Huygens, R.B.C. (2000): Ars Edendi. A Practical Introduction to Editing Medieval Latin Texts. Turnhout: Brepols.
Keeline, T. (2017): "The Apparatus Criticus in the Digital Age". The Classical Journal 112:3, 343–364.
Kiss, D. (2013, 2017): Catullus online. http://www.catullusonline.org (last access 2019.01.31).
Maas, P. (1927): "Textkritik". In: A. Gercke; E. Norden (eds.) Einleitung in die Altertumswissenschaft. Vol. 1, fasc. 2. Leipzig: Teubner. (Transl. by B. Flower based on the 3rd rev. ed. from 1957: Oxford: Clarendon, 1958).
Monella, P. (2018): "Why Are There No Comprehensively Digital Scholarly Editions of Classical Texts?" In: A. Cipolla (ed.): Digital Philology: New Thoughts on Old Questions. Padova: libreriauniversitaria.it, 141–159. (Paper first published online in April 2012).
New Testament Virtual Manuscript Room (NTVMR) (2019). http://ntvmr.uni-muenster.de (last access 2019.01.31).
Pasquali, G. (1934): Storia della tradizione e critica del testo. Firenze: Le Monnier (2nd edition 1952).
Pierazzo, E. (2015a): Digital Scholarly Editing: Theories, Models and Methods. Farnham: Routledge.
Pierazzo, E. (2015b): "TEI beyond XML". Paper given at the TEI Conference and Members' Meeting 2015, Lyon, October, 28–31. http://tei2015.huma-num.fr/en/papers/#140 (last access 2019.01.31).
Reeve, M.D. (2011): Manuscripts and Methods: Essays on Editing and Transmission. Roma: Edizioni di Storia e Letteratura.
RIDE. A review journal for digital editions and resources. Published by the Institut für Dokumentologie und Editorik (IDE).
Roelli, Ph.; Macé, C. (eds.) (2015): Parvum lexicon stemmatologicum. A Brief Lexicon of Stemmatology. Helsinki: Helsinki University Homepage. https://doi.org/10.5167/uzh-121539.
Roelli, Ph. (ed.) (forthcoming): Stemmatology in the Digital Age.
Sahle P. (2008–): A Catalog of Digital Scholarly Editions, version 3.0. http://www.digitale-edition.de (last access 2019.01.31).
Sahle, P. (2010): "Zwischen Mediengebundenheit und Transmedialisierung. Anmerkungen zum Verhältnis von Edition und Medien". editio – International Yearbook of Scholarly Editing 24, 23–36.

Sahle, P. (2013): Digitale Editionsformen, Zum Umgang mit der Überlieferung unter den Bedingungen des Medienwandels – Befunde, Theorie und Methodik. Norderstedt: BoD.
Sahle, P. (2016): "What Is a Scholarly Digital Edition (SDE)?". In: M. Driscoll; E. Pierazzo (eds.): Digital Scholarly Editing: Theory, Practice and Future Perspectives. Cambridge: OBP, 19–39. DOI: 10.11647/OBP.0095.
Stählin, O. (1914): Editionstechnik. Ratschläge für die Anlage textkritischer Ausgaben. Leipzig: Teubner. (Completely revised version of the first edition from 1909).
Tarrant, R.J. (2016): Texts, Editors, and Readers: Methods and Problems in Latin Textual Criticism. Cambridge: Cambridge University Press.
TEI Consortium (2019): TEI P5: Guidelines for Electronic Text Encoding and Interchange. http://www.tei-c.org/guidelines/p5/ (last access 2019.01.31).
Tempestini, S.; Spadini, E. (eds.) (2015–2018): La Commedia di Boccaccio, versione beta 0.2. https://boccacciocommedia.unil.ch (last access 2019.01.31).
Timpanaro, S. (2005): The Genesis of Lachmann's Method. Chicago: The University of Chicago Press. (Original Italian edition from 1961).
Trovato, P. (2017): Everything you Always Wanted to Know about Lachmann's Method: A Non-standard Handbook of Genealogical Textual Criticism in the Age of Post-Structuralism, Cladistics, and Copy-text. Padova: Libreriauniversitaria.it. (Original Italian edition from 1961).
van Zundert, J. (2018): "On Not Writing a Review About Mirador. Mirador, IIIF, and the Epistemological Gains of Distributed Digital Scholarly Resources". Digital Medievalist 11. http://doi.org/10.16995/dm.78.
Warren, M. (2013): "The Politics of Textual Scholarship". In: N. Freistat; J. Flanders (eds.): Cambridge Companion to Textual Scholarship. Cambridge: Cambridge University Press, 119–134. https://doi.org/10.1017/CCO9781139044073.007.
West, M.L. (1973): Textual Criticism and Editorial Technique. Leipzig: B.G. Teubner.
Witt, J.C. (ed.) (2011): Petrus Plaoul. Commentarius in libros Sententiarum: Editiones electronicas. http://petrusplaoul.org (last access 2019.01.31).
Witt, J.C. (2018): "Digital Scholarly Editions and API Consuming Applications". In: R. Bleier; M. Bürgermeister; H.W. Klug; F. Neuber; G. Schneider (eds.): Digital Scholarly Editions as Interfaces. Norderstedt: BoD, 219–247. https://kups.ub.uni-koeln.de/9118/ (last access 2019.01.31).

Oliver Bräckel, Hannes Kahl, Friedrich Meins
and Charlotte Schubert

eComparatio – a Software Tool for Automatic Text Comparison

Abstract: The following paper gives a short description of the software-tool eComparatio that was originally intended as a tool for the comparison of different text editions. An example of its original purposes will be given, the larger part of the paper consists of a detailed description of the actual comparison process in detail. In a final section, some differences to similar text comparison tools for plain text will be given.

1 Some preliminary remarks

To explain why there are different versions of "a text" and why it might be necessary to compare them seems – at least while approaching the readers of a volume entitled "Digital Classical Philology" – like carrying coals to Newcastle. The eComparatio software tool we will be presenting in the following pages, however, has its origins not so much in the "purely philological" realm of collating and editing.[1] It is rather grounded in the daily needs and practical experience of those who are working as historians or literary scientists with the so-called "classical" and "canonical" texts, which oftentimes happen to be at hand in several different editions. In the following paper, we are trying to show that the software could be a useful tool for textual criticism in a narrower sense as well, and that it is also taking some steps towards this direction in its latest development.

We will therefore try to illustrate the idea of eComparatio as a useful tool for ancient historians (and scholars working with different text editions in general),

1 The software was developed by Hannes Kahl during a project funded by the DFG from March 2014 to March 2016 and developed further in 2016 in the follow-up project "Annotating and Editing with Canonical Text Services" funded by the Andrew W. Mellon foundation and conducted in cooperation with Christopher Blackwell from Furman University in Greenville, SC. The following paper is mainly a summary of presentations from the DHd conference in Cologne and the "52. Deutscher Historikertag" in Münster (Germany). Further documentation and the software itself are available online at http://www.ecomparatio.com and eComparatio on GitHub via the homepage http://www.eaqua.net (last access 2019.01.31).

Oliver Bräckel, Hannes Kahl, Friedrich Meins, Charlotte Schubert, Universität Leipzig

https://doi.org/10.1515/9783110599572-013

and we will also try to give some insight into the unique comparison method. A concluding section is aiming at a comparative analysis of eComparatio and some other similar tools concerning their different applications.

2 An example from practice

The famous fragment B1 of Anaximander plays an important role in the reconstruction of the world views of the Pre-Socratic philosophers. In this fragment, Anaximander discusses the origin (*arché*) of the world. The fragment is part of a paraphrase ascribed to Theophrastus, which in turn is handed down to us by Simplicius – hence telling the paraphrase from the direct quotation is made even more complicated here. Kirk et al. (2001) point out that Theophrastus' interpretation shows a strong Aristotelian influence,[2] an impression which might even be increased by the fact that Simplicius quotes the passage in a commentary on Aristotle.

In modern editions, the textual context of the fragment considered relevant for the interpretation varies profoundly (see Figure 1). Furthermore, the editions differ with regard to their interpretation of what exactly is to be considered as part of the verbatim quotation. *Die Fragmente der Vorsokratiker* marks the whole phrase ἐξ ὧν δὲ ἡ γένεσίς ἐστι τοῖς οὖσι, καὶ τὴν φθορὰν εἰς ταῦτα γίνεσθαι κατὰ τὸ χρεών. διδόναι γὰρ αὐτὰ δίκην καὶ τίσιν ἀλλήλοις τῆς ἀδικίας κατὰ τὴν τοῦ χρόνου τάξιν [...] as actual "B"-fragment. Scholars as Vogel (1963) and Mansfeld (1983 and 2009) are following this notion. Kirk et al. (2001) take κατὰ τὸ χρεών to be the only original part of the first sentence, and so does Graham (2010). The main argument for this line of interpretation is the terminological application of certain words in Aristotle and the Peripatetics, wherefore Kirk et al (2001). consider the bigger part of the sentence to be an adjunct by Theophrastus himself.[3]

In cases like this, a helpful overview of different editions of fragments as well as of the source texts can be provided to the scholar by the eComparatio tool. An even more interesting insight is highlighted by the tool concerning the editorial history of the verbatim part of the fragment itself (see Figure 2).

In the oldest edition of the text, the Aldina of Franziskus Asulanus from 1526 A.D., the word ἀλλήλοις is missing. This is grammatically valid, since δίκην or τίσιν διδόναι are known collocations with the meaning "being punished", and do

2 Cf. Kirk et al. (2001, 115).
3 Cf. Kirk et al. (2001, 129, 133).

Figure 1: Parallel view of Anaximander B1 in different editions, of Simplicius as well as of Pre-Socratics.

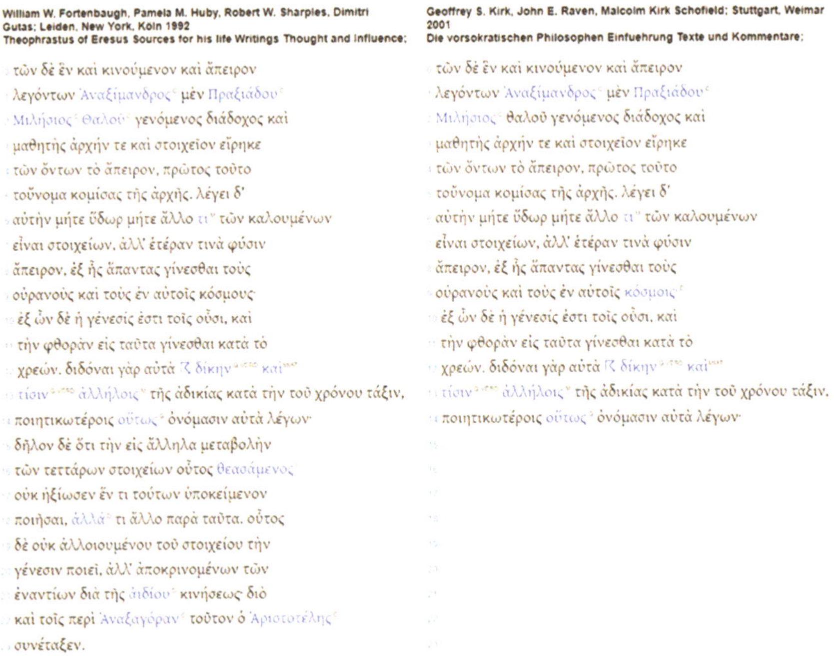

Figure 1 (continued)

not need an indirect object.[4] With regards to content, the trade-off between the "existing things" – often considered to be a central aspect of the fragment – would go missing. In its place, there would be a hendiadys denoting a rather undefined "punishment" the "being things" are suffering. Similar phrases are, after all, found in Hippolytus[5] and other parts of Theophrastus.[6]

In fact, there seems to be no evidence in the manuscripts for this reading. But Diels in his edition of Simplicius did obviously not consider it as one of the typesetters' "levissim[i] errores", but as a deliberate conjecture by Asulanus.[7]

4 Cf. LSJ, s.v. τίσις: "freq. in Hdt., τίσιν δοῦναί τινος suffer punishment for an act, or s.v. δίκη 3: the object or consequence of the action, atonement, satisfaction, penalty, δίκην ἐκτίνειν, τίνειν, Hdt.9.94, S.Aj.113: adverbially in acc., 'τοῦ δίκην πάσχεις τάδε;' A.Pr.614; freq. δίκην or δίκας διδόναι suffer punishment, i.e. make amends (but δίκας δ., in A.Supp.703 (lyr.), to grant arbitration); 'δίκας διδόναι τινί τινος' Hdt.1.2, cf. 5.106".

5 Cf. Haer. I, 6, 1f (DK 12 A2, B2).

6 Cf. Theophrastus, Phys, op. fr. 2 Diels (DK 12 A9, B1).

7 This might also be indicated by the transposition of the nouns.

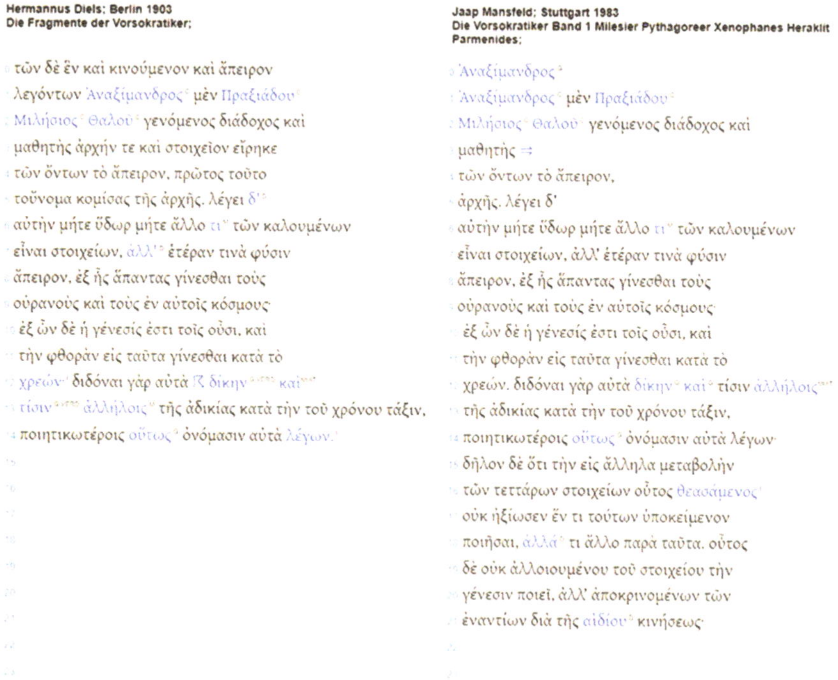

Figure 1 (continued)

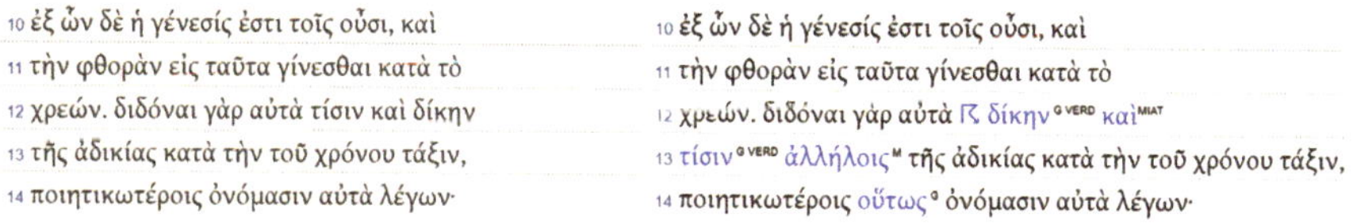

Figure 2: The Text of the Aldina (on the left hand) juxtaposed to that of Kirk et al. (2001).

According to Diels, some of these were rather unfortunate, some at least worth considering. He therefore included the reading into his apparatus in which he was striving for a more or less detailed representation of the vulgate to make a comparison possible.[8]

8 Cf. Diels (1882, vii); Mansfeld (2009, 10 note 1) sees the version of the Aldina as an "improvement for the worse". He impressively describes the consequences of this reading for modern philosophy up to the 19th century, which he points out to be the basis of what he calls a "mythical interpretation [...] according to which the coming to be of things from the divine

This might be sufficient as an example for the cases in which a simple overview and highlighted synopsis of different editorial choices can be helpful. That might even be more so the case if one considers the growing corpora of "digital" and "digitized" editions that are already at hand in the classics or are in the making. Some of them strive for scholarly accuracy and are based more or less on the state-of-the-art editions,[9] others are rather trying to broaden the spectrum by providing more and more versions and editions of the "canonical" texts.[10] The possibilities established by this can be productively enhanced by a tool that helps to point out the sometimes fundamental textual differences at the first glance even for the cursory reader.

3 An (hopefully) exoteric description of eComparatio's comparison algorithm

Generally speaking, there are two kinds of text-comparison software. The first kind compares texts as lists of words, the other kind compares checksums that represent the text. eComparatio can be attributed to the first group, as, for example, also is the common "diff" algorithm. eComparatio is neither a completely new software, nor is it a technical improvement of the underlying method in a narrower sense.

eComparatio still differs from other comparison programs in some fundamental aspects, first of which is the "expansion" of the technical notion of equality – we will get back to that point in the following section. The second aspect is the "maximisation" of the results. This means that the results of the text-comparison are designed to meet the requirements of a utilisation in the context of a digital edition. One aspect of this "maximisation" is the classification of different kinds of textual differences. This aspect should become clear from the section thereafter.

Apeiron is an act of injustice towards it." This interpretation is still being passed down as a result of some of its champions being "canonical" themselves by now.

9 For example the Bibliotheca Teubneriana Latina (https://www.degruyter.com/view/db/btl) or the TLG (http://stephanus.tlg.uci.edu/): last access 2019.01.31.

10 Cf. the Perseus Project (http://www.perseus.tufts.edu/hopper/) and Brepolis (http://www.brepolis.net/): last access 2019.01.31.

3.1 The "expansion" of equality

To illustrate the pertinent question, we have to engage in some kind of "geometrisation" regarding our (technical, this is to be said, rather than mathematical or philosophical) notion of "equality". The analogy runs as follows: on a straight line, if two points are equal, this means they are the same point. If they are not, their relation can be expressed in form of a difference with an algebraic sign (e.g. *+2* or *-2*). If we want to generalise from this "geometrisation", we could say that equality is directionless, while non-equality is oriented. This also means that there are always at least two possible expressions of the same "non-equality", depending on the point of reference. Transferred to the realm of text, the most simple case would be that a given text t1 contains one word more than a given text t2 or that t2 contains one word less than t1.[11] Already this rather trivial assumption leads to a central problem when it comes to the comparison of texts as lists of words, i.e., as "sequences": in order to establish the fact that a word contained in sequence 2 is *not* part of sequence 1, one would – normally – have to compare both sequences mutually, because it is not possible to actually compare something *not* included in the first sequence, or, more specific, something which cannot be addressed properly because the total number of words is smaller than in the other sequence.

There are certain more complex problems when it comes to comparing texts in practice, and those examples might clarify what we mean when we are talking about the "expansion" of the technical notion of equality. In fact, especially the case mentioned above of one word missing or being more than in the other text in a certain passage, can be understood not just as difference when it comes to the text as a whole. E.g., this might on a larger scale be the case in the likely scenario in which a bigger part of a given text differs from the passage of the juxtaposed sequence that is expected to be its counterpart, but could indeed be seen as "equal" to another passage in that text.

This is where our notion of "partial non-equality" comes into play. This category covers the spectrum in which parts or single words of a whole text differ from the other text, and could be either "healed" through omitting parts of it,[12] by modifying it, or might still occur in the other text at another position. This, on the one hand, might point towards a different kind of difference (a

11 If a word is "different" according to our everyday concept, this could be considered something more *and* less in each of the texts on the technical level. This case, however, is not part of what shall be illustrated here, as will hopefully become more obvious from the following.

12 Which would most likely indicate a "true" difference (two different words at the same positions of two sequences, the blind spot of the "geometrical" analogy above).

commutation, a parenthesis, a diplography, or the like), and, even more importantly, on the other hand offers the opportunity to set a new starting point for the comparison at the position(s) where the word shows up again.

In short, this "expansion" of the notion of equality is the basis for a constantly repeated search for possible matches, even in the case of an apparent difference. In the next sections, this process and how it is also leading to the above mentioned "maximisation" of results will be illustrated.

3.2 The comparison process

eComparatio compares any given number of versions of a text. While the final results are the outcome of comparisons of each single version with every other, we shall concentrate at this point on the comparison of two versions.

The basic assumption – as with every comparison software – is the general similarity of the texts. The algorithm starts comparing the first words in both texts, which are represented as mere lists of words or as "sequences". As long as the words on the corresponding positions show no difference, they will be considered equal. As soon as we encounter a difference, the case of logical ambiguity is on hand: in this case, the software will check at first if equality can be established by applying certain modifications (i.e., identifying the difference as a difference in diacritics, punctuation, capitalization, ligatures, homophonous letters as u and v in Latin, a different orthography, etc.): aBcd ... / abcd .... If this is the case, the comparison will go on at the next position in the list, e.g. position 3 in text 1 and in text 2.

If equality cannot be established in this way, the search goes on: if the next position (i.e. p3) is equal again, it will be most certainly a different word: axcd / abcd, i.e., a "true difference".

If there is a single word inserted in text 1, it should be able to establish equality by omitting a word: axbc ... / abcd ... can be "healed" by omitting "x". If a single word is inserted in text 2, t1p3 and t2p4 should be equal again: abcd ... / axbcd .... If this is both not the case, the algorithm will start to search text 2 for the next word that equals p3 from t1 (the next "c[s])" in t2), to look if the passage either continues after an intermission of undefined length, or if it does not. In the second case, "c" is identified as a word "more" in t1 than in t2.

In the first case, the neuralgic point is the identification of the right connecting point in t2, i.e., the right "c". In this case, the distance as well as the following equalities and non-equalities are decisive.

The key point in this procedure is that the software is constantly keeping track of the "logical value" of the single relations of the positions compared in the different texts. The highest level of "equality" is based on the above mentioned assumption that in two texts, which more often than not are similar, the same strings (i.e. combination of letters in their numerical representation) at two corresponding positions indeed do represent two "equal" words. The hierarchy of logical validity goes from this via the different states of "partial" inequality already mentioned (containing the cases in which certain kinds of "difference" can be attributed), down to states of logically unsound or rather unreliable states.

To convert those cases of unreliable logical value into a state of "partial inequality", again, the basic assumption is the general similarity of the texts. The algorithm will, as a last step, search the passages identified as unreliable at first for equalities with regard to overall length, to intervals, and, if those measures of "symmetrical" comparison fail, by reading those passages in the opposite direction, also identify commutations and contortions.

3.3 The "maximisation" of results

The self-documentation of the comparison process generates a static representation of the single steps and of the logical decisions that rule the comparison. Those decisions, as has been shown in the section above, establish different categories of what can be addressed as "differences" on the level of the textual comparison. On the one hand, the categorisation of differences distinguishes eComparatio from other similar software. The self-documentation, on the other hand, paves the way for representing the result in rather different visual and analytic forms and ways, and it enables the user to change on the fly what we could call "base-text".

4 The application of eComparatio compared with some similar software tools

Apart from eComparatio, there is obviously plenty of other software designed for the purpose of comparing texts in a similar fashion, and it seems to be reasonable here to highlight the differences to illustrate the place of eCompartio in this area of research. The point here is to show the differences in approach in the sense of an environmental analysis, to give the user a better understanding which software might be the first choice due to her or his specific concerns.

There are two tools which shall be discussed here: Juxta[13] and CollateX.[14] Both are, as eComparatio, comparison tools for plain text that needs no further formatting.

4.1 Juxta

Juxta "is an open-source tool for comparing and collating multiple witnesses to a single textual work." It is also originally provided for "scholars and editors who want to examine the history of a text from manuscript to print versions".[15] While it is possible to download an older version of Juxta, you can also use a browser application in a beta status, the most recent version.

Other than eComparatio, Juxta has its focus on modern philologies. As a result of this, Juxta does not contain special features designed to work with texts in the classical languages: For example, the user does not have the opportunity to choose whether the Latin u/v and the Greek diacritics are valued as differences or not, as he or she has in eComparatio. This and the special classification and statistical analysis based on this differentiation are not possible in Juxta.

An even more important difference that has its roots in the different approaches and needs in the different philologies is the following: Juxta seems to be designed with the routines of copy-text editing in mind. Therefore, its emphasis lies on a representation of the results of the comparison in form of a single base-text, in which all differences to the other texts are shown. Another possibility is the contrasting juxtaposition of two single witnesses. Thus there is no overall view like the synopsis in eComparatio. The latter one, which allows an actual contrasting juxtaposition of all witnesses and highlights the particular differences in each of the comparison texts, seems to be more convenient for the procedure of collating in classical philology.

The apparatus automatically generated by the tools are in both cases what one could call an "apparatus of variants". This might serve in any case as a basis when it comes to comparing textual witnesses that can be categorised on the same level. In the case of Juxta, a feature for continuative hierarchising is in the making, but still in a test phase yet. In general, it can be said that the apparatus is designed rather with regard to the conventions of modern philologies.

13 http://www.juxtasoftware.org (last access 2019.01.31).
14 https://collatex.net (last access 2019.01.31).
15 http://www.juxtasoftware.org/about/ (last access 2019.01.31).

eComparatio provides an HTML-export of the data of the apparatus, and it is possible to change the base text on the fly. A further hierarchisation of the output-data has to be carried out manually.

4.2 CollateX

Similar to Juxta, CollateX[16] seems to concentrate rather on the needs of modern philology. One of the main differences with eComparatio, again, lies in the possibility to determinate the specific category of a textual difference. Another advantage of eComparatio is the statistical evaluation of the results of the comparison. Relating to different representations, CollateX provides two different views. At first, there is a graphic representation of the text which is a very useful tool for identifying the relations of the text with regard to possible dependencies. Secondly, there is an "Alignment Table", on which two texts are juxtaposed, and the differences are highlighted at a word level. An option similar to the synopsis of eComparatio does not exist. The number of comparison texts is arbitrary in both tools, but eComparatio seems to run more smoothly when it comes to longer texts, at least when it comes to the browser-based versions of the tools. One of the main differences between both tools is the choice of a base-text and the arbitrary change of this base-text, which is not possible with CollateX.

5 Conclusion

The paper has given a short overview of the original purposes of eComparatio and has tried to show why the software tool can actually be helpful not only to historians and scholars working with different (digitised and digital) editions, but could also be of interest to those who want to compare texts with other objectives. Some features of the software such as the possibility to compare an arbitrary number of versions of a text of (theoretically) also arbitrary length, the HTML-output of apparatus-data for further use, or the possibility to change the base text on the fly, have been pointed out to be valuable aspects on the side of usability.

16 CollateX can be used in a browser version as Demo (https://collatex.net/demo/: last access 2019.01.31). A downloadable version is provided. To examine the main features of this tool, the demo version should be sufficient.

The most important point in our view, however, is the unique comparison algorithm itself, which is not only able to classify the differences found, but also manages contortions and commutations in the texts to be identified, a problem with which comparison software based on diff algorithms often struggles. The concept of "partial differences" or "extended" equality furthermore leads to a high resilience of the algorithm especially when the number of differences – in particular the length of the inserted passages in one or the other text – grows.

Bibliography

Asulanus, F. (1526): In Aristotelis Physicorum libros commentaria. Simplicii Commentarii in octo Aristotelis physicae auscultationis libros cum ipso Aristotelis textu. Venedig: F. Asulanus.

Diels, H. (1882): Commentaria in Aristotelem Graeca. Vol. IX, Simplicii in Physicorum libros quattuor priores. Berlin.

Diels, H. (1903): Die Fragmente der Vorsokratiker. Berlin: Weidmannsche Buchhandlung.

Graham, D.W. (2010): The Texts of the Early Greek Philosophy, Cambridge: Cambridge University Press.

Kirk, G.S.; Raven, J.E.; Schofield, M. (2001): Die Vorsokratischen Philosophen. Einführung, Texte und Kommentare. Stuttgart-Weimar: J.B. Metzler.

Mansfeld, J. (1983): Die Vorsokratiker, Band 1. Stuttgart: Philipp Reclam jun. Verlag

Mansfeld, J. (2009): "Bothering the Infinite. Anaximander in the Nineteenth Century And Beyond". Antiquorum Philosophia 2009:3, 9–68.

Appendix

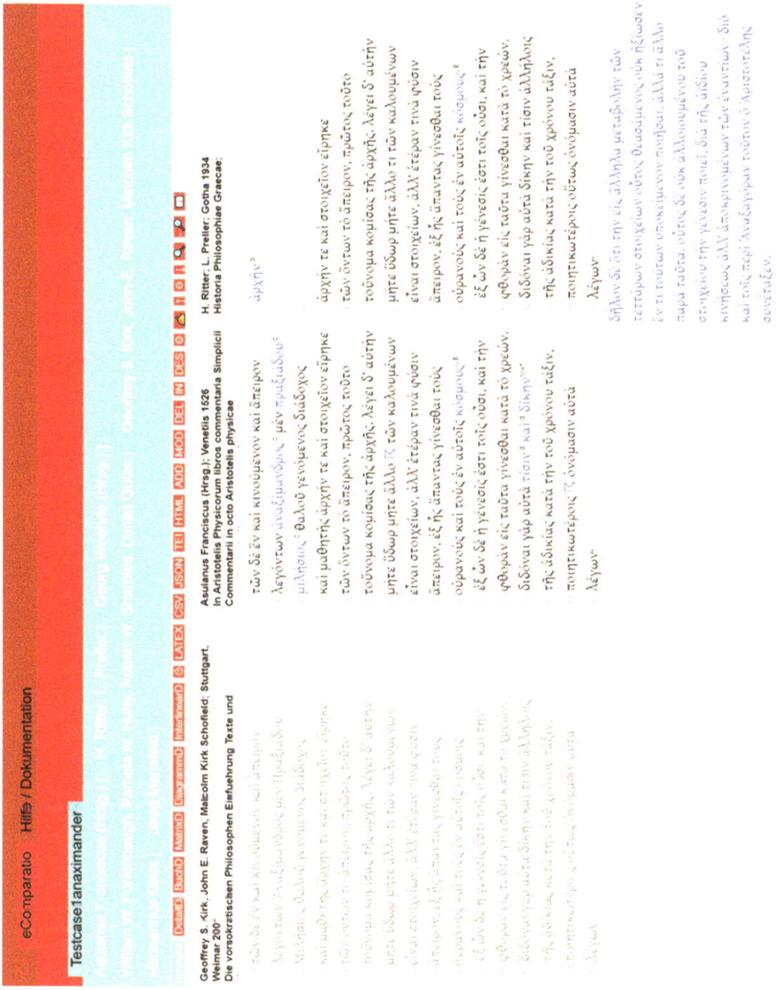

Figure 3: The synopsis provides the user with an exactly aligned juxtaposition of the chosen base text and the texts it is compared with. Differences are highlighted in every single one of the texts checked against the base text.

Georg Woehrle (Hrsg.); Berlin, Boston 2012
Die Milesier Anaximander und Anaximenes;

τῶν δὲ ἓν καὶ κινούμενον καὶ ἄπειρον
λεγόντων Ἀναξίμανδρος μὲν Πραξιάδου
Μιλήσιος Θαλοῦ[C] γενόμενος διάδοχος
καὶ μαθητὴς ἀρχήν τε καὶ στοιχεῖον εἴρηκε
τῶν ὄντων τὸ ἄπειρον, πρῶτος τοῦτο
τοὔνομα κομίσας τῆς ἀρχῆς. λέγει δ' αὐτὴν
μήτε ὕδωρ μήτε ἄλλο τι τῶν καλουμένων
εἶναι στοιχείων, ἀλλ' ἑτέραν τινὰ φύσιν
ἄπειρον, ἐξ ἧς ἅπαντας γίνεσθαι τοὺς
οὐρανοὺς καὶ τοὺς ἐν αὐτοῖς κόσμους·[E]
ἐξ ὧν δὲ ἡ γένεσίς ἐστι τοῖς οὖσι, καὶ τὴν
φθορὰν εἰς ταῦτα γίνεσθαι κατὰ τὸ χρεών.
διδόναι γὰρ αὐτὰ δίκην καὶ τίσιν ἀλλήλοις
τῆς ἀδικίας κατὰ τὴν τοῦ χρόνου τάξιν,
ποιητικωτέροις οὕτως ὀνόμασιν αὐτὰ
λέγων·

William W. Fortenbaugh, Pamela M. Huby, Robert W. Sharples, Dimitri Gutas; Leiden, New York, Köln 1992
Theophrastus of Eresus Sources for his life Writings

τῶν δὲ ἓν καὶ κινούμενον καὶ ἄπειρον
λεγόντων Ἀναξίμανδρος μὲν Πραξιάδου
Μιλήσιος Θαλοῦ[C] γενόμενος διάδοχος
καὶ μαθητὴς ἀρχήν τε καὶ στοιχεῖον εἴρηκε
τῶν ὄντων τὸ ἄπειρον, πρῶτος τοῦτο
τοὔνομα κομίσας τῆς ἀρχῆς. λέγει δ' αὐτὴν
μήτε ὕδωρ μήτε ἄλλο τι τῶν καλουμένων
εἶναι στοιχείων, ἀλλ' ἑτέραν τινὰ φύσιν
ἄπειρον, ἐξ ἧς ἅπαντας γίνεσθαι τοὺς
οὐρανοὺς καὶ τοὺς ἐν αὐτοῖς κόσμους·[E]
ἐξ ὧν δὲ ἡ γένεσίς ἐστι τοῖς οὖσι, καὶ τὴν
φθορὰν εἰς ταῦτα γίνεσθαι κατὰ τὸ χρεών.
διδόναι γὰρ αὐτὰ δίκην καὶ τίσιν ἀλλήλοις
τῆς ἀδικίας κατὰ τὴν τοῦ χρόνου τάξιν,
ποιητικωτέροις οὕτως ὀνόμασιν αὐτὰ
λέγων·

Hermannus Diels; Berlin 1903
Die Fragmente der Vorsokratiker;

τῶν δὲ ἓν καὶ κινούμενον καὶ ἄπειρον
λεγόντων Ἀναξίμανδρος μὲν Πραξιάδου
Μιλήσιος Θαλοῦ[C] γενόμενος διάδοχος
καὶ μαθητὴς ἀρχήν τε καὶ στοιχεῖον εἴρηκε
τῶν ὄντων τὸ ἄπειρον, πρῶτος τοῦτο
τοὔνομα κομίσας τῆς ἀρχῆς. λέγει δ'[D] αὐτὴν
μήτε ὕδωρ μήτε ἄλλο τι τῶν καλουμένων
εἶναι στοιχείων, ἀλλ'[D] ἑτέραν τινὰ φύσιν
ἄπειρον, ἐξ ἧς ἅπαντας γίνεσθαι τοὺς
οὐρανοὺς καὶ τοὺς ἐν αὐτοῖς κόσμους·[E]
ἐξ ὧν δὲ ἡ γένεσίς ἐστι τοῖς οὖσι, καὶ τὴν
φθορὰν εἰς ταῦτα γίνεσθαι κατὰ τὸ χρεών·
διδόναι γὰρ αὐτὰ δίκην καὶ τίσιν ἀλλήλοις
τῆς ἀδικίας κατὰ τὴν τοῦ χρόνου τάξιν,
ποιητικωτέροις οὕτως ὀνόμασιν αὐτὰ
λέγων.

Jaap Mansfeld; Stuttgart 1983
Die Vorsokratiker Band 1 Milesier Pythagoreer Xenophanes Heraklit Parmenides;

Ἀναξίμανδρος[G]
Ἀναξίμανδρος μὲν Πραξιάδου
Μιλήσιος Θαλοῦ[C] γενόμενος διάδοχος
καὶ ⇒
τῶν ὄντων τὸ ἄπειρον,
ἀρχῆς. λέγει δ' αὐτὴν
μήτε ὕδωρ μήτε ἄλλο τι τῶν καλουμένων
εἶναι στοιχείων, ἀλλ' ἑτέραν τινὰ φύσιν
ἄπειρον, ἐξ ἧς ἅπαντας γίνεσθαι τοὺς
οὐρανοὺς καὶ τοὺς ἐν αὐτοῖς κόσμους·[E]
ἐξ ὧν δὲ ἡ γένεσίς ἐστι τοῖς οὖσι, καὶ τὴν
φθορὰν εἰς ταῦτα γίνεσθαι κατὰ τὸ χρεών.
διδόναι γὰρ αὐτὰ δίκην καὶ τίσιν ἀλλήλοις
τῆς ἀδικίας κατὰ τὴν τοῦ χρόνου τάξιν,
ποιητικωτέροις οὕτως ὀνόμασιν αὐτὰ
λέγων·

Figure 3 (continued)

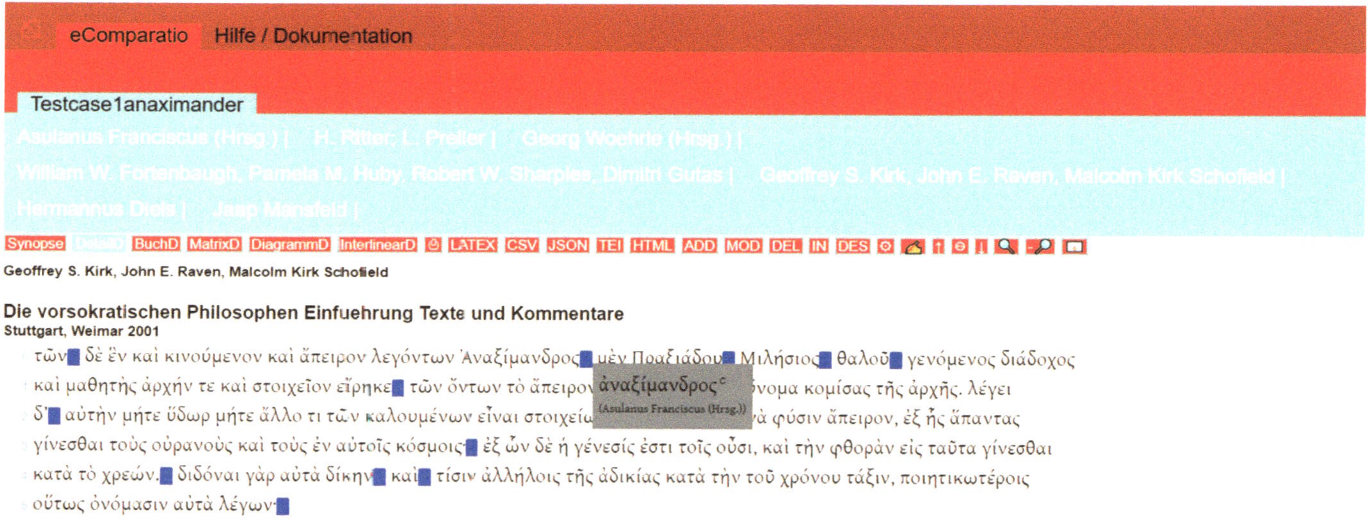

Figure 4: The detail view shows the comparison results as indices in the base text. By clicking the index mark, all differences occurring in other versions of the text regarding the particular word are displayed.

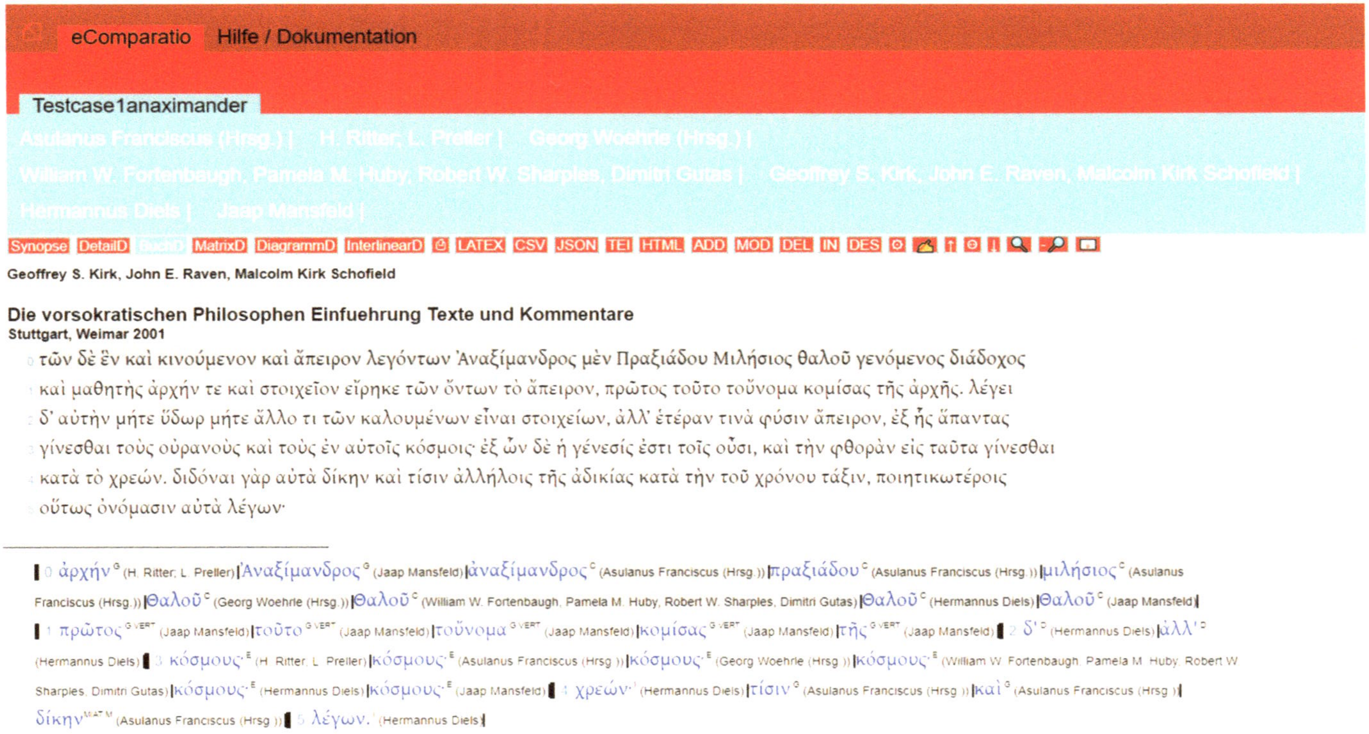

Figure 5: The book view imitates the apparatus of a printed edition. The apparatus can be adapted to personal needs by the user.

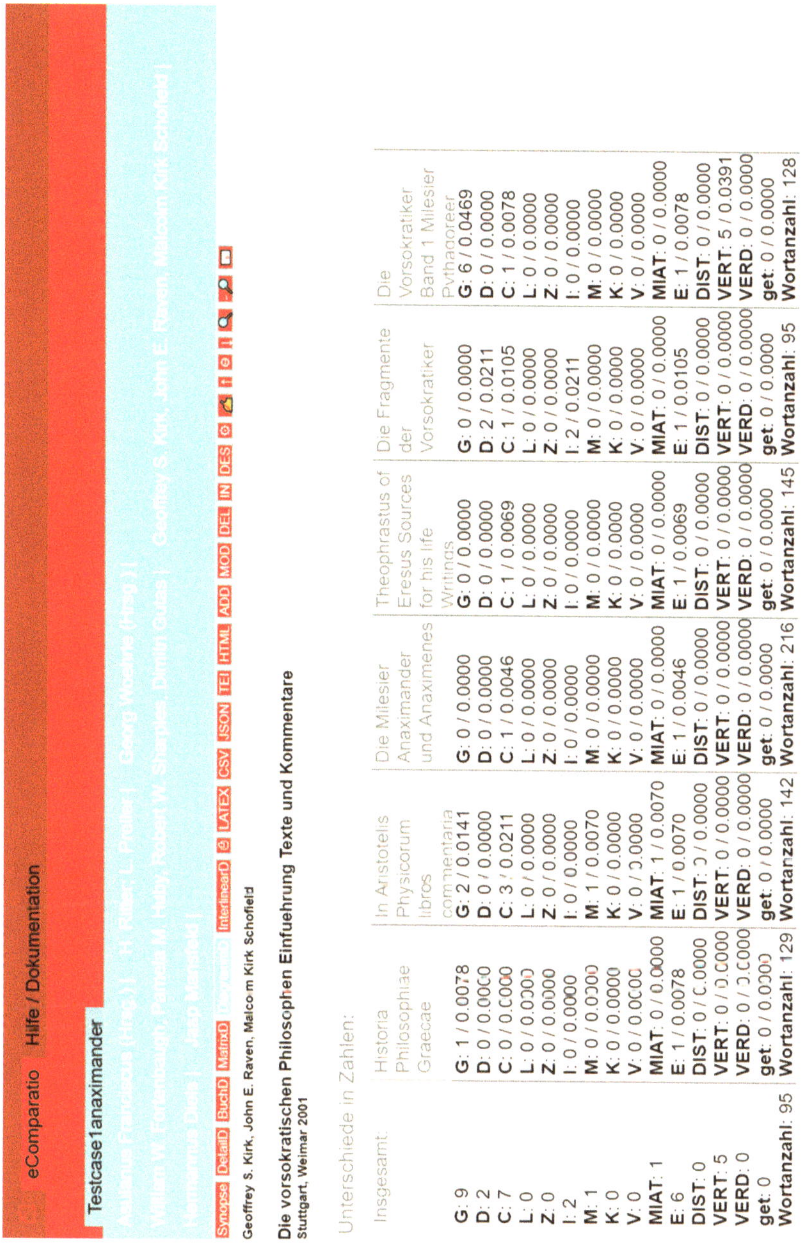

Figure 6: The classification of differences can be used for various statistical analyses.

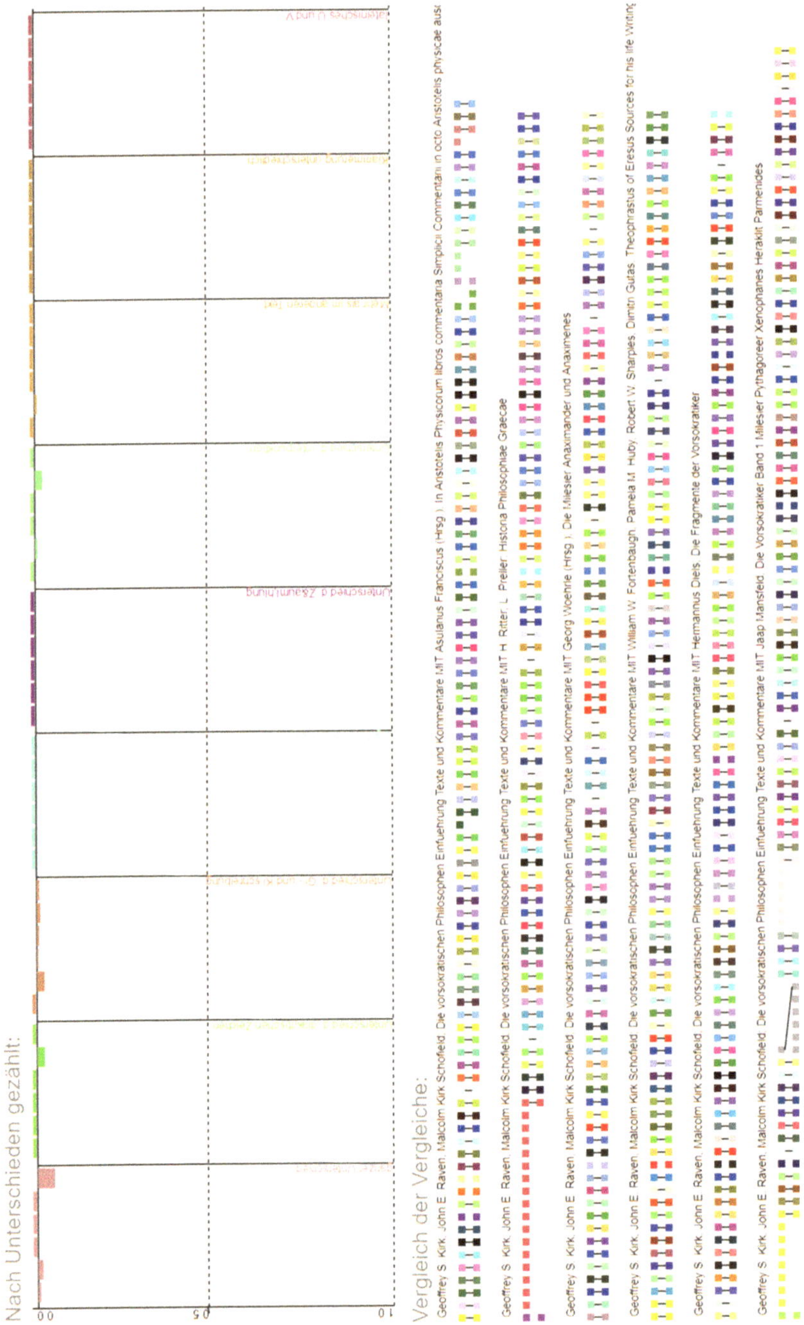

Figure 6 (continued)

Casey Dué and Mary Ebbott

The Homer Multitext within the History of Access to Homeric Epic

Abstract: Through a series of descriptive vignettes, this paper considers "access" at selected points within the long history of the Homeric epics to investigate our own principles of access in the Homer Multitext. We examine modes of access to the *Iliad* and commentary on it in four historical eras (5th-century BCE Athens, 2nd-century BCE Alexandria, 1st-century CE Rome, and 15th-century CE Venice). Using the contexts of these historical moments, we then reflect on our own point in that history: how are we as editors replicating, replacing, or reviving modes or limitations of access through the structures and intentional editorial decisions of the digital Homer Multitext?

Introduction

The Homer Multitext (HMT) has its origins and purpose in the use of digital tools to better reveal, represent, and investigate the Homeric epics and their oral, traditional nature. Questions about the significance and consequence of access within the project arose as soon as we had acquired high-resolution digital photographs of three manuscripts of the *Iliad* from the Biblioteca Marciana in Venice (Marciana 821, 822, 841) in 2007. What do we mean by access, and what would access to these manuscripts look like within the HMT? What would it take to provide meaningful access to the texts they contain? Some of these questions were answered immediately and definitively: the Homer Multitext would publish those photographs under a Creative Commons license allowing for reuse by anyone even before we had used them in our own editions. As the team of HMT editors began work on creating digital editions from these and other manuscripts, we were confronted with further questions related to access: who is our intended audience or user, what will different users need from the editions, how will paradigms of scholarship shift now that access to the manuscripts will be more readily available and now that we can begin to ask questions about the texts and scholia that were simply not possible before?

These questions of access to the epic poetry – and to commentary on and interpretation of that poetry – have accompanied the Homeric epics through

Casey Dué, University of Houston
Mary Ebbott, College of the Holy Cross

https://doi.org/10.1515/9783110599572-014

much of their long history. After we look at selected points within that history and consider the shape of access at each one, we can ask how we are replicating, replacing, or reviving certain kinds of access through the digital medium and through the structures and intentional editorial decisions of the HMT. We have chosen four points in this long history to examine what access to the *Iliad* and commentary on it looked like, and each of them will provide some context and some questions to consider about our own point in that history.

Athens in the late 5th century BCE

It is a summer day. The moon is waning. It is the last week of Hekatombaion, and the annual festival of the Panathenaia is beginning.[1] If it is the Great Panathenaia this year, celebrated every four years, there will be a weeklong series of events involving contests of both musical and athletic skills. The festival culminates in an elaborate procession in honor of Athena and the dedication of her new *peplos*. Then there will be a sacrifice of a *hekatomb*, one hundred cattle, providing a feast of meat for everyone there. On this first day of the festival, the musical competitions are held.

In a large performance space (venues throughout the centuries may have included the Agora, the Pnyx, the Odeon of Perikles, and much later the Theater of Dionysus), an international lineup of Homeric performers (rhapsodes) perform the epics of Homer, which have been strictly defined for this event as the *Iliad* and the *Odyssey*. The audience, numbering in the thousands, has access to these poems in performance, in a state-organized religious festival in honor of the patron goddess of the *polis*. The rhapsodes are competing for significant cash prizes, and they are held to specific rules. Each one must perform his assigned part, an episode between 500 and 800 lines long that is part of the defined narrative sequence. The rhapsode who performs the next episode in the sequence must be able to pick up the narrative thread where the last performer left off. Thus even as they compete with one another, the rules of the competition result in the rhapsodes connecting their performances to one another and cooperating to perform the complete narrative. This state-sanctioned and state-sponsored performance of the Homeric epics is its most authoritative in Athens.

Four years is a long time to wait for access to these poems again. It seems that the same rhapsodes who perform at the Panathenaia and other religious

1 For our description of the performance of the *Iliad* and *Odyssey* at the Panathenaia we are indebted to Connelly (2014), Nagy (2002), Neils (1992; 2007), and Shapiro (1992; 2015).

festivals in other *poleis* can also offer a performance in the hopes of the audience paying them directly. Athenians might have access to the Homeric epics more often through a performance of that kind. Ion, the professional rhapsode in Plato's dialogue named for him, provides an example.[2] He has come to Athens for the Panathenaia having just competed in Epidauros (*Ion* 530a–b). Socrates expresses his hope that Ion will show him his skill in performing Homeric epic *and* in explaining it – that is, his expertise in being an interpreter of the poet's *dianoia*, or intention (530c–d). Thus rhapsodes in some situations provide commentary on the poetry as well. These other possible performances are implied when Socrates asks Ion about the emotional effects of his performance (535b–e). Ion agrees to Socrates' suggestion that a rhapsode would naturally pick either the exciting or the sad parts. The rhapsode selects which parts of the epics he wants to sing (or the audience might request a particular part), and he chooses the most emotionally affecting parts in order to get paid.

At the Panathenaia, the rules require that the whole song be sung in a particular order. When a rhapsode is performing on his own, the audience's preferences influence the choice of episodes and how they are performed. Such individual performances by rhapsodes, including explanation of the poetry, are also alluded to by the 4th-century Athenian orator Isocrates (*Panathenaicus* 18–19, 33),[3] who disparages those who recite and explain Homeric epic in the Lyceum. What is the significance of this location for the performances that Isocrates criticizes? The Lyceum is a center of education, and men of a certain social class, at least, would have an education in which these epics held the greatest prominence.[4] In two of Xenophon's dialogues about Socrates – his teacher as well as Plato's – an interlocutor is said to know or possess all of Homer's verses. In Xenophon's *Symposium*, Nikeratos relates "My father, taking care that I should become a good man, compelled me to learn all of Homer's verses. And now I could speak the whole *Iliad* and *Odyssey* 'by mouth' [i.e., 'by heart']."[5] Euthydemos in the *Memorabilia* is asked by Socrates whether he wants to be a rhapsode, "for they say that you have acquired all of Homer's verses."[6] Euthydemos demurs, not, it seems, because he couldn't perform them, but because he considers rhapsodes "entirely silly" (πάνυ ἠλιθίους). These educated

2 See Nagy (1996; 2002) for more on this dialogue and the performance of Homeric epic in the 5th century.

3 (Nagy 1996, 122–125).

4 See Robb (1994) and Yamagata (2012).

5 ὁ πατὴρ ὁ ἐπιμελούμενος ὅπως ἀνὴρ ἀγαθὸς γενοίμην ἠνάγκασέ με πάντα τὰ Ὁμήρου ἔπη μαθεῖν: καὶ νῦν δυναίμην ἂν Ἰλιάδα ὅλην καὶ Ὀδύσσειαν ἀπὸ στόματος εἰπεῖν, *Symposium* 3.5.

6 καὶ γὰρ τὰ Ὁμήρου σέ φασιν ἔπη πάντα κεκτῆσθαι, *Memorabilia* 4.2.10

young men have been taught Homeric epic so thoroughly that each now seems to have access to any and all of it through his own memory. Their learning it by heart, so that it is something they "own", suggests that they can now access it without need for a text, if there ever was one.

In Classical Athens, Homeric epic was *heard* in many venues and situations, and these informal and formal performances provided access both to the poetry and to interpretation and thoughts about it. As we move ahead in time to the 2nd century BCE and to a different place – Alexandria, Egypt – we also shift to considering a proliferation of *texts*. Performance of the epics still occurred into the Roman era, but our next historical moment is focused on access to texts.

Alexandria in the 2nd century BCE

Overlooking the city's great harbor on the Mediterranean is the famous Library of Alexandria, established by Ptolemy Soter, a promoter of scholarship.[7] Its monumental collection grows each time a ship comes into that harbor: city officials collect whatever books are on board and bring them to the Library to be copied. The confiscated books are kept by the Library, and the copies returned to the owners, who had to hope they got a better deal in whatever business brought them to the city. What else might you expect from a Library with the purpose of collecting "all the books in world"?

Access to the Library's holdings might have been restricted to those scholars associated with the institution. (A smaller "sister" library, also founded by the Ptolemies, seems to have been available nearby and was more open.) Those privileged scholars in the famous Library might have been able to see hundreds of thousands of scrolls, rolled up with protective covers on, perhaps with a tag on the end to identify the contents. Under the Library directorship of Zenodotus in the 3rd century, Callimachus had created his Tables (*Pinakes*) that gave some account of the Library's holdings as representative of human knowledge: a collection of that size needs some way of being organized.

When it comes to the *Iliad*, collecting all the books in the world means collecting many copies, and as it happens, many *versions* of it. Three heads of the Library – Zenodotus of Ephesus [c. 284 – c. 260 BCE], Aristophanes of Byzantium [c. 194–180 BCE], and Aristarchus of Samothrace [sometime after

7 Our description of the Library and Egyptian papyri of the *Iliad* relies on Berti (2016), Heller-Roazen (2002), Morgan (1998), Nagy (1996). See also Finkelberg (2006), McNamee (1981), and Porter (1992).

180–145/4 BCE] – took advantage of the possibility afforded by the collection to compare these many versions. In the commentaries (*hupomnēmata*) that Aristarchus wrote on the *Iliad*, he makes remarks and judgments on these many versions, which included the work of his predecessors in Alexandria and even scholars at other libraries, such as Crates at the rival library in Pergamum, as well as texts collected from several places around the Mediterranean, called in the scholia the "city" (*politikai*) copies. For scholars in a center of learning such as the Library of Alexandria at this time, access was abundant.

To judge by the number of papyri of the *Iliad* that survive from this period, the epic was also a popular text outside of the library. The general reader, whoever he may have been, had access to the *Iliad* in a common or standard version. As we move past the middle of the 2nd century, greater standardization is seen in the papyri. The texts found in the papyri are also simpler, usually without commentary or comparison to other texts, and are found throughout Egypt.

A subset of the papyri of the *Iliad* from this era have been identified as "school texts." Such papyri come from several locations in Egypt, including smaller towns and villages, and are a high proportion of papyri finds from the 2nd century BCE. To judge from the absolute number of these Homeric school texts found, the fact that they are about two-thirds of the total number found, and that the school texts of the *Iliad* far outnumber those of the *Odyssey* (86 vs 11), it seems that anyone who received some sort of education was introduced to the *Iliad*. Homeric epic was part of early education and continued to be central throughout formal education. This access may have been of a limited sort – for example, learning the first lines of the *Iliad* as a writing or memorization exercise – yet encounters with the *Iliad* in education were frequent.

From a beginning student learning to read and write to international scholars consulting texts from everywhere Homeric epic was known, a proliferation of texts in this period granted differing levels of access. The *Iliad* was both the foundation and the pinnacle of Greek learning. That status would continue under the Roman Empire.

Rome in the 1st century CE

An elaborate dinner party, one meant to impress, must offer entertainment as well as lavish food. The *Iliad* and *Odyssey*, now centerpieces of education for those classes distinguished by their learning in Greek, might show up in many forms: as subject matter for beautiful wall paintings within the dining room, as allusions embedded in dinner conversation between learned hosts and guests, or even more directly in performance, for at this dinner party the host has hired entertainers to act out episodes from the epics.

The dinner party that allows us this glimpse, albeit a satirical one, of the varieties of access to Homer in 1st-century CE Rome is the one given by the affluent and ostentatious freedman Trimalchio in Petronius' *Satyricon*. Trimalchio has wealth to match his limitless aspirations of status and esteem.[8] But as Petronius portrays him, Trimalchio's former life has not prepared him for the life to which he aspires. While his guests are entertained by a group of *Homeristai* who act out episodes from the Homeric epics in Greek, Trimalchio reads along in a Latin crib.

The character of Trimalchio is being mocked for his intellectual pretensions and their attendant class aspirations: his attempts to display his own erudition is woefully confused, a hopeless jumble of half-remembered Greek myths. Trimalchio understands that among elite Romans "one ought to know philology even in the midst of dinner" (*oportet etiam inter cenandum philologiam nosse* 39),[9] and he claims to possess libraries in both Latin and Greek (48), but he cannot understand the performance of the *Homeristai* without a Latin translation to guide him, and he mangles the plot of the *Iliad* when he speaks about it, indiscriminately mixing in an episode narrated in the Epic Cycle (and Greek tragedy), with dramatic culinary results.

By contrast we can assume that Petronius' learned audience *does* know their Homer, and so can understand just how much Trimalchio gets wrong. The *Satyricon* as a whole relies on its own audience's familiarity with the *Iliad* and *Odyssey* for its full effect of "playfulness and irony" with Homeric epic's grandeur.[10] Trimalchio's feast, with its many Homeric allusions and in-jokes, reveals the various ways that Romans of different social classes might have encountered the Homeric poems in the Early Empire.

Most Romans probably did not experience Homer in books but in dramatic public performances in the tradition of mimes and pantomimes. In the Hellenistic world, and as early as the time of Demetrius of Phalerum in the late 4th century BCE, the performances of Homeric epic became more and more theatrical, performed at festivals along with mimes, pantomimes, and dances.[11] By the early Roman Empire, "Homeric performances had essentially become the

---

8 For the Homeric elements in the Satyricon, see Cameron (1969), Horsfall (1989), Farrell (2004), Hurka (2007), Schmeling (2002), and Ypsilanti (2010).

9 Or possibly, as Ruden translates it, "you've gotta know a little literature, even if it's only for the dinner table."

10 (Ypsilanti 2010, 221).

11 (Nagy 1996, 153–186). See also González (2013, 447–465) with additional citations *ad loc.*

prerogative of other Homerists – actors, mimes, and pantomimes, who came to be included in official performances and contests in the 2nd century CE, so popular had they become."[12] These more popular forms of Homeric entertainment are reflected in the performance of the *Homeristai* at Trimalchio's dinner when they act out battles scenes with shields and spears for the entertainment of Trimalchio's guests.

Trimalchio seems to think that he should know Homer if he is to impress high-class guests, even as his attempts to display his "philology" give his ignorance away. But why? The Romans connected their own foundational stories, their earliest history, to the Trojan War.[13] By the 1st centuries BCE and CE frescoes in Roman houses depict Homeric landscapes and scenes: "elite Romans, like the Etruscans before them, surrounded themselves with visual Iliads and, especially, Odysseys."[14] Roman letters from this time also display a deep familiarity with the poems on the part of educated Romans. Cicero, for example, not only quotes the epics but does so in playful ways that suggest intimate knowledge of them by both writer and audience.[15]

How did these elite Romans come by this familiarity? What did they have access to that a man like Trimalchio couldn't have? First and foremost was their education. As Farrell (2004, 267) describes it, "Easy familiarity with Homer was the mark of an expensive education." Children from wealthier Roman families were brought up with knowledge of Greek literature and especially Homer, as well as the Roman poets such as Livius Andronicus (who translated the *Odyssey* into Latin), Naevius, Ennius, and, later, Virgil.[16] Horace attests to the *Iliad*'s role in his education: *Romae nutriri mihi contigit atque doceri/iratus Grais quantum nocuisset Achilles* "It was my fate to be brought up in Rome and to be taught/ how much the angered Achilles harmed the Greeks," *Epistles* 2.2.41–42. If Trimalchio did not know Greek and therefore did not have "easy familiarity with Homer," he would always be out of place among the educated elite, no matter how much wealth he amassed.

What does access to Homer in written form look like at this point in time? How did a poet like Virgil, for example, come to know the *Iliad* and *Odyssey* so intimately?[17] Given the limitations of our evidence, we have to essentially work

12 (Gangloff 2018, 147).
13 Joseph Farrell (2004, 254) has demonstrated that Homer pervaded Roman life, especially for elite Romans. See also Tolkhien (1897, 1900).
14 (Farrell 2004, 262).
15 (Farrell 2004, 266).
16 See Horace, *Satires* 1.6.71–78, *Epistles* 2.1.28–71 and 2.2.41–42, and Quintilian 1.8.5.
17 See Nelis (2010) for his exploration of this question.

backwards, deducing what works Virgil must have consulted via the allusions we recognize to them, but we know little that is certain about his working methods.[18] Libraries, both private and public, existed in and around Augustan Rome, though it is not clear who had borrowing privileges (if anyone did), or how easily texts were accessed.[19] Cicero, for example, not only owned a great many books, he frequently borrowed books from his wealthy equestrian friend Atticus, who seems to have owned (or had access to) everything.

Both Virgil and Cicero came from families who could afford to provide them with an education. Virgil's patron, moreover, was Maecenas, and by extension, Augustus, putting him among "elite Romans," however elite is defined. Whether through personal collection, consultation of libraries, or borrowing from friends or literary patrons, Virgil had access to the *Iliad* and *Odyssey*, Greek tragedy, and the scholarly material that has been transmitted in the Homeric scholia.[20] In addition to books, Virgil may have also had access to Homeric scholars. Aristonicus, whose work is excerpted in the scholia of the Venetus A manuscript of the *Iliad*, was in Rome during Virgil's lifetime and at least one point of contact can be found between Aristonicus' scholarly publications and Virgil's *Aeneid*.[21]

In Rome, the educated elite had easy access to Homer, even before the adoption of the codex book form or the establishment of public libraries at gymnasia or Trajan's grand public library, dedicated in 112/113 CE.[22] Virgil could thus also expect his audience to be knowledgable about Homeric epic. They grew up surrounded by works of art depicting Homeric episodes that they could easily interpret, they learned vast stretches of the *Iliad* and *Odyssey* by heart in school, and they could buy, borrow, and consult texts of the poem on papyrus scrolls. Taking the fictional Trimalchio as a counterexample, we can surmise that non-elite Romans were not educated in the same way and that a lack of knowledge about Homeric epic marked their social status. On the other hand, they had a kind of access to the *Iliad* and *Odyssey* in the form of

18 For a similar approach to reconstructing the library of Plato, see Staikos (2013).

19 As Nicholas Horsfall (2016, 19) has observed, "Everything depended of course on who you were, and who your friends were." For the libraries attested in Virgil's lifetime, see the evidence compiled in Horsfall (2016, 28–29), as well as Horsfall (1993), Casson (2001, 61–123), Nelis (2010, 15–16), Bowie (2013), and Houston (2014). See also the other articles about libraries in the Roman Empire collected in König et al. (2013).

20 The scholarly literature on this topic is vast, but both Nelis (2010) and Horsfall (2016, 17–27) provide overviews with additional bibliography *ad loc.*

21 (Horsfall 2016, 23). On Virgil's access to and familiarity with Homeric scholarship see also Schlunk (1974).

22 On all three of these see Casson (2001, 80–108).

various types of popular entertainment. As we move ahead a thousand years and more, access to texts remains a central question.

Venice in the 15th century CE, by way of 10th century Byzantium

As we look through the deluxe 10th-century manuscript of the *Iliad*, so full of writing on most of its pages, the unusual features stand out. The stain in the margin of one parchment folio perhaps made by red wine around the base of stemmed glass. Pages beautifully written in a 15th-century hand, five hundred years after the manuscript's construction, with empty margins. An invaluable but confusing set of front matter, rebound out of order. A set of 12th-century illustrations, including one that covers up some text. Anachronisms and anomalies like these in the Venetus A manuscript of the *Iliad* give us a glimpse into the Byzantine and Renaissance experience of accessing Homer in manuscript form.

Homer was transmitted from antiquity to the Middle Ages and beyond through the work of literary scholars and philosophers and through education. The *Iliad* and *Odyssey* remained the centerpieces of Greek education from Classical times through the Byzantine Empire. As Christianity developed, Homeric poetry was read through allegorical interpretation and continued to be important in the Christian Byzantine culture. Even beyond allegory, Homer was cited as an authority alongside scripture in both secular and Christian rhetoric.[23]

The Romans who read Homer during imperial times would have done so on papyrus scrolls. Eventually, parchment codices, which resemble modern books in their shape and construction, superseded scrolls as the medium for transmitting literature.[24] Alexandrian and Roman scholars had published their scholarly works and commentaries on the poems in separate scrolls, which could be keyed to the Homeric texts by means of critical signs.[25] The earliest surviving manuscripts of the *Iliad* and *Odyssey* contain both the texts of the poems themselves and excerpts from the scholarly commentaries of antiquity, copied into their margins. These writings in the margins, known as *scholia*, explain points of grammar, usage, the meaning of words, interpretation of the poetry, and arguments about the correct text and the authenticity of verses. Only a small number of the nearly 200 medieval manuscripts of the *Iliad* are deluxe editions complete with scholia.

23 (Browning 1992).
24 (Casson 2001, 124–135); (Ebbott 2009); (Reynolds and Wilson 2014, 34–36).
25 (Pfeiffer 1968, 218); (Nagy 2004, 33–34); (Bird 2009); (Schironi 2018 and forthcoming).

Who had access to such deluxe editions? Who purchased them, read them, and benefitted from their learned commentaries? For whom was the Venetus A, so lavishly produced, initially made? We simply do not know. While we can learn much about how this manuscript was constructed from the document itself,[26] we don't know anything about who commissioned or originally owned this artifact. But its contents reveal that this was no school text, nor was it meant for a casual reader. Not only are difficult points of grammar and punctuation and obscure vocabulary discussed throughout, but the work of the Alexandrian editors who were attempting to establish the correct text of the poem is quoted and discussed extensively. In assembling so much learned commentary into a single document, the Venetus A becomes itself a work of scholarship.

We *do* know something about a later owner, the Greek Cardinal Basileus Bessarion. He acquired both the Venetus A and the Venetus B (an 11th-century manuscript, also in Venice's Marciana Library) in the 15th century CE and donated them together with his entire collection of Greek manuscripts to the Republic of Venice, thereby forming the Marciana library's initial collection.[27] Basileus Bessarion began collecting books at a very early age, and initially on a very constrained budget, when he was a student of philosophy in the Byzantine city of Mistra, in the Peloponnese. As his career in the church advanced, his ability to acquire manuscripts increased, and so did his desire to amass a great library. In 1437 the Byzantine Emperor John VIII Philologus made him Metropolitan of Nicaea and dispatched him to Italy to participate in the decades-long negotiations between the Western and Eastern churches. These negotiations brought Bessarion to the city of Venice in 1438. This *Serenissima Repubblica di Venezia* came to represent for Bessarion a hope for a "Second Byzantium."

Over the next decades, Bessarion's efforts toward building an all-encompassing library of Greek learning took on a new urgency. When news of the fall of Constantinople came to Italy, Bessarion wrote to Michael Apostolis, from whom he had already borrowed, bought, and copied a great number of books, including works on Homeric epic by Quintus of Smyrna. Formerly, he said to his friend, he had collected books for his own pleasure. Now that Constantinople was in the hands of the Ottoman Sultan, he wanted to acquire all Greek literature, to keep it in some safe place, where it would be accessible to all readers until Greece was once again free.

---

26 (Allen 1899); (Dué 2009); (Dué and Ebbott 2014); (Kalavrezou 2009).

27 For more on Bessarion and the historical context in which he acquired and then donated the Venetus A to the Republic of Venice, see Blackwell and Dué (2009), as well as Labowski (1979).

Is the wine glass stain in the Venetus A Bessarion's? There is probably no way to know. But it is quite possible that the nineteen folios of the Venetus A that are written in a 15th century hand, folios that no doubt were lost from the original manuscript during the centuries between its construction and Bessarion's acquisition of it and had to be replaced, are the work of Bessarion's own hand. Because the parchment used was so durable, manuscripts were typically rebound and repaired at many points in their history. It is possible that during the rebinding of the Venetus A required to add Bessarion's replacement folios, some of the front matter (which preserves excerpts from Proclus' *Chrestomathy*, including a summary of most of the now lost poems of the Epic Cycle) was rebound out of order.

Three centuries earlier, an owner of the Venetus A copied an excerpt from Heliodorus' novel, the *Aithiopika*, into a blank portion of a folio in the front matter, perhaps confusing the *Aithiopika* with the similarly titled epic poem the *Aithiopis*. Soon after (within a century) someone had painted over it and also added to the margins in the front matter illustrations of scenes from the Epic Cycle. As manuscripts changed owners through the centuries and went through varying periods of neglect and care, and as the needs and desires of readers evolved, manuscripts of the *Iliad* and *Odyssey* both gained and lost valuable material.

When Bessarion donated his manuscript collection to the Republic of Venice in 1468, his collection became a public library that offered access to the works of philosophers, scientists, and theologians, and that was responsible for the rediscovery in Europe of such authors as Athenaeus and Ptolemy the Geographer. Nowhere is the depth and significance of Bessarion's gift more apparent than in his donation of two complete manuscripts of the Homeric *Iliad*. These are now known from their catalogue entries in the Marciana library as Marciana 822 [= Marcianus Graecus Z. 454], the Venetus A, and Marciana 821 [= Marcianus Graecus Z. 453], the Venetus B. Both contain the text of the *Iliad*, surrounded by scholia, which preserve the research and editorial work of the scholars of Ptolemaic Alexandria and Rome. These two manuscripts are now at the heart of the Homer Multitext, a project that provides access to the Homeric epics, Homeric scholarship, and the historical artifacts that transmit them in digital form.

Access in the 21st century – location unrestricted

Bessarion's gift of the Venetus A and B manuscripts of the *Iliad* to the Republic of Venice has given us access to the Homeric scholarship of antiquity. If not for its preservation in the margins of these manuscript, much of that scholarship would be lost. Through access to that scholarship we can better reconstruct

Archaic performance traditions, the editorial practices of Hellenistic and Roman scholars, and the centrality of the Homeric epics in Greek education across the centuries.

In the centuries that followed Bessarion's donation, new technologies allowed for new means of access to the *Iliad*.[28] The first printed edition of the Greek text of the *Iliad* (without scholia) was made in Florence in 1488–1489. The Venetus A and B manuscripts of the *Iliad* were not published until 1788, when Jean Baptiste d'Anse de Villoison rediscovered them, so to speak, in the Marciana Library in Venice and published an edition of the *Iliad*, drawing on the texts of both manuscripts, and included their scholia in the back of the book. Prior to that time, they remained in keeping, publicly available, but not, apparently, accessed.[29] In 1901, a photographic facsimile of the Venetus A by Domenico Comparetti was published, allowing a new kind of access to the manuscript outside of the Marciana library. Other editions of the epic poem and other editions of the scholia (always separate from one another) were produced in the 19th and 20th century.

How does the Homer Multitext fit into this long history of the *Iliad* and the commentary on it? What can we learn from these other eras as we continue to think intentionally about what we want access to mean in this digital age? Will digital editions like the Homer Multitext replace print editions, and what would it mean to do so? First we should note that this history shows us that different technologies – access afforded by oral performance vs. written text, scrolls vs. codices, manuscripts vs. printed books – overlap for a long time before one ever replaces the other completely, if that ever happens. Perhaps, then, we should consider how digital media allow us to *revive* the manuscripts and make them more accessible, rather than simply replace the print edition. What else is worth reviving from this long history? What do we want to replicate from the past, and what do we want to avoid replicating?

Picture the audience of thousands at the Panathenaia listening to the performance of the *Iliad*. Scale of access is one element in our decision making: how to give the greatest number of people access. Those thousands in Athens were all experiencing that performance at the same time in the same space.

28 (Ebbott 2009).

29 This is not to say that they were never accessed, just that they were not widely known. The scholar Martino Filetico evidently consulted them while they were still in there possession of Bessarion, and about a century later the Venetian scholar Vettore Fausto transcribed the Venetus A's scholia and critical signs for books 19–22 of the *Iliad* into his own copy of the 1488 *editio princeps* of the *Iliad*, now Marcianus Graecus IX 35. (On these early consultations see Pontani's (2001) review of Pincelli (2000) as well as Erbse (1969, xv–xvi).)

Digital technologies can also create large-scale access, without limitations by time or space. Bessarion wanted to preserve manuscripts and the learning they contained, and so he moved them out of Byzantium and provided the beginning of a public library. If the digital photographs of those manuscripts he donated are likewise going to help preserve their contents for further generations to access, our policy that allows duplication and distribution uncontrolled by the HMT is one way of enabling such preservation. Yet we must also be attentive to the rapid obsolescence of digital technologies. The Venetus A parchment codex continues to survive after a thousand years – what can and must we do to ensure that those photographs and our digital editions will be accessible in another decade, let alone in another millennium?

Now recall the multitude of texts of the *Iliad* that the Library of Alexandria gathered in its quest to collect all the books in the world. At that point in history, a select few had access to a great number of witnesses to the epic, and they were able to create editions and commentary from sources that no longer survive. The HMT seeks to replicate the multiplicity of that collection and the comparison of complete witnesses that the Library enabled. (Recall that Bessarion, too, acquired more than one version of the *Iliad* with scholia for his collection.) Although we cannot recover all of what the Alexandrian scholars had access to, by publishing our manuscripts as we have, with no fees and under a Creative Commons 4.0 non-commercial-attribution-share alike license, we can give access to the surviving information and revive complete versions of the scholia, at least.

At the same time, we seek to replace the model in which only a privileged few have access to the manuscripts. One profound shift that has already been realized by the digital access to the manuscripts is the involvement of undergraduates in the creation of the digital editions, together with new kinds of research that those digital editions make possible. Even in our own lifetimes, consulting manuscripts and being a textual editor were activities reserved for only a rare few: the rest of us had to rely on their editions. In the past decade, more than 100 undergraduate students have contributed to the creation of a complete digital edition of the Venetus A manuscript. With many more manuscripts, papyri, and other sources to be added, that number will continue to grow. Through the published digital photographs of the Venetus A manuscript, one of our summer undergraduate researchers, working for 40 hours per week for 9 weeks, has spent more time closely examining the texts it contains, on its very pages, than anyone had access to for centuries. We have seen that undergraduates from a range of institutions in the United States and the Netherlands are more than capable of reading the minuscule and semiuncial scripts, deciphering the ligatures and also the dense expression of the scholia, applying structured markup to defined elements of the contents, and formulating and pursuing creative research that emerges from their intense familiarity with the manuscript – both its contents and its physical form and layout.[30] Greater access has thus already changed the "received wisdom" of who can read manuscripts and who can contribute to our understanding of the textual history of the epics.

Another practice of past access that we want to replace: the edition of the *Iliad* that seeks to reconstruct an hypothesized "original". We seek to supersede that approach with a clear picture of the multiformity with which the *Iliad* has been transmitted to us. The Homer Multitext allows each surviving document to be viewed and considered on its own terms. Our recently completed digital edition of the text and scholia of the Venetus A manuscript of the *Iliad* provides a complete transcription of every page of the manuscript, spatially linked to the already published high-resolution images. The transcriptions are encoded in XML and are freely available in both human- and machine-readable form via the HMT. Digital tools, some already available and some still in development, allow users to interact with and search the text in a variety of ways. This fundamental editorial decision, to represent each historical instantiation of the *Iliad* as a whole worthy of study (alone and in comparison with other historical instantiations), is one that we arrived at over the course of many years of experimentation, theorizing, and reflection. In the end we concluded that proceeding in this way is the only way to accurately represent the history and transmission of a poem composed in performance. We do not want to replicate the mistakes of scholars over the millennia who have sought in vain to recover a single authoritative text from an oral tradition in which, to paraphrase Albert Lord, there was quite simply no original to be found.[31]

We have also decided not to simply replicate the practice of the *apparatus criticus*, and that decision also has a basis in considerations of access. We have argued elsewhere the problems inherent in a typical apparatus.[32] To be blunt, the conventional *apparatus* is a barrier rather than a means to access (and to be even blunter, some people seem to like that about it). Only the most specialized consulters of an *apparatus criticus* can decode what it is attempting to convey, and even they will be often at a loss as to what the original sources actually say. There are types of information, such as how the layout of the page creates relationships between texts, that an *apparatus* simply cannot convey. Digital

30 For just two examples, see Blackwell et al. (2016), and Churik and Smith (forthcoming). For more examples, see the posts on the Homer Multitext blog with the label "undergraduate research": http://homermultitext.blogspot.com/search/label/undergraduate research (last access 2019.01.31).

31 (Lord 1960, 100–101).

32 See, e.g., Dué and Ebbott (2009; 2010, 153–159; 2016).

tools of textual analysis, developed for texts in many languages across many formats of publication, also make the conventional *apparatus* obsolete.

There are many questions remaining about future developments of the project. How will a user of the Homer Multitext make comparisons between readings? In fact, during this phase of the project we have chosen not to worry excessively about how precisely our data will be used to make such comparisons. Instead, we have forefronted our efforts not to replicate the contempt aimed at Trimalchio by those who knew their Homer "better" than he did. A related question about access that we continue to confront is the role of translation of the texts (whether the poetry or the scholia), or what kinds of other contextual information are necessary to aid nonspecialists in their navigation of the texts. As our digital editions are published, what will we need to add to increase access and invite more researchers and readers into the study of the epics? On a conceptual level, the editors of the Homer Multitext have concluded that making the evidence of the historical sources available to every individual reader, thereby allowing them the tools to understand and even make editorial judgements for themselves, is the kind of access we want to provide. It is time, and now possible, to reach new audiences and ask new questions.

Bibliography

Allen, T. (1899): "On the Composition of Some Greek Manuscripts: The Venetian Homer". Journal of Philology 26, 161–181.

Berti, M. (2016): "Greek and Roman Libraries in the Hellenistic Age". In: S. White Crawford; C. Wassen (eds.): The Dead Sea Scrolls at Qumran and the Concept of a Library. Studies in the Documents of the Judean Desert Series. Leiden and Boston: Brill, 31–54.

Bird, G. (2009): "Critical Signs – Drawing Attention to 'Special' Lines of Homer's *Iliad* in the Manuscript Venetus A". In: C. Dué (ed.): Recapturing a Homeric Legacy: Images and Insights from the Venetus A Manuscript of the Iliad. Cambridge, MA: Harvard University Press, 89–115.

Blackwell, C.; Dué, C. (2009): "Homer and History in the Venetus A". In: C. Dué (ed.): Recapturing a Homeric Legacy: Images and Insights from the Venetus A Manuscript of the Iliad. Cambridge, MA: Harvard University Press, 1–18.

Blackwell, C.; Roughan, C.; Smith, D. (2016): "Citation and Alignment: Scholarship Outside and Inside the Codex". Manuscript Studies 1, 5–27.

Bowie, E. (2013): "Libraries for the Caesars". In: K. König; K. Oikonomopoulou; G. Woolf (eds.): Ancient Libraries. Cambridge: Cambridge University Press, 237–260.

Browning, R. (1992): "The Byzantines and Homer". In: R. Lamberton; J. Keaney (eds.): Homer's Ancient Readers. Princeton: Princeton University Press, 134–148.

Cameron, H. (1969): "The Sybil in the *Satyricon*". Classical Journal 65, 337–339.

Casson, L. (2001): Libraries in the Ancient World. New Haven: Yale University Press.

Churik, N.; Smith, D. (forthcoming): "Design and Layout of the Richest Manuscript of the *Iliad*". Anvil Academic. http://anvilacademic.org/projects/d-neel-smith-and-nikolas-churik-design-and-layout-of-the-richest-manuscript-of-the-iliad/ (last access 2019.01.31).
Comparetti, D. (ed.) (1901): Homeri Ilias cum scholiis. Codex venetus A, Marcianus 454 phototypice editus. Leiden: Sijthoff.
Connelly, J.B. (2014): The Parthenon Enigma. New York: Vintage Books.
Dué, C. (ed.) (2009): Recapturing a Homeric Legacy: Images and Insights from the Venetus A Manuscript of the Iliad. Cambridge, MA: Harvard University Press.
Dué, C.; Ebbott, M. (2009): "Digital Criticism: Editorial Standards for the Homer Multitext". Digital Humanities Quarterly 3: 1. http://www.digitalhumanities.org/dhq/vol/003/1/000029/000029.html (last access 2019.01.31).
Dué, C.; Ebbott, M. (2010): Iliad 10 and the Poetics of Ambush: A Multitext Edition with Essays and Commentary. Cambridge, MA, and Washington, DC: Center for Hellenic Studies.
Dué, C.; Ebbott, M. (2014): "An Introduction to the Homer Multitext Edition of the Venetus A manuscript of the *Iliad*". The Homer Multitext. http://www.homermultitext.org/manuscripts-papyri/VenA-Introduction-2014.html (last access 2019.01.31).
Dué, C.; Ebbott, M. (2016): "The Homer Multitext and the System of Homeric Epic". Classics@ 14. https://chs.harvard.edu/CHS/article/display/6524 (last access 2019.01.31).
Ebbott, M. (2009): "Text and Technologies: The *Iliad* and the Venetus A". In C. Dué (ed.): Recapturing a Homeric Legacy: Images and Insights from the Venetus A Manuscript of the Iliad. Cambridge, MA: Harvard University Press, 31–56.
Erbse, H. (ed.) (1969–1988): Scholia Graeca in Homeri Iliadem (scholia vetera). 7 Vols. Berlin: De Gruyter.
Farrell, J. (2004): "Roman Homer". In: R. Fowler (ed.): The Cambridge Companion to Homer. Cambridge: Cambridge University Press, 254–271.
Finkelberg, M. (2006): "Regional Texts and the Circulation of Books: The Case of Homer". Greek, Roman, and Byzantine Studies 46, 231–248.
Gangloff, A. (2018): "Rhapsodes and Rhapsodic Contests in the Imperial Period". In: J. Ready; C. Tsagalis (eds.) (2018): Homer in Performance: Rhapsodes, Narrators, and Characters. Austin: University of Texas Press, 130–150.
González, J. (2013): The Epic Rhapsode and His Craft: Homeric Performance in a Diachronic Perspective. Washington, DC: Center for Hellenic Studies.
Heller-Roazen, D. (2002): "Tradition's Destruction: On the Library of Alexandria". October 100, 133–153.
Horsfall, N. (1989): "'The Uses of Literacy' and the 'Cena Trimalchionis': I". Greece & Rome 36, 74–89.
Horsfall, N. (1993): "Empty Shelves on the Palatine". Greece & Rome 40, 58–67.
Horsfall, N. (2016): The Epic Distilled: Studies in the Composition of the Aeneid. Oxford: Oxford University Press.
Houston, G. (2014): Inside Roman Libraries: Book Collections and their Management in Antiquity. Chapel Hill, NC: The University of North Carolina Press.
Hurka, F. (2007): "Die literarisch gebildeten literarischen Barbareien des Trimalchio". In: L. Castagna; E. Lefèvre (eds.): Studien zu Petron und seiner Rezeption. Berlin and New York: De Gruyter, 213–225.
Kalavrezou, I. (2009): "The Twelfth-Century Illustrations in the Venetus A". In: C. Dué: Recapturing a Homeric Legacy: Images and Insights from the Venetus A Manuscript of the Iliad. Cambridge, MA: Harvard University Press, 117–132.

König, J.; Oikonomopoulou, K.; Woolf, G. (eds.) (2013): Ancient Libraries. Cambridge: Cambridge University Press.
Labowsky, L. (1979): Bessarion's Library and the Biblioteca Marciana: Six Early Inventories. Sussidi Eruditi 31. Roma: Edizioni di storia e letteratura.
Lord, A. (1960): The Singer of Tales. Cambridge, MA: Harvard University Press.
McNamee, K. (1981): "Aristarchus and 'Everyman's' Homer". Greek, Roman, and Byzantine Studies 22:3, 247–255.
Morgan, T. (1998): Literate Education in the Hellenistic and Roman Worlds. Cambridge: Cambridge University Press.
Nagy, G. (1996): Poetry as Performance: Homer and Beyond. Cambridge, MA: Harvard University Press.
Nagy, G. (2002): Plato's Rhapsody and Homer's Music: The Poetics of the Panathenaic Festival in Classical Athens. Washington, DC: Center for Hellenic Studies.
Nagy, G. (2004): Homer's Text and Language. Urbana and Chicago, IL: University of Illinois Press.
Neils, J. (ed.) (1992): Goddess and Polis: The Panathenaic Festival in Ancient Athens. Hanover, NH and Princeton, NJ: Princeton University Press.
Neils, J. (2007): "Replicating Tradition: The first celebrations of the Greater Panathenaia". In: O. Palagia; A. Choremi-Spetsieri (eds.): The Panathenaic Games. Oxford: Oxbow Books, 41–51.
Neils, J. (ed.) (2015): Worshipping Athena: Panthenaia and Parthenon. Madison, WI: University of Wisconsin Press.
Nelis, D. (2010): "Vergil's Library". In: J. Farrell; M. Putnam (eds.): A Companion to Vergil's Aeneid and its Tradition. Malden and Oxford: Wiley-Blackwell, 13–25.
Pfeiffer, R. (1968): A History of Classical Scholarship: From the Beginnings to the End of the Hellenistic Age. Oxford: Oxford University Press.
Pincelli, M. (ed.) (2000): Martini Philetici In corruptores Latinitatis. Roma: Edizioni di storia e letteratura.
Pontani, F. (2001): Review of M. Pincelli, Martini Philetici In corruptores Latinitatis (Rome, 2000). Bryn Mawr Classical Review 2001. 03.22.
Porter, J. (1992): "Hermeneutic Lines and Circles: Aristarchus and Crates on the Exegesis of Homer". In: R. Lamberton; J. Keaney (eds.): Homer's Ancient Readers. Princeton: Princeton University Press, 67–114.
Reynolds, L.; Wilson, N. (2014): Scribes and Scholars: A Guide to the Transmission of Greek & Latin Literature. 4th ed. Oxford: Oxford University Press.
Robb, K. (1994): Literacy and Paideia in Ancient Greece. Oxford: Oxford University Press.
Ruden, S. (2000): Petronius/*Satyricon*. Indianapolis, IN: Hackett Publishing.
Schironi, F. (2018): The Best of the Grammarians: Aristarchus of Samothrace on the Iliad. Ann Arbor, MI: University of Michigan Press.
Schironi, F. (forthcoming): "Early Editions". In: C. Pache (ed.): Cambridge Homer Encyclopedia. Cambridge: Cambridge University Press.
Schlunk, R. (1974): The Homeric Scholia and the Aeneid: A Study of the Influence of Ancient Homeric Literary Criticism on Vergil. Ann Arbor, MI: University of Michigan Press.
Schmeling, G. (2002): "(Mis)uses of Mythology in Petronius". In: J.F. Miller; C. Damon; K.S. Myers (eds.): Vertís in Usum: Studies in Honor of Edward Courtney. München and Leipzig: K.G. Saur, 152–163.

Shapiro, H. (1992): "*Mousikoi Agones*: Music and Poetry at the Panathenaia". In: J. Neils (ed.): Goddess and Polis: The Panathenaic Festival in Ancient Athens. Hanover, NH and Princeton, NJ: Princeton University Press, 53–76.

Shapiro, H. (2015): "Democracy and Imperialism: The Panathenaia in the Age of Perikles". In: J. Neils (ed.): Worshipping Athena: Panathenaia and Parthenon. Madison, WI: University of Wisconsin Press, 215–225.

Staikos, K. (2013): Books and Ideas: The Library of Plato and the Academy. trans. N. Koutras. New Castle, DE: Oak Knoll Press.

Tolkhien, J. (1897): De Homeri auctoritate in cotidiana Romanorum vita. Jahrbücher für classiche Philologie Suppl. 23. Leipzig.

Tolkhien, J. (1900): Homer und die römische Poesie. Leipzig: T. Weicher.

Yamagata, N. (2012): "Use of Homeric References in Plato and Xenophon." Classical Quarterly 62:1, 130–144.

Ypsilanti, M. (2010): "Trimalchio and Fortunata as Zeus and Hera: Quarrel in the 'Cena' and 'Iliad'". Harvard Studies in Classical Philology 105, 221–237.

Monica Berti

Historical Fragmentary Texts in the Digital Age

Abstract: This paper describes how the digital revolution is changing the way scholars access, analyze, and represent historical fragmentary texts, with a focus on traces of quotations and text reuses of ancient Greek and Latin sources. The contribution presents two different projects: 1) the Digital Fragmenta Historicorum Graecorum (DFHG), which is a digital collection of ancient Greek fragmentary historians enriched with functionalities for accessing and analyzing their texts; 2) the Digital Athenaeus, which provides experimental tools for reading the text of the *Deipnosophists* of Athenaeus of Naucratis and getting information about citations of authors and works that are preserved in it.

Introduction

In the last two centuries generations of scholars have been publishing many critical editions of historical fragmentary texts of Greek and Latin sources. These publications are the result of an intense work for individuating and assembling traces of quotations and text reuses of authors whose works are now mostly lost. Classical scholarship has adopted the word *fragmenta* to name these traces and describe their transmission in our textual heritage.[1] In this case the term doesn't refer to broken off pieces of material objects bearing textual evidence, but to the output of philological analyses of researchers who have to dig into the context of literary texts to individuate references to authors and works.[2] The goal of this paper is to describe how the digital revolution is changing the way scholars evaluate and represent fragmentary texts, while preserving the lesson of a long established editorial and philological tradition.[3]

---

1 (Most 1997).
2 (Berti 2012; 2103).
3 A detailed description of this topic is forthcoming in a monograph by Monica Berti entitled *Digital Editions of Historical Fragmentary Texts*.

Monica Berti, Universität Leipzig

https://doi.org/10.1515/9783110599572-015

Classical scholarship and fragmentary texts

Glenn Most individuates two main phases in the history of modern scholarship on collecting fragmentary texts:[4] 1) the humanist and early modern phase that began in the second half of the sixteenth century and was interested more in publishing the very best fragments of the most important authors than in producing complete, critical, and exhaustive collections, and 2) the romantic and contemporary phase that began in the second half of the eighteenth century and brought a new attempt to understand the totality of the past beyond the few surviving canonical works. The second phase was fundamental for developing a new scholarship on ancient literary fragments that took off in the middle and the second half of the nineteenth century, when scholars began to establish rigorous philological methods for producing big collections of fragmentary texts belonging to many different genres, as for instance epic poetry, comedy, tragedy, philosophy and historiography.

These important efforts in collecting fragmentary texts depend not only on an interest in looking for every possible trace of the past, but also on the fact that fragmentary literature covers a significant percentage of what has been preserved from our tradition.[5] Given the fragmentary state of ancient evidence and its complexity, counting the amount of textual fragments and calculate its proportion in relation to what has survived from the past is a difficult task that can't produce complete and definitive results, first of all because it is not possible to establish with precision and uniquely what is a fragmentary text. In spite of that, digital libraries of Greek and Latin sources allow us to undertake this task at least in a provisional way.

According to statistics performed on the online Thesaurus Linguae Graecae (TLG) for the period of time between the eighth century BC and the sixth century CE, about 50% of authors is represented by fragmentary authors (Figure 1). Within this group, more than 80% is represented by authors who are completely lost (e.g., Hellanicus), and about 18% by authors who have both fragmentary and still extant works (e.g., Sophocles) (Figure 2).[6]

---

4 (Most 2009, 15–17).

5 As far as it concerns ancient Greek historiography, Strasburger (1977, 9–15) tried to quantify the "land of ruins" of this genre and came to the conclusion that the tradition has preserved only about 2.5% of what was originally written, with a *ratio* of 1 to 40 between what is still extant and what is lost.

6 These percentages are based on TLG data as of early 2018: http://stephanus.tlg.uci.edu (last access 2019.01.31). For more information on this data and other digital collections,

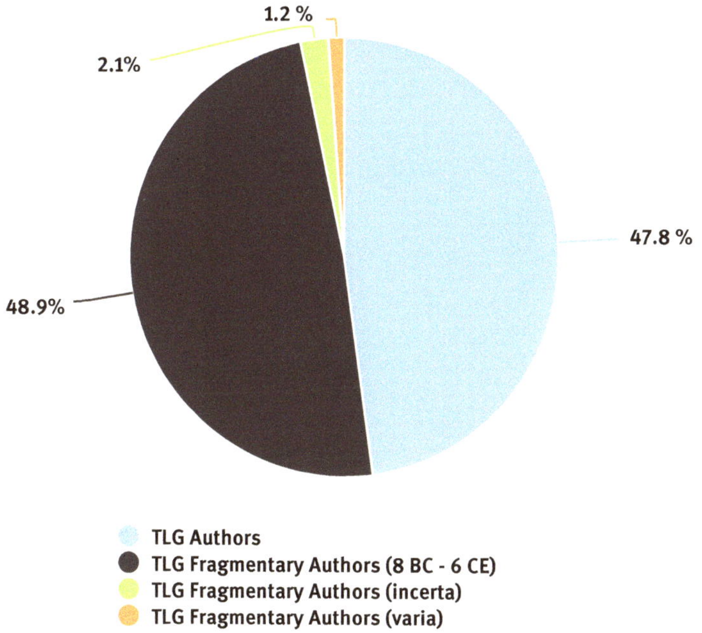

Figure 1: Fragmentary authors in the Thesaurus Linguae Graecae (TLG).

These percentages reflect the situation of Greek literature and the amount of fragmentary authors, showing the importance of working on this kind of evidence for improving our knowledge of Classical sources. As mentioned before, traditional scholarship has given an extraordinary contribution to the critical reconstruction of the intellectual personality of many lost authors by establishing philological criteria to study and edit them with the technology of the printed book. Today digital tools offer a new environment that requires us to rethink the way we analyze and represent this kind of evidence. In the following paragraphs we will describe concrete opportunities and challenges of the digital revolution by presenting two projects focused on ancient Greek fragmentary texts.

---

see http://www.dfhg-project.org/Fragmentary-Texts (last access 2019.01.31). A detailed description of these resources will be available in the monograph mentioned at note 3.

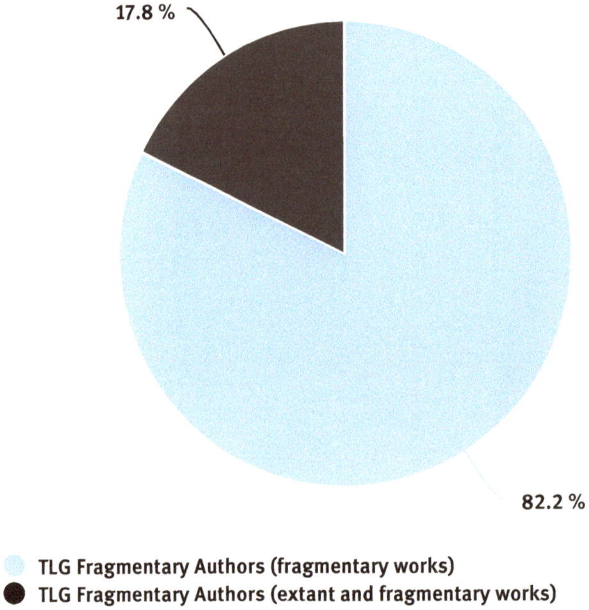

Figure 2: Fragmentary authors in the Thesaurus Linguae Graecae (TLG).

Fragmentary texts and the digital revolution

Digital Classical philology is working on two main challenges. The first one is the conversion of printed editions of Greek and Latin sources into a machine readable format that preserves their textual and editorial heritage.[7] The second challenge is the publication of new digital critical editions that make use of computational technologies and help define standards and scholarly models that are different from those developed through the technology of traditional books.[8] The first generation of digital libraries has digitized the reconstructed

7 In this regard a lot of work is currently developed by the Open Greek and Latin (OGL) project at the University of Leipzig. See also the contributions by Leonard Muellner and Samuel J. Huskey in this volume.

8 On this aspect see the paper by Franz Fischer in this volume. On the technology of the printed book, see Borsuk (2018).

text of single editions of Classical works.[9] The goal of the second generation of digital libraries is to publish multiple editions of the same work, reproduce the critical apparatus and all other paratextual elements (prefaces, introductions, indexes, bibliographies, notes, etc.), and generate collaborative environments for critical editing of Greek and Latin sources.[10]

Fragmentary works are directly involved in this process because they consist of quotations and text reuses preserved by still extant sources. This means that also in this case efforts are focused both on the digitization of printed critical editions of fragmentary authors and on the implementation of a new model for representing fragments inside digital contexts. The Digital Fragmenta Historicorum Graecorum (DFHG) and the Digital Athenaeus are two projects focused on these aspects for dealing with fragmentary authors and works in a digital environment.

The Digital Fragmenta Historicorum Graecorum (DFHG)

The Digital Fragmenta Historicorum Graecorum (DFHG) is the digital version of the five volumes of the *Fragmenta Historicorum Graecorum* (FHG), which is the first big collection of ancient Greek historical fragments published by Karl Müller.[11] The FHG is a collection of quotations and text reuses (*fragmenta*) extracted from many different sources pertaining to 636 ancient Greek fragmentary historians. Except for the first volume, authors are chronologically distributed and date from the sixth century BC through the seventh century CE. Fragments are numbered sequentially and arranged by works and book numbers with Latin translations, commentaries, and critical notes. A separate appendix at the end of the first volume includes the *Marmor Parium* and the Greek text of the *Marmor Rosettanum* with translations and commentaries.[12]

9 Examples are the TLG, the Perseus Digital Library, and the PHI Latin Texts.

10 For reasons of space, we only refer to two generations of digital libraries, but see Babeu (2011, 2–3) on "several generations of digital corpora in Classics".

11 (Müller 1841–1873). The project is available online at http://www.dfhg-project.org (last access 2019.01.31). See also Berti (2019).

12 Two digital projects are currently developed on the *Marmor Parium* and the *Marmor Rosettanum*: see Berti and Stoyanova (2014) and Berti et al. (2016c).

The fifth volume collects Greek and Syriac historical fragments preserved in Armenian texts.[13]

The DFHG is not a new edition of ancient Greek fragmentary historians, but a digital experiment to provide textual, philological, and computational methods for representing fragmentary authors and works in a digital environment. The reason for choosing the collection of the FHG depends on different factors: 1) an interest in Greek fragmentary historiography, which offers many examples of reuse of prose texts whose complexities are shared by other genres of fragmentary literature;[14] 2) the necessity of digitizing printed editions and preserving them not only as image files but also as structured machine readable collections, that can be accessed for experimenting with text mining of historical languages; 3) the importance of the FHG for understanding more recent editions of Greek historical fragments and in particular *Die Fragmente der griechischen Historiker* (FGrHist) by Felix Jacoby, who spent his life to change and improve the collection created by Karl Müller;[15] 4) the fact that the corpus of the FHG is open (i.e., free of copyright) and big enough to perform computational experiments and obtain results.[16]

The DFHG is an ongoing project that has been developing many tools and services not only for accessing the entire collection of the FHG, but also for providing a new digital and philological model that can be applied to other collections of fragmentary authors. The complete text of the five volumes of the FHG has been converted into a machine readable format with Optical Character Recognition (OCR) systems as part of the Open Greek and Latin (OGL) project at the University of Leipzig.[17] The digital version of the FHG has been produced starting from the OCR output by creating an SQL database for delivering web services and tools. Web pages are generated using the Ajax technique to retrieve data from the database and increase the usability of the huge amount of FHG contents. Functionalities of the DFHG are

13 On the collection of the FHG, see Petitmengin (1983) and Grafton (1997).

14 (Berti 2012; 2103).

15 (Jacoby 1909; 2015).

16 The FHG is a corpus of more than 2 million words (in Greek, Latin, and French) with more than 600,000 Greek tokens.

17 On OCR for ancient Greek and Latin see the contribution by Bruce Robertson in this volume. Even if nowadays it is possible to obtain good results when OCRing nineteenth century editions of ancient Greek and Latin sources, errors are still present in OCRed texts. The DFHG project is working on OCR post-correction and also includes an experimantal editing environment for manual corrections.

presented below and descriptions are grouped according to tools and add-ons developed by the project.[18]

1. Visualization of DFHG Contents. Contents of the DFHG can be browsed by selecting the entire collection or one single volume in the homepage of the project. The slide in/out navigation menu represents the whole structure of volumes, books, authors, works and fragments collected in the printed edition, and it is available for the entire collection and for each volume.[19] The "Expand All" and "Collapse All" functions allow scholars to navigate the FHG with a comprehensive view of the structure of the whole collection by expanding and collapsing every volume, book, author and work down to the fragment level. This structure is very helpful because the printed version of the FHG does not contain detailed tables of contents of its volumes.[20] Following each navigation menu element, users are able to jump to the relevant section of the FHG without reloading the page. The navigation menu gives access to the following contents as they are arranged in the FHG: *volumina* (FHG I-V), *praefationes* (FHG I, II, IV and V), *libri* and other volume divisions (FHG I-V), list of authors, works, books and fragments (FHG I-V), *Index Nominum et Rerum* (FHG I), *Index Marmoris Rosettani* (*Table de mots grecs, et des principaux faits expliqués*) (FHG I) and *addenda et corrigenda* (FHG I-V).[21] The DFHG main page of the entire collection and of each volume allows to visualize and navigate the following contents: a) introductions to FHG authors with notes;[22] b) five-item rows for each fragment with the following data: (1) the number of the fragment with links to the relevant page of the printed edition of the FHG, to the *Index Nominum et Rerum* and the *Index Marmoris Rosettani*, and to the OpenNLP POSTagger for Ancient Greek, (2) a reference to the source text of the fragment (sometimes with

18 Tools and add-ons are available through the homepage of the project with detailed descriptions and instructions.

19 The menu faithfully represents the arrangement of authors and fragments in the FHG.

20 The FHG only provides an *index auctorum* and an *index titulorum* at the end volume IV.

21 FHG III doesn't have a *praefatio*. Still missing in the DFHG are the *index auctorum*, the *index titulorum*, and the *index nominum et rerum* of volume II-IV that are published at the end of FHG IV, and the *indices* of the two sections of FHG V. Also, *addenda et corrigenda* in the DFHG are represented as separate web pages at the end of each volume due to the fact that their integration in the relevant passages of the collection would have required too much manual work.

22 FHG I has a unique introduction at the beginning of the volume, which has been split into sections corresponding to each author of the volume and inserted at the beginning of the relevant author section in the DFHG. In this case the DFHG follows the model of the other FHG volumes, where almost every author has a separate introduction in the relevant section.

a short or long commentary), (3) the Greek or the Latin text of the fragment, (4) the Latin (or French) translation/summary of Greek fragments, and (5) the Latin (or French) commentary to the text of the fragment;[23] c) two- or three-item rows for still surviving sources (e.g., Apollodorus' *Bibliotheca*, the *Marmor Parium*, and the *Marmor Rosettanum* in FHG I, or Diodorus Siculus in FHG II) with (1) the Greek text, (2) the Latin (or French) translation, and (3) the commentary sometimes with notes. The grey sidebar of the main page shows the original arrangement of pages in the FHG with links to the printed edition available through Google Books.

2. Search through the DFHG. The DFHG Digger filters the FHG according to authors, works, work sections and book numbers. By typing and selecting through a live search, users can display the desired part of the collection. It is possible to combine filters using logical AND/OR expressions to get a more precise selection.[24] DFHG contents (introductions, fragments, translations, commentaries and source texts) are searchable in two different ways: (1) by highlighting words in the DFHG main page of the entire collection or of a single volume, and (2) by searching words directly in the DFHG Search tool. Results show the number of occurrences in each DFHG author and are organized by authors and works, and searched words are highlighted in the texts of the DFHG. When available, results display also inflected forms and lemmata through Morpheus, the Suda On Line, and the Liddell-Scott Lexicon in the CITE Architecture (see below).[25]
3. Integration with external resources. One of the main goals of the project is to integrate the DFHG with external resources such as textual collections, authority lists, dictionaries, lexica and gazetteers. The DFHG main page is currently connected to the printed edition of the FHG, to the 8,427 entries of the *Index Nominum et Rerum* (FHG I), to the 249 entries of the *Index Marmoris Rosettani* (FHG I) and to the OpenNLP POSTagger for Ancient Greek; the DFHG search tool is connected to the corresponding fragment in the main page, to Morpheus, the Suda On Line and the Liddell-Scott Lexicon in the CITE Architecture. These resources allow users to get information about the texts of

23 On the OpenNLP POSTagger see Celano et al. (2016). On its integration in the DFHG, see below.

24 Combining for example author name and work title, like CHARON and ΠΕΡΣΙΚΑ.

25 Morpheus is the morphological parsing and lemmatizing tool of the Perseus Project, the Suda On Line is the digital version of the lexicon Suda, and the Liddell-Scott Lexicon in the CITE Architecture is the digital version of the LSJ lexicon published as a CITE collection (see the paper by Chistopher W. Blackwell and Neel Smith in this volume).

the fragments of the FHG by obtaining results concerning the morphology of words, their syntactic function, their meaning, and the disambiguation of named entities. As far as it concerns ancient Greek and Latin, all these resources already offer significant results, but are not complete and still require a work of disambiguation and correction. The goal is to make use of these resources to automatically disambiguate and annotate part of the DFHG data, which in turn offers a collection of parsed texts for enriching external libraries of Greek and Latin sources. In this regard, the DFHG project is working on named entities recognition and on the creation of a complete DFHG thesaurus by including other external authority lists. Figure 3 shows an example with some of the DFHG occurrences of the Greek word Εὐρώπη, which is both a personal and a place name. The lemmatization of the inflected forms automatically identifies the word both in the Lexicon of Greek Personal Names (LGPN) and in Pleiades.[26] A further work of analysis of the contexts of the DFHG fragments, where this word appears, provides an overview of the use of Εὐρώπη in Greek historiography both as a personal and a place name.

4. Data Citation. Each DFHG menu element has a unique identifier expressed as a URN (Uniform Resource Name). The syntax of each URN represents the editorial work of Karl Müller, who has arranged fragments in a sequence and has attributed them to fragmentary authors, works, work sections and book numbers. The following examples show different levels of granularity of these URNs, that are used to identify and cite fragmentary authors and works down to the fragment level.
   - `urn:lofts:fhg.1.hecataeus` identifies the author Hecataeus in FHG I;
   - `urn:lofts:fhg.1.hecataeus.hecataei_fragmenta` identifies the whole section of Hecataeus' fragments in FHG I;
   - `urn:lofts:fhg.1.hecataeus.hecataei_fragmenta.genealogiae` identifies Hecataeus' Γενεαλογίαι in FHG I;
   - `urn:lofts:fhg.1.hecataeus.hecataei_fragmenta.genealogiae.liber_secundus` identifies the second book of Hecataeus' Γενεαλογίαι in FHG I;
   - `urn:lofts:fhg.1.hecataeus.hecataei_fragmenta.genealogiae.liber_secundus:350` identifies fragment 350 of the second book of Hecataeus' Γενεαλογίαι in FHG I.

26 LGPN is originally a printed edition that collects all ancient Greek personal names attested on written sources from the eighth century BC down to the late Roman Empire (http://www.lgpn.ox.ac.uk: last access 2019.01.31). Pleiades is a community-built gazetteer and graph of ancient places (https://pleiades.stoa.org: last access 2019.01.31).

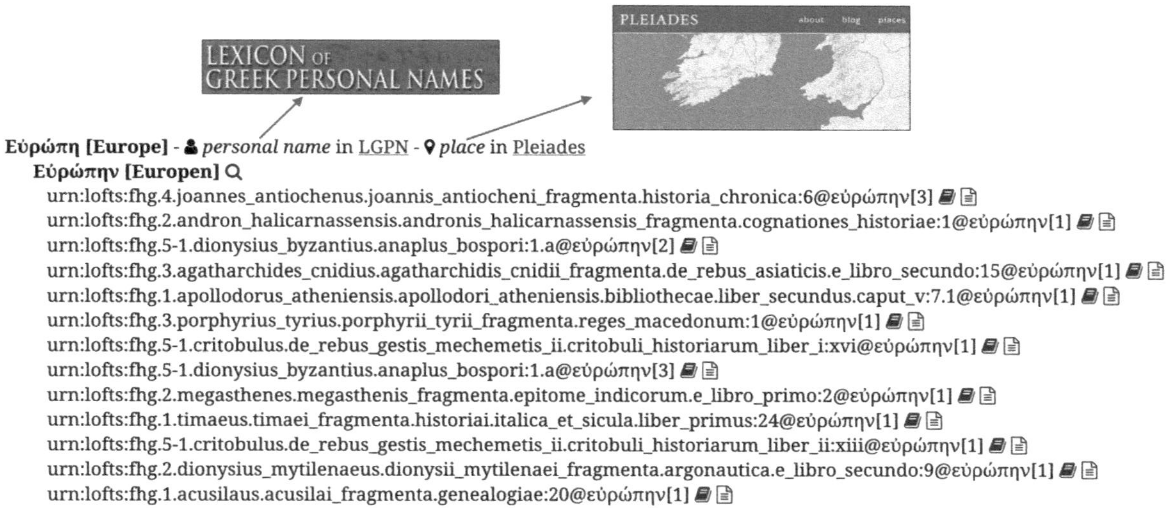

Figure 3: Named entity disambiguation in the DFHG.

A URN identifies itself as a urn in the LOFTS domain, whose acronym stands for the Leipzig Open Fragmentary Texts Series (LOFTS) and represents the domain of textual fragments.[27] Work titles in the URN are expressed in the Latin translation provided by Müller in the FHG. URNs are combined with a URL prefix (http://www.dfhg-project.org/DFHG/#) to generate stable links. The DFHG project provides also CITE URNs according to the guidelines of the CITE Architecture.[28] CITE URNs are accessible through the DFHG API, the DFHG Fragmentary Authors Catalog, and the Müller-Jacoby Table of Concordance (see below). By using URN identifiers, it is possible to export citations of DFHG fragments and source texts down to the word level. By selecting the desired portion of text, users get a URN that identifies the selection.[29] The DFHG provides also a URN Retriever, which is a tool for retrieving and citing passages and words in the fragments by typing the corresponding URN. For example:
   - Hellanicus' fragment 1 corresponds to `urn:lofts:fhg.1.hellanicus.hellanici_fragmenta.phoronis:1`;
   - the beginning of Hellanicus' fragment 1 (Ἑλλάνικος ὁ Λέσβιος τοὺς Τυῤῥηνούς φησι, Πελασγοὺς πρότερον καλουμένους, ἐπειδὴ κατῴκησαν ἐν Ἰταλίᾳ, παραλαβεῖν ἣν ἔχουσι προσηγορίαν) corresponds to `urn:lofts:fhg.1.hellanicus.hellanici_fragmenta.phoronis:1@ἑλλάνικος[1]-προσηγορίαν[1]`.
5. Data export. The DFHG provides a web API that can be queried with author names and fragment numbers. The result is a JSON output containing every piece of information about the requested fragment.[30] The DFHG automatically exports data to CSV and XML files. XML files are generated both as EpiDoc XML and well formed XML. EpiDoc XML files represent the structure of the printed edition of the FHG and are based on guidelines specifically developed for the DFHG project as part of the EpiDoc community.[31] Well formed XML files collect information about fragments and source texts of the FHG.
6. DFHG Fragmentary Authors Catalog. This tool searches and visualizes the 636 Greek fragmentary historians whose quotations and text reuses are collected in the FHG. The catalog enables users to search the database by

27 (Berti et al. 2016a; Berti 2018).

28 See the paper by Christopher W. Blackwell and Neel Smith in this volume.

29 For example `urn:lofts:fhg.1.ephorus.ephori_fragmenta.historiae.liber_tertius:37@περιθοῖδαι[1]-ἰξίονος[1]` identifies the sentence Περιθοῖδαι, δῆμος τῆς Οἰνηίδος φυλῆς, ἀπὸ Πειρίθου τοῦ Ἰξίονος in Ephorus' fragment 37.

30 For example http://www.dfhg-project.org/DFHG/api.php?author=ACUSILAUS&fragment=10 (last access 2019.01.31).

31 (Berti et al. 2014–2015).

authors (e.g., Hippys Rheginus) and volumes (e.g., FHG II). Results display data about the exact location of authors in the FHG, their chronology according to the arrangement by Müller, pages with links to both the digital and the printed version of the FHG, CITE URNs of DFHG authors (e.g., `urn:cite:lofts:fhg.1.hellanicus`), and places corresponding to the geographical epithet of each FHG author used by Müller with links to Pleiades canonical URIs.[32] This data can be also visualized in the Fragmentary Authors Map and in the Fragmentary Authors Chart, which represent the geographical distribution of FHG authors and their arrangements in the volumes of the printed edition.[33]

7. DFHG Witnesses Catalog. This tool searches and visualizes authors and works (witnesses) that preserve quotations and text reuses of FHG fragmentary historians. The catalog allows users to search the database by FHG authors (e.g., Phanodemus) and works (e.g., ATTIKA), by witnesses (authors and works, as for instance Harpocration or the *Deipnosophistae*), and by editions, manuscripts and inscriptions cited in the FHG as sources of fragments (e.g., Bethe. *Pollucis Onomasticon* I. Lipsiae 1900, the *Codex Palatinus Graecus* 398, and *IG* XII.5.444). Results display witnesses (authors and works) with Perseus Catalog URNs (e.g., `urn:cite:perseus:author.728` and `urn:cts:greekLit:tlg0016.tlg001`), literary and geographical epithets and dates of witnesses (authors) according to the TLG, the Perseus Catalog, Pleiades and the Brill's New Pauly, passages of works (witnesses) that preserve quotations and text reuses with detailed information about the corresponding *fragmenta* in the DFHG and links to the URN Retriever, and finally references to inscriptions, manuscripts and editions cited in the FHG as sources of fragments.[34] This data can be also visualized in the Witnesses Map, the Witnesses (Authors and Works) Charts, and the Witnesses

32 Authors in FHG I don't have geographical epithets, but places have been added in the DFHG because they are known. As for other volumes, missing geographical epithets in the FHG correspond to missing places in the DFHG.

33 Future work will also provide a catalog of fragmentary work titles, which is available in the *index titulorum* of the printed edition. In this case the goal is to extract data concerning these titles by annotating each of their occurrences in the text of the FHG.

34 On the difficulties of attributing literary and geographical epithets to ancient authors and on the issues concerning their chronology, see Berkowitz and Squitier (1990, xvii–xxii). Links to resources concerning editions, manuscripts and inscriptions are progressively added to the DFHG Witnesses Catalog.

Timeline. These resources complement the printed edition of the FHG, which lacks an index of source texts of the fragments.[35]

8. Müller-Jacoby Table of Concordance. This tool finds correspondences between fragmentary historians published in the FHG and in the FGrHist, including the *continuatio* and the BNJ. Given that Jacoby Online is a work in progress, as soon as new BNJ authors are published they are also included in the DFHG table of concordance.[36] Users can search the database by FHG, FGrHist, and BNJ (1 and 2) data. Results display, in addition to information from the DFHG and Jacoby Online, corresponding data in other editions of Karl Müller related to the FHG and links to the Perseus Catalog.[37] This table of concordance complements the FGrHist and Jacoby Online, which offer incomplete or abstent correspondences to FHG authors.[38] The goal is to go beyond these collections and generate expanded catalogs of Greek fragmentary historians with corresponding data from printed and digital editions.
9. Text Reuse Detection. The DFHG project offers experimental text reuse functionalities for automatic text reuse detection of FHG authors in their witnesses. Users can insert XML file URLs or select one of the PerseusDL / Open Greek and Latin editions available in the DFHG.[39] Results display quotations and text reuses of FHG authors within their source texts. The DFHG allows scholars to download complete XML files of the source texts of the fragments with `dfhg` attributes that mark up the presence of DFHG text reuses in the relevant passages of the source texts. DFHG text reuse detection is based on the Smith-Waterman algorithm that performs local sequence alignment to detect similarities between strings.[40]

---

35 The need of complete indices of source texts of historical fragments has been shown by Bonnechère (1999).

36 I'm very grateful to the team working on Jacoby Online for sending me updates about new published authors.

37 Only for corresponding authors in the FHG, FGrHist, and BNJ. More information is available in the homepage of the table of concordance.

38 The FGrHist has incomplete *Konkordanzen*. Jacoby Online doesn't include correspondences with authors in the FHG.

39 PerseusDL is the Perseus Digital Library collection of Greek and Latin texts. OGL is the Open Greek and Latin collection, which includes also the Free First Thousand Years of Greek texts (see the paper by Leonard Muellner in this volume).

40 For an overview of the Smith-Waterman algorithm, see https://en.wikipedia.org/wiki/Smith–Waterman_algorithm (last access 2019.01.31).

The Digital Athenaeus: annotation of text reuse entities

The Digital Athenaeus is a project that provides scholars with experimental tools for accessing the text of the *Deipnosophists* of Athenaeus of Naucratis and getting information about citations of authors and works that are preserved in it.[41] The reason for choosing this work is due to its importance as a rich collection of text reuses (*fragmenta*) of ancient Greek authors who belong to many different literary genres.[42] The *Deipnosophists* offers the opportunity to experiment with a new way of representing fragmentary texts inside their context of transmission, which is the main concern when collecting evidence about reused authors and works. Textual fragments are a form of hypertext and a digital environment permits to annotate and visualize them as reuses within their context. This possibility allows to go beyond the limits of printed editions, where extended chunks of texts conserving *fragmenta* of other texts are extracted, decontextualized, and reprinted in other editions.[43]

The Digital Athenaeus aims at providing an inventory of authors and works cited by Athenaeus and at implementing a data model for identifying, analyzing, and citing uniquely instances of text reuse in the *Deipnosophists*. This means extracting and annotating a wide variety of elements that pertain to text reuse, such as names of quoted authors, titles and descriptions of quoted works, and in general the language of the text reuse itself. The Greek text of the *Deipnosophists* in the Digital Athenaeus is based on the Teubner edition of Georg Kaibel (1887–1890) and the project is producing tools and services for reading the text and generating text reuse related data that are described in the following pages.[44]

1. Casaubon-Kaibel Reference Converter. This is a tool for finding concordances between the two different reference systems used in the editions of the *Deipnosophists* by Isaac Casaubon (1597) and Georg Kaibel (1887–1890).[45] This resource is not only helpful for getting the correspondence between passages of the two editions, but most importantly for generating machine readable citations based on Kaibel references, because they are canonical, independent of any particular manifestation of the text, and valid across

41 http://www.digitalathenaeus.org (last access 2019.01.31).

42 (Berti et al. 2016b).

43 (Almas and Berti 2013).

44 Tools and services are available through the homepage of the project with detailed descriptions and instructions.

45 On the two systems, see Lenfant (2007).

editions and translations.[46] Causabon citations are by definition tied to page-breaks in his particular edition and are therefore not logical. Kaibel citations are based on books and paragraphs corresponding to precise chunks of text and are well suited to a digital environment.[47] Given that in printed editions scholars traditionally make use of Casaubon citations, the Casaubon-Kaibel Reference Converter automatically converts Casaubon citations into Kaibel citations, in order to create URNs based on the CITE Architecture, as for example `urn:cts:greekLit:tlg0008.tlg001.perseus-grc2:1.4` (= Ath., *Deipn.* 1.4).[48] In addition to the converter, which also includes links to the printed editions of Casaubon and Kaibel, the tool provides a web API with a JSON output for integrating data into external services.

2. CTS URN Retriever. This tool allows to retrieve and cite paragraphs, passages, and words in the Greek text of the *Deipnosophists*. For example:
   - Ath. *Deipn.* 3.7 corresponds to `urn:cts:greekLit:tlg0008.tlg001.perseus-grc2:3.7`;
   - the second occurrence of the word βίβλου in Ath. *Deipn.* 1.1 corresponds to `urn:cts:greekLit:tlg0008.tlg001.perseus-grc2:1.1@βίβλου[2]`;
   - the quotation of the words of Antiphanes (ἀεὶ δὲ πρὸς Μούσαισι καὶ λόγοις πάρει, ὅπου τι σοφίας ἔργον ἐξετάζεται) in Ath. *Deipn.* 1.4 corresponds to `urn:cts:greekLit:tlg0008.tlg001.perseus-grc2:1.4@ἀεὶ[1]-ἐξετάζεται[1]`.

   Each URN is combined with a URL prefix (http://www.digitalathenaeus.org/tools/KaibelText/index.php#) to produce stable links for visualizing every citation in the whole text of the *Deipnosophists*, which is browsable by books and paragraphs through a slide in/out navigation menu. The text is based on the edition by Kaibel and each paragraph is connected to the corresponding entries in the *indices scriptorum* of the *Deipnosophists* (see below) and to the OpenNLP POSTagger for Ancient Greek for getting automatic information about the morphology of each word. Using CTS URNs, it is possible to export citations of the *Deipnosophists* down to the word level. The Search tool allows to search the entire text and, when available, results display also inflected forms and lemmata from Morpheus, the Suda On Line, and the Liddell-Scott Lexicon in the CITE Architecture.

---

46 (Berti et al. 2016b, 124–125).

47 Every scholar of Athenaeus knows the ambiguity of Casaubon references, because it's difficult to identify with precision the begining and the end of his paragraphs.

48 `tlg0008.tlg001.perseus-grc2` identifies the edition by Kaibel in the Perseus Catalog. See Berti et al. (2016b).

3. Indices Scriptorum. One of the goals of the Digital Athenaeus is to experiment with semi-automatic annotations of data related to text reuse. This is the reason why the project has produced digital versions of indices of authors and works published in the printed editions of the *Deipnosophists* by August Meineke, Georg Kaibel, and S. Douglas Olson. SQL databases of these indices have been created starting from OCR outputs of the printed editions and have been enriched with automatically converted Kaibel references and with links to external resources for reading the whole context of each reference. Dynamic graphs generate graphic visualizations of the indices (Figure 4) and a web API with a JSON output allows to integrate data into external services. These indices offer lists of author names and work titles cited by Athenaeus and they can be considered as already disambiguated lists of named entities (author names and work titles) to be mapped on to the text of the *Deipnosophists* to obtain a first set of annotations pertaining to text reuse.[49]
4. Book Stream. This tool shows an automatic alignment of index entries extracted from the indices by Meineke, Kaibel, and Olson. The resource is based on the alignment of Kaibel references that have been automatically generated by the conversion of Casaubon references included in the printed versions of the indices. Each entry in the book stream is linked to the database of each index. Each paragraph of the *Deipnosphists* is linked to Index to Text, which is an experimental tool based on the Levenshtein distance for producing an automatic alignment of the index entries with their corresponding forms in the Greek text of the *Deipnosophists*.[50] Given that index entries are in Latin or in English, the Levenshtein distance has to be adjusted to generate the closest possible results between the indices and the Greek text.[51] A further work of manual correction and a comparison with data obtained from named entities extraction (see below) will enable to create a complete and correct alignment.
5. Named Entities Digger and Concordance. These tools allow to search inflected forms of detected named entities (with transliteration) as they appear in the

49 This is not the case of the index by Olson, because it includes not only authors but also other personal names. The Digital Athenaeus offers also the index *dialogi personae* by Georg Kaibel, because this is a list of the names of the sophists who participate in the dialogues described by Athenaeus and who actually quote many authors and works.

50 For an overview of the Levenshtein distance, see https://en.wikipedia.org/wiki/Levenshtein_distance (last access 2019.01.31).

51 The threshold can be changed by users in the online version.

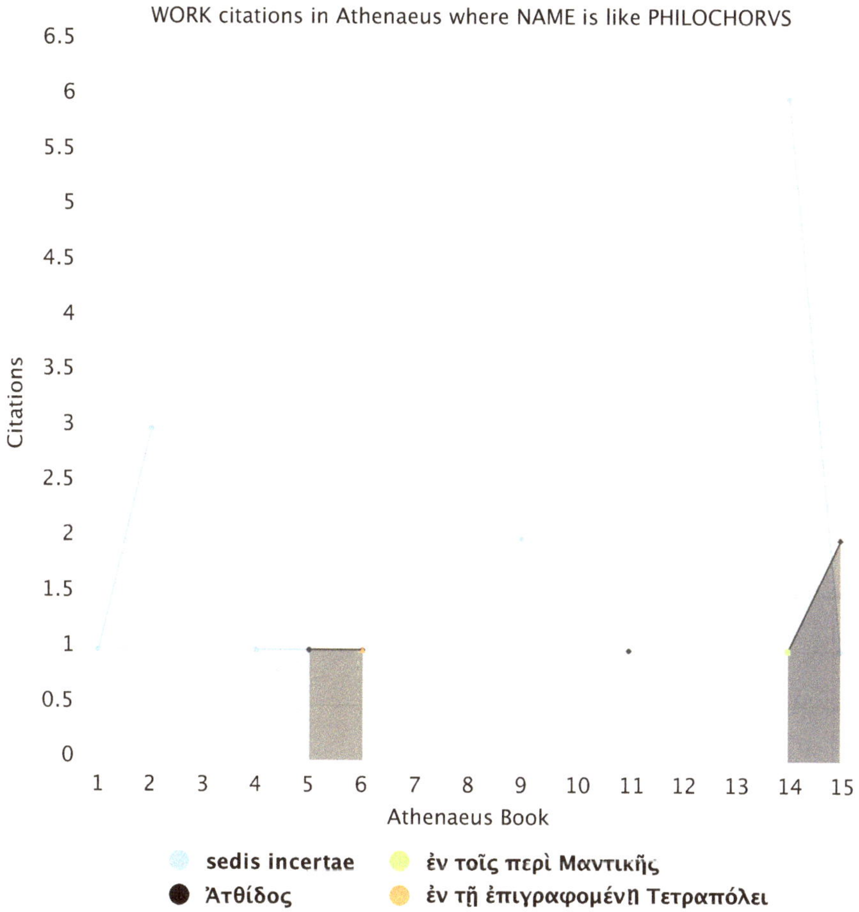

Figure 4: Digital Athenaeus dynamic graph.

Deipnosophists (e.g., Αἰσχύλου [Aischylou]) and visualize their immediate context. The tools are the result of semi-automatic extraction of named entities and are connected to external resources and authority lists: Logeion, the TLG, LGPN, Pleiades, VIAF, an annotated EpiDoc XML file of the *Deipnosophists* (ed. Gulick) in the PerseusDL, and the Index of Ancient Greek Lexica (DC3 – Duke Collaboratory for Classics Computing). Thanks to the lemmatization of detected named entities, it is possible to compare lemmata with the datasets of these external resources and obtain provisional lists of partially disambiguated named entities, such as personal names, place names, constellations, ethnic, festivals, groups, languages, months and titles. Every form of detected named entities has a CTS URN and, if present, can be visualized in the *indices scriptorum* by Meineke, Kaibel and Olson for further disambiguation.

Conclusion

The two projects described in this paper show how many possibilities the digital environment offers for accessing and analyzing Classical sources that are preserved through quotations and text reuses in later texts. The digitization of Greek and Latin sources is increasing the number of textual data at our disposal, allowing us to work with big quantities of resources in a way that was not possible in a printed world. Language technologies offer techniques and models for accessing these resources, structuring their content, and extracting information from them. Classical fragmentary texts require a further effort to manage challenges and issues concerning their philological ambiguities and complexities. The projects presented in this paper aim at offering a first selection of these challenges, issues, and needs that future generations of scholars will be able to address, expand, and implement.

Bibliography

Almas, B.; Berti, M. (2013): "Perseids Collaborative Platform for Annotating Text Re-Uses of Fragmentary Authors". In: DH-Case 2013. Collaborative Annotations in Shared Environments: Metadata, Vocabularies and Techniques in the Digital Humanities. Florence, September 10, 2013. ACM Publication. DOI: 10.1145/2517978.2517986.

Babeu, A. (2011): Rome Wasn't Digitized in a Day. Building a Cyberinfrastructure for Digital Classics. Washington, D.C.: Council on Libraries and Information Resources.

Berkowitz, L.; Squitier, K.A. (eds.) (1990): Thesaurus Linguae Graecae. Canon of Greek Authors and Works. 3rd ed. New York and Oxford: Oxford University Press.

Berti, M. (2012): "Citazioni e dinamiche testuali. L'intertestualità e la storiografia greca frammentaria". In: V. Costa (ed.): Tradizione e Trasmissione degli Storici Greci Frammentari II. Tivoli: Edizioni Tored, 439–458.

Berti, M. (2013): "Collecting Quotations by Topic: Degrees of Preservation and Transtextual Relations among Genres". Ancient Society 43, 269–288. DOI: 10.2143/AS.43.0.2992614.

Berti, M. (2018): "Annotating Text Reuse within the Context: The Leipzig Open Fragmentary Texts Series (LOFTS)". In: U. Tischer; U. Gärtner; A. Forst (eds.): Text, Kontext, Kontextualisierung. Moderne Kontextkonzepte und antike Literatur. Hildesheim, Zürich, and New York: Olms, 223–234.

Berti, M. (2019): "Digital Fragmenta Historicorum Graecorum (DFHG)". In: Digital Humanities 2019. Book of Abstracts. Utrecht, July 8–12, 2019.

Berti, M.; Almas, B.; Dubin, D.; Franzini, G.; Stoyanova, S.; Crane, G.R. (2014–2015): "The Linked Fragment: TEI and the Encoding of Text Reuses of Lost Authors". Journal of the Text Encoding Initiative 8. DOI: 10.4000/jtei.1218.

Berti, M.; Almas, B.; Crane, G.R. (2016a): "The Leipzig Open Fragmentary Texts Series (LOFTS)". In: N.W. Bernstein; N. Coffee (eds.): Digital Methods and Classical Studies. DHQ Themed Issue 10: 2. http://www.digitalhumanities.org/dhq/vol/10/2/000245/000245.html (last access 2019.01.31).

Berti, M.; Blackwell, C.W.; Daniels, M.; Strickland, S.; Vincent-Dobbins, K. (2016b): "Documenting Homeric Text-Reuse in the *Deipnosophistae* of Athenaeus of Naucratis". In: G. Bodard; Y. Broux; S. Tarte (eds.): Digital Approaches and the Ancient World. BICS Themed Issue 59:2, 121–139. https://doi.org/10.1111/j.2041-5370.2016.12042.x.

Berti, M.; Jushaninowa, J.; Naether, F.; Celano, G.G.A; Yordanova, P. (2016c). "The Digital Rosetta Stone. Textual Alignment and Linguistic Annotation". In: M. Berti; F. Naether (eds.): Altertumswissenschaften in a Digital Age: Egyptology, Papyrology and Beyond. Proceedings of a conference and workshop in Leipzig, November 4–6, 2015. Universität Leipzig: Publikationsserver der Universität Leipzig. http://nbn-resolving.de/urn:nbn:de:bsz:15-qucosa-201522 (last access 2019.01.31).

Berti, M.; Stoyanova, S. (2014): "*Digital Marmor Parium*. For a Digital Edition of a Greek Chronicle". In: S. Orlandi (ed.): Information Technologies for Epigraphy and Cultural Heritage. Proceedings of the First EAGLE International Conference. Roma: Sapienza Università Editrice, 319–324.

Bonnechère, P. (1999): Die Fragmente der griechischen Historiker. Indexes of Parts I, II, and III. Indexes of Ancient Authors. Leiden and Boston: Brill.

Borsuk, A. (2018): The Book. Cambridge, MA and London: The MIT Press.

Celano, G.G.A; Crane, G.; Majidi, S. (2016): "Part of Speech Tagging for Ancient Greek". Open Linguistics 2:1, 393–399. DOI: 10.1515/opli-2016-0020.

Grafton, A. (1997): "*Fragmenta Historicorum Graecorum*: Fragments of Some Lost Enterprises". In: G.W. Most (ed.): Collecting Fragments. Fragmente Sammeln. Göttingen: Vandenhoeck & Ruprecht, 124–143.

Jacoby, F. (1909): "Ueber die Entwicklung der griechischen Historiographie und den Plan einer neuen Sammlung der griechischen Historikerfragmente". Klio 9:9, 8–123.

Jacoby, F. (2015): "On the Development of Greek Historiography and the Plan for the New Collection of the Fragments of the Greek Historians". The 1956 Text with the Editorial Additions of Herbert Bloch. Trans. by Mortimer Chambers and Stefan Schorn. Histos Supplement 3. Newcastle upon Tyne: Newcastle University.

Lenfant, D. (2007): "Athénée: Texte et systèmes de référence". In: D. Lenfant (ed.): Athénée et les fragments d'historiens. Actes du colloque de Strasbourg (16–18 juin 2005). Paris: De Boccard, 383–385.

Martin, T.R.; Berti, M. (2017): "Open Greek and Latin Data for the Challenges of the Fragmentary State of the Primary Sources for the Pentekontaetia". Mouseion (special issue on Open Greek and Latin) 14:3, 409–436.

Most, G.W. (1997): Collecting Fragments. Fragmente sammeln. Göttingen: Vandenhoeck und Ruprecht.

Most, G.W. (2009): "On Fragments". In: W. Tronzo (ed.): The Fragment. An Incomplete History. Los Angeles: Getty Research Institute, 9–20.

Müller, K. (1841–1873): Fragmenta Historicorum Graecorum. I-V. Paris: Ambroise Firmin-Didot.

Petitmengin, P. (1983): "Deux têtes de pont de la philologie allemande en France: Le *Thesaurus Linguae Graecae* et la *Bibliothèque des auteurs grecs* (1830–1867)". In: M. Bollack; H. Wismann (eds.): Philologie und Hermeneutik im 19. Jahrhundert. Volume 2. Göttingen: Vandenhoeck & Ruprecht, 76–107.
Strasburger, H. (1977): "Umblick im Trümmerfeld der griechischen Geschichtsschreibung". In: Historiographia Antiqua. Commentationes Lovanienses in honorem W. Peremans septuagenarii editae. Volume 6. Symbolae A. Leuven: Leuven University Press, 3–52.

Linguistic Annotation and Lexical Databases for Greek and Latin

Giuseppe G.A. Celano

The Dependency Treebanks for Ancient Greek and Latin

Abstract: The article aims to be an introduction to the dependency treebanks currently available for Ancient Greek and Latin, i.e., the Ancient Greek and Latin Dependency Treebank (AGLDT), the Index Thomisticus Treebank (IT-TB), the PROIEL Treebank, and the SEMATIA Treebank. Their pipelines for creation of morphosyntactic annotations are presented so as to highlight major commonalities and differences. All treebanks share the same basic underlying formalism, whereby syntactic words are connected to each other to form labeled directed acyclic graphs, and their annotation schemes, although different, are comparable to a very large extent.

1 An introduction to the dependency treebank formalism

A dependency treebank is a corpus containing a symbolic representation of the syntax of one or more texts. It can be defined as a set of sentences parsed according to the linguistic formalism of dependency grammar. Most treebanks for Ancient Greek and Latin, i.e., the Ancient Greek and Latin Dependency Treebank (AGLDT), the Index Thomisticus Treebank (IT-TB), the PROIEL Treebank, and the SEMATIA Treebank, are dependency treebanks. Even if, in the present article, I deal only with dependency treebanks, most of what follows in the present section could also be applied, mutatis mutandis, to describe constituency treebanks, such as the Nestle 1904 and SBNLGT Treebanks,[1] the major difference being that in dependency treebanks all nodes except the ROOT node are paired with tokens,[2] while in constituency treebanks non-terminal nodes, which represent phrases, such as VPs or PPs, are also licensed.

The parsed sentences in a treebank are formally represented as labeled directed acyclic graphs, where each token, excluding the ROOT node, is annotated

1 The treebanks and relative documentation can be accessed at https://github.com/biblicalhumanities/greek-new-testament/tree/master/syntax-trees (last access 2019.01.31).
2 The term is here used to mean a syntactic word, i.e., the unit for syntactic analysis.

Giuseppe G.A. Celano, Universität Leipzig

https://doi.org/10.1515/9783110599572-016

for its linguistic head and syntactic function. The graphs for each sentence can be visualized as trees (hence the name of "tree-bank"), whose vertices/nodes, excluding the ROOT node, correspond to a sentence's tokens and whose directed edges depict syntactic dependencies (i.e., head-dependent relationships) specified for syntactic functions.

Figure 1 shows an example of a parse tree. Tokens are connected via labeled arrows (i.e., edges with direction from heads to dependents): for example, αὐτόν is a dependent of ὀνομάζουσι and its syntactic function is OBJ (i.e., it is the object of its head ὀνομάζουσι). Notably, the original sentence in Figure 1 contains the graphic word ἐγῷμαι, where two syntactic words, ἐγὼ and οἶμαι, are merged together by crasis. This phenomenon well illustrates the necessity of keeping the concept of graphic word and token/syntactic word distinct in treebanking: even if, in Ancient Greek and Latin, the ratio between tokens and graphic words is very close to one (i.e., one graphic word usually corresponds to one token), there exist cases where graphic words clearly need to be split (e.g., Latin enclitic *que* also requires tokenization).

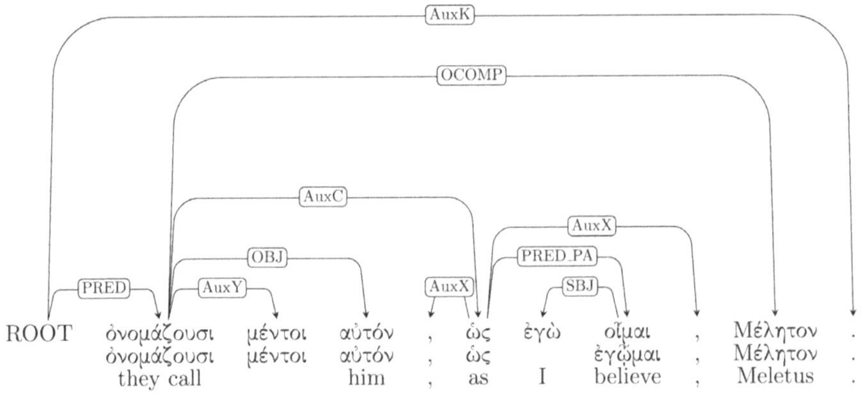

Figure 1: A dependency tree from Plato's *Euthyphro* (2b).

Each token in a parse tree can only have one head (also called "governor"), while one head can have more than one dependent. This translates, graphically, into one or more arrows originating from a token (e.g., ὀνομάζουσι has four dependents), but only one arrowhead per token. In the constituency/dependency grammar parlance, it is common to also describe relationships between tokens as kinship relationships: for example, ὀνομάζουσι is the parent of μέντοι, αὐτόν, ὡς, and Μέλητον, which are in turn its children. These latter tokens are, with respect to each other, siblings, in that they have a common parent.

In this regard, it is noteworthy that the dependency formalism fits perfectly into the XML/XPath/XQuery data model,[3] in that each sentence graph could be serialized as an element node whose child and descendant elements represent the linguistic tree structure (see Figure 2). The XML Path language 3.1 provides a tool to smoothly query such elements, by allowing traverse along a rich set of axes, such as `parent::`, `descendant::`, or `following-sibling::`.[4]

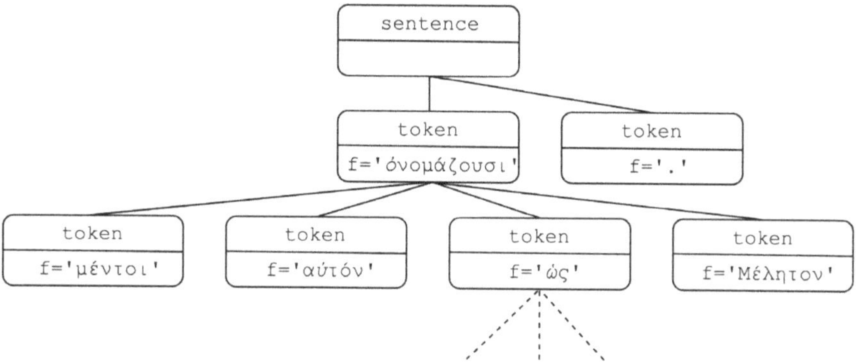

Figure 2: An XML serialization of the sentence in Figure 1.

The dependency formalism used for treebanks offers a model for syntactic annotation, which is, like any model, a trade-off between description completeness/ accuracy and simplicity, the latter being required to make the entire process of annotation of large data sets doable. One of the clearest limitations of the dependency model is that all relationships are formally represented as dependency relationships (i.e., subordinate relationships). This poses a challenge when it comes to representing non-subordinate relationships, such as constituents coordinated by conjunctions such as καί or *et* ("and"), appositions, or, as in Figure 1, parenthetical clauses.

3 https://www.w3.org/TR/xml/; https://www.w3.org/TR/xpath-datamodel-31/; https://www.w3.org/TR/xpath-functions-31/; https://www.w3.org/TR/xquery-31/ (last access 2019.01.31).

4 Interestingly, the XML structures of the serializations of both the AGLDT and the PROEIL Treebank privilege readability by keeping unaltered the token order of original texts: tokens are serialized as sibling elements and the linguistic dependency structure is expressed via internal links. On the contrary, the Prague Markup Language (Pajas 2010) used for the IT-TB shows a closer mapping between the parent-child relationships of the linguistic structure and those of the XML structure.

In the dependency formalism, such non-subordinate structures are formally represented, like any other, as subordinate relationships in order to preserve the simplicity of the model. Notwithstanding, they have to be correctly interpreted as *technical* dependencies,[5] their linguistic reality being different. This is even clearer with punctuation marks, which are commonly part of a syntactic tree, although their syntactic relevance is often questionable (especially for ancient texts, where punctuation is usually added by modern editors). The ROOT node can also be interpreted as a technical node: in the AGLDT, it typically governs the verb of the main clause, which receives the syntactic label PRED, and the final punctuation mark, which always receives the syntactic label AuxK.

Differently from constituency treebanks, constituents such as noun phrases or subordinate clauses are not explicitly annotated in a dependency treebank. However, most of them can be indirectly identified combining morphological and syntactic information. In the AGLDT, for example, a noun and its dependents can be taken to form an NP; similarly, a node labeled with AuxC, used to annotate a subordinate conjunction, and its dependents form a subordinate clause; a finite verb form with syntactic label ATR plus its dependents is a relative clause.

A treebank typically contains morphological annotation and lemmatization, which are layers of annotation preliminary to syntactic annotation. Further annotation layers, such as, for example, pragmatics or semantics, can also be added. All dependency treebanks for Ancient Greek and Latin contain morphological annotation and lemmatization. Only a few Ancient Greek and Latin texts have also been enriched with some semantic and/or pragmatic annotation (see following sections).

The pipeline for the creation of a treebanked text typically includes the following steps:

- automatic tokenization of an original text,
- automatic morphological (and syntactic) annotation,
- manual correction of the tokenization/morphosyntactic annotation.

Even though original texts can be in any format, they are usually available as TEI/EpiDoc XML, which is the standard for text encoding. Each treebank has developed its own algorithms to perform both tokenization and morphosyntactic annotation. The automatic morphosyntactic annotation is now usually performed via statistical POS taggers/parsers which have been previously trained on gold data annotated manually or by rule-based algorithms.

5 https://www.cil19.org/cc/en/abstract/contribution/754/index.html (last access 2019.01.31).

Manual annotation for a given text is usually performed by one, two, or three annotators. The one-annotator model is the "scholarly model": annotation reliability is assumed because of the expertise of the annotator, who is a trained advanced scholar. In the two-annotator model, one expert annotator's annotation is reviewed by another expert annotator (whose judgment therefore prevails). The three-annotator model requires that the annotations of two annotators are adjudicated by a third expert annotator, who resolves discrepancies.

Layers of annotations are not provided as pure stand-off markup.[6] Morphosyntactic (and pragmatic) annotation is usually attached to tokens within the same file. Even when the layers of annotations are kept separate, as in the Prague Markup Language (PML) used for the IT-TB, references to offsets in the (unannotated) original texts are not given – the tokenization of an original text therefore becomes the new base text. The original physical format for all treebanks is some flavor of XML. Since the schemas adopted are rather simple, it is also possible to easily convert the XML formats to other formats, such as CoNLL.

In the following sections, I will describe the Ancient Greek and Latin dependency treebanks in more detail, trying to offer an overview whose aim is to describe the main features, commonalities, and differences of the treebanks. I introduce the AGLDT in Section 2, while in Section 3 the IT-TB is presented. I outline the PROEIL Treebank in Section 4 and the SEMATIA Treebank in Section 5. Section 6 contains some conclusive remarks.

2 The Ancient Greek and Latin Dependency Treebank

The Ancient Greek and Latin Dependency Treebank is the oldest treebank for Ancient Greek and Latin (Bamman and Crane 2011). The project started at Tufts University in 2006 and is currently continued mostly at Leipzig University. The treebank contains entire texts or parts of texts belonging to classical antiquity, the choice of which reflect research interests of the annotators. The current release is 2.1. Most of the annotations have been performed by single scholars or university students under the supervision of a teacher.

6 A recently approved DFG-project ("Revising, standardizing, and expanding the Ancient Greek and Latin Dependency Treebank") aims, among other things, to provide stand-off annotation for the AGLDT using PAULA XML: http://gepris.dfg.de/gepris/projekt/408121292?language=en (last access 2019.01.31).

The Ancient Greek part of the treebank currently contains 557,922 tokens. It includes the annotations of (parts of) the following works: *Ilias*, *Odysseia*, *Hymnus in Demetrem*, Aeschylus' and Sophocles' tragedies, Hesiod's *Theogonia*, *Operae et dies*, and *Scutum*, Plato's *Euthyphro*, Lysias' *De caede Eratosthenis*, *In Alcibiadem I*, *In Alcibiadem II*, *In Pancleonem*, Plutarch's *Alcibiades* and *Lycurgus*, Aesop's *Fabulae*, Athenaeus' *Deipnosophistae*, Diodorus Siculus' *Bibliotheca Historica*, Herodotus' *Historiae*, Polybius' *Historiae*, Pseudo Apollodorus' *Bibliotheca*, and Thucydides' *Historiae*.

The Latin part of the treebank contains 79,697 tokens. The following works have been (partly) annotated: Augustus' *Res Gestae*, Jerome's *Vulgata*, Ovid's *Metamorphoses*, Sallust's *Bellum Catilinae*, Caesar's *Commentarii de Bello Gallico*, Cicero's *In Catilinam*, Vergil's *Aeneid*, Petronius's *Satyricon*, Phaedrus' *Fabulae*, Propertius' *Elegiae*, Suetonius' *Vita Divi Augusti*, and Tacitus' *Historiae*.

As Ancient Greek and Latin are morphologically rich languages, the morphological annotation of each token in the AGLDT treebank is based on tagsets[7] identifying both parts of speech and morphological features.[8] It is to be noted that, differently from syntactic annotation, most of the Ancient Greek and Latin texts have been annotated without specific morphological guidelines. Guidelines for the annotation of Ancient Greek morphology have been added from release 2.0.[9]

The lack of morphological guidelines is a common feature of all the Ancient Greek and Latin dependency treebanks. Since writing guidelines is a labour-intensive task, all projects have given priority to syntactic guidelines, syntax being arguably more complex to annotate. It is however acknowledged that morphological guidelines are needed. While morphological annotation for most tokens may seem uncontroversial, there are a number of known phenomena requiring rules.

These include, for example, distinction of the category noun/adjective (e.g., is *Athenienses* always an adjective?) or definition of the category "pronoun," the latter being able to be used to cover examples such as ἐγώ and ἐμός (= possessive

7 They are documented at https://github.com/PerseusDL/treebank_data/tree/master/v1/greek (Ancient Greek) and https://github.com/PerseusDL/treebank_data/tree/master/v1/latin (Latin) (last access 2019.01.31).

8 The annotations have been performed using the full-fledged Arethusa annotation tool, which also allows automatic tokenization and sentence split – which, as any other piece of annotation, can then be manually corrected. It is accessible at http://sosol.perseids.org/sosol/, while its code, including the one for the tagsets, is documented at https://github.com/alpheios-project/arethusa (last access 2019.01.31).

9 (Celano 2014).

adjective). Similarly, rules are needed to consistently annotate, for example, ὁ and τις, which could be articles (definite and indefinite, respectively) or pronouns. Another example is the distinction between relative adverbs and conjunctions: when Latin *ubi* means "when", it tends to be annotated as a subordinate conjunction, but when it means "where" as a relative adverb. Many of such morphological issues are treated in the Guidelines for the Ancient Greek Dependency Treebank 2.0.[10] Guidelines for Latin morphology are missing.

Technically, morphological annotation has been performed semi-automatically, a morphological analyzer suggesting an annotation, which is then validated by an annotator.[11] It is physically encoded as a 9-character long string, whose first position represents the POS and the following ones the morphological features. For example, the morphology of βασιλέα corresponds to "n-s—ma-," which stands for noun ("n"), singular ("s"), masculine ("m"), and accusative ("a"). Each position in the string always corresponds to a definite morphological category having definite values represented by letters. For example, the third position always encodes "number" with three possible values: singular ("s"), plural ("p"), and dual ("d"). Similarly, the seventh position always encodes "gender" and can take three values: masculine ("m"), feminine ("f"), and neuter ("n"). When a category is not relevant for a certain word form, a hyphen is used to mean lack of that morphological feature. For example, the feature "person" is always encoded in second position: as nouns are not specified for "person", the string for βασιλέα shows a hyphen.

Syntactic annotation for both Ancient Greek and Latin has been performed following an annotation scheme informed by the guidelines for the analytical layer (i.e., syntax) of the Prague Dependency Treebank 2.0.[12] The initial guidelines for Ancient Greek and Latin comprise 19 and 20 syntactic labels, respectively. In general, dependency rules, as well as the meaning of the labels, used to annotate Ancient Greek and Latin are very similar.

The initial guidelines for Ancient Greek and Latin, as most other guidelines, present syntactic descriptions which cannot necessarily be complete, but represent a compromise between annotation feasibility and description completeness. The guidelines for Ancient Greek have been further extended by the

10 (Celano 2014).

11 The morphological analyzer used is Morpheus (Crane 1991), which is integrated into the Arethusa annotation framework. A POS tagger has been more recently used for Ancient Greek (Celano et al. 2016).

12 (Hajič et al. 1999).

annotation guidelines for the AGDT 2.0.[13] Their novelty consists in making the annotation rules more precise by incorporating H.W. Smyth's *Greek Grammar for Colleges* (henceforth SG; Smyth 1920) both notionally and formally via hyperlinks to the relevant sections of the Perseus digital edition.[14] Many definitions are also provided with treebanked examples to make them clearer. On the contrary, the *Guidelines for the Syntactic Annotation of Latin* remain the only documentation for syntactic annotation of Latin (but see Section 3 for the *Rules of Annotation for the Analytical Layer of the Index Thomisticus Treebank*).[15]

The basic unit for syntactic annotation is the sentence, whose end is formally defined by the presence of a strong punctuation mark, such as a full stop or a colon. Prototypically, a sentence has a main verb, which is annotated as the linguistic root of the dependency tree and gets the label PRED (= "predicate"). Problematic is the case where a main verb is missing: in this case, an elliptical node functioning as the main verb is usually added. If a sentence starts with a coordinating conjunction, as is often the case in both Ancient Greek and Latin, the conjunction is chosen as the linguistic root (COORD), while its associated verb is made dependent on it with the label PRED_CO.

The suffix _CO is added to any node depending on a coordinate conjunction. Appositions are similarly encoded: the appositive nodes get labels depending on their syntactic function within a clause, which are terminated by the suffix _AP.

The sentence in Figure 3 shows the annotation style for appositions in Latin: *Fulvius* and *filius* are both annotated as subjects and get the suffix _AP. Notably, this annotation style differs from how apposition is treated in Ancient Greek and Latin traditional grammars, where apposition is conceptualized of as an independent syntactic function and not as a coordinate structure. According to this latter, *Fulvius* should be annotated as SBJ depending on *erat* and *filius* as APOS depending on *Fulvius*. This annotation style is favored for Ancient Greek starting from the guidelines 2.0.

The label OBJ is meant to captures all arguments not being SBJ, PNOM, or OCOMP. This means that it is not only used for direct objects, but also for a great variety of other complements "required" by a given verb. These include, for example, indirect objects and prepositional objects, such as those governed by verbs of motion. Admittedly, the notion of argument is notoriously difficult

---

13 (Celano 2014).

14 http://www.perseus.tufts.edu/hopper/text?doc=Perseus%3Atext%3A1999.04.0007 (last access 2019.01.31).

15 (Bamman et al. 2007). In the present and following sections, I will focus on the most noteworthy annotation phenomena/questions; for more details the reader is referred to the guidelines and data of each treebank.

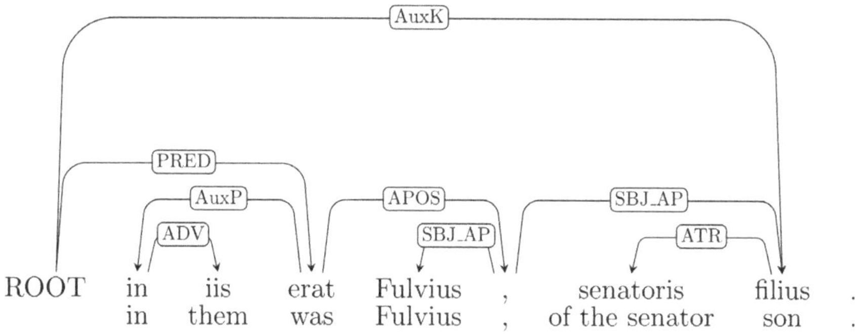

Figure 3: A dependency tree showing apposition.
Note: The example is drawn from Bamman et al. 2007, p. 28. The syntactic label of *iis* is however questionable: I would rather consider it as OBJ.

to define and both the original guidelines for both Ancient Greek and Latin do not attempt to define it precisely[16], therefore leaving to the annotator the task of identifying them.

The syntactic function "predicate nominal" (PNOM) is prototypically meant to capture complements depending on the copula. The Ancient Greek guidelines 2.0 further specify that this same label should also be used for complements, including supplementary participles not in indirect discourse, which depend on copulative verbs, a list of which is given in SG 917. Similarly, the label OCOMP is used for object complements and, according to the Ancient Greek guidelines 2.0, for supplementary participles not in the indirect discourse depending on verbs of perceiving and finding (SG 2110–2115).

The label ADV ("adverbial") is used to tag dependents being adjuncts. Contrary to OBJ nodes, adverbials are those dependents which are not verb specific and could therefore potentially modify any verb. Typical adjuncts are, for example, temporal modifications. The annotation schemes for Ancient Greek and Latin also include a number of Aux- labels to annotate dependents whose function is "auxiliary", which usually correspond to function words, such as prepositions and conjunctions.

The Ancient Greek guidelines 2.0 also provide rules for the annotation of a third annotation layer, which is called "advanced syntax layer", whose nature is at the interface between syntax and semantics.[17] More precisely, it can

16 See, however, https://github.com/PerseusDL/treebank_data/blob/master/AGDT2/guidelines/Greek_guidelines.md#obj (last access 2019.01.31).
17 (Celano 2015).

be defined as a syntax-driven semantic layer corresponding to categories such as "genitive of possession" or "purpose clause" elaborated by traditional grammars and summarized in Smyth (1920). This layer of annotation is currently available only for the annotated passages of Aesop's fables and Diodorus Siculus' *Bibliotheca Historica*.

The advanced syntax layer has been designed as an algorithm which, starting from the morphological annotation of any given token, guides the annotator, through successive steps, towards a more specific, semantic annotation. For example, a noun morphologically tagged as a genitive, can be further annotated – depending on its function within the clause – as "genitive proper > genitive of possession" or as "ablatival genitive > genitive of cause". An underlying assumption for the creation of this layer is that classicists are familiar with its categories, which are considered useful for the study and description of the language.

The Ancient Greek and Latin Dependency Treebank is released in a native XML format. The XML schema is very simple and intuitive. Each text is contained in a `treebank` element, which is the outermost element of the XML file. The `treebank` element has `sentence` elements as children, which contain `word` elements, each of which conveys the morphosyntactic information relative to a sentence token. The `word` elements are specified for at least six attributes: the `id` attribute content is an integer signaling the position of a given token in the sentence; the `form` attribute contains the actual word form for the given token, while the `lemma` attribute its lemma; the `postag` attribute content is the 9-character long string standing for the morphological analysis; the `relation` attribute shows the syntactic function the given token bears with respect to its head, which is referred to, in the `head` attribute, via the integer of the ID of its corresponding `word` element.[18]

3 The Index Thomisticus Treebank

The Index Thomisticus Treebank (IT-TB)[19] is, together with the Latin Dependency Treebank (LDT) (see Section 2), the oldest treebank for Latin.[20] It has been run, since its inception, at the Catholic University of Milan. It contains

18 Many texts also contain cite attributes containing the corresponding cts:urn identifier: https://www.homermultitext.org/hmt-doc/index.html (last access 2019.01.31).

19 The IT-TB is described in more detail, in this volume, in the contribution by Marco Passarotti.

20 (McGillivray et al. 2009); (Passarotti 2011).

parts of Thomas Aquinas' *Summa Theologica* which have been annotated for morphology ("morphological layer") and syntax ("analytical layer"). It currently consists of 277,547 tokens.[21] Part of the data (28,886 tokens) has also been annotated for pragmatics and semantics ("tectogrammatical layer"). The annotation has been performed by a single scholar and then reviewed by another scholar.

The IT-TB relies on the data provided by the *Index Thomisticus* (IT),[22] which is one of the first projects in what we would now call Digital Humanities/ Computational Linguistics: it aimed to digitize all works of Thomas Aquinas and POS tag and lemmatize them.

The morphological annotation of the IT-TB[23] is, due to its historical connection with the IT, the most peculiar one when compared to the morphological layers of the other treebanks. While morphological annotation in the LDT (see Section 2) and the PROIEL Treebank (see Section 4) reflects the categorization elaborated by traditional grammar, the IT-TB is freer in this respect: parts of speech are, for example, identified by a combination of two values: the first describes "flexional categories", most of which specify declension/conjugation type, while the second gives information for "flectional types" ("Nominal", "Participial", "Verbal", "Invariable", and "Pseudo-lemma"). For example, *multitudinis* is tagged as "C1", where "C" stands for "third declension" and "1" for "Nominal". Similarly, *pigmentaria* is annotated as "A1", i.e., "first declension" and "Nominal", while *et* is tagged as "04", i.e., "invariable" and "invariable".

These examples show that a mapping from the IT-TB morphological categories to the more widely known of the LDT is not always possible (without recourse to external resources such as dictionaries or morphological analyzers). The "Nominal" category, for example, can correspond to either a noun or an adjective. Similarly, a token labeled as "04" could be a conjunction, such as "et", or an adverb, such as "bene".

The IT-TB shares the same annotation guidelines for syntax with the LDT (Bamman et al. 2007; see Section 2 for more details). They have also been complemented by the *Rules of Annotation for the Analytical Layer of the Index Thomisticus Treebank* (henceforth RALIT).[24]

21 The calculations on the PML format have been performed on the release available at https://itreebank.marginalia.it/view/download.php on 2018.10.13 (excluding the more recent Golden Age texts).

22 http://www.corpusthomisticum.org/it/index.age (last access 2019.01.31).

23 Documentation for the tagset is available at https://itreebank.marginalia.it/doc/Tagset_IT.pdf and https://itreebank.marginalia.it/doc/Tagset_IT_README.txt (last access 2019.01.31)

24 (Passarotti 2016).

In RALIT annotation issues are addressed, which are particularly (but not exclusively) relevant to Thomas Aquinas' Latin. These include sentences starting with a conjunction, such as *sed* or *quia*. The case of sentences introduced by *quia* is particularly interesting in that it has to do with the phenomenon of ellipsis, which is notoriously difficult to deal with theoretically and therefore also regulate. While the introduction of elliptical nodes in a sentence raises a number of theoretical issues (especially when it comes to comparing different annotations of the same text, elliptical nodes altering the initial token number), it is clear that building of a syntactic tree often requires them. As to the specific case of *quia*, it is stated in RALIT that it is treated as the linguistic root of the tree and the verb depending on it receives the label PRED. In this case, therefore, no elliptical node is added. In general, adequate treatment of ellipsis currently remains one of the major challenges for treebanking.

Interestingly, in RALIT an annotation rule for the construction "ita ... sicut" is also given. The adverb *ita* is made the head of the subordinate clause introduced by *ut*. This kind of syntactic construction is very frequent in both Ancient Greek and Latin. Typically, a pronoun or an adverb anticipates a following subordinate clause, which is usually introduced by a conjunction. Such a clause is of an explicative nature with respect to the anaphor/cataphor in the superordinate clause. English shows a similar construction with clauses introduced by, for example, "to such an extent that" or "to the point that", where the subordinate conjunction "that" introduces the clause explaining what the extent/point is. This construction can take different forms: the kind of the anaphor/cataphor can be a pronoun, an adverb, or a noun, while the subordinate clause can be introduced by different conjunctions (or even be an infinitive clause). The subordinate clause is in traditional grammar described as being in apposition to the anaphor/cataphor (SG 991).

The IT-TB also provides tectogrammatical annotation for a subset of its morphosyntactically annotated sentences.[25] The guidelines for this layer of annotation are based on the annotation manual for the tectogrammatical layer of the Prague Dependency Treebank[26] complemented by the *Guidelines for*

25 The tectogrammatical layer is also, together with the morphological and analytical layers, made available for some Latin texts of the Golden Age: https://itreebank.marginalia.it/doc/15-01-2018_all_resources_all_formats.zip (last access 2019.01.31). A syntactically-based valency lexicon and semantically-based valency lexicon have also been created: https://itreebank.marginalia.it/view/resources.php (last access 2019.01.31).

26 (Mikulová 2006).

Tectogrammatical Annotation of Latin Treebanks: The Treatment of some Specific Constructions, which provide rules for specific Latin constructions.[27]

The tectogrammatical layer provides a description for the pragmatics and semantics of a given sentence. Particularly noteworthy are the formalisms for semantic (macro)roles (called "functors"), coreference, and topic-focus articulation. Since a tectogrammatical tree is meant to represent the semantics and pragmatics of a sentence, its tree structure is different from the corresponding syntactic tree, which has to do with surface syntax: prepositions, for example, are not assigned separate nodes in a tectogrammatical tree, but are merged with nodes of the nouns they govern, in that they enable functor identification (and therefore semantic roles).

The IT-TB is released in different formats. All three annotation layers are available only in the PML (Prague Markup Language) language, which is an XML format specifically designed to encode the linguistic annotation layers for the Prague Dependency Treebank. The PML format keeps the three annotation layers physically separate and links them via IDs. Notably, the XML syntax encoding linguistic trees is informed by the parent-child relationships between linguistic nodes (see Pajas 2010 for the full specification). The morphosyntactic annotation is also available in two other common formats: CoNLL and Tiger XML.

4 The PROIEL Treebank

The PROIEL Treebank originates from the PROIEL (Pragmatic Resources in Old Indo-European Languages) project, which was run at Oslo University between 2008 and 2013. The project produced morphosyntactic (and partly pragmatic) annotation for the Greek New Testament and its translations into the following Old Indo-European languages: Latin, Gothic, Armenian, and Old Church Slavonic.[28]

After the end of the PROIEL project, the PROIEL Treebank has continued to be augmented with new Ancient Greek and Latin texts, mainly belonging to classical antiquity (see also Eckhoff (2017) for the PROEIL Treebank family). Currently, it comprises, besides the Greek and Latin New Testaments, (parts of) the following works: Herodotus' *Histories*, Sphrantzes' *Chronicles*, Caesar's *De*

27 (Passarotti and Gonzáles Saavedra 2015).
28 (Haug et al. 2008); (Haug et al. 2009).

Bello Gallico, Cicero's *Epistulae ad Atticum* and *De Officiis*, *Peregrinatio Aetheriae* and Palladius' *Opus Agriculturae*. The Ancient Greek part of the treebank consists of 250,455 tokens, while the Latin part of 225,064 tokens (release 20180408).[29] Annotations are stored in files containing detailed metadata for each text, such as the source of the text, tagset abbreviations and their expansions, and names of annotators and reviewers.[30]

The morphological annotation[31] for both Latin and Ancient Greek is very similar to that of the Ancient Greek and Latin Dependency Treebank. The parts of speech acknowledged are however more numerous (i.e., 27). This is mainly due to subcategorizations of more general parts of speech: for example, pronouns are classified as demonstrative, indefinite, interrogative, personal, personal reflexive, possessive, possessive reflexive, reciprocal, and relative. Similarly, nouns are of two types: common and proper. On the contrary, the morphological features are essentially the same as those of the AGLDT, with minor deviations. Remarkably, some of them are defined on a purely morphological basis, in that specific values for morphologically ambiguous terminations are allowed: for example, the gender for an adjective such as *cotidianis* is annotated as "masculine, feminine or neuter", even though the gender of its governing noun can disambiguate it.

The syntactic annotation is based on an annotation scheme[32] similar to those for the AGLDT, in that it also relies on the annotation guidelines for the analytical layer of the Prague Dependency Treebank. Also in the PROEIL Treebank argument structure is annotated. Besides subjects and objects (the latter corresponding mostly, but not exclusively, to arguments in the accusative case), arguments conveyed by oblique cases or prepositional phrases are distinguished through the label OBL. In the case of prepositional phrases, the label is used for both the preposition and its dependent noun. If the preposition introduces an adjunct, it receives the label ADV, but the dependent noun is still annotated as OBL, being always considered an oblique argument – on the contrary, in the AGLDT prepositions are always annotated as AuxP and their

29 The numbers do not consider punctuation marks, which are not encoded as token elements.
30 The treebank can be downloaded at https://github.com/proiel/proiel-treebank/releases (last access 2019.01.31).
31 See https://proiel.github.io/handbook/developer/#apis-and-libraries for the code documenting, among other things, text preprocessing (last access 2019.01.31).
32 (Haug 2010).

dependent nouns can get the label OBJ or ADV depending on whether they are or are not arguments.

Differently from the AGLDT, a specific label (XOBJ) is used to mark the syntactic function of predicative complements depending on verbs such as *esse*, *videari*, or *creare*. The distinction between subject and object complements is marked via a system called *slash notation*, which consists in the addition of a dependency relation of the subject or object on the predicative complement. The XOBJ label is also used to annotate infinitives depending on auxiliary verbs such as *posse* and *velle* or on the passive forms of verbs such as *putare* and *dicere* (e.g., *dicitur ad urbem venisse*, with *venisse* receiving the XOBJ label). The PROIEL Treebank also has specific labels for partitives (PART), conjunct participles (XADV), and complement sentences (COMP).[33]

Remarkably, in the PROEIL Treebank function words such as prepositions and subordinate conjunctions take the labels describing the syntactic function of the phrases they heads, while in the AGLDT it is the governed nouns or verbs that receive such labels, prepositions and conjunctions being tagged with function labels (AuxP and AuxC, respectively).

Parts of the Ancient Greek and Latin texts have also been annotated for information structure.[34] This includes addition of pro-drop subjects and of a few labels mostly pertaining to the information status of referents. In particular, the "new" and "old" labels are the ones which prototypically help identification of foci and topics in a sentence.[35]

The PROIEL Treebank is released in a native XML format, which includes all annotation layers. The XML structure is very similar to that of the AGLDT (See Section 2), with `sentence` elements containing `token` elements, each of which has at least 9 attributes. Among these two are peculiar: `citation-part`, which contains the passage reference and `presentation-after`, which contains any punctuation mark following the given token. Optionally, the information-status attribute can be present. The slash notation, which adds further dependency relations, is encoded in slash elements within `token` elements. The morphosyntactic information is also made available in a CoNLL format.

33 A precise description of these labels is outside the scope of the present article. The reader is referred to the guidelines for a detailed account of all their uses.

34 (Haug et al. 2014).

35 All possible information-structure labels are listed in each treebank file. The information structure-annotation is currently best readable when accessing the texts at http://foni.uio.no:3000/, where a visualization for each single annotation layer is provided (last access 2019.01.31).

5 The SEMATIA Treebank

The SEMATIA Treebank[36] aims to provide morphosyntactic annotations for papyri using the formalism of the AGLDT.[37] It is currently maintained at Helsinki University and contains 313 papyrological texts[38] coming from the Duke Databank of Documentary Papyri.[39]

The fragmentary nature of papyri represents one of the biggest challenges for annotation. As is known, more or less extensive parts of a text may be missing, which the papyrologist tries to interpret and integrate. Moreover, documentary papyri usually do not have word division, which often, as one can imagine, raises ambiguities. The complexity of papyri is mirrored in the heavy markup contained in the original TEI XML documents, which challenges automatic extraction of the text itself.[40]

For this reason, two annotated versions of a given papyrus are provided in the SEMATIA Treebank: one for the original text (also called "original layer") and one for the same text after editorial intervention. Moreover, sections of a papyrus written by different authors also receive separate annotations.

Texts are preprocessed and annotated using the Arethusa annotation framework (see note 8). The morphological annotation is facilitated by the Morpheus morphological analyzer, whose outputs however require to be frequently corrected because it is based on Classical Greek and Classical Latin and the lexicon of papyri differs from them in many respects.[41] The SEMATIA Treebank is released in the same XML format as the AGLDT.

6 Conclusion

In the present paper, I have overviewed the existing dependency treebanks for Ancient Greek and Latin, with the aim not to describe them exactly but to present their most relevant features and how they relate to each other.

---

36 The SEMATIA Treebank is available at https://sematia.hum.helsinki.fi and https://github.com/ezhenrik/sematia-tb (last access 2019.01.31).

37 (Vierros 2018).

38 There are 19,340 tokens for Ancient Greek and 1,400 tokens for Latin in the data sets available at https://github.com/ezhenrik/sematia-tb on 2018.10.13.

39 http://papyri.info/ (last access 2019.01.31).

40 (Vierros and Henriksson 2017).

41 See also Celano (2018).

There currently exist four dependency treebanks for Ancient Greek and Latin: the AGLDT contains texts from classical antiquity, while the IT-TB (mainly) contains Thomas Aquinas' *Summa Theologica*; the PROIEL Treebank originally contained the New Testament and some of its translations into Old Indo-European languages, but texts from classical antiquity have subsequently been added; the SEMATIA Treebank contains documentary papyri.

The AGLDT and the IT-TB share the same Latin syntactic guidelines, while the AGLDT and the SEMATIA treebank the same Ancient Greek and Latin syntactic guidelines. The PROEIL treebank has developed its own syntactic guidelines for both Ancient Greek and Latin, even though they are similar to the ones adopted by the AGLDT, all relying on the annotation guidelines for the analytical layer of the Prague Dependency Treebank. Some treebanks also provide a few texts annotated for semantics/pragmatics.

Despite some differences, it is safe to say that the morphosyntactic annotation of one treebank can be converted into that of another treebank to a large extent: this is also evidenced by the ongoing work to convert the original annotation schemes into the Universal Dependencies[42] one. The original format of all treebanks is XML, but none of them has so far adopted pure stand-off annotation (i.e., where tokens are referenced to the offsets of the original unannotated text).

Acknowledgements: This research has been funded by the Deutsche Forschungsgemeinschaft (DFG, German Research Foundation: project number 408121292).

Abbreviations

AGLDT	=	Ancient Greek and Latin Dependency Treebank
AGDT	=	Ancient Greek Dependency Treebank
IT	=	Index Thomisticus
IT-TB	=	Index Thomisticus Treebank
LDT	=	Latin Dependency Treebank
SG	=	H. W. Smyth's *Greek Grammar for Colleges*, 1920

42 http://www.universaldependencies.org (last access 2019.01.31).

Bibliography

Bamman, D.; Passarotti, M.; Crane, G.; Raynaud, R. (2007): Guidelines for the Syntactic Annotation of Latin Treebanks. https://github.com/PerseusDL/treebank_data/blob/master/v1/latin/docs/guidelines.pdf (last access 2019.01.31).

Bamman, D.; Crane, G. (2011): "The Ancient Greek and Latin Dependency Treebank". In: C. Sporleder; A. van Den Bosch; K. Zervanou (eds.): Language Technology for Cultural Heritage. Berlin and Heidelberg: Springer, 79–89.

Celano, G.G.A. (2014): Guidelines for the Annotation of the Ancient Greek Dependency Treebank 2.0. https://github.com/PerseusDL/treebank_data/edit/master/AGDT2/guidelines (last access 2019.01.31).

Celano, G.G.A.; Crane, G. (2015): "Semantic Role Annotation in the Ancient Greek Dependency Treebank". In: D. Markus; E. Hinrichs; A. Patejuk; A. Przepiórkowski (eds.): Proceedings of the Fourteenth International Workshop on Treebanks and linguistic Theories (TLT14). Warszawa: Institute of Computer Science, 26–34.

Celano, G.G.A; Crane, G.; Majidi, S. (2016): "Part of Speech Tagging for Ancient Greek". Open Linguistics 2:1, 393–399. https://doi.org/10.1515/opli-2016-0020.

Celano, G.G.A. (2018): "An Automatic Morphological Annotation and Lemmatization for the IDP Papyri". In: N. Reggiani (ed.): Digital Papyrology II. Berlin and Boston: De Gruyter, 139–148.

Crane, G. (1991): "Generating and Parsing Classical Greek". Literary and Linguistic Computing 6, 243–245.

Eckhoff, H.; Bech, K.; Bouma, G.; Eide, K.; Haug, D.; Haugen, O.E.; Jøhndal, M. (2017): "The PROIEL Treebank Family: A Standard for Early Attestations of Indo-European Languages". Language Resources and Evaluation 52, 29–65.

Hajič, J.; Panevová, J.; Buráňová, E.; UrešOvá, Z.; Bémová, A.; (in cooperation with) Kárník, J.; Štěpánek, J.; Pajas, P. (1999): Annotations at Analytical Level: Instructions for Annotators. https://ufal.mff.cuni.cz/pdt2.0/doc/manuals/en/a-layer/html/index.html (last access 2019.01.31).

Haug, D.T.T.; Jøhndal, M.L. (2008): "Creating a Parallel Treebank of the Old Indo-European Bible Translations". In: C. Sporleder; K. Ribarov (eds.): Proceedings of the Second Workshop on Language Technology for Cultural Heritage Data (LaTeCH). Association for Computational Linguistics, 27–34.

Haug, D.T.T.; Jøhndal, M.L.; Eckhoff, H.M.; Hertzenberg, M.J.; Müth, A. (2009): "Computational and Linguistic Issues in Designing a Syntactically Annotated Parallel Corpus of Indo-European Languages". Traitement automatique des langues 50:2, 17–45.

Haug, D.T.T. (2010): PROEIL Guidelines for Annotation. http://folk.uio.no/daghaug/syntactic_guidelines.pdf (last access 2019.01.31).

Haug, D.T.T.; Eckhoff, H.M.; Welo, E. (2014): "The Theoretical Foundations of Givenness Annotation". In: K. Bech; K.G. Eide (eds.): Information Structure and Syntactic Change in Germanic and Romance languages. Amsterdam: John Benjamins, 17–52.

McGillivray, B.; Passarotti, M.; Ruffolo, P. (2009): "The Index Thomisticus Treebank Project: Annotation, Parsing and Valency Lexicon". Traitement Automatique des Langues 2009, 103–127.

Mikulová, M.; Bémová, A.; Hajič, J.; Hajičová, E.; Havelka, J.; Kolárová, V.; Kučová, L.; Lopatková, M.; Pajas, P.; Panevová, J.; Razímová, M.; Sgall, P.; Štěpánek, J.;

Urešová, Z.; Veselá, K.; Žabokrtský, Z.; (translation) Součková, K.; Böhmová, A.; Čermáková, K.; Havelka, J.; Corness, P. (2006): Annotation on the Tectogrammatical Layer in the Prague Dependency Treebank: Annotation Manual. http://ufal.mff.cuni.cz/pdt2.0/doc/manuals/en/t-layer/html/index.html (last access 2019.01.31).

Pajas, P. (2010): The Prague Markup Language (version 1.1). http://ufal.mff.cuni.cz/jazz/pml/doc/pml_doc.pdf (last access 2019.01.31).

Passarotti, M. (2011): "The State of the Art of Latin and the Index Thomisticus Treebank Project". In: M. Ortola (ed.): Corpus Anciens et Bases de Données, ALIENTO. Échanges Sapientiels en Méditerranée 2, 301–320.

Passarotti, M.; Gonzáles Saavedra, B. (2015): Guidelines for Tectogrammatical Annotation of Latin Treebanks: The Treatment of some Specific Constructions. https://itreebank.marginalia.it/doc/Guidelines_tectogrammatical_Latin.pdf (last access 2019.01.31).

Passarotti, M. (2016): Rules of Annotation for the Analytical Layer of the Index Thomisticus Treebank.https://itreebank.marginalia.it/doc/Guidelines_analytical_latin_specific-constructions.pdf (last access 2019.01.31).

Smyth, H.W. (1920): Greek Grammar for Colleges. New York: American Book Company.

Treebank: Annotation Manual. http://ufal.mff.cuni.cz/pdt2.0/doc/manuals/en/t-layer/html/index.html (last access 2019.01.31).

Vierros, M.; Henriksson, E.; (2017): "Preprocessing Greek Papyri for Linguistic Annotation". In: M. BüChler; L. Mellerin (eds.): Journal of Data Mining and Digital Humanities. Special Issue on Computer-Aided Processing of Inter-textuality in Ancient Languages. https://jdmdh.episciences.org/paper/view?id=1385 (last access 2019.01.31).

Vierros, M. (2018): "Linguistic Annotation of the Digital Papyrological Corpus: Sematia". In: N. Reggiani (ed.): Digital Papyrology II. Berlin and Boston: De Gruyter, 105–118.

Marco Passarotti

The Project of the Index Thomisticus Treebank

Abstract: The paper introduces the project of the Index Thomisticus Treebank (IT-TB). The IT-TB is a dependency-based treebank based on the corpus of the Index Thomisticus by father Roberto Busa (IT), which includes the *opera omnia* of Thomas Aquinas, for a total of approximately 11 million words. Currently, the IT-TB is the largest Latin treebank available, with more than 350,000 nodes in around 17,000 sentences. The annotation covers the entire books 1, 2 and 3 of *Summa contra Gentiles*, plus excerpts from *Scriptum super Sententiis Magistri Petri Lombardi* and *Summa Theologiae*. The paper details the multi-layer annotation style of the IT-TB and its background theoretical motivations. The conversion process to the now widely used Universal Dependencies style is described as well. Across more than a decade, the project has developed a number of linguistic resources and NLP tools for Latin connected to the IT-TB. As for the resources, the paper presents the syntax-based subcategorization lexicon IT-VaLex and the valency lexicon Latin Vallex. As for the tools, the automatic dependency parsing process is described, highlighting the core issue of portability of NLP tools across the wide diachronic and diatopic span of Latin texts. A section is dedicated to automatic morphological analysis of Latin, introducing the analyzer Lemlat and its recent enhancement with information on derivational morphology and a new set of lexical entries covering a large *Onomasticon* (from Forcellini dictionary) and Medieval Latin (from Du Cange glossary).

1 Introduction

The name of the Italian Jesuit Roberto Busa is quoted in almost every introduction to Computational Linguistics or Digital Humanities. His often recounted

Note: The author gratefully acknowledges the support of the project LiLa (Linking Latin. Building a Knowledge Base of Linguistic Resources for Latin). This project has received funding from the European Research Council (ERC) European Union's Horizon 2020 research and innovation programme under grant agreement No 769994.

Marco Passarotti, Università Cattolica del Sacro Cuore, Milano

https://doi.org/10.1515/9783110599572-017

meeting in New York with the founder of IBM, Thomas Watson Sr., in 1949 is considered one of the funding moments of the discipline.[1]

Similarly, the Index Thomisticus (IT), the most important outcome of that meeting, is usually mentioned among the first annotated textual corpora available in machine-readable format.[2] The result of thirty years of work and funding from IBM, the IT contains the *opera omnia* of Thomas Aquinas (118 texts) as well as 61 texts by other authors related to Thomas, for a total of approximately 11 million tokens. The corpus is morphologically tagged and lemmatized and it is available on paper, CD-ROM and on-line (http://www.corpusthomisticum.org).

Already at the time when the IT was just published, Busa planned to enhance the corpus with syntactic metadata. After a number of pilot attempts since the Nineties, the process of syntactic annotation of the IT started in 2006 with the so-called Index Thomisticus Treebank (IT-TB; http://itreebank.marginalia.it), which today represents the largest syntactically annotated corpus for Latin available.

Father Busa, who died in 2011, had the opportunity to see the start of the project and followed its first steps. In December 2009, he gave his last speech at a scientific event, the eighth edition of the international workshop on *Treebanks and Linguistic Theories* (http://tlt8.unicatt.it). The talk of Busa was entitled *From Punched Cards to Treebanks: 60 Years of Computational Linguistics*. The following excerpt from the unpublished transcription of that talk epitomizes both the objective and the motivation of the IT-TB:

> The [. . .] aim is to construct a summa of the entire syntax of Aquinas with statistics and percentages of each grammatical element, including punctuation marks (this is the Index Thomisticus Treebank project): this will then serve as a yardstick to compare or contrast the Latin grammar of St Thomas with that of others in other languages as well.

The objective of Busa was huge: to perform the syntactic annotation of the entire corpus of Thomas Aquinas' works not only to get a deep knowledge of his language and, thus, philosophy, but also to be able to compare Latin with other languages. This sounds like a plan perfectly fitting the needs of current research in the area of linguistic resources. The Universal Dependencies project (http://universaldependencies.org), which the IT-TB takes part of, represents

1 (Passarotti 2013, 17).
2 (Busa 1974–1980).

today the most rising effort from the research community to build a common annotation style for an ever growing number of languages. Starting from the empirical description of the syntactic constructions of a single language, this can be compared with those of other languages thanks to shared formats, schemes and tools. The IT-TB today contributes to such common effort, providing evidence about the specific variety of Latin represented by the works of Thomas Aquinas.

Across more than a decade, the IT-TB has grown into a larger project, which has gone beyond the construction of the treebank of Thomas Aquinas' texts. Starting from the IT-TB, the project has built a number of other linguistic resources and tools for automatic processing of Latin, making the CIRCSE research center in Milan (where the project is run since its beginning) an internationally known hub in the field and contributing to lead Latin out of its status of under-resourced language, which was still the case in mid 2000s when the IT-TB was started.

This paper wants to provide an overview of the IT-TB project, by detailing both the theoretical and the practical aspects connected to the building and the use of its resources and Natural Language Processing (NLP) tools for Latin.

The paper is organized as follows. Section 2 describes the main linguistic resource of the project, namely the IT-TB, presenting the theoretical framework supporting its annotation style, and its recent conversion into the Universal Dependencies style. Section 3 details two lexical resources strictly related to the IT-TB: the syntactic subcategorization lexicon IT-VaLex and the valency lexicon Latin Vallex. Section 4 deals with NLP tools for Latin. First, it introduces the version 3.0 of the Latin morphological analyzer Lemlat, particularly focusing on its enhancement with information about derivational morphology. Second, it presents the state of the art of automatic dependency parsing of the IT-TB, sketching the problem of portability of NLP tools for Latin across time and space. Finally, Section 5 concludes the paper by discussing a number of open challenges in the field and by looking at the near future of the IT-TB project as well as of the several linguistic resources and NLP tools for Latin built so far, presenting the objectives of the new ERC-Consolidator Grant LiLa, which is run at CIRCSE.

2 The Index Thomisticus Treebank

2.1 Theoretical background

The IT-TB is a dependency treebank based on a subset of the IT. The project is carried out at the CIRCSE research center of the Università Cattolica del Sacro Cuore in Milan, Italy (http://centridiricerca.unicatt.it/circse).[3]

The dependency-based annotation style of the IT-TB is grounded on Functional Generative Description (FGD),[4] a theoretical framework developed in Prague and intensively applied and tested while building the Prague Dependency Treebank of Czech (PDT).

FGD is based on the assumption that language must be considered as a form-meaning composite. Consistently and like the PDT, the IT-TB features three layers of annotation ordered as follows:[5]

(1) a morphological layer: disambiguated morphological annotation and lemmatization;
(2) an "analytical" layer: annotation of surface syntax (the "form");
(3) a "tectogrammatical" layer: annotation of underlying syntax (the "meaning").

Both analytical and tectogrammatical layers describe the sentence structure with dependency tree-graphs, respectively named "analytical tree structures" (ATSs) and "tectogrammatical tree-structures" (TGTSs).

In ATSs every word and punctuation mark of the sentence is represented by a node of a rooted dependency tree. The edges of the tree correspond to dependency relations labeled with (surface) syntactic functions called "analytical functions" (like Subject, Object, etc.).

---

3 (Passarotti 2010). The IT-TB is freely available from the IT-TB website under a Creative Commons Attribution-NonCommercial-ShareAlike 3.0 Unported License. Data can be queried by using PML Tree Query (PML-TQ), a highly portable query language and search engine (Pajas and Štěpánek 2009). PML-TQ is available both as a local extension of the tree editor TrEd (http://ufal.mff.cuni.cz/tred/) and as an on-line implementation which, in the case of the IT-TB, enables users to run queries on the linguistic resources of the IT-TB project (http://itreebank.marginalia.it/view/resources.php). The portion of the IT-TB annotated at the analytical layer is accessible also through the web-based treebank search and visualization application TüNDRA (Martens and Passarotti 2014) as part of the web infrastructure of linguistic resources and tools CLARIN (https://www.clarin.eu: last access 2019.01.31).

4 (Sgall et al. 1986).

5 (Hajič et al. 2000).

TGTSs describe the underlying structure of the sentence, conceived as the semantically relevant counterpart of the grammatical means of expression (described by ATSs). The nodes of TGTSs represent content words only, while function words and punctuation marks are left out. The nodes are labeled with semantic role tags called "functors", which are divided into two classes according to valency: (a) arguments, called "inner participants", i.e. obligatory complements of verbs, nouns, adjectives and adverbs: Actor, Patient, Addressee, Effect and Origin; (b) adjuncts, called "free modifications": different kinds of adverbials, like Place, Time, Manner etc. TGTSs feature two dimensions that represent respectively the syntactic structure of the sentence (the vertical dimension) and its information structure ("topic-focus articulation", TFA), based on the underlying word order (the horizontal dimension). Also ellipsis resolution and coreference analysis are performed at the tectogrammatical layer and are represented in TGTSs through newly added nodes (ellipsis) and arrows (coreference).

2.2 Analytical layer

During the first three years of the project, the analytical annotation of the IT-TB was performed fully manually. Since 2009, analytical data are annotated in semi-automatic fashion by using various combinations of stochastic parsers trained on different subsets of the IT-TB (see Section 4.1), whose output is manually checked by two human annotators.

Currently the number of analytically annotated nodes in the IT-TB is around 370,000, corresponding to approximately 23,000 sentences excerpted from three works of Thomas Aquinas: *Scriptum super Sententiis Magistri Petri Lombardi* (*Sent.*), *Summa contra Gentiles* (*ScG*) and *Summa Theologiae* (*ST*). In particular, the IT-TB includes the following texts annotated at the analytical layer:

A. concordances of the lemma *forma* in *Sent.*, *ScG* and in the first 76 *quaestiones* of *ST*;
B. entire first, second and third books and chapters 1–11 of the fourth book of *ScG*.

Analytical annotation is performed according to a specific manual for the syntactic annotation of Latin treebanks,[6] which was developed on the basis of the PDT guidelines for analytical annotation.[7]

6 (Bamman et al. 2007).
7 (Hajič et al. 1999).

Figure 1 reports the ATS of the following sentence from the IT-TB: "tunc enim unaquaeque res optime disponitur cum ad finem suum convenienter ordinatur;" ('So, each thing is excellently arranged when it is properly directed to its purpose;') (*ScG* I, ch. 1, no. 2).

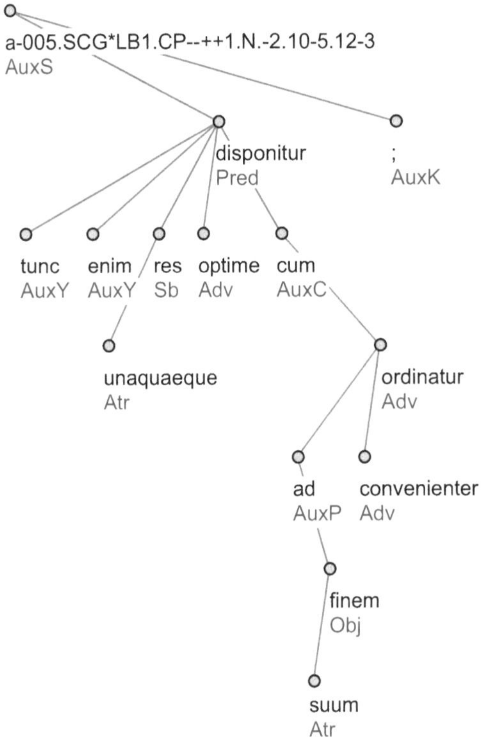

Figure 1: An analytical tree structure.

Except for the technical root of the tree (which reports the textual reference of the sentence), each node in the ATS corresponds to either one word or punctuation mark in the sentence. Nodes are arranged from left to right according to surface word order; they are connected in governor-dependent fashion and each relation is labeled with an analytical function. For instance, the relation between the word *res* and its governor *disponitur* is labeled with the analytical function Sb (Subject), i.e. *res* is the subject of *disponitur*. Four kinds of analytical functions that occur in the tree are assigned to auxiliary sentence members, namely AuxC (subordinating conjunctions: *cum*), AuxK (terminal punctuation marks), AuxP (prepositions: *ad*) and AuxY (sentence adverbs: *enim*, *tunc*).[8]

2.3 Tectogrammatical layer

The tectogrammatical annotation workflow of the IT-TB is based on TGTSs automatically converted from ATSs.[9] Conversion is performed by adapting to Latin a number of ATS-to-TGTS scripts provided by the NLP framework Treex.[10] The TGTSs that result from conversion are then checked and refined manually by two independent annotators. The annotation guidelines are those for the tectogrammatical layer of the PDT.[11]

So far, the first 2,000 sentences of *ScG* have been fully annotated at tectogrammatical level (corresponding to approximately 28,000 nodes).[12] Figure 2 shows the TGTS corresponding to the ATS of the sentence reported in Figure 1.

Since only nodes for content words can occur in TGTSs, auxiliary sentence members labeled with analytical functions AuxC, AuxK and AuxP are collapsed. Analytical functions are replaced with functors. The nodes for the lemmas *enim* and *tunc* are both assigned the functor PREC, since they represent expressions linking the clause to the preceding context; they are given nodetype "atom" (atomic nodes), which is used for adverbs of attitude, intensifying or modal expressions, rhematizers and text connectives.[13] *Res* is the Patient (PAT) of *dispono*, as it is the syntactic subject of a passive verbal form (*disponitur*).[14] Both the adverbial forms of *bonus* (*optime*) and *convenio* (*convenienter*) are labeled with functor MANN, which expresses manner by specifying an

8 The other analytical functions occurring in this sentences are the following: Adv (adverbs and adverbial modifications, i.e. adjuncts), Atr (attributes), AuxS (root of the tree), Obj (direct and indirect objects), Pred (main predicate of the sentence).

9 (González Saavedra and Passarotti 2014).

10 (Popel and Žabokrtský 2010).

11 (Mikulová et al. 2006).

12 Also some texts excerpted from the Latin Dependency Treebank of Classical Latin (LDT; Bamman and Crane 2007) were annotated at the tectogrammatical layer in the context of the IT-TB project. In particular, these are 100 sentences from Caesar and Cicero, and the entire text of *Bellum Catilinae* by Sallust (Passarotti and González Saavedra 2018).

13 (Mikulová et al. 2006, 17).

14 Conversely, syntactic subjects of active verbal forms are usually labeled with the functor ACT (Actor). However, this does not always hold true, since the functor of the subject depends on the semantic features of the verb.

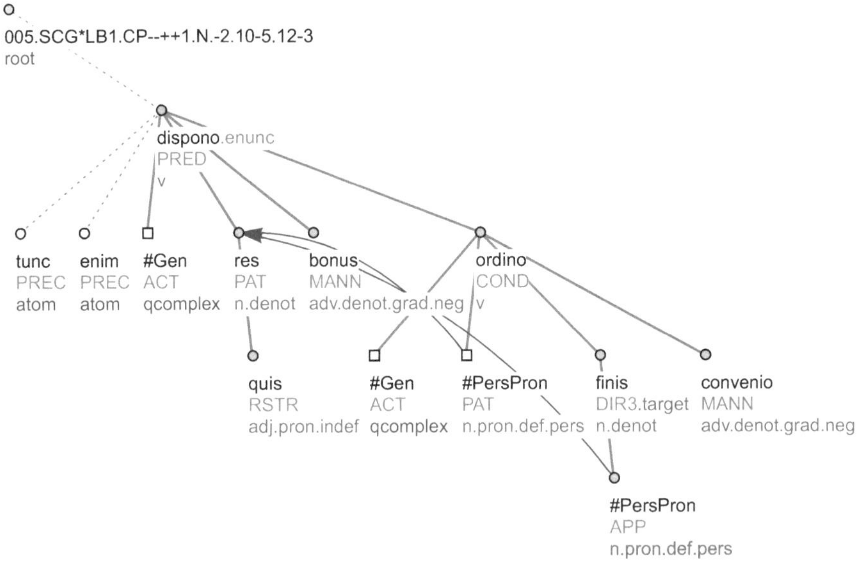

Figure 2: A tectogrammatical tree structure.[15]

evaluating characteristic of the event, or a property. *Unusquisque* is a pronominal restrictive adnominal modification (RSTR) that further specifies the governing noun *res*. The clause headed by *ordinatur* (lemma: *ordino*) is assigned the functor COND, as it reports the condition on which the event expressed by the governing verb (*disponitur*; lemma: *dispono*) can happen. The lemma *finis* is assigned the functor DIR3 (Directional: to), which expresses the target point of the event. *Finis* is then specified by an adnominal modification of appurtenance (APP).

Three newly added nodes occur in the tree (square nodes), to provide ellipsis resolution of those arguments of the verbs *dispono* and *ordino* that are missing in the surface structure. *Dispono* is a two-argument verb, the two arguments being respectively the Actor and the Patient, but only the Patient is explicitly expressed in the sentence, i.e. the syntactic subject *res*. The missing argument, i.e. the Actor (ACT), is thus replaced with a "general argument" (#Gen), because the coreferred element of the omitted modification cannot be clearly identified

15 In the default visualization of TGTSs, word forms are replaced with lemmas.

with the help of the context. The same holds also for the Actor of the verb *ordino* (#Gen), whose Patient (#PersPron, PAT) is coreferential with the noun *res*, as well as the possessive adjective *suus* (#PersPron, APP). In the TGTS, these coreferential relations are shown by the blue arrows linking the two #PersPron nodes with the node for *res*.[16]

The nodes in the TGTS are arranged from left to right according to TFA, which is signaled by the color of the nodes (white nodes: topic; yellow nodes: focus). A so-called "semantic part of speech" is assigned to every node: for instance, "denotational noun" is assigned to *finis*.[17] Finally, the illocutionary force class informing about the sentential modality is assigned to the main predicate of the sentence *dispono* ("enunciative").

2.4 The Index Thomisticus Treebank in Universal Dependencies

Universal Dependencies (UD)[18] is one of the most notable projects currently ongoing in computational linguistics. The project, run by contributors from the research community, aims at creating a collection of dependency treebanks for different languages built according to a cross-linguistically consistent annotation style meant to complement (but not to replace) the single language/treebank-specific schemes.

Started in 2014 with the first set of guidelines, the project has published a new release of the collection of the treebanks roughly every six months. Version 2 (v2), which introduces a new set of guidelines, was released in March 2017. The current version is 2.2 (July 2018). It includes 122 treebanks and 71 languages.

The IT-TB is part of UD since version 1.2 (November 2015), thanks to an automatic conversion procedure from ATSs to UD.[19] The UD annotation guidelines show a number of differences from those of the IT-TB original scheme for ATSs. Figure 3 presents the UD v2 compliant tree of the sentences whose ATS is shown in Figure 1.

From Figure 3 it stands out clearly that one of the basic annotation principles of UD is that fundamental dependencies do hold between content words, while function words depend on the content word they modify. For instance,

---

16 #PersPron is a "t-lemma" (tectogrammatical lemma) assigned to nodes representing possessive and personal pronouns (including reflexives).

17 (Mikulová et al. 2006, 47).

18 http://universaldependencies.org (last access 2019.01.31); (Nivre 2015).

19 (Cecchini et al. forthcoming).

one can see that in the UD tree of Figure 3 there is a direct dependency relation between the main predicate of the sentence (*disponitur*) and that of the subordinate clause *ordinatur*, while this is not the case in the ATS of Figure 1, where such relation is mediated by the the subordinating conjunction (*cum*). Consistently, in UD trees prepositions depend on the head of the prepositional phrase. In Figure 3, the node for the preposition *ad* depends on *finem* (thus creating a direct relation between the content words *ordinatur* and *finem*), while the opposite holds in the ATS of Figure 1, resulting in an indirect relation between *ordinatur* and *finem*.

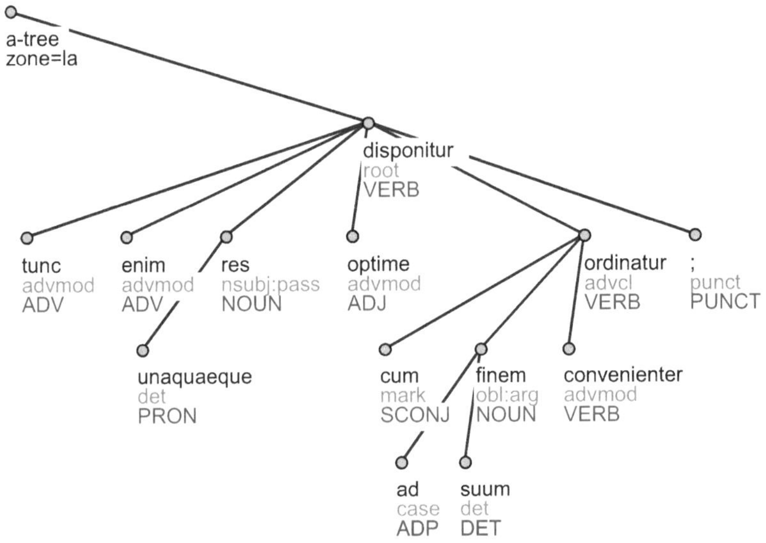

Figure 3: A UD v2 tree.

3 Subcategorization and valency lexica

Following the basic assumption of frame semantics,[20] according to which the meaning of some words can be fully understood only by knowing the frame elements that are evoked by that word, valency lexica for several languages are today available.[21] These lexica play an important role in NLP thanks to their

20 (Fillmore 1982).

21 See, for instance, PropBank (Kingsbury and Palmer 2002), FrameNet (Ruppenhofer et al. 2006) and PDT-Vallex (Hajič et al. 2003), which were first created in intuition-based fashion

large applicability in tasks like semantic role labeling, word sense disambiguation, automatic verb classification, selectional preference acquisition and also treebanking.[22]

As for Latin, the IT-TB project has developed two lexica for Latin based on the notion of valency: IT-VaLex and Latin Vallex.

3.1 IT-VaLex

IT-VaLex is a corpus-driven syntactic subcategorization lexicon whose entries (verbs only) are automatically induced from the analytical layer of annotation of the IT-TB.[23]

Being developed in corpus-driven fashion, IT-VaLex fully reflects the empirical evidence shown by corpus data and can always be rebuilt using a new version of the source treebank. The lexicon provides a full account of the syntactic subcategorization behavior of the verbs in the IT-TB. This means that only those arguments that are explicitly realized by a lexical item in the text are reported in IT-VaLex, thus resulting in cases where, for instance, typically three-argument verbs (like *do* 'to give') are assigned a subcategorization frame featuring only one argument (e.g. the subject), reflecting the fact that, among the three possible arguments, only one is realized by a lexical item in the occurrences of the verb represented by that frame.

Each entry in IT-VaLex corresponds to a verbal token in the treebank. All those tokens that share a common lemma are then collected together, to build the lexical entry of that lemma in the lexicon.

Subcategorization frames are enhanced with a number of properties concerning their occurrences in the IT-TB. These are the voice of the verb, the morpho-syntactic and syntactic features of its arguments and the order of the verb and its arguments in the sentence.

For example, one of the patterns referring to the active instances of the verb *compono* 'to join' in the lexicon is "A_Sb[nom]+V+Obj[acc]+(cum)Obj[abl]". "A" stands for "active" and the sign "+" links the elements in the linear order in

---

and then checked and refined by using data taken from corpora. Examples of valency lexica automatically acquired from annotated corpora are VALEX (Korhonen et al. 2006) and LexShem (Messiant et al. 2008).

22 (Urešová 2004).

23 (McGillivray and Passarotti 2009). The same structure of IT-VaLex is resembled by a lexicon created from the Latin Dependency Treebank and described by McGillivray (2013, 31–60).

which they appear in the sentence. Sb and Obj are analytical functions. The case of the arguments is enclosed in square brackets and the preposition *cum* introducing the ablative argument is in round brackets. This pattern thus corresponds to those active occurrences of *compono* preceded by a nominative subject and followed by an accusative argument and an ablative argument introduced by the preposition *cum*, like in the following sentence of Thomas Aquinas "intellectus componit privationem cum subiecto" ('The intellect links privation to the subject') (*Sent.* III, Dist. 6, Q. 2, Art. 1).

Currently IT-VaLex includes 1,276 lexical entries, corresponding to 65,535 verbal occurrences in the IT-TB. The lexicon is downloadable from the IT-TB website and can be queried through a dedicated web graphical interface (http://itreebank.marginalia.it/itvalex). Complex queries can be run by merging different search criteria, namely the number of arguments, their order, their morpho-syntactic labels and their lemma.

3.2 Latin Vallex

Latin Vallex is a valency lexicon built in conjunction with the tectogrammatical annotation of the IT-TB and the LDT performed by the IT-TB project.[24]

Each valency-capable word occurring in the semantically annotated portion of the two treebanks is assigned one frame entry in Latin Vallex. These can be verbs (*do* 'to give'), adjectives (*contrarius* 'opposite'), nouns (*descriptio* 'representation') and adverbs (*similiter* 'similarly').

The structure of the lexicon resembles that of the valency lexicon for Czech PDT-Vallex in the theoretical context of FGD. On the topmost level, the lexicon is divided into word entries. A word entry consists of a non-empty sequence of frame entries relevant for the lemma in question, where each different frame entry usually corresponds to one of the lemma's senses. Each frame entry contains a description of the valency frame itself and of the frame attributes. A valency frame is a sequence of frame slots. Each frame slot represents one complement of the given lemma. The surface morphological features of the frame slots are recorded, coming from the the textual evidence provided by the tectogrammatical annotation of the two Latin treebanks Latin Vallex is built on. Attributes are functors used to express types of relations between lemmas and their complements. The functors reported in the frame entries of Latin Vallex are those for inner participants ('arguments'). Also some free

24 (Passarotti et al. 2016).

modifications ('adjuncts') can enter the frame entries and are recorded as optional slots. The most frequent functors for adjuncts appearing in Latin Vallex are the locative and directional ones, which are mostly used in the frame entries for motion verbs.[25] For instance, the prototypical frame entry for the verb *venio* features three slots, whose functors are ACT, DIR1 (Direction-From) and DIR3 (Direction-To).

Presently, Latin Vallex includes 1,373 lexical entries and 3,406 frame entries. Like the treebanks which is based on, it is downloadable from the website of the IT-TB and can be queried either locally via TrEd or online through a PML-TQ implementation (http://itreebank.marginalia.it/view/resources.php). Users can move between a specific frame entry in the lexicon and its occurrences in the source treebanks.

4 Natural Language Processing tools

4.1 Morphological analysis; Lemlat and word formation Latin

Lemlat is a morphological analyzer for Latin whose version 3.0 was recently released.[26]

Among the available morphological analyzers for Latin,[27] Lemlat has proved to be the best performing together with LatMor[28] and the one provided with the largest lexical basis. In versions 1.0 and 2.0, this consists in the collation of three Latin dictionaries[29] for a total of 40,014 lexical entries and 43,432 lemmas. In version 3.0, the lexical basis of Lemlat was further enlarged at CIRCSE by adding the *Onomasticon* provided by the fifth edition of the Forcellini Dictionary.[30]

25 (Mikulová et al. 2006, 503–514).

26 (Passarotti et al. 2017). For details about credits of the different versions of Lemlat see http://www.lemlat3.eu/about/credits/ (last access 2019.01.31).

27 The main ones are *Words* (http://archives.nd.edu/words.html), Lemlat (http://www.lemlat3.eu), *Morpheus* (https://github.com/tmallon/morpheus), reimplemented in 2013 as *Parsley* (https://github.com/goldibex/parsley-core), the PROIEL Latin morphology system (https://github.com/mlj/proiel-webapp/tree/master/lib/morphology) and *LatMor* (http://cistern.cis.lmu.de) (last access 2019.01.31). Morpheus, Parsley and LatMor are all capable of analyzing word forms into their morphological representations including vowel quantity.

28 For the results of a comparison between the morphological analyzers for Latin see Springmann et al. (2016, 389) and Passarotti et al. (2017, 28).

29 GGG: (Georges and Georges 1913–1918); (Glare 1982); (Gradenwitz 1904).

30 (Budassi and Passarotti 2016).

Most recently, in the context of the IT-TB project the lexical basis of Lemlat was enhanced by CIRCSE also with *Glossarium Mediae et Infimae Latinitatis*, a reference dictionary for Medieval Latin comprising approximately 86,000 lemmas.[31] This makes Lemlat able to analyze the inflected forms of more than 150,000 Latin lemmas spread over a large diachronic span.

4.1.1 Word form analysis

Given an input word form recognized by Lemlat, the tool produces in output the corresponding lemma(s) and a number of tags conveying (a) the part of speech of the lemma(s) and (b) the morphological features of the input word form. The analysis is run on types rather than on tokens, which means that no contextual disambiguation is performed.

If the analyzed word is morphologically derived, its derivation process is provided by reporting the base lemma and the word formation rule applied (see Section 4.1.2). For instance, the word form *amabilem* is analyzed by Lemlat as singular masculine/feminine accusative of the adjective *amabilis* 'lovable', which is derived from the verb *amo* 'to love' via a word formation rule that builds second class deverbal adjectives with suffix *-bil-*.

The lexical database of Lemlat 3.0 is available at https://github.com/CIRCSE/LEMLAT3, where also a Command Line Interface (CLI) implementation of the tool for Linux, OSX and Windows can be downloaded.

4.1.2 Derivational morphology

The information on derivational morphology provided by Lemlat is taken from Word Formation Latin (WFL; Litta et al. 2016), a derivational morphology resource for Latin built by CIRCSE in the context of a project funded by the EU Horizon 2020 Research and Innovation Programme under the Marie Skłodowska-Curie Individual Fellowship.

WFL connects the lemmas of the GGG lexical basis of Lemlat by word formation rules (WFRs). Each morphologically derived lemma is assigned a WFR and is paired with its base lemma. All those lemmas that share a common (not derived) ancestor belong to the same "morphological family". For instance, nouns *amator*

31 (Du Fresne Du Cange et al. 1883-1887).

'lover' and *amor* 'love', and adjective *amabilis* all belong to the morphological family whose ancestor is the verb *amo*.

WFL can be accessed via a web application (http://wfl.marginalia.it), where WFR-based relations between the lemmas of a morphological family are represented in a tree graph. In such graph, a node is a lemma, and an edge is the WFR applied to derive the output lemma from the input one (or two, in the case of compounds), along with any affix used. For example, Figure 4 shows a part of the derivation tree for the lemma *amo*. One can see that *amabilis* derives from *amo* and it is in turn the input for two other derived lemmas: *amabilitas* 'loveliness' and *inamabilis* 'repugnant'. Clicking on an edge shows the lemmas built by the WFR concerned in that edge. Lemmas are provided both as a tree graph and as an alphabetical list.

4.2 Dependency parsing

So far, the IT-TB is the treebank providing the training set that allowed to achieve the best accuracy rates for dependency parsing of Latin.[32] This is not surprising, not only because the IT-TB is the largest Latin treebank available, but also because its texts are written in quite a formal variety of Medieval Latin and are very consistent, as they are written by one author only.

The parser developed by Ponti and Passarotti achieves a Labeled Attachment Score (LAS) of 86.5 and an Unlabeled Attachment Score (UAS) of 90.97 and it is the one currently used in the IT-TB project to process automatically the sentences of the IT before double manual checking.[33] The parser was trained on a version of the IT-TB including around 250,000 nodes. Six different stochastic dependency parsers were first trained and tested. The best performing one was then provided with an ad-hoc feature model for Medieval Latin and its settings were tuned. Then, a combination of the outputs of two shift-reduce parsers and one graph-based parser was performed.

The quite high accuracy rates for syntactic parsing achieved on the IT-TB data must be considered carefully when generalizing about the automatic processing of Latin. Indeed, performances of stochastic NLP tools depend heavily on the training set which their models are built on. This problem is particularly hard when Latin is concerned, because Latin texts show a high degree of variation resulting from (a) a wide time span (covering more than two millennia),

32 (Ponti and Passarotti 2016).
33 (Buchholz and Marsi 2006).

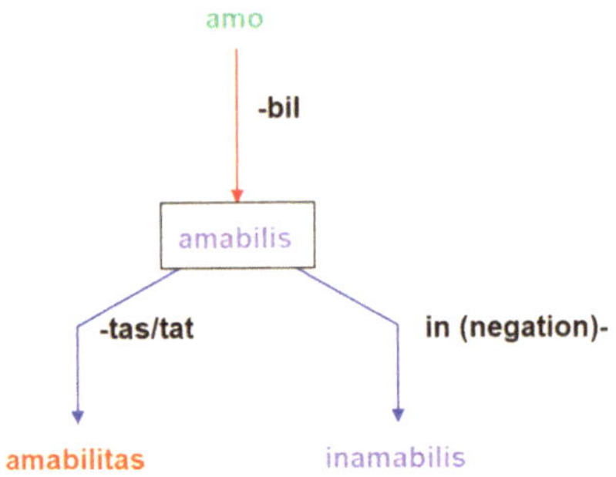

Figure 4: Derivation tree for *amo* (part).

(b) a large variety of genre (ranging from literary to philosophical, historical and documentary texts) and (c) a big diatopic diversity (spread all over Europe and beyond). As a matter of fact, Ponti and Passarotti show that when the best performing IT-TB-based dependency parser is applied on texts from the Classical era taken from the LDT, results drop dramatically: e.g. 28.2 on Caesar and 23.9 on Ovid. This is strictly related to the remarkable incongruity between the varieties of Latin represented in the training set (IT-TB) and in the test data (LDT).

5 Conclusion and future work

Building a linguistic resource is a labor-intensive work, which today goes beyond the simple development of a new collection of (annotated) linguistic data. In a virtuous circle, several different kinds of actors are concerned: textual resources are made of words, which are described in lexical resources and represent the main object of analysis of NLP tools, which in turn tend to achieve better accuracy rates when trained on larger empirical evidence provided by textual data. This is why, in more than a decade the IT-TB project has developed a number of lexical resources and NLP tools connected with the annotated data of the treebank.

The annotation work is also diverse. Beside continuing the analytical annotation of the IT-TB, a core task of the project is to enlarge the available set of sentences annotated at the tectogrammatical layer, to address the current need of semantic annotation in textual resources. The task is time-consuming because the portion of work that can be performed automatically is still very limited and annotators must have a deep understanding of the text both at intra- and inter-sentential level.

Beside linguistic annotation of textual data, there are three other open issues.

First, lexical resources must be enlarged and refined to be able to cover and process a larger (and more diverse) set of Latin data.

Second, the three Latin treebanks available in UD, namely the IT-TB, the LDT and PROIEL,[34] must be harmonized, as they still show differences in tokenization, lemmatization, PoS-tagging and syntactic analysis.

Third is assessing the degree of portability of NLP tools for Latin. As shown in Section 4.2, the sociolinguistic aspects connected to Latin texts open new challenges for the NLP world. Indeed we do not deal with one Latin only, but with several varieties of Latin, which can even heavily differ one from the other. Building sets of annotated empirical data to train stochastic NLP tools to process all such varieties is out of reach of current research. Instead, trying to make NLP processes more dynamic, enabling them to automatically adapt to the specific variety of language they deal with, would represent a major advance not only in the field of resources for Latin but overall in computational linguistics. In this respect, Latin is a perfect case study language, where developing and evaluating techniques, methods and tools for dynamic domain-adaptation in NLP. The harmonization of the three Latin treebanks in UD is a mandatory step also towards such objective, providing a set of texts annotated with a common scheme which can be used as a test bed for different NLP tasks.

This paper focuses on the resources and tools for Latin built by the IT-TB project. They represent just an example of those currently available, as there exists a huge number of digitized Latin texts (and lexical resources as well) built by various projects around the world, spread in different repositories and recorded in various data formats.[35] This is a limit, because linguistic resources become even more useful when linked with each other, which makes it possible to exploit the contribution each of them gives to linguistic analysis. The increasing complexity and diversity of linguistic resources and NLP tools that have become available throughout the last decades have led to a growing interest in their sustainability and interoperability.[36] This was partially approached by building large infrastructures of linguistic resources, like CLARIN (https://www.clarin.eu), DARIAH (http://www.dariah.eu) and META-SHARE (http://www.meta-share.org). However, these represent collections of resources and tools, which can be used and queried from one common place on the web, more than interconnections between them to make the whole greater than the sum of its parts.

34 (Haug and Jøhndal 2008).

35 (Bagnall and Heath 2018).

36 (Ide and Pustejovsky 2010).

Instead, making linguistic resources interoperable requires that all types of information related to a particular word/text get integrated into a common representation. Currently, the most rising approach to make linguistic resources interoperable (and potentially enhanced with NLP web-services) is to apply to them the principles of Linked Data and thus to build a Linguistic Linked Open Data cloud.[37]

The ERC-Consolidator Grant LiLa (Linking Latin. Building a Knowledge Base of Linguistic Resources for Latin: https://lila-erc.eu), recently started at CIRCSE, wants to connect and, ultimately, to exploit the wealth of linguistic resources and NLP tools for Latin assembled so far, in order to bridge the gap between raw language data, NLP and knowledge descriptions. To this aim, the project will build a Knowledge Base for Latin by using the Linked Data paradigm to combine data from disparate linguistic resources, provide NLP web-services and ultimately include also Latin into the multilingual Linguistic Linked Open Data cloud.

Bibliography

Bagnall, R.S.; Heath, S. (2018): "Roman Studies and Digital Resources". The Journal of Roman Studies 108, 1–19.

Bamman, D.; Crane, G. (2007): "The Latin Dependency Treebank in a Cultural Heritage Digital Library". In: Proceedings of The Workshop on Language Technology for Cultural Heritage Data (LaTeCH 2007). Prague, Czech Republic: Association for Computational Linguistics, 33–40.

Bamman, D.; Passarotti, M.; Crane, G.; Raynaud, S. (2007): Guidelines for the Syntactic Annotation of Latin Treebanks. Boston, MA: Tufts University Digital Library. http://hdl.handle.net/10427/42683 (last access 2019.01.31).

Buchholz, S.; Marsi, E. (2006): "CoNLL-X Shared Task on Multilingual Dependency Parsing". In: Proceedings of the Tenth Conference on Computational Natural Language Learning. Association for Computational Linguistics, 149–164.

Budassi, M.; Passarotti, M. (2016): "Nomen Omen. Enhancing the Latin Morphological Analyser Lemlat with an Onomasticon". In: Proceedings of the 10th SIGHUM Workshop on Language Technology for Cultural Heritage, Social Sciences, and Humanities (LaTeCH 2016). Stroudsburg, PA: Association for Computational Linguistics, 90–94.

Busa, R. (1974-1980): Index Thomisticus. Stuttgart-Bad Cannstatt: Frommann-Holzboog.

Cecchini, F.M.; Passarotti, M.; Marongiu, P.; Zeman, D. (forthcoming): "Challenges in Converting the Index Thomisticus Treebank into Universal Dependencies". In: Proceedings of the Universal Dependencies Workshop 2018 (UDW 2018).

37 (Chiarcos et al. 2013).

Chiarcos, C.; Cimiano, P.; Declerck, T.; McCrae, J.P. (2013): "Linguistic Linked Open Data (LLOD). Introduction and Overview". In: Proceedings of the 2nd Workshop on Linked Data in Linguistics (LDL-2013). Pisa, Italy: Association for Computational Linguistics, i–xi.

Du Fresne Du Cange, C. (1883-1887): Glossarium Mediae et Infimae Latinitatis. Niort: L. Favre.

Fillmore, C. (1982): "Frame Semantics". In: Linguistics in the Morning Calm. Selected Papers from SICOL-1981. Seoul: Hanshin Publishing Co., 111–137.

Forcellini, A. (1940): Lexicon Totius Latinitatis. Padova: Typis Seminarii.

Georges, K.E.; Georges H. (1913-1918): Ausführliches Lateinisch-Deutsches Handwörterbuch. Hannover: Hahn.

Glare, P.G.W. (1982): Oxford Latin Dictionary. Oxford: Oxford University Press.

González Saavedra, B.; Passarotti, M. (2014): "Challenges in Enhancing the Index Thomisticus Treebank with Semantic and Pragmatic Annotation". In: Proceedings of the Thirteenth International Workshop on Treebanks and Linguistic Theories (TLT-13). Tübingen, Germany: Department of Linguistics, University of Tübingen, 265–270.

Gradenwitz, O. (1904): Laterculi Vocum Latinarum. Leipzig: Hirzel.

Hajič, J.; Panevová, J.; Buránová, E.; Urešová, Z.; Bémová, A. (1999): Annotations at Analytical Level. Instructions for annotators. Prague: Institute of Formal and Applied Linguistics. http://ufal.mff.cuni.cz/pdt2.0/doc/manuals/en/a-layer/pdf/a-man-en.pdf (last access 2019.01.31).

Hajič, J.; Böhmová, A.; Hajičová, E.; Vidová Hladká, B. (2000): "The Prague Dependency Treebank: A Three-Level Annotation Scenario". In: A. Abeillé (ed.): Treebanks: Building and Using Parsed Corpora. Amsterdam: Kluwer, 103–127.

Hajič, J.; Panevová, J.; Urešová, Z.; Bémová, A.; Kolárová-Rezníčková, V.; Pajas, P. (2003): "PDT-VALLEX: Creating a Large Coverage Valency Lexicon for Treebank Annotation". In: J. Nivre; E. Hinrichs (eds.): TLT 2003. Proceedings of the Second Workshop on Treebanks and Linguistic Theories. Volume 9 of Mathematical Modelling in Physics, Engineering and Cognitive Sciences. Växjö, Sweden: Växjö University Press, 57–68.

Haug, D.; Jøhndal, M. (2008): "Creating a Parallel Treebank of the Old Indo-European Bible Translations". In: K. Ribarov; C. Sporleder (eds.): Proceedings of the Language Technology for Cultural Heritage Data Workshop (LaTeCH 2008). Marrakech, Morocco: ELRA, 27–34.

Ide, N.; Pustejovsky, J. (2010): "What does Interoperability Mean, anyway? Toward an Operational Definition of Interoperability for Language Technology". In: Proceedings of the Second International Conference on Global Interoperability for Language Resources (ICGL). Hong Kong.

Kingsbury, P.; Palmer, P. (2002): "From Treebank to Propbank". In: Proceedings of the Third International Conference on Language Resources and Evaluation (LREC 2002). Las Palmas, Gran Canaria: ELRA.

Korhonen, A.; Krymolowski, Y.; Briscoe, T. (2006): "A Large Subcategorization Lexicon for Natural Language Processing Applications". In: Proceedings of the Fifth International Conference on Language Resources and Evaluation (LREC 2006). Genoa: ELRA, 1015–1020.

Litta, E.; Passarotti, M.; Culy, C. (2016): "Formatio formosa est. Building a Word Formation Lexicon for Latin". In: A. Corazza; S. Montemagni; G. Semeraro (eds.): Proceedings of the Third Italian Conference on Computational Linguistics (CLiC–it 2016). Naples: Accademia

University Press, Collana dell'Associazione Italiana di Linguistica Computazionale. Vol. 2, 185–189.
Martens, S.; Passarotti, M. (2014): "Thomas Aquinas in the TüNDRA: Integrating the Index Thomisticus Treebank into CLARIN-D". In: Proceedings of the Ninth International Conference on Language Resources and Evaluation (LREC 2014). Reykjavik: ELRA, 767–774.
McGillivray, B.; Passarotti, M. (2009): "The Development of the Index Thomisticus Treebank Valency Lexicon". In: Proceedings of LaTeCH-SHELT&R Workshop 2009. Athens: ACL, 43–50.
McGillivray, B. (2013): Methods in Latin Computational Linguistics. Leiden and Boston: Brill.
Messiant, C.; Korhonen, A.; Poibeau, T. (2008): "LexSchem: A Large Subcategorization Lexicon for French Verbs". In: Proceedings of the Sixth International Conference on Language Resources and Evaluation (LREC 2008). Marrakech: ELRA, 533–538.
Mikulová, M.; Bémová, A.; Hajič, J.; Hajičová, E.; Havelka, J.; Kolářová, V.; Kučová, L.; Lopatková, M.; Pajas, P.; Panevová, J.; Razímová, M.; Sgall, P.; Štěpánek, J.; Urešová, Z.; Veselá, K.; Žabokrtský, Z.; Součková, K.; Böhmová, A.; Čermáková, K.; Havelka, J.; Corness, P. (2006): "Annotation on the Tectogrammatical Layer in the Prague Dependency Treebank Institute of Formal and Applied Linguistics". Prague: Institute of Formal and Applied Linguistics. http://ufal.mff.cuni.cz/pdt2.0/doc/manuals/en/t-layer/html/index.html (last access 2019.01.31).
Nivre, J. (2015): "Towards a Universal Grammar for Natural Language Processing". In: Gelbukh A. (ed.): Computational Linguistics and Intelligent Text Processing. CICLing 2015. Cham: Springer, 3–16.
Pajas, P.; Štěpánek, J. (2009): "System for Querying Syntactically Annotated Corpora". In: G. Geunbae Lee; S. Schulte Im Walde (eds.): Proceedings of the ACL-IJCNLP 2009 Software Demonstrations. Singapore: World Scientific Publishing Co Pte Ltd, 33–36.
Passarotti, M. (2010): "Leaving Behind the Less-Resourced Status. The Case of Latin through the Experience of the Index Thomisticus Treebank". In: 7th SaLTMiL Workshop on Creation and Use of Basic Lexical Resources for Less-Resourced Languages. La Valletta: ELRA, 27–32.
Passarotti, M. (2013): "One Hundred Years Ago. In Memory of Father Roberto Busa SJ". In: F. Mambrini; M. Passarotti; C. Sporleder (eds.): Proceedings of the Third Workshop on Annotation of Corpora for Research in the Humanities (ACRH-3). Sofia: Bulgarian Academy of Sciences, 15–24.
Passarotti, M.; González Saavedra, B.; Onambele, C. (2016): "Latin Vallex. A Treebank-based Semantic Valency Lexicon for Latin". In: Proceedings of the Tenth International Conference on Language Resources and Evaluation (LREC 2016). Portorož: ELRA, 2599–2606.
Passarotti, M.; Budassi, M.; Litta, E.; Ruffolo, P. (2017): "The Lemlat 3.0 Package for Morphological Analysis of Latin". In: G. Bouma; Y. Adesam (eds.): Proceedings of the NoDaLiDa 2017 Workshop on Processing Historical Language. Gothenburg: Northern European Association for Language Technology Proceedings Series 32, 24–31.
Passarotti, M; González Saavedra, B. (2018): "The Treebanked Conspiracy. Actors and Actions in Bellum Catilinae". In: J. Hajič (ed.): Proceedings of the 16th International Workshop on Treebanks and Linguistic Theories (TLT16). Prague: Institute of Formal and Applied Linguistics, 18–26.

Ponti, E.M.; Passarotti, M. (2016): "Differentia compositionem facit. A Slower-Paced and Reliable Parser for Latin". In: Proceedings of the Tenth International Conference on Language Resources and Evaluation (LREC 2016). Portorož: ELRA, 683–688.

Popel, M.; Žabokrtský, Z. (2010): "TectoMT: Modular NLP Framework". In: H. Loftsson; E. Rögnvaldsson; S. Helgadóttir (eds.): Proceedings of IceTAL, 7th International Conference on Natural Language Processing. Berlin, Heidelberg and New York: Springer, 293–304.

Ruppenhofer, J.; Ellsworth, M.; Petruck, M.R.L.; Johnson, C.R.; Scheffczyk, J. (2006): FrameNet II. Extendend Theory and Practice. https://framenet.icsi.berkeley.edu/fndrupal/node/5400 (last access 2019.01.31).

Sgall, P.; Hajičová, E.; Panevová, J. (1986): The Meaning of the Sentence in its Semantic and Pragmatic Aspects. Dordrecht: D. Reidel.

Springmann, U.; Schmid, H.; Najock, D. (2016): "LatMor: A Latin Finite-State Morphology Encoding Vowel Quantity". In: G. Celano; G. Crane (eds.): Treebanking and Ancient Languages: Current and Prospective Research (Topical Issue). Open Linguistics 2:1, 386–392.

Urešová, Z. (2004): The Verbal Valency in the Prague Dependency Treebank from the Annotator's Point of View. Bratislava: Jazykovedný ústav Ľ. Štúra, SAV.

Federico Boschetti

Semantic Analysis and Thematic Annotation

Abstract: This contribution aims at investigating some methods, resources and tools devoted to the semantic analysis and the thematic annotation. The first part, devoted to the paradigmatic axis, describes available lexico-semantic resources for the classical languages, which belong to accomplished or on-going projects. Starting from Minozzi's Latin WordNet, the structure of multilingual lexico-semantic networks mapped on the original (American English) Princeton WordNet will be discussed and criticized. The automated procedures to create the basis for a new Ancient Greek WordNet from bilingual dictionaries (mainly: the LSJ) will be illustrated and the on-going project named Homeric Greek WordNet, validated by students and scholars, will be presented. Furthermore, the difficulties to map the conceptual nodes related to the ancient world on a modern semantic network will be discussed. The second part of the contribution, devoted to the syntagmatic axis, is focused on the semantic and thematic annotation of classical and biblical texts. The top-down approach to the annotation of themes and motifs in the Memorata Poetis Project is illustrated and pros and cons are discussed. In that project, devoted to the study of multilingual and multicultural intertextuality, a taxonomy of thematic labels established a priori is shared by all the members of the project. Finally, the bottom-up approach of Euporia is discussed. In this approach, folksonomies are created by the annotators, and the labels are grouped and organized in ontologies a posteriori, during an incremental process of revision.

1 Introduction

The notion of "dead languages" is deceiving: it is better to focus the attention on the complex relations between continuous and discontinuous traditions. Ancient Greek and classical Latin evolved towards modern languages through continuous, oral traditions and partially survive through discontinuous, literary traditions:[1] the linguistic resources discussed in this chapter are based only on the latter.

1 See Mondin (2014).

Federico Boschetti, Istituto di Linguistica Computazionale "A. Zampolli", CNR, Pisa

https://doi.org/10.1515/9783110599572-018

When the transmission of linguistic knowledge, interrupted by calamitous events or just by a progressive decline in interest, is revitalized through a renewed focus on ancient literatures, i.e. in written texts that do not correspond to the current language of the native speakers, we must be aware of the wide discrepancy between the communicative competence of the sender of the literary message and the competence of the new receiver. The communicative competence involves not only linguistic, but also extra-linguistic aspects of the communication, such as the socio-cultural context in which the linguistic act (spoken or written) is performed: the notion of communicative competence has been introduced by Hymes (1966) precisely to overtake the dichotomy between linguistic competence and linguistic performance proposed by Chomsky (1965).

Even when we are in front of a genuine text, such as (under certain conditions) an epigraph, not corrupted by errors due to the transmission along the centuries, what we can recognize objectively, unequivocally, is just the signifier (*signifiant*, according to Saussure) layer, not the signified (*signifié*) layer. Textual meaning is always open to multiple interpretations and the hermeneutic space is wider according to the distance between the communicative competence of the message addresser and the competence of the addressee.

In this chapter we present digital resources and computational instruments to study ancient Greek and Latin words from a semantic point of view and to investigate classical texts from a thematic point of view. Section 2 is devoted to semantic analysis from three different perspectives. Distributional semantics is based on quantitative methods applied to textual corpora, in order to recognize semantic similarities among words that share similar contexts. WordNets are lexico-semantic resources based on information extracted from monolingual or bilingual dictionaries, in which words with the same meaning are grouped and associated to conceptual nodes that establish various semantic relations (e.g. hypernymy/hyponymy, or holonymy/meronymy) with other conceptual nodes. Finally, the Dynamic Lexicon is a lexical resource based on the alignment of ancient Greek and Latin texts with their translations into modern languages, such as English. Section 3 is devoted to the thematic analysis of classical (and modern) literary texts, by following different methodologies. Topic modeling is based on automated procedures for the identification of word/document clusters. By applying a top-down approach, intertextual relations are identified by human annotators among multilingual texts. On the contrary, by applying a bottom-up approach, patterns relevant for an interdisciplinary study of ancient texts (e.g. from a philological and anthropological perspective) are observed.

2 Semantic analysis

Semantic analysis concerns the paradigmatic axis, even if it can exploit the syntagmatic axis for dealing with contextual information necessary to determine the word meaning. In this section two different approaches are discussed: the first one is based on the assumption that meaning is self-contained in textual corpora, because semantic similarity is latent behind the noisy variety of lexical choices. The second one is based on the assumption that bilingual dictionaries can be used to group together ancient Greek or Latin synonyms that share the same translation.

2.1 Distributional semantics

Distributional Semantics is based on the so called "distributional hypothesis" formulated by Firth (1957, 11): "You shall know a word by the company it keeps". According to this hypothesis, the word meaning is inferable by the contexts in which the word is used, i.e. by the other words of the documents in which it occurs. In order to calculate the similarity, it is necessary to create a vector space based on matrices of word co-occurences and apply statistical or computational methods to reduce the original, high dimensional space to a lower dimensional space with less information noise.[2] In order to reduce the dimensions, Singular Value Decomposition is applied or, more recently, Recurrent Neural Networks are used.[3]

2.1.1 Synchronic perspective

As described by Boschetti (2018), the exploration of semantic spaces can be applied both to an entire corpus or to consistent subcorpora divided by genres (e.g. Epics, Tragedy, Philosophy, etc.). Semantic similarities due to the co-occurrence in similar contexts are identified by the proximity in the reduced vector space but they are not labeled: they can be synonyms, antonyms, hyper-/hyponyms or co-hyponyms, holo-/meronyms or co-meronyms, etc. As relevant examples, we will observe in the semantic space of the Ancient Greek corpus two case studies: co-hyponyms and antonyms.

2 See Lenci (2008).
3 See Mikolov (2013).

Abstract terms that belong to traditional and highly repeated lists, such as virtues, feelings or emotions are easily clustered. We are interested to explore how are grouped virtues that constitute traditional paradigms, such as faith, hope and charity, compared to other positive qualities, such as ὑγίεια, soundness.

As shown in Figure 1, clusters are sharply defined. On the right side of the plot we find some physical virtues frequently mentioned by ancient philosophers and writers. On the left side of the plot are distributed the seven virtues of the Christian tradition, clearly divided in two groups: the theological virtues (ἀγάπη, charity; ἐλπίς, hope and πίστις, faith) on the top of the chart and the cardinal virtues (ἀνδρεῖα, manliness; δικαιοσύνη, justice; φρόνησις, prudence and σωφροσύνη, temperance) on the bottom part of the chart.

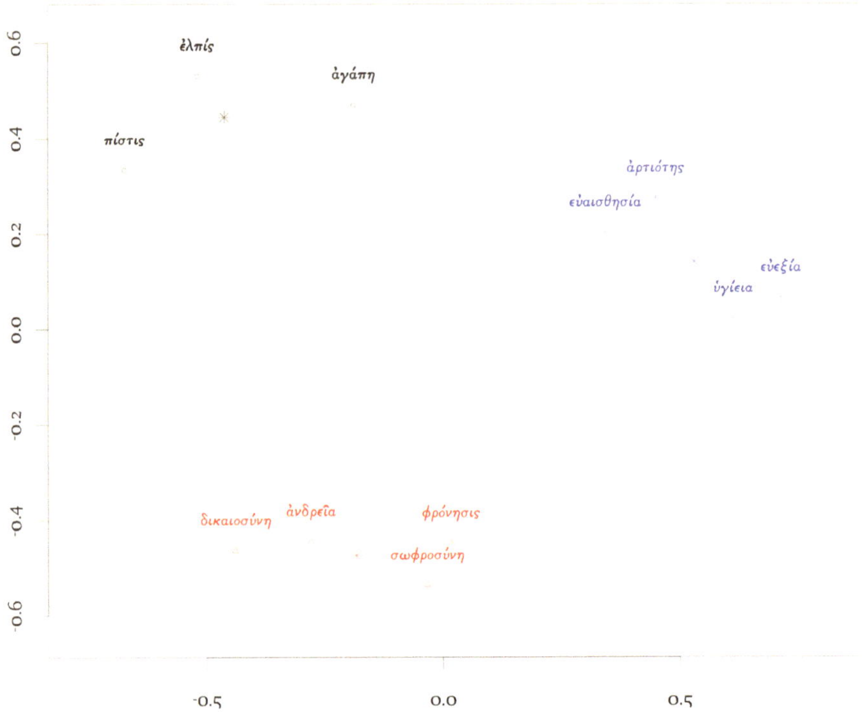

Figure 1: Semantic spaces: clusters of virtues.

Antonyms appear in similar contexts, in which opposite properties of the same terms are expressed, in particular when the couple of antonyms is constituted by adjectives that can occur with a restricted selection of names.

As shown in Figure 2, tight proximity in the semantic space is observed for domain-specific terms, such as ἔμψυχος (animate) and ἄψυχος (inanimate), commonly used in philosophical and medical texts. On the contrary, couples of antonyms that can be used in any context, such as μέγας (big) and μικρός (small), are more spaced.

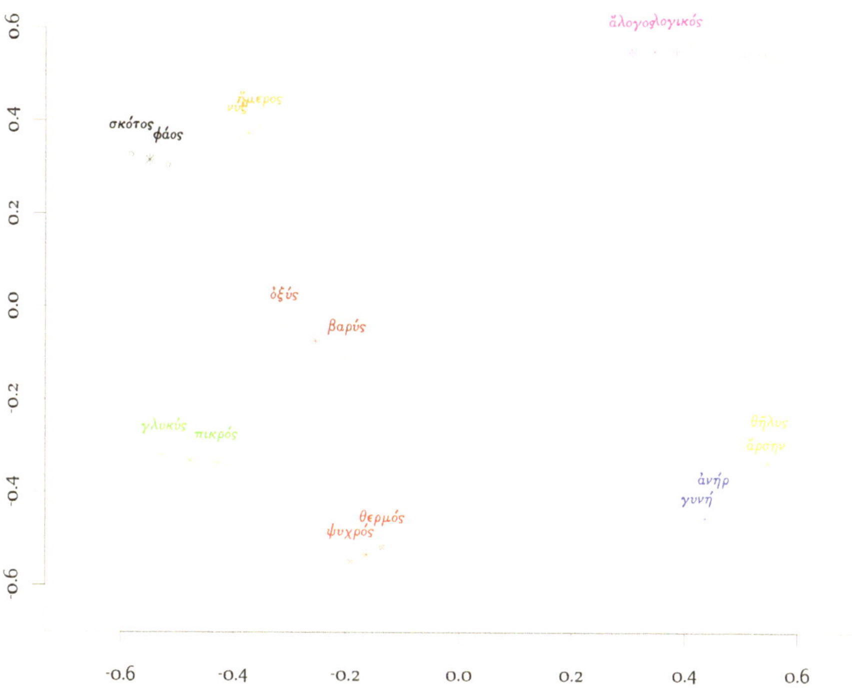

Figure 2: Semantic spaces: clusters of antonyms.

The identification of semantic similarity, combined with other linguistic information, such as frequency, diachronic distribution, genre distribution, etc. is useful to evaluate textual variants, in order to provide evidence that one word could be a trivial gloss for the other (*lectio facilior*). Finally, it is worth to note that O' Donnell (2005) applied these exploratory methods to the Greek of the New Testament.

2.1.2 Diachronic perspective

A large corpus of literary texts distributed along the centuries, such as the corpus of the entire ancient Greek Literature, can be chronologically partitioned according to historical periodizations. Semantic spaces constructed on the different subcorpora can show the semantic shift of relevant terms. For example, before and after Christ, many terms, such as θάνατος (dead), ἀνάστασις (resurrection) and ἀθανασία (immortality), sensitively change their semantic associations.[4]

2.2 WordNets

WordNets are lexico-semantic resources, in which the terms belonging to the open parts of speech (nouns, verbs, adjectives and adverbs) are grouped into sets of synonyms (called synsets) associated to conceptual nodes, which are described by a gloss. Words are interlinked by lexical relations, such as derivation (e.g. *style* / *stylish*) or antonymy (i.e. the relation between the contraries: e.g. *big* / *small*) and conceptual nodes are interlinked by semantic relations, such hypernymy / hyponymy (i.e. the relations between general and specific terms: e.g. *container* / *bottle*), holonymy / meronymy (i.e. the relations between compound and component: e.g. *charriot* / *wheel*).

The original project, usually called Princeton WordNet (PWN, available at https://wordnet.princeton.edu) in order to be distinguished by its derivatives, aimed at the creation of a lexical database for English, useful for computational linguists and cognitive scientists.[5] Along the last decades many initiatives have extended PWN, in order to create an interrelated network of multilingual lexico-semantic resources. The Global WordNet Association (http://globalwordnet.org) provides a platform for discussing, sharing and connecting multilingual wordnets created by independent organizations.

EuroWordNet (EWN)[6] (http://projects.illc.uva.nl/EuroWordNet/) and MultiWordNet (MWN)[7] (http://multiwordnet.fbk.eu) are authoritative examples for modern (e.g. Italian, Spanish or Romanian) and ancient (e.g. Latin) languages.

In EWN and in MWN conceptual nodes of the new languages are aligned to the conceptual nodes of PWN by different philosophies, which are well expressed by Pianta et al. (2002, 1):

> There are at least two models for building a multilingual wordnet. The first model, adopted within the EuroWordNet project, consists of building language specific wordnets

4 See Rodda (2017) and Boschetti (2018).
5 See Fellbaum (1998).
6 See Vossen (1998).
7 See Pianta et al. (2002).

independently from each other, trying in a second phase to find correspondences between them (Vossen, 1998). The second model, adopted within MultiWordNet (MWN), consists of building language specific wordnets keeping as much as possible of the semantic relations available in the Princeton WordNet (PWN). This is done by building the new synsets in correspondence with the PWN synsets, whenever possible, and importing semantic relations from the corresponding English synsets; i.e., we assume that if there are two synsets in PWN and a relation holding between them, the same relation holds between the corresponding synsets in the new language.

2.2.1 Latin WordNet

Latin WordNet (LWN), developed at the University of Verona by Minozzi (2009), is part of the MultiWordNet Project. After the automated extraction of Latin-English couples from bilingual dictionaries and the projection on the PWN conceptual network, synsets have been manually validated. According to the model adopted by MWN, the conceptual structure of PWN constitutes the backbones for the synsets of the other languages. With modern western languages the correspondence is quite tight, but ancient languages are the expression of different conceptualizations. MWN has some mechanisms to afford this issue: the creation of new conceptual nodes, peculiar to a specific language, that in English can be expressed by a periphrasis (lexical gap); the linkage of words to a PWN conceptual node more general (a hypernym) or more specific (a hyponym); the implicit suppression of semantic relations among intermediate conceptual nodes.

This last case is exemplified in Figure 3, which is a screenshot captured from the MWN website, related to the hypernyms of the Latin term *aquila* in its different senses. For the first sense (eagle as bird of pray), PWN follows the complete taxonomy with the indication, in English, of the phylum *cordate* and the subphylum *vertebrate*, whereas the current version of LWN does not associate any lexical values to the intermediate conceptual nodes between *animal* and *avis*. Considering that MWN has not a diachronic perspective and that the Linnean taxonomy is expressed in Latin, the flatten hierarchy [*aquila*] < [*ales, avis, volucris*] < [*animal, animalis, bellua, bestia, pecus*], which is suitable for the ancient conceptualization, could be enlarged in a future version of LWN with the intermediate synsets related to the phylum (*cordata*) and related to the subphylum (*vertebrata*).

In many cases LWN accepts modern senses, in agreement with the modus operandi of the *Lexicon Recentis Latinitatis*.[8] Accordingly, for instance, *cliens* can have the meaning of "any computer that is hooked up to a computer

---

8 See Egger (2004).

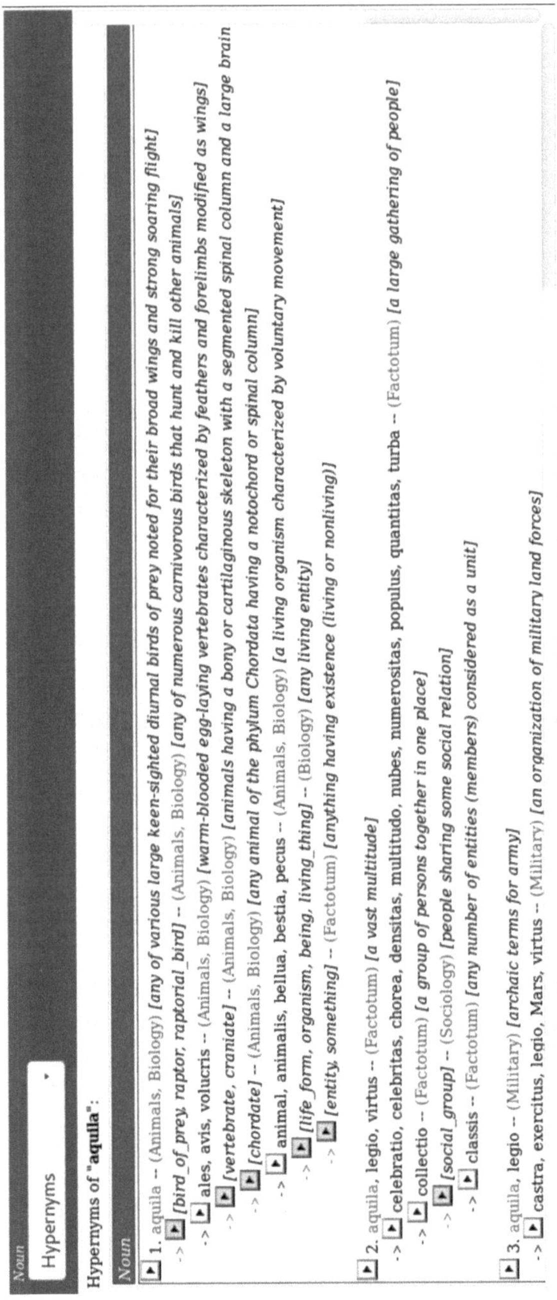

Figure 3: Latin WordNet: hypernyms of *aquila*.

network", hyponym of *machina*, which is in turn, among other senses, a "4-wheeled motor vehicle; usually propelled by an internal combustion engine", hyponym of *vehiculum*. Thus, LatinWordNet addresses the problem of polysemy from a modernist perspective.

LWN is used to improve search engines with query expansion mechanisms, which take into account synonyms and other semantically related terms. It is a precious resource also for computational linguistic studies. For instance, McGillivray (2014) used LWN to study verbal selectional preferences for the lexical fillers in specific argument roles. Thanks to the relations of hypernymy / hiponymy,it is possible to identify semantic categories (such as food or drink) preferred by verbs (such as *edo* or *bibo*) for the argument roles (such as the affected theme).

2.2.2 Ancient Greek WordNet

In collaboration with the Perseus Project and the Alpheios Project, the CNR-ILC of Pisa is developing Ancient GreekWordNet (AGWN). As described by Bizzoni et al. (2014), three Greek-English digital dictionaries provided by the Perseus Project have been used to bootstrap AGWN: the Liddell-Scott-Jones,[9] the Middle-Liddell[10] and Autenrieth's Homeric Lexicon.[11] Greek words have been grouped in synsets, thanks to the common English translation, and they have been linked by the relation of near equivalence to the synsets in PWN containing the same English word. In this way, the conceptual nodes of AGWN are independent from the conceptual node of PWN, even if they are interlinked, and they can receive a different gloss, more appropriate for the ancient world.

By exploiting WordNet Domains,[12] which associate each synset of PWN to a specific domain (or to the generic *factotum* domain), synsets related to modern concepts in chemistry, computer science, telecommunication etc. have been automatically filtered out. For instance, the English word *bat* assumes in different domains specific senses, glossed by "a nocturnal mouselike mammal [...]" in the domain of *Animals* and *Biology* and glossed by "an implement used in baseball by the batter" in the domain of *Baseball*. The latter sense can be filtered out by the identification of the anachronistic domain, so that the ancient Greek word νυκτερίς (bat, as an animal) is associated only to the correct conceptual node, whose gloss is modified in "a nocturnal mouselike animal"

9 See Liddell et al. (1940).
10 See Liddell and Scott (1889).
11 See Autenrieth (1891).
12 See Bentivogli et al. (2004).

(as shown in Figure 4). Indeed, LWN can have a modernist perspective, because Latin is still in use (e.g. to write encyclicals on current topics), whereas Ancient Greek WordNet must be focused only on the conceptual representation of the ancient world.

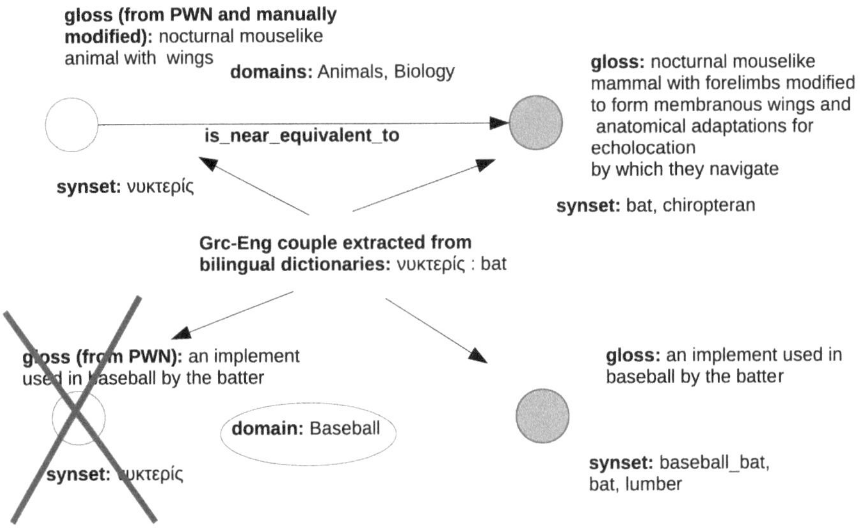

Figure 4: Linkage between AGWN and PWN.

Misaligned polysemy between ancient Greek and English and residual anachronisms remain the main source of error: the current version of AGWN, available at http://www.languagelibrary.eu/new_ewnui, is just experimental and still very noisy.

2.2.3 Homeric Greek WordNet

From the original Ancient Greek WordNet, a narrower project has been developed on the Homeric lexicon. The Homeric Greek WordNet filters only the synsets that contains at least one word attested in the *Iliad*, the *Odyssey* or both the poems.

By focusing our attention on a single author, we had the following goals: a) synchronic perspective on the archaic period; b) usage of a specific sense supported by textual evidence as in historic dictionaries; c) limited number of synsets to check. The ongoing project, accessible at http://cophilab.ilc.cnr.it/hgwnWeb/, engages students for the validation of synsets (last access 2019.01.31).

As shown in Figure 5, first of all students must check if the synset is active or not (because it expresses an anachronism), if the synset is near equivalent (the default) or loosely approximated to the correspondent PWN and they may modify the gloss accordingly. Then, they must score the pertinence of each Greek word, according to the following scale: a) word unrelated with the meaning of the synset; b) word vaguely related to the synset due to any undeclared reason; c) word that is not synonym but establishes another semantic relation (declared in the notes) with the remaining words of the synset; d) word that fits the meaning of the synset, but is posthomeric; e) word that fits the meaning of the synset and is attested in Homer in that specific sense, as declared in the notes.

2.2.4 Dynamic Lexicon

The Dynamic Lexicon[13] is based on syntactic annotated corpora (treebanks), aligned with modern translations at the granularity of word (or phrase) to word (or phrase). The Dynamic Lexicon (DL), currently extended also to ancient Greek, allows to study collocations, verbal valency, argument structures and selectional preferences.

Considering that both AGWN and the DL are multilingual resources to study the lexicon of Ancient Greek texts and their translations, and considering that both are works in progress, Berti et al. (2016) combined them, in order to improve the accuracy by mutual correction.

3 Thematic annotation

Thematic annotation is performed on the syntagmatic axis by the identification of general topics (themes) and their recurrent, concrete or symbolic actualizations (motifs), even if the definition and distinction of theme and motif is quite controversial.[14] The main advantages are the possibility to explore the documents of a large corpus by thematic similarities and the possibility to compare multilingual texts, independently by their lexical content. In this section three different approaches are discussed: the first is an automated method to group documents according to word clusters; the others are manual methods to annotate texts: in particular, the second is a top-down approach in which the index

13 See Bamman and Crane (2008).
14 See Segre (1985) and Ciotti (2014).

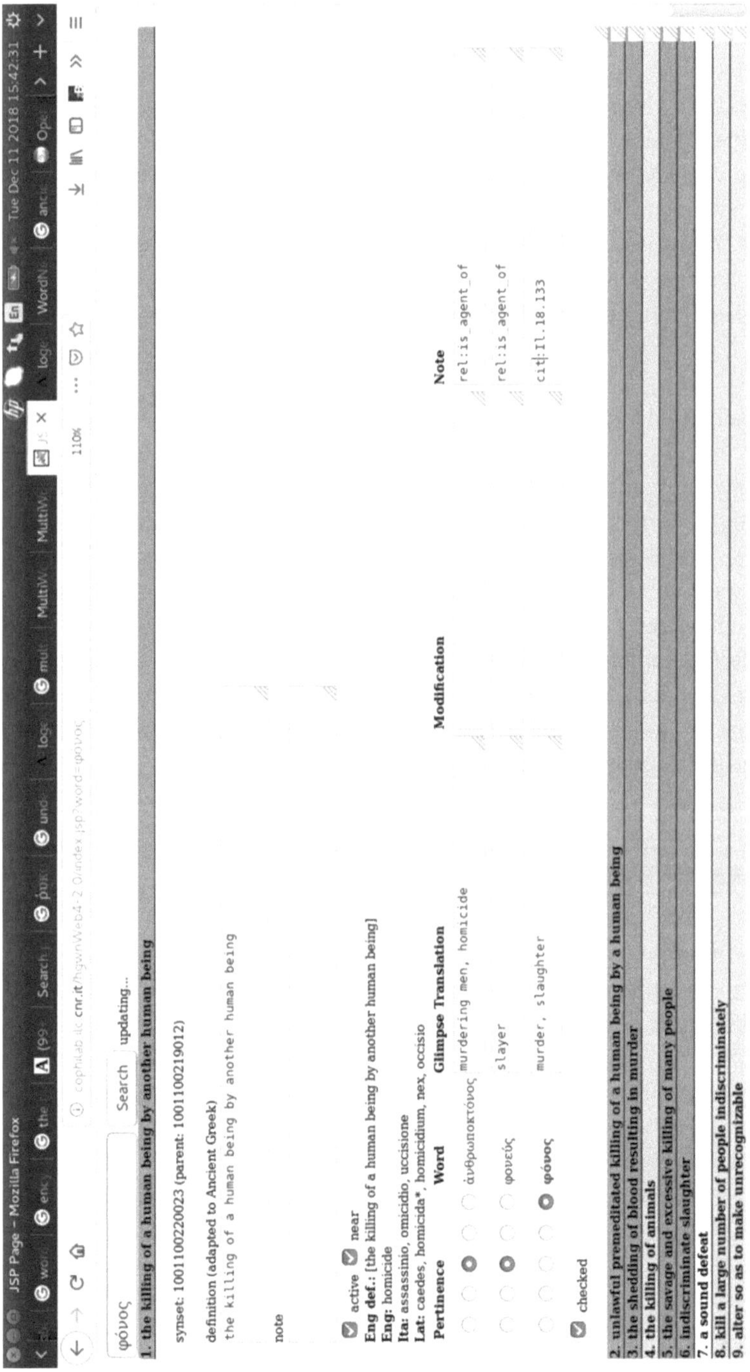

Figure 5: Homeric Greek WordNet.

of themes and motifs are established a priori, and the third is a bottom-up approach in which texts are annotated by an open set of descriptors, reorganized a posteriori in ontologies.

3.1 Topic modeling

As pointed out in Koentges (2016):

> Topic modelling is "a method for finding and tracing clusters of words (called 'topics' in shorthand) in large bodies of texts". A topic can be described as a recurring pattern of co-occurring words. Topic models are probabilistic models that are often based on the number of topics in the corpus being assumed and fixed. The simplest and probably one of the most frequently applied topic models is the latent Dirichlet allocation (LDA).

Topic modeling is useful to identify similarities between documents and to find surprising outliers that need more investigation in large textual corpora, according to the principles of the distant reading.[15]

3.2 Top-down approach

A top-down approach to manual annotation of themes and motifs is based on a basic knowledge of the corpus that must be annotated as whole and a solid (literary, linguistic, stylistic, etc.) theory built on previous studies or created on samples of the same or analogous corpora.

A top-down approach is suitable to extend large corpora with new annotated documents according to homogeneous criteria and clear guidelines. As an example, below we present a project that follows this paradigm.

3.2.1 Memorata Poetis

Memorata Poetis[16] is a large intertextual project based on the annotation of themes and motifs related to short poems (e.g. epigrams or sonnets) in ancient Greek, Latin, Italian, English and Arabic literature.

The principal investigator (from the Univesity Ca' Foscari in Venice) established with his collaborators an index of themes and motifs at the beginning of

15 See Moretti (2013).

16 See Mastandrea (2017).

the project, after a preliminary study of thematic repertories of the last centuries. The index is hierarchically structured in three levels, and the top level is constituted by these six topics: *Animalia, Arbores et virentia, Dei et heroes, Homines, Loca, Res.* The intermediate level specifies the upper one; for example *Arbores et virentia* is divided in *Arborum species, Flores, Fructus, Usus arborum, herbarum, florum et fructuum.* Finally, the lowest level provides the highest degree of details. For example, *Flores* is divided into *Crocus, Flores deis deabusque consecrati, Flores in mythologia, Hyacinthus, Laus florum, Lilium, Metamorphosis in flores, Narcissus, Papaver, Rosa, Serta florum, Viola.*

As shown in Figure 6, it is possible to run search on the multilingual, annotated corpus of Memorata Poetis, in order to find co-occurrent themes and motifs: in this specific case for the individuation of the co-occurence of the floral motifs rose and violet, independently by their lexical expression in the different languages: ῥόδον (e.g. *anthologia Graeca* 5, 144) or *rosa* (e.g. *anthologia Latina* 24) for the rose and λευκόιον (e.g. *anthologia Graeca* 5, 144), ἴον (e.g. *anthologia Graeca* 4, 2) or *violae* (e.g. *anthologia Latina* 24) for the violet.

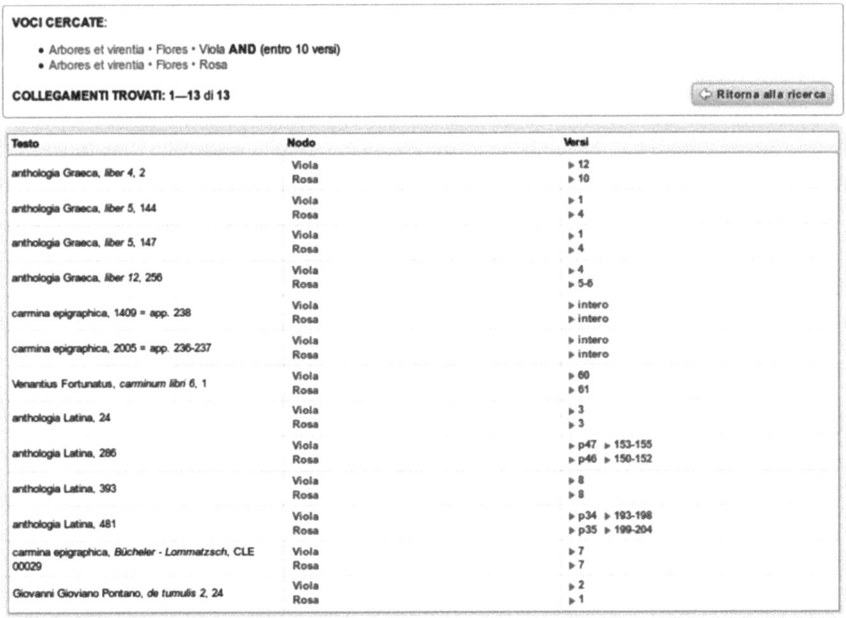
VOCI CERCATE:

- Arbores et virentia • Flores • Viola **AND (entro 10 versi)**
- Arbores et virentia • Flores • Rosa

COLLEGAMENTI TROVATI: 1—13 di 13

Ritorna alla ricerca

Testo	Nodo	Versi
anthologia Graeca, *liber 4*, 2	Viola Rosa	▸ 12 ▸ 10
anthologia Graeca, *liber 5*, 144	Viola Rosa	▸ 1 ▸ 4
anthologia Graeca, *liber 5*, 147	Viola Rosa	▸ 1 ▸ 4
anthologia Graeca, *liber 12*, 256	Viola Rosa	▸ 4 ▸ 5-6
carmina epigraphica, 1409 = app. 238	Viola Rosa	▸ intero ▸ intero
carmina epigraphica, 2005 = app. 236-237	Viola Rosa	▸ intero ▸ intero
Venantius Fortunatus, *carminum libri 6*, 1	Viola Rosa	▸ 60 ▸ 61
anthologia Latina, 24	Viola Rosa	▸ 3 ▸ 3
anthologia Latina, 286	Viola Rosa	▸ p47 ▸ 153-155 ▸ p46 ▸ 150-152
anthologia Latina, 393	Viola Rosa	▸ 8 ▸ 8
anthologia Latina, 481	Viola Rosa	▸ p34 ▸ 193-198 ▸ p35 ▸ 199-204
carmina epigraphica, *Bücheler - Lommatzsch*, CLE 00029	Viola Rosa	▸ 7 ▸ 7
Giovanni Gioviano Pontano, *de tumulis 2*, 24	Viola Rosa	▸ 2 ▸ 1

Figure 6: Memorata Poetis Search Engine.

A hierarchical index of themes and motifs established a priori, which uses Latin as metalanguage, was necessary to assign clear guidelines for the annotation to large and heterogeneous groups of collaborators to the project, but it has drawbacks.

The first is due to the aprioristic creation of the index, that can be only exceptionally modified along the project. The second, strictly related with the first, is due to the adaptation of the observed phenomena to the descriptors available in the model, instead of an adaptation of the model to the observed phenomena. The last drawback is due to the hierarchical structure of the index, which inhibits traversal relations. For instance, *Laudes animalium* (praises of animals) is under *Animalia* and *Laus florum* (praise of flowers) is under *Arbores et virentia > Flores*, without a link between them.

3.3 Bottom-up approach

The knowledge acquired on the themes and motifs actually contained in the corpus of Memorata Poetis Project during the annotation phase and the study a posteriori of the relevant traversal relations among the items of the index are the basis for the ontological reorganization of the index discussed by Khan et al. (2016) for a more efficient querying of the corpus by the integration of textual content, annotations according to the original taxonomy and new ontological information. For example, acts of speech, such as praises, have been identified and grouped in order to be used in query expansions, independently from the object of the praise.

3.3.1 Euporia

Taking advantage of this experience and following new trends in manual annotation popularized by CATMA (http://catma.de), we applied a bottom-up approach for research and educational purposes through the annotation tool Euporia.[17] Euporia is based on Domain-Specific Languages (DSLs) to define the syntax of the annotations, on the CITE (http://cite-architecture.github.io/about) framework for the stand-off reference to the target texts, on open tagsets (personomies, defined by a single scholar or folksonomies, defined by teams), refined during periodical revisions and, finally, on the identification of ontological relations among the items of the eventual tagset.

17 See Mugelli et al. (2016).

Figure 7 illustrates the annotation by G. Mugelli to Aesch. *Ag.* 228–237. The DSL created in collaboration with the LAMA Lab (University of Pisa) for the study of rituals in the ancient Greek tragedies permits the annotation of continuous, discontinuous or overlapping textual sequences by hashtags belonging to an open tagset related to objects, actions, properties involved in rituals presented or mentioned on the stage. The DSL allows the annotation of variant readings (marked by @vl, *varia lectio*), alternative interpretations (marked by @vi, *varia interpretatio*) and conditional readings or interpretations (marked in curly braces and possibly negated by the exclamation mark), in order to define constraints for new readings or interpretations.

Figure 7: Euporia Annotation.

For instance,
☛ [233 πέπλοισι.. προνωπῆ] @vi:233_3 #supplicatio Bonanno2006 ☚
means that Bonanno (2006) suggests to interpret the verse as a supplication and
☛ [233 παντὶ θυμῷ] {@vi:233_3} #animus_supplicis ☚
means that, if we accept the Bonanno's interpretation, παντὶ θυμῷ is referred to a suppliant, otherwise, if we do not accept Bonanno's interpretation, as expressed by
☛ [233 παντὶ θυμῷ] {!@vi:233_3} #animus_sacrificantis ☚
then παντὶ θυμῷ should be referred to a sacrificer.

As described by Khan et al. (2018), the personomy (i.e. the open tagset created by G. Mugelli) is linked to an upper ontology for common concepts and to a domain ontology for the specific concepts related to rituals in ancient Greek tragedies. By exploiting both the ontological relations (e.g. the relation is_a_type_of) and the original hashtags, the search engines allows query expansion, as shown in Figure 8, in which different types of animals are searched as raised victims in a sacrifice.

Figure 8: Euporia Search.

4 Conclusion

In conclusion, we discussed semantic investigations based on a variety of methods, at different levels of granularity (words or discourse) and with different degrees of automation. All these methods should be considered exploratory, in order to identify regions of interest inside monolingual or multilingual (sub)corpora.

Bibliography

Autenrieth, G. (1891): A Homeric Dictionary for Schools and Colleges. New York, NY: Harper and Brothers.

Bamman, D.; Crane, G.R. (2008): "Building a Dynamic Lexicon from a Digital Library". In: Larsen; A. Paepke; J. Borbinha; M. Naaman (eds.): Proceedings of JCDL'08, Pittsburgh, PA, June 16–20, 2008. New York, NY: ACM.

Bentivogli, L.; Forner, P.; Magnini, B.; Pianta, E. (2004): "Revising WordNet Domains Hierarchy: Semantics, Coverage, and Balancing". In: G. Sérasset; S. Armstrong; C. Boitet;

A. Popescu-Belis; D. Tufis (eds.): COLING 2004. Proceedings of the Workshop on Multilingual Linguistic Resources (MLR2004), Geneva, Switzerland, August 28, 101–108.

Berti, M.; Crane, G.R.; Yousef, T.; Bizzoni, Y.; Boschetti, F.; Del Gratta, R. (2016): Ancient Greek WordNet meets the Dynamic Lexicon: The Example of the Fragments of the Greek Historians. In: V.B. Mititelu; C. Forăscu; C. Fellbaum; P. Vossen (eds.): Proceedings of the Eighth Global WordNet Conference, Bucharest, Romania, January 27–30, 2016, 34–38.

Bizzoni, Y.; Boschetti, F.; Del Gratta, R.; Diakoff, H.; Monachini, M.; Crane, G.R. (2014): "The Making of Ancient Greek WordNet". In: N. Calzolari; K. Choukri; T. Declerck; H. Loftsson; B. Maegaard; J. Mariani; A. Moreno; J. Odijk; S. Piperidis (eds.): Proceedings of LREC 2014. Reykjavik: ELRA, 1140–1147.

Bonanno, M.G. (2006): "Assenza, più acuta presenza. Ifigenia nell'«Agamennone» di Eschilo". Lexis 24, 199–210.

Boschetti, F. (2018): Copisti Digitali e Filologi Computazionali. Roma: CNR Edizioni. http://hdl.handle.net/20.500.11752/OPEN-89 (last access 2019.01.31).

Chomsky, N. (1965): Aspects of the Theory of Syntax. Cambridge, MA: MIT Press.

Ciotti, F. (2014): "Tematologia e metodi digitali: Dal markup alle ontologie". In: B. Alfonzetti; G. Baldasarri; F. Tomasi (eds.): I cantieri dell'italianistica. Ricerca, didattica e organizzazione agli inizi del XXI secolo. Roma: Adi editore, 1–10.

Egger, C. (2004): Lexicon Recentis Latinitatis. Città del Vaticano: Libraria Editoria Vaticana.

Fellbaum, C. (1998): WordNet: An electronic lexical database. Cambridge, MA: MIT Press.

Firth, J.R. (1957): Papers in Linguistics 1934–1951. London: Oxford University Press.

Hymes, D. (1966): "Two Types of Linguistic Relativity". In: W. Bright (ed.): Sociolinguistics. The Hague: Mouton, 114–158.

Khan, A.F.; Arrigoni, S.; Boschetti, F.; Frontini, F. (2016): "Restructuring a Taxonomy of Literary Themes and Motifs for More Efficient Querying". MATLIT: Materialities of Literature 4:2, 11–27.

Khan, A.F.; Mugelli, G.; Boschetti, F.; Frontini, F.; Bellandi, A. (2018): "Using Formal Ontologies for the Annotation and Study of Literary Texts". In: AIUCD 2018 – Book of Abstracts, 31 January – 2 February 2018, Bari: Associazione per l'Informatica Umanistica e la Cultura Digitale, 246–248.

Koentges, T. (2016): "Topic Modelling of Historical Languages in R". https://www.dh.uni-leipzig.de/wo/topic-modelling-of-historical-languages-in-r (last access 2019.01.31).

Lenci, A. (2008): "Distributional Semantics in Linguistic and Cognitive Research". Italian Journal of Linguistics 20:1, 1–31.

Liddell, H.G.; Scott, R. (1889): An Intermediate Greek-English Lexicon. Oxford: Clarendon Press.

Liddell, H.G.; Scott, R.; Jones, H.S.; McKenzie, R. (1940): A Greek-English Lexicon. Oxford: Clarendon Press.

Mastandrea, P. (ed.) (2017): Strumenti digitali e collaborativi per le Scienze dell'Antichità. Venezia: Edizioni Ca' Foscari.

McGillivray, B. (2014): Methods in Latin Computational Linguistics. Leiden and Boston: Brill

Mikolov, T.; Sutskever, I.; Chen, K.; Corrado, G.; Dean, J. (2013): "Distributed Representations of Words and Phrases and their Compositionality". In: C.J.C. Burges; L. Bottou; M. Welling; Z. Ghahramani; K.Q. Weinberger (eds.): Proceedings of the 26th International Conference on Neural Information Processing Systems – (NIPS'13), Volume 2. Curran Associates Inc., USA, 3111–3119. arXiv:1310.4546 [cs.CL].

Minozzi, S. (2009): "The Latin WordNet Project". In: P. Anreiter; M. Kienpointner (eds.): Latin Linguistics Today. Akten des 15. Internationalem Kolloquiums zur Lateinischen Linguistik. Innsbruck: Institut für Sprachen und Literaturen der Universität Innsbruck, 707–716.
Mondin, L. (2014): Introduzione allo studio del latino. Venezia. https://www.docsity.com/it/introduzione-allo-studio-del-latino/616038 (last access 2019.01.31).
Moretti, F. (2013): Distant Reading. London: Verso.
Mugelli, G.; Boschetti, F.; Del Gratta, R.; Del Grosso, A.M.; Khan, A.F.; Taddei, A. (2016): "A User-Centred Design to Annotate Ritual Facts in Ancient Greek Tragedies". Bulletin of the Institute of Classical Studies 59:2, 103–120.
O'Donnell, M.B. (2005): Corpus Linguistics & The Greek of the New Testament. Seffield, TN: Sheffield Phoenix Press.
Pianta, E.; Bentivogli, L.; Girardi, C. (2002): "MultiWordNet: Developing an Aligned Multilingual Database". In: Proceedings of the First International Conference on Global WordNet, Mysore, India, January 21 –25.Global WordNet Association.
Rodda, M.A.; Lenci, A.; Senaldi, M.S.G. (2017): "Panta rei: Tracking Semantic Change with Distributional Semantics in Ancient Greek". Italian Journal of Computational Linguistics 3:1, 11–24.
Segre, C. (1985): "Tema/motivo". In: Avviamento all'analisi del testo letterario. Torino: Einaudi, 331–356.
Vossen, P. (ed.) (1998): EuroWordNet: A Multilingual Database with Lexical Semantic Networks. Dordrecht: Kluwer.

Notes on Contributors

Alison Babeu has served as the Digital Librarian and Research Coordinator for the Perseus Project since 2004. During her time at Perseus she has worked on a variety of diverse projects, from research into historical newspaper digitization to the development of cyberinfrastructure for digital classics as well as helping to manage the metadata for its flagship Greek and Latin collections. Before coming to Perseus, she worked as a librarian at both the Harvard Business School and the Boston Public Library. She has a BA in History from Mount Holyoke College and an MLS from Simmons College. Her current projects include the ongoing development of and support for the Perseus Catalog and helping manage the work of the Open Greek and Latin Project. Her current research interests include digital libraries and digital humanities; metadata creation and cataloging; and new roles for librarians in supporting the complex world of digital scholarship.

Monica Berti is Assistant Professor of Digital Humanities at the University of Leipzig, where she teaches courses in Digital Classics and Digital Philology. She has been working since 2008 with the Perseus Digital Library at Tufts University. Her research interests are focused on ancient Greece and the digital humanities and she has extensively published and led projects in both fields. She is currently working on representing quotations and text reuses of ancient lost works and she is leading the Digital Fragmenta Historicorum Graecorum (DFHG) and the Digital Athenaeus projects. As part of her teaching activities, she is program director of SunoikisisDC, which is an international consortium of Digital Classics programs developed by the University of Leipzig in collaboration with the Harvard's Center for Hellenic Studies and the Institute of Classical Studies London.

Christopher W. Blackwell is the Louis G. Forgione University Professor of Classics and Adjunct Professor of Computer Science at Furman University in Greenville, South Carolina, USA. He holds a BA in Classics from Marlboro College and a PhD in Classics from Duke University. He has been co-Project Architect of the Homer Multitext since its inception. He has published books and articles on Greek history, Alexander the Great, intellectual property law, digital humanities, and historical botany.

Federico Boschetti graduated in Classics at the University "Ca' Foscari" of Venice in 1998. In 2005 he discussed his PhD thesis in Classical Philology at the University of Trento (joint supervision by the University of Lille III) and in 2010 he discussed his PhD in Cognitive and Brain Sciences – Language, Interaction and Computation at the University of Trento. Since 2011 he has been a confirmed researcher at the Institute of Computational Linguistics "A. Zampolli" of the CNR of Pisa. He taught Digital Humanities at the Venice International University in 2014, 2015 and 2017. He currently teaches Digital Philology at the University of Pisa. He has collaborated with the Perseus Project at Tufts University in Medford (MA) in 2009 and 2013. He is a member of the editorial board of *Lexis*, a journal of Classical Philology.

https://doi.org/10.1515/9783110599572-019

Oliver Bräckel is a PhD Candidate in Ancient History. He worked on several projects both in the fields of Classics and Digital Humanities funded by BMBF, DFG and the Mellon Foundation. Currently he is employed as a research assistant in the Department of History at the University of Leipzig.

Patrick J. Burns is the ACLS Postdoctoral Fellow for the Quantitative Criticism Lab (University of Texas at Austin) where he conducts research on computational approaches to historical-language text, working at the intersection of literary criticism, philology, and big data. He has published articles in these areas, including "Creating Stoplists for Historical Languages" for *Digital Classics Online* and "Measuring and Mapping Intergeneric Allusion in Latin Poetry using Tesserae" for a special issue on Computer-Aided Processing of Intertextuality in Ancient Languages for the *Journal of Data Mining and Digital Humanities*. Patrick is also the Latin tools developer for the Classical Language Toolkit, an open-source project dedicated to text analysis and natural language processing research for historical languages. He received his doctorate in Classics from Fordham University and has worked as a researcher for the Institute for the Study of the Ancient World (New York University).

Hugh A. Cayless is a Senior DH Research Developer with the Duke Collaboratory for Classics Computing (DC3). He is a member and past Chair of the TEI Technical Council and is the Treasurer of the TEI Consortium. His current research interests include the development of tools and techniques for publishing digital critical editions, digital epigraphy and papyrology, and APIs for digital publication systems. Hugh holds a PhD in Classics and a Master's degree in Information Science, both from UNC Chapel Hill.

Giuseppe G.A. Celano is a DFG Project Leader at the NLP Department of the University of Leipzig. His current work focuses on revising, expanding, and standardizing the Ancient Greek and Latin Dependency Treebank, of which he is a co-editor. His research interests lie at the crossroads of computer science, linguistics, and philology.

Neil Coffee is Professor of Classics at the State University of New York at Buffalo. His interests include Latin epic poetry, Roman social history, ancient philosophy, and digital approaches to literary and intellectual history. He is the author of *The Commerce of War: Exchange and Social Order in Latin Epic* and *Gift and Gain: How Money Transformed Ancient Rome*. His forthcoming co-edited volume is *Intertextuality in Flavian Epic Poetry* (De Gruyter 2019). He leads the Tesserae Project, which uses computational methods to study intertextuality among classical and later authors. He founded and serves as Co-Chair of the Digital Classics Association.

Casey Dué is Professor and Director of Classical Studies at the University of Houston, as well as Executive Editor at the Center for Hellenic Studies in Washington, DC. She is the author most recently of *Achilles Unbound: Multiformity and Tradition in the Homeric Epics* (Washington, DC, 2018). Other publications include *Homeric Variations on a Lament by Briseis* (Lanham, MD, 2002), *The Captive Woman's Lament in Greek Tragedy* (Austin, TX, 2006), and (with Mary Ebbott) *Iliad 10 and the Poetics of Ambush: A Multitext Edition with Essays and Commentary* (Washington, DC, 2010). She is the co-editor (together with Mary Ebbott) of the Homer Multitext (http://www.homermultitext.org).

Mary Ebbott is a Professor in the Classics Department at the College of the Holy Cross in Worcester, Massachusetts. She is co-Editor of the Homer Multitext, co-author with Casey Dué of *Iliad 10 and the Poetics of Ambush*, and author of *Imagining Illegitimacy in Classical Greek Literature* and of articles on the Homeric epics and on Athenian tragedy.

Franz Fischer was coordinator and researcher at the Cologne Center for eHumanities (CCeH), University of Cologne. He created digital editions of William of Auxerre's treatise on liturgy and of Saint Patrick's *Confessio* and coordinated the Marie Skłodowska Curie Initial Training Network DiXiT. Franz Fischer has been serving on the Digital Medievalist Executive Board since 2014 and is editor-in-chief of the *Digital Medievalist* Journal. He is a founding member of the Institute for Documentology and Scholarly Editing (IDE), teaching at summer schools and publishing SIDE, a series on digital editions, palaeography and codicology, and RIDE, a review journal on digital editions and resources. Starting from May 2019 he is Associate Professor at Università Ca' Foscari Venezia, where he is also director of the Centre for Digital and Public Humanities.

Gerhard Heyer holds the Chair on Natural Language Processing at the Computer Science Department of the University of Leipzig. His field of interest is focused on automatic semantic processing of natural language text with applications in the area of information retrieval and search as well as Digital Humanities. Until he moved to Leipzig, he was responsible within the Olivetti Group for establishing research and development in electronic publishing and natural language processing. Gerhard Heyer has published numerous papers on natural language processing, including the well known book *Text Mining: Wissensrohstoff Text* by W3L/Springer. He is conducting several research projects funded by the EU, the German Research Foundation (DFG), and industrial funding.

Samuel J. Huskey is an Associate Professor and the Chair of the Department of Classics and Letters at the University of Oklahoma. He has led the Digital Latin Library project since its inception in 2012. He is also the Information Architect for the Society for Classical Studies. In addition to his work in digital humanities computing, his current projects include a translation of Boccaccio's minor Latin works and an edition of Calpurnius Siculus' bucolic poetry.

Hannes Kahl is a PhD Candidate in Ancient History and Computer Science. He worked as software developer in several projects both in the fields of Classics and Digital Humanities funded by BMBF, DFG and the Mellon Foundation. Currently he is working on a research project in the Department of History at the University of Leipzig with the aim of developing a tool for the in-depth indexing of digitized journals.

Friedrich Meins holds a PhD in Ancient History. He worked in several projects both in the fields of Classics and Digital Humanities funded by BMBF, DFG and the Mellon Foundation. Currently he is employed as a postdoctoral research assistant in the Department of History in Leipzig.

Leonard Muellner is Professor Emeritus of Classical Studies at Brandeis University and a Senior Fellow of the Center for Hellenic Studies, Washington, DC. His scholarly interests center on Homeric epic, with special interests in historical linguistics, anthropological approaches to the study of myth, and the poetics of oral traditional poetry. His published works include *The Meaning of Homeric EUKHOMAI through its Formulas*, Innsbruck, 1976, *The Anger of Achilles: Mênis in Greek Epic*, Ithaca (NY), 1996, repr. ppbk., 2005, and several articles, including "The Simile of the Cranes and Pygmies. A Study of Homeric Metaphor," *Harvard Studies in Classical Philology*, vol. 93, 1990, 59–101, and "Grieving Achilles," in *Homeric Contexts: Neoanalysis and the Interpretation of Oral Poetry*, Berlin, 2012, 187–210; an article by him on Visual and Verbal Art and Memory will appear in the Chinese journal *National Art* in Spring, 2019.

Marco Passarotti is Associate Professor at Università Cattolica del Sacro Cuore (Milan). His main research interests deal with building, using and disseminating linguistic resources and natural language processing tools for Latin. A pupil of one of the pioneers of humanities computing, father Roberto Busa SJ, since 2006 he heads the Index Thomisticus Treebank project. In 2009, he founded the CIRCSE research centre of computational linguistics at Università Cattolica. Currently, he is Principal Investigator of an ERC-CoG Grant (2018–2023) aimed at building a Linked Data based Knowledge Base of resources and tools for Latin. He organized and chaired several international scientific events. He co-chairs the series of workshops on Corpus-based Research in the Humanities (CRH). He teaches Computational Linguistics at Università Cattolica (Milan) and at the University of Pavia.

Bruce Robertson is Professor of Classics and Head of Department at Mount Allison University in New Brunswick, Canada, where, following PhD studies at the University of Toronto, he has taught for twenty years. He has been involved in several initiatives related to the use of computer technologies to better understand the Greek and Roman past, including a historical markup language, a web app for graphical treebanking, and, for the past seven years, large-scale, high-quality OCR for ancient Greek and Latin. The latter endeavor has seen him contribute to many digitization projects around the world. Currently, he also serves as the Vice-President of the Classical Association of Canada.

Charlotte Schubert is Professor of Ancient History and Chair of the Department of History at the University of Leipzig. Her research focuses on the history of Athenian democracy and the history of Ancient Medicine as well as on Digital Classics (development of the web portal eAQUA, co-founder and co-editor of the Open Access eJournal *Digital Classics Online*). She is currently working on various Digital Classics projects and on a larger study on *Isonomia in Antiquity*.

Neel Smith is Professor of Classics and Chair of the Department of Classics at the College of the Holy Cross in Worcester, Massachusetts, USA. He holds a PhD from the University of California, Berkeley. He has been co-Project Architect of the Homer Multitext since its inception. He has published and presented on Classical archaeology, ancient science, and digital methods in classical studies.

James K. Tauber is the founder and CEO of Eldarion, a software company focused on Python and Web development. He has been involved in open source and Web standards for over two decades and was in the original working group that developed XML. Trained in both linguistics and classical philology, Tauber has worked on the application of digital methods to the study of Ancient Greek for 25 years and recently led the development of the new Scaife Viewer for the Perseus Digital Library. He is a Fellow of the Python Software Foundation, a member of the Unicode Consortium, and a participant in the Open Greek and Latin project.

Jochen Tiepmar graduated from the University of Leipzig in 2013 with a MSc degree in Computer Science in the Department for Natural Language Processing (NLP). After graduating, he was a member of the project *The Library of a Billion Words*. The goal of this ESF-funded project was to create an infrastructure for a digitalization workflow for documents and part of this infrastructure was a Canonical Text Service (CTS). After evaluating the solutions that were available at the time, he decided to implement a CTS suitable for needs in the digital humanities. While working at ScaDS (Scalable Data Solutions), a BMBF-funded project with the goal to build a competence center for Big Data related problems, he received his PhD in Computer Science with a dissertation entitled *Implementation and Evaluation of the Canonical Text Service Protocol as Part of a Research Infrastructure in the Digital Humanities*. Currently he is teaching in the NLP department and in the department for Computational Humanities at the University of Leipzig.

Index

This Index lists names of people working in digital classical philology and names of projects related to the topics of this book.

https://doi.org/10.1515/9783110599572-020